ArtScroll Judaica Classics®

Rabbi Nosson Scherman / Rabbi Meir Zlotowitz
General Editors

A PROJECT OF THE

Mesórah Heritage Foundation

DAYS

Published by

Mesorah Publications, ltd

ניצוצות וליקוטים מספר שפת אמת
על עניני אלול וימים נוראים

OF AWE

Ideas and Insights of the

SFAS EMES

on the High Holy Days

Anthologized and Adapted by
Rabbi Yosef Stern

FIRST EDITION
First Impression . . . July 1996

Published and Distributed by
MESORAH PUBLICATIONS, Ltd.
4401 Second Avenue
Brooklyn, New York 11232

Distributed in Europe by
J. LEHMANN HEBREW BOOKSELLERS
20 Cambridge Terrace
Gateshead, Tyne and Wear
England NE8 1RP

Distributed in Israel by
SIFRIATI / A. GITLER — BOOKS
4 Bilu Street
P.O.B. 14075
Tel Aviv 61140

Distributed in Australia & New Zealand by
GOLDS BOOK & GIFT CO.
36 William Street
Balaclava 3183, Vic., Australia

Distributed in South Africa by
KOLLEL BOOKSHOP
22 Muller Street
Yeoville 2198, Johannesburg, South Africa

ARTSCROLL JUDAICA CLASSICS®
DAYS OF AWE
© Copyright 1996, by MESORAH PUBLICATIONS, Ltd.
4401 Second Avenue / Brooklyn, N.Y. 11232 / (718) 921-9000

ISBN:
0-89906-023-4 (hard cover)
0-89906-024-2 (paperback)

Typography by CompuScribe at ArtScroll Studios, Ltd.
4401 Second Avenue / Brooklyn, N.Y. 11232 / (718) 921-9000

Printed in the United States of America by Noble Book Press Corp.
Bound by Sefercraft Inc., Quality Bookbinders, Brooklyn, N.Y.

ברכה לראש משביר

למע"כ האי גברא יקירא הנדיב הדגול והחשוב
איש האשכולות

הרה"ח **יחיאל בן ציון פישאהף** הי"ו

ומשפחתו שיחיו לאוי"ט
שתמכו בהוצאת הספר

לעילוי נשמת זוגתו אמם היקרה
האשה הדגולה והחשובה רודפת צדקה וחסד

מרת **מינדל** ע"ה

(למשפחת אורבך)

נפטרה ביום הרביעי כ"ד תשרי תשמ"ט

ולעילוי נשמות הוריהם
אביו הרבני רודף צדקה וחסד

הרה"ח מוהר"ר **דוב פישאהף** ז"ל

נכד הגה"צ חסידא ופרישא

מוה"ר **זאב נחום** זצ"ל

אבדק"ק ביאלה, מח"ס אגודת אזוב

אמו האשה החשובה

מרת **מירל** ע"ה

בניהם: **אהרן אשר ויעקב יצחק**
ובנותיהם: **רבקה, ברײנדל ורחל**

כולם נהרגו על קדה"ש, ונקבע היאהרצייט כ"ה אדר ב'

חותנו הרבני הנעלה

מוה"ר **ישראל ניידר** ז"ל

נפטר י"ג תשרי תשל"ט

חמותו האשה החשובה

חיה זיסע ע"ה

נפטרה ז' שבט תשל"ה

ב״ה ה׳ שמות תשנ״ב לפ״ק

לכב׳ ידידי היקר והנכבד הרה״ג חו״ב נותן טעם לשבח הרב
דוד אלעווסקי שליט״א
שלום רב!

בנידון הספר המבאר את השפ״א לסוכות אשר חיבר הרב
יוסף שטערן שליט״א – הנה כידוע לך אינני נותן הסכמות
באופן עקרוני. ובפרט כאשר השפה האנגלית אינה שגורה בפי
לא שייך בכלל שאני אעבור ע״ז ואסכים עליו. אבל כפי
ששמעתי מכם שאנשים חשובים שבחו את הספר הנני מצרף גם
ברכתי להרב המחבר שליט״א שיצליח.

והנני בזה ידידך הדורש״ט

פינחס מנחם אלטר

פנחס מנחם אלטר

Rabbi CHAIM P. SCHEINBERG
Rosh Hayeshiva "TORAH-ORE"
and Morah Hora'ah of Kiryat Mattersdorf

הרב חיים פינחס שיינברג
ראש ישיבת "תורה-אור"
ומורה הוראה דקרית מטרסדורף

יום ד' לש"ק פ' כי תצא, י"א אלול תשנ"ה.
פעיה"ק ירושלים תובב"א.

מכתב ברכה

שונה תורתינו הקדושה מספרי אומות העולם, באשר התורה באה לידי תכליתה כשהיא מלמדת לאדם את האמת, ויש בזה שני חלקים דהיי' א' ידיעה האמת, וב' המעשה שהיא חיי האמת, שעם כל הקושי הכרוכה בקנין ידיעת התורה ע"י עמל רב במחשבה בחריפות ובישוב הדעת, מ"מ עוד יותר קשה לאדם ללחום עם יצרו ולחיות את כל אורחות חייו על פי דעת התורה.

ובדורינו מצינו של"ע ירד קרן התורה פלאים ממה שהי' בדורות הקודמים, בזה שנלקו הלבבות בטמטום עצום מרב כל, וקשה מאד לעורר את הלבבות הסתמים והאטומים לשאיפת התורה והאמת, וכדי לחזור ולקרבן נצרך שפה מיוחדת המדברת אליהן בהסברת פנים ומושכן אחרי התורה.

וספרי "שפת אמת" הצליחו מאד בזה בדורינו בכוללם יחד את שני העניינים, הא' ה"אמת", והב' ה"שפה" המשתף גם את הלב בעבודה, ומעוררה לקיים את המעשה, ונמצא שמתוך הספרים מתעורר האדם לשלימות בין באמונה פשוטה ותמה בקיום המצוות, ובין בידיעה בתורה בעמקות ובחריפות, ועי"ז גם יכול לעשות את המצוות בהבנה ובטעם בכל הלב ובכל הנפש החפצה.

וכידוע בגלל דקותן של הענינים, לפעמים קשה אפי' לגדולים לעמוד על בוריין במקורן, ולכן עוד יותר קשה למסרן בשפה אחרת, וכדי לעשות כן דרושה מלאכת אומנות יתירה. ובי"ה זכה האי גברא רבא איש האשכולות ש"ב **הרה"ג רבי יוסף שטרן שליט"א**, רב דביהכ"נ אגודת אחים בפלעטבוש נ.י., שכבר נתפרסם כסופר מהיר המנצח על עבודה זו בהצלחה מרובה, והספרים הראשונים של ליקוטים והסברים בלשון ענגליש על המועדים ועל ליל הסדר כבר נתקבלו ברבים בחשק עז, ועכשיו שלח את ידו לעניני הימים הנוראים וחנוכה ופורים, ומתכונן בעה"ה להמשיך אח"כ בשפת אמת על התורה.

ועל כן כל המסייעו בעבודתו הכבירה הוא ממזכי ומחזיקי תורה לרבים, שהיא זכות גדולה לברכה ולהצלחה בכל העניינים הרוחניים והגשמיים כמבואר ברז"ל.

ותפלתינו שזכותו של השפת אמת זצ"ל תעמוד לסייע שיתקבלו הספרים החדשים לא פחות ועוד יותר ממה שנתקבלו הראשונים, ושהנג"ל ימשיך בעבודתו עבודת הקודש ללמוד וללמד תורה ברבים בכל האופנים כיד ה' הטוב עליו מתוך הרחבת הדעת, ושיעמיד דורות ישרים אשר מהם ירוו' רב נחת אמיתית, ושיפוצו מעיינותיו חוצה, ושנזכה לראות בהרמת קרן התורה לאמיתה והיראה הטהורה בהכרת האמת, בביאת משיח צדקינו ובבנין בית המקדש במהרה בימינו אמן.

הכו"ח לכבוד התורה ולומדי',

חיים פינחס שיינברג

רחוב פנים מאירות 2, ירושלים, ת. ד. 6979, טל. 371513-(02), ישראל
2, Panim Meirot St., Jerusalem, P.O.B. 6979, Tel (02)-371513, Israel

מכתב ברכה מאת כ״ק האדמו״ר מנאוואמינסק שליט״א
לספרי הקודם על הגדה של פסח

(718) 436-1133

RABBI YAAKOV PERLOW
1569 - 47TH STREET
BROOKLYN, N.Y. 11219

יעקב פרלוב
ביחמו״ד עדת יעקב נאוואמינסק
ברוקלין, נ.י.

בס״ד ו/ם ד ב' והזכא תערף

נפוד גפאת ידידי, הרב העולה והנעלה
איה וכ״ל נעים ..., שלום ורב ....

תשואות חן חן ... על ... הפריה לטויי פסח
... לבן רחבי ... את ... הקדוא והבב
על חינך ה... ביד, נאשהו .. עם רצים
כך ... כ... על ... על ..., הנגל והפלוא לתרגם
להגד את ... הלחוים של ... יוראל ותענורות
... ... רחקים ... האחם כל ... ...
... הדף ... את ... ...
... ... כאייית .... יחדו הכל
... ... ה

יעקב פרלוב

Publisher's Preface

To publish this work is a high honor. *Sfas Emes* is a name that has evoked respect and awe for a hundred years, as a commentary on the Talmud and as a collection of penetrating insights on the Torah and Festivals. One of the last generation's great *roshei yeshiva* said:

> "There is hardly a Torah commentary that I have not studied, but always I come back to the *Sfas Emes*. Every year I go through it again and I never fail to see new ideas that I never noticed before." .

Rabbi Yosef Stern is one of the countless *talmidei chachamim* whose fascination with *Sfas Emes* has enriched his own life and, through him, the lives of many who attend his classes and lectures. Now, he goes a giant step further. He has taken the major ideas of the *Sfas Emes* on the High Holy Days and presented them in clear, cogent, stimulating essays, topic by topic. Connoisseurs of this classic know that the *Sfas Emes* on these two festivals are expecially challenging and seminal.

At the very least, this book will vastly enrich all who read it. At best, it will introduce many of its readers to the original, so that they too will mine its vast storehouse of ideas and comments.

This book is not a translation, for the *Sfas Emes* cannot be translated. It pulls together strands of thought on individual topics from the over thirty years of comment collected in the original, and weaves the ideas into a clear and coherent tapestry. To those familiar with the *Sfas Emes*, it will be a reminder, a refresher, and a treasury of insights they may have overlooked. To those unfamiliar with it, the book will be an electrifying adventure in Torah thought.

We express our appreciation to Rabbi Stern for undertaking this daunting work.

We likewise are grateful to all those whose talents have been harnessed in producing a work so significant. They may all be proud to have made an important contribution to the Torah growth of countless people.

Rabbis Meir Zlotowitz/Nosson Scherman

Rosh Chodesh Tammuz 5756
June 1996

Author's Preface

כי גם בעוסקו בעוה"ז אם כל רצונו מגעגע להתדבק בהש"י עי"ז עצמו
יש עלי' לכל הדברים שעוסק בהם. וע"ש זה נקרא רצון מל' ריצה שלא
בהדרגה שע"י הרצון יכולין להפוך הכל רצונו לעלות להש"י. (שפ"א
ראה תרל"ג)

Even while one is involved in matters of this world, if his sole
desire is to cling to Hashem this yearning [not only leaves a
profound impact on the individual] but also elevates the entire
material world.

The term רָצוֹן, ordinarily translated as *grace* or *will*, is
actually derived from רִיצָה, *running*. One who possesses an
intense desire [to come close to Hashem] can soar and vault
spiritually and pursue goals that are ordinarily unattainable. In
fact he will succeed in transforming everything in this world
— the curses as well as the blessings — into a source of
blessing.   (Free Translation of *Sfas Emes* Re'eh 5632)

The summer is drawing to its close. The earth receives the
final glow of the sun and its fruits approach their full maturity.
Everything that grows and lives seeks to extract the maximum
benefit from the last rays of the year. The apple paints itself
with its final shade of red, the wine receives its richest sparkle.
The ground gives its last sap, the cornstalks grow to their limit.
The bee seeks the last drop of honey in the flower before it
vanishes. The squirrel drags the last grain of corn to his winter
store. The returning swallow carries the last straw to the nest.
There is no time to be lost; the end is in sight. The Master
will soon call . . .
              (*Collected Writings Volume II* Rabbi S.R. Hirsch)

The two selections, one from the *Sfas Emes* himself (though not necessarily in the context of *Elul*) and the other a small segment culled from
Rav Samson Raphael Hirsch's classic depiction of *Elul*, help capture the
essence of those climactic final days of the year. These are not only
days of grace and goodwill but also an annual opportunity for extraordinary
growth.

Not only man, but also the entire natural world prepares for its annual rendezvous with its Creator, as Rav Samson Raphael Hirsch so magnificently portrays.[1]

Just as that great Chassidic master, the *Sfas Emes*, derives the extraordinary tempo of these days from the very name of the month, יְמֵי רָצוֹן, so too Rav Samson Raphael Hirsch — writing at about the same time as the *Sfas Emes* but addressing a vastly different audience — visualizes all of nature joining man in urgent preparation for Rosh Hashanah's judgment.

Having enjoyed the *zechus* of taking the reader through the Three Festivals utilizing the prism of the *Sfas Emes*, enriching the Seder night through the publication of the *Haggadah* based on the *Sfas Emes* insights (and presenting Chanukah and Purim from his perspective), we now continue the yearly cycle with the fourth volume in this series.

While the material in this volume primarily deals with the Days of Awe, spanning the period from the joyous renewal of *Elul* to the unique experience of Yom Kippur afternoon, in reality this volume encompasses much more — Life itself! Life in this world (עוֹלָם הַזֶּה) and life in the World to Come (עוֹלָם הַבָּא). Life of the Body, and of the Divine Spark embedded in the soul (נְקוּדָה פְּנִימִיּוּת). Lives of ordinary people pouring out their heart in *Tefillah* and the lives of the *Avos*, Avraham and Yitzchak, interconnected and the *Akeidah*. Life before sinning and life of the repentant Jew. Daily life here on earth — and the supernatural life which the Jew enjoys on Yom Kippur.

ঙ্গ How to Use This Volume

To appreciate this commentary fully, the reader should consider the following observations:

☐ This work is not a translation of the *Sfas Emes*. Such a project, even if it were judged to be an appropriate undertaking, is well beyond the capabilities of this writer.

☐ This work makes no attempt to follow the sequence presented in the writings of the *Sfas Emes*. Instead we have selected, rearranged, and often "expanded" insights that were first said at Chassidic gatherings (*tischen*) over a period of 35 years, from 5631 to 5665 (1871-1905), in an attempt to render them more easily accessible to the contemporary reader.

☐ This work makes no attempt to present an exhaustive treatment of the *Sfas Emes's* insights on any particular topic, much less on the High Holidays (*Yamim Noraim*) as a whole. Apart from considerations of space, the sheer volume and profundity of the *Sfas Emes's* writings

---

1. This thought is uncannily similar to the Sfas Emes's interpretation of וְכָל בָּאֵי עוֹלָם that all living beings — not only man — are being judged on Rosh Hashanah.

preclude the possibility of reproducing everything he wrote about the High Holidays. Wherever possible, we have provided references to the original sources in the writings of the *Sfas Emes* on the Torah and High Holidays so that those readers with a command of Hebrew can appreciate his insights in their original format. Even for such readers, however, we feel that this work will be a valuable digest and commentary on concepts that are often difficult to grasp fully in their original, very terse, style.

☐ In this volume we have provided the reader with Hebrew excerpts extracted from virtually every piece of *Sfas Emes* discussed in this text. While hardly intended to be exhaustive, these Hebrew excerpts represent a crosssection of the *Sfas Emes's* ideas, and hopefully, will motivate the reader to explore further the original Hebrew.

☐ Perhaps most importantly, while we have done everything possible to present the thoughts of the *Sfas Emes* in easily accessible form, we make no claim that this volume will make for light reading. As with most works on the basic principles of Torah, it is best read in small portions, and requires time to absorb and assimilate. Over the course of time, however, it is hoped that such an approach will yield substantial cumulative effects. It is the author's fervent wish and prayer that the reader will pick up this book again and again, each time finding a new idea to be treasured and savored by a Jew thirsting to drink from the rich spiritual springs of the Festival cycle.

☐ Finally, many of the *Sfas Emes'* writings, by virtue of the profundity and obscurity, are subject to varying interpretations. While many people have assisted in the preparation of this volume for publication, the author alone assumes responsibility for its interpretations of this Torah classic, which are his own and most likely mirror his perceptions. May Hashem protect us from errors.

❦ ❦ ❦

The reader should consider the undertone of joy that permeates this volume. While one would expect שִׂמְחָה to be a major theme of *The Three Festivals* and of the *Haggadah,* even this volume featuring the High Holidays is dominated by optimism and joy.

The reader is also urged to read carefully the following section entitled ''A Tribute to the Gerrer Rebbe זצ״ל.'' *Klal Yisrael* was shocked by his sudden passing shortly after Purim. It is our fervent wish that these few words of appreciation will stimulate the reader to study further and be inspired by this *tzaddik's* legacy.

May the time come speedily when the lofty ideals of the *Sfas Emes* will be realized, when the universe will be suffused by דַּעַת ה׳. In the immortal words of Yirmiyahu (a verse that my father זצ״ל noted was on the front page of the original *Horeb,* published by Rav Samson Raphael Hirsch): וְלֹא יְלַמְּדוּ עוֹד אִישׁ אֶת רֵעֵהוּ וְאִישׁ אֶת אָחִיו לֵאמֹר דְּעוּ אֶת ה' כִּי כוּלָּם יֵדְעוּ אוֹתִי לְמִקְטַנָּם וְעַד גְּדוֹלָם נְאֻם ה' כִּי אֶסְלַח לַעֲוֹנָם וּלְחַטָּאתָם לֹא אֶזְכָּר עוֹד, *They will no longer teach — each man and his fellow, each man his brother — saying, "Know Hashem!" For all of them will know Me, from their smallest to their greatest — the word of Hashem — when I will forgive their iniquities and will no longer recall their sins (31:33).*

~§ Acknowledgments

To the sponsors:

Mr. and Mrs. Benzion Fishoff whose generous support made possible the publication of this volume of *Sfas Emes.* Mr. Fishoff, himself a Holocaust survivor, whose story is presented in the recent publication *From Ashes to Renewal* (Agudath Israel, 1995), has served as an invaluable link between the pre-war Chassidic court of the *Imre Emes* and the contemporary Ger community. His generosity to numerous Torah causes, and especially Ger *Mosdos* throughout the world, is legendary. May Hashem bless Mr. Fishoff and his family with the strength to perpetuate his numerous philanthropic endeavors לְאוֹרֶךְ יָמִים וְשָׁנִים.

To my family:

In memory of my dear father החבר ר' חיים בן החבר ר' יוסף ז"ל who exemplified all year long the יִרְאַת ה', אַהֲבַת ה', and מִדּוֹת טוֹבוֹת highlighted during the יָמִים נוֹרָאִים.

May Hashem grant my mother שתחי' the opportunity to perpetuate the דֶרֶךְ that she shared with her husband. May she have *nachas* from her children and grandchildren and good health לְאוֹרֶךְ יָמִים וְשָׁנִים.

To my dear parents-in-law, Rabbi and Rebbetzin Scheinberg, who have raised an entire generation of *talmidim* in more than four decades in *chinuch.* May Hashem grant them long and healthy years and continued *nachas* from their children and grandchildren.

To my *eishes chayil,* who has given me constant encouragement to complete this project in the face of the numerous challenges and distractions of daily life. Her efforts to maintain a comparatively tranquil working atmosphere, despite the enormous responsibilities of raising a family, can never be forgotten. May Hashem grant us the merit to witness together בָּנִים וּבְנֵי בָנִים עוֹסְקִים בַּתּוֹרָה וּבְמִצְוֹת.

To all those who have contributed to this volume:

To my editors R' Pinchos Asher Rohr and Mrs. Ethel Gottlieb for their superb dedication and highly professional work. The entire volume benefited from their expertise in overall editing, checking sources, annotating and ensuring that the manuscript conform to the high standards of the ArtScroll series.

To R' David Olewski, Menahel of Mesivta Beis Yisrael, for his guidance and advice and for his invaluable liaison to the Gerrer community.

Yasher Koach to Michael Reminick, Dovid and Chaim Wanounou, Simcha Glen, and Menachem Stern for their logistical support.

To my "fellow travelers," Reb Mechel Stern and Reb Moshe Yaroslawitz, who patiently served as a "sounding board" for many of these Torah thoughts.

To the staff of Mesorah Publications:

To Rabbi Nosson Scherman, a Torah educator, writer, and lecturer of great note who has championed this project through many vicissitudes. Were it not for his involvement and accessibility, in spite of his frenetic schedule, this book would never have seen the light of day.

To Rabbi Meir Zlotowitz for his painstaking attention to every detail of the project. The superb quality of all ArtScroll productions are a testament to his superior abilities.

My appreciation to R' Avrohom Biderman who helped coordinate the final production of this book. Also to the typesetting department — Mrs. Esther Feierstein, Mrs. Dvory Bick, Yehuda Gordon, Udi Herskovits, Toby Heilbrun, and Toby Brander for their patient and skillful typing and retyping. To Chaya Gitty Loevy for her painstaking care and aesthetic taste in paginating this volume. Thanks as well to R' Eli Kroen for his striking cover design. The beautiful design makes it as pleasing to the eye as it is to the mind.

I am appreciative of Mrs. Faygie Weinbaum's reading and corrections, as well as that of Mrs. Mindy Stern.

To the members of Congregation Agudas Achim of Midwood where I have been privileged to serve as their Rav and to its president Mr. Arthur Pearlman.

My thanks to Rabbi Moshe Kolodny, Director of Orthodox Archives of Agudath Israel, for his invaluable assistance in preparing the tribute to the Gerrer Rebbe זצ"ל.

Above all, I must express my total gratitude to Hashem. No human effort could possible reach fruition were it not for Hashem's unceasing help in every minute detail of the project.

Yosef Stern

Rosh Chodesh Tammuz 5756
June 1996

Table of Contents

Aseres Yemei Teshuvah

Yom Kippur

A Tribute to the
Gerrer Rebbe, זצ"ל

Klal *Yisrael* was shocked by the sudden passing of the Gerrer Rebbe, כ״ק אדמו״ר הרב הגאון ר׳ פינחס מנחם אלתר זצ״ל (the last surviving grandson of the *Sfas Emes* זצ"ל), on the 16th of Adar, 5756 (March 7, 1996). The following tribute to this unforgettable Torah giant is based on the *piyut* מַרְאֵה כֹהֵן, recited during *Mussaf* of Yom Kippur and is culled from various sources including *Dos Yiddishe Vort*, *HaModia*, and the *Yated Neeman*.

אֱמֶת מַה נֶּהְדָּר הָיָה כֹהֵן גָּדוֹל בְּצֵאתוֹ מִבֵּית קָדְשֵׁי הַקֳּדָשִׁים בְּשָׁלוֹם בְּלִי פֶגַע

*True! How majestic was the Kohen Gadol as he left the
Holy of Holies in peace, without injury*

כְּאֹהֶל הַנִּמְתָּח בְּדָרֵי מַעְלָה

*Like the heavenly canopy stretched out over those who
dwell above*

The Rebbe זצ"ל always emphasized the need to soar heavenward, to reach higher spiritual levels. He would insist that nothing — neither misfortune nor tragedy — should prevent a Jew from attaining his spiritual potential.

כִּבְרָקִים הַיּוֹצְאִים מִזִּיו הַחַיּוֹת

*Like the lightning bolts emanating from the radiance of
the Chayos*

The Rebbe's smile! Who can forget that unforgettable smile that would soothe even the most depressed? Who can forget the radiance and the sheer joy with which he confronted every challenge of life?

כְּגֹדֶל גְּדִילִים בְּאַרְבַּע קְצָווֹת

Like the tzitzis fringes attached to the four corners

By placing the *tzitzis* on the four edges of a garment, we are emphasizing the essential unity of *Klal Yisrael*. No matter how far we may have been dispersed, even to the furthest reaches of the earth, we still converge, just as the fringes of the *tzitzis* are gathered (cf. *Sfas Emes Shelach* 5660).

The Rebbe זצ"ל was always concerned about *achdus*, the elusive goal of Jewish unity, working tirelessly to promote unity of all Torah-true Jews. During his brief tenure as Rebbe he would travel to the furthest reaches to stimulate his *chassidim* and all of *Klal Yisrael*, visiting the United States, Canada and England.

כִּדְמוּת הַקֶּשֶׁת בְּתוֹךְ הֶעָנָן

Like the image of the rainbow amid the cloud

Despite the numerous clouds in his personal life (the loss of a young child, and the tragic passing of his beloved son Rav Aryeh זצ"ל, a *talmid chacham* of note), he would encourage others, sharing their burden of suffering. He agreed to accept the position of Rebbe (upon the passing of his brother, HaRav Simcha Bunim Alter זצ"ל, known as the לֵב שִׂמְחָה, in 1992), only after he could relate to the travails of his numerous petitioners *as if they were his own*.

Once a virtual stranger informed the Rebbe that his wife had given birth to a daughter. Departing from precedent, the Rebbe toasted this young man with a *LeChaim*. He later explained: Since I have shared the suffering of the first 29 petitioners, I am entitled to share the joy of the first bit of happy news that I heard today.

It is widely speculated that the tragic spate of terrorist bombings, and their numerous fatalities "broke the Rebbe's heart." Just as the suffering of Jewish soldiers conscripted during the Russo-Japanese war may have contributed to the premature passing of his grandfather (the *Sfas Emes*) (cf. *The Three Festivals*, p. 22), so too *Klal Yisrael's* recent tragedies took an enormous toll on the Rebbe.

כְּוֶרֶד הַנָּתוּן בְּתוֹךְ גִּנַּת חֶמֶד

Like a rose that is placed amid a precious garden

Great Torah personalities do not suddenly "emerge," as if by chance; they are painstakingly planted and nurtured by previous generations.

The Rebbe was the scion of great *tzaddikim*, he was the last surviving grandson of the *Sfas Emes* and the youngest child of the *Imrei Emes* (refer to our tribute to him in *Days of Joy*).

Just as one zealously guards a precious and delicate rose, so too the *Imrei Emes* זצ״ל was intimately involved in the spiritual growth and development of his son, Pinchas Menachem, securing for him the best tutors and carefully outlining a program of study, stimulating him to attain his full potential. During the German bombardment of Warsaw, his father spared no effort to keep Pinchas Menachem (who had just celebrated his *bar mitzvah*) at his side. Through a series of miracles — abetted by enormous bribes to the Gestapo — the *Imrei Emes* and his son were able to flee the Warsaw Ghetto and eventually reach Eretz Yisrael.

בְּעֹז אֲשֶׁר הִלְבִּישׁ טָהוֹר לַמִּטַּהֵר

Like the strength with which the Pure One garbed the one who became pure

The Rebbe זצ״ל was not only a devoted son, but also a loyal follower of his two older brothers who had preceded him as Rebbe, Rav Yisrael Alter (known as the בֵּית יִשְׂרָאֵל, who presided from 1948 to 1977, and Rav Simcha Bunim Alter, the לֵב שִׂמְחָה, who served from 1977 to 1992). Upon assuming the mantle of leadership, he perpetuated and furthered many of the practices begun by his predecessors, such as awaking before dawn to study Torah, insisting on unpretentious *simchos* even for the affluent, encouraging the daily study of a page of *Talmud Yerushalmi* (as well as the more traditional *Daf Yomi*), and fostering the annual convocation of all Gerrer institutions (איחוד מוסדות גור).

כְּזֵר הַנָּתוּן עַל מֵצַח מֶלֶךְ

Like a crown that is placed on a king's forehead

Anyone witnessing the enormous reverence accorded to the Rebbe by the throngs of pilgrims coming to his "*tish*" every Shabbos, and especially Yom Tov, enjoyed a taste of spiritual royalty. Not merely royalty, but rather *royalty resurrected*. During the tenure of the Rebbe זצ״ל, as many people thronged the Gerrer *Bais HaMedrash* as had during the heyday of pre-war Poland. (Refer to the tribute to the *Imrei Emes* for a description of that era.)

כְּחֶסֶד הַנִּתָּן עַל פְּנֵי חָתָן

Like the graciousness granted to a bridegroom's face

The Rebbe זצ"ל epitomized kindness in all its manifestations: financial assistance to the impoverished, a sounding board and receptive ear to the infirm and to those overwhelmed with life's burdens, and words of advice to all those who sought his counsel. He displayed an extraordinary kindness to children, and was keenly interested in their progress. I remember the Rebbe asking a parent whether it would be all right to offer his *kinderlach* a small chocolate bar!

But he also *demanded* kindness, insisting that many of *Klal Yisrael's* problems stem from עַיִן רָעָה, our unwillingness to tolerate the success of others (a concept best expressed through the Yiddish term *"farginnen"*). While we may *preach* the ideal of וְאָהַבְתָּ לְרֵעֲךָ כָּמוֹךָ, *love your fellow as yourself,* true אַהֲבַת יִשְׂרָאֵל requires *active practice* — seeking the success of others as well as ourselves; it requires an עַיִן טוֹבָה, a *good* and *tolerant eye.*

כְּטֹהַר הַנָּתוּן בִּצְנִיף טָהוֹר

Like the purity that was placed upon the turban pure

The Rebbe זצ"ל fought valiantly for moral purity, insisting upon exemplary moral standards for Jews worldwide and especially in Israel. In particular, he utilized his considerable influence to combat the rash of abortions threatening *Klal Yisrael's* survival, and to insist upon higher standards in the media.

כְּמַלְאָךְ הַנִּצָּב עַל רֹאשׁ דֶּרֶךְ

Like an angel stationed on a highway

The Gerrer Rebbe, serving for many decades as Rosh Yeshiva of Yeshivas Sfas Emes, was the מוֹרֶה דֶּרֶךְ, *the spiritual mentor* (cf. *Moed Kattan* 17a, comparing a Torah teacher to an angel).

כְּשָׂרֵי צְבָאוֹת בְּרֹאשׁ עַם קֹדֶשׁ

Like the leaders of hosts at the head of a holy people

As a member and later chairman of the Moetzes Gedolei HaTorah (Rabbinical Advisory Board) of Agudath Israel in *Eretz Yisrael,* he was a general and supreme strategist on behalf of *Klal Yisrael,* offering his sage advice on all matters affecting Torah Jewry.

As a small child, while the Rebbe זצ״ל was reviewing the story of Yaakov's dream of a ladder entrenched on earth whose head reached heavenward, the *Imrei Emes* asked him: "Why didn't Yaakov dream that he had climbed the ladder?" The future Rebbe responded: "Look at the following *passuk*: וְהִנֵּה ה׳ נִצָּב עָלָיו, *And behold! Hashem was standing above the ladder.* Why climb the ladder when Hashem is already present, already hovering above the ladder?"

This, then, was the Rebbe זצ״ל's motif, already stated as a young child: Always be prepared to grow, to climb, but never lose sight of the ultimate objective — to remain humble in Hashem's presence — וְהִנֵּה ה׳ נִצָּב עָלָיו — זְכוּתוֹ יָגֵן עָלֵינוּ וְעַל כָּל יִשְׂרָאֵל.

Elul

יְמֵי רָצוֹן
Days of Grace

The month of Elul is commonly thought of as a time of Divine goodwill (עֵת רָצוֹן), but this term raises questions: Since Hashem is eternal and unchanging, how can He be said to show one quality — such as goodwill — at some times and different qualities at others? Indeed, how can His kindness be limited to a particular time frame, since we know He is מָלֵא רַחֲמִים, *constantly* filled with mercy?

We must therefore say that the prevalence of Divine goodwill in Elul does not result from any change in Hashem's nature, Heaven forbid, but rather reflects an increased capacity on Israel's part to absorb His kindness. Normally Hashem's kindness, being infinite, is beyond our ability to assimilate. In Elul, however, this kindness is channeled through the י״ג מִדּוֹת הָרַחֲמִים, the *Thirteen Attributes* [lit. *measures*] *of Mercy*, which scale it down to proportions we can appreciate. The concept of *measures* suggests finite limits which are set by Hashem to His otherwise limitless Attributes so that mortals can benefit. Every Elul (and other instances described as periods of Divine goodwill, e.g. *Shalosh Seudos*) the Jewish people acquire the capacity to benefit from the י״ג מִדּוֹת הָרַחֲמִים, the *Thirteen Attributes of Mercy*. Similarly, the Jewish people can make the most of the Divine light of Torah (cf. *Mishlei* 6:23, נֵר מִצְוָה וְתוֹרָה אוֹר, *a commandment is a lamp and the Torah is light*) that prevails at such times.

On our part, however, we must do everything in our power to make ourselves into suitable vessels to receive Hashem's mercies, even in a more limited and finite form. We can do this by circumscribing limits for ourselves, as Shlomo HaMelech wrote (*Shir HaShirim* 8:10), אֲנִי חוֹמָה, *I am a wall*, for unless we control our wants and desires, we are certain to dissipate Hashem's bounty. When we place boundaries and limits on our passions we can focus on fulfilling the Divine will. Consequently, Hashem will limit His boundless Attributes so that every Elul, Israel may benefit from them.   (*Elul 5631*)

במנחה בשבת עת רצון וכן בחודש אלול ימי רצון. והלא השי״ת
אין בו שינוי והוא למעלה מן הזמן. רק הפי׳ שהשינוי הוא בהזמן.

Actually the term עֵת רָצוֹן is extremely precise. Certainly Hashem Himself remains fixed and unchanging at all times, and is indeed totally beyond any limits of time (a quality described in Hebrew as לְמַעֲלָה מִן הַזְמַן, *above time*). In our time-bound world, however, periods of time do change. Thus Elul is a *time* of goodwill, a month in which *time* itself is altered and becomes capable of receiving Hashem's bounty from the world above the bounds of time. Consequently, we in this temporal world (עוֹלָם הַזֶּה) are capable of making a connnection with the timeless ideals of the World to Come (עוֹלָם הַבָּא) and elevating ourselves to a far more spiritual existence.   (*Elul 5634*)

ימי אלול המה ימי רצון כמ״ש בספרים דכתי׳ כי מי גוי גדול אשר
לו אלקים קרובי׳ וגו׳ בכל קראנו אליו ולכן בימים הללו שבנ״י
משתוקקין לשוב לה׳ כן נפתח למעלה שערי תשובה . . .

The fact is that any time Israel opens its heart to Hashem in sincere prayer to draw close to Him is a time of Divine goodwill, as Moshe proclaimed (*Devarim* 4:7), כִּי מִי גוֹי גָּדוֹל אֲשֶׁר לוֹ אֱלֹהִים קְרֹבִים אֵלָיו כַּה׳, אֱלֹהֵינוּ בְּכָל קָרְאֵנוּ אֵלָיו, *For which is a great nation that has a God Who is close to it, as is* HASHEM, *our God, whenever we call to Him?* If Hashem is close to us whenever we call to Him, then especially in Elul, a month filled with prayers and fervent desire to be as close to Hashem as possible, the Gates of Prayer and Repentance are certain to be open.   (*Likutim*)

וכמו שהחטא נשאר לדורות. . .ממילא התשובה שעשו אז ותקנו
החטא. בוודאי הי' ג''כ לדורות. ומרע''ה תיקן בשורש נשמות
בנ''י בשמים . . . לכן בנקל עכ''פ לנו לתקן גופי החטאים. וע''י
שלוחות שניות היו בדרך בעלי תשובות. נשאר ההארה שלהם גם
עתה יותר מהימים של הלוחות הראשונות כי בע''ת אתיין
בחילא סגי.

The special quality of these days, to kindle our aspirations to return to
Hashem, has its roots in the first Elul Israel experienced as a nation,
when the people were steeped in intense repentance over the Sin of the
Golden Calf. The Sages tell us that that sin was not completely expiated
at the time; instead Hashem amortized the punishment we deserved and
continually extracts it in small portions whenever we need to be
punished for other offenses (cf. *Rashi, Shemos* 32:34). We may assume
that the profound desire to return to Hashem we felt that first Elul also
continues to reverberate in our national soul during this month — even
today and throughout all generations.

Another factor contributes to the special grace these days have for
penitents. The Sages (*Devarim Rabbah* 3:12) relate that Moshe's prayers
to reinstate the souls of the Jewish people to Hashem's favor after the
Sin of the Golden Calf rent every corner of the heavens (cf. *Rashi,
Shemos* 1:1, where the heavenly roots of Jewish souls are compared to
stars). As a result, during these days it is easier for us to rectify our
sins and to restore our souls to their original pure state. If anything, we
can make ourselves even stronger than before, since sincere penitents
have even greater power to serve Hashem than those who have never
sinned. (*Elul* 5643)

כי תבוא תרמ''א: ולפי מה שאדם דופק כל ימי השנה כך נפתח לו
באלה הימים . . . ובימים אלו מבקשין בשמים שיתעוררו בנ''י
בתשובה כמ''ש קול דודי דופק . . .

During these days so imbued with Divine goodwill, Hashem eagerly
awaits for us to return, and indeed pleads with us to seek out the Divine
spark in our midst and allow it to guide us back to Him. We are aided
in this process by a special gift that is in force during Elul: the Thirteen Measures of Mercy which facilitate our return. This multifaceted

nature of *teshuvah* is sublimely depicted by Shlomo *HaMelech* in *Shir HaShirim* (5:2): קוֹל דּוֹדִי דוֹפֵק: פִּתְחִי לִי אֲחֹתִי רַעְיָתִי יוֹנָתִי תַמָּתִי שֶׁרֹאשִׁי נִמְלָא טָל, *The voice of my Beloved knocks, "Open for Me, My sister, My beloved, My dove, My perfection, for My head is filled with dew."* Hashem pleads with us to open our hearts to Him, and assures us that He is filled only with mercy (the Thirteen Divine Measures are often symbolized by dew in the literature of *Kaballah*) for us.

From this we can learn how important it is for us to persist in calling out to Hashem throughout the year. Even though our prayers may seem to go unheard and unanswered as we are offering them, once Elul comes and the gates of heaven are opened by our sincere desire to repent and to return to Hashem, then all our prayers from the entire year surge through them and find a warm and loving reception in Hashem's ears. *(Ki Savo 5641)*

⊰ לוּחֹת שְׁנִיּוֹת / The Second Tablets ⊱

שופטים תרנ״ח: הראשונים היו ברצון הקב״ה בעצמו ואחרונים
נתרצה הקב״ה לנו כמ״ש מתרצה ברחמים ומתפייס בתחנונים.

As we said above, the extraordinary nature of Elul and its status as a period of grace can be traced back to the first Elul Israel experienced as a nation. Having just undergone spiritual depression and ostracism following the Sin of the Golden Calf, the people were restored to Hashem's good graces on Rosh Chodesh Elul, when Moshe ascended Mount Sinai for his final stay. This initiated a forty-day period of rapprochement between the Creator and Israel culminating in the granting of the Second Tablets on Yom Kippur, a time justly known in our history as יְמֵי רָצוֹן, *days of Divine goodwill.*

In this section we shall elaborate on the unique significance of the Second Tablets, focusing in particular on their importance to later generations during the month of Elul. We shall also consider the relationship between Israel's return to Hashem that first Elul and the annual process of *teshuvah* which occurs every year at this time.

Our sincere return to Hashem during that first Elul illustrates how much power we have to arouse Hashem's goodwill simply by displaying initiative and a desire to return to Him. Although the First Tablets were also given in an ambiance of Divine Grace (cf. *Rashi Devarim* 9:18 who describes this period as יְמֵי רָצוֹן, *days of goodwill*), Hashem's goodwill at that time came not so much in response to Israel's petition to draw close to Him but rather as a unilateral grant of favor to His beloved people. That first Elul, however, having betrayed Hashem's expectations for them through their involvement with the Golden Calf, Israel now had to traverse the long road back on its own initiative and to re-earn Hashem's grace on the strength of its own merits. By heeding Moshe's earnest prayers and accepting the people's heartfelt repentance, Hashem made a clear commitment never to spurn our initiatives to return to Him. Thus the liturgist describes Hashem as מִתְרַצֶּה בְּרַחֲמִים וּמִתְפַּיֵּס בְּתַחֲנוּנִים, *The One Who becomes favorable through compassion and becomes appeased through supplications*, perhaps a reference to that first Elul, when Hashem accepted Israel's initiative and showed the Jewish people how to find a path back to Him in all future Eluls. *(Shoftim 5658)*

☙ First Tablets — Merit
Second Tablets — Sincere Repentance

> וצריך איש ישראל להתחזק באלה הימ' יום שקרבנו הקב"ה
> ברצון כי לוחות הראשונות היו בחי' הבחירה בבנ"י ובאחרונות
> בחי' התקרבות כמ"ש תבחר ותקרב. ומ"מ עיקר הברית הי'
> באחרונות . . .

The First Tablets were given by Hashem to a virtuous nation, as yet untainted by the Sin of the Golden Calf, as a symbol that He had selected us from among all other peoples. The Second Tablets, however, were an even more potent sign that Hashem still wanted to draw us close to Him even after our sin. The relationship between the two events is captured succinctly by the Psalmist (65:5): אַשְׁרֵי תִּבְחַר וּתְקָרֵב, *Happy is the [nation] whom You choose and draw near*. Hashem *chose* us to receive the First Tablets on the basis of our merits and then welcomed our sincere repentance and drew us back to Him again to give us the Second Tablets. *(Elul 5661)*

לכן בנקל עכ״פ לנו לתקן גופי החטאים. וע״י שלוחות שניות היו בדרך בעלי תשובות. נשאר ההארה שלהם גם עתה יותר מהימים של הלוחות הראשונות כי בע״ת אתיין בחילא סגי.

To understand how the Second Tablets signaled Hashem's acceptance of our repentance, let us remember that the forty-day period Moshe spent on Mount Sinai to receive them is observed annually by Jews throughout the world as a month of introspection and repentance — Elul. The first forty-day period, in contrast, is not commemorated. Surely this is impressive testimony to the higher status of returning penitents vis-a-vis a nation of as-yet untested *tzaddikim* receiving the Torah for the first time.

(*Elul 5643*)

חודש אלול ניתקן לתשובה שבו קיבל מרע״ה לוחות אחרונות שעיקר תשובה לתורתך כנ״ל. . .כי למה נצרך מרע״ה להיות מ׳ יום שניים הלא כבר למד מקודם מ׳ יום . . . הי׳ תורה זו באופן אחר כמו לבע״ת לא כמו שהי׳ מקודם . . .

Why did Hashem require Moshe to spend a second forty-day period on Mount Sinai simply to receive the Second Tablets, when he had surely mastered the entire Torah during his first stay? In light of the above discussion, however, the explanation appears clear: During Moshe's first stay on the mountain, he was given preparation to teach the Torah to a nation of *tzaddikim*, as befitted the nation's status at that time. Now that the people had sinned and struggled to repent, he had to be equipped with an entirely different methodology suitable to their changed condition as pentitents. The special needs of the *baal teshuvah* in attaining Torah knowledge are alluded to in *Berachos* 34b, בְּמָקוֹם שֶׁבַּעֲלֵי תְשׁוּבָה עוֹמְדִים אֵין צַדִּיקִים גְּמוּרִים יְכוֹלִים לַעֲמֹד, *In the place* [i.e. the approach to learning Torah] *where the baalei teshuvah stand, even the completely righteous are unable to stand.*

(*Likutim*)

ולפי שהאחרונות היו הלוחות מלמטה והכתב מלמעלה ה״ז כריתות ברית והתקרבות התחתונים לעליונים . . .

Let us consider further the permanent impact left by the Second Tablets on our people. Hashem sealed His relationship with us in the form of a covenant (בְּרִית), as the Torah states (*Shemos* 34:10): הִנֵּה אָנֹכִי כֹּרֵת בְּרִית נֶגֶד כָּל עַמְּךָ, *Behold! I seal a covenant before your entire people.* The Second Tablets, which were made of stone hewn by Moshe, typified covenants in which both parties commit themselves to contribute to the common good.

In contrast, there was no need for Israel to play a role in preparing the First Tablets, since at that time they had attained the spiritual heights of angels as the Psalmist says (82:6): אֱלֹהִים אַתֶּם וּבְנֵי עֶלְיוֹן כֻּלְּכֶם, *You are angelic, sons of the Most High are you all.* However, in the aftermath of the Golden Calf, when they were reduced in stature to ordinary human beings residing on earth, it was more appropriate for Israel to have a part in fashioning the material base on which the Torah was given

(Elul 5661)

Although the human involvement in the Second Tablets might seem to detract from their importance, actually they speak to the condition of the contemporary Jew far better than the First Tablets, even though these were made entirely by Hashem. So removed is our generation from the experience of Mount Sinai that we cannot possibly aspire to reach the lofty levels proffered by the First Tablets. The Second Tablets, however, precisely because they embody human participation, continue to act as the backbone of our national existence until this very day.

(ibid.)

וגם הראשונות היו בקולי קולות ובאחרונות אמר הקב"ה אין לך
יפה מן הצניעות. . .הענין כי בראשונות הי' הכוונה לתקן כל
העולם . . . אך עמלק הרשע ימ"ש הוא גרם חטא העגל. . .ולכן
היו האחרונות בצינעה להיות מיוחד רק לבנ"י.

Apart from the composition of the Second Tablets, the circumstances under which they were given also differ significantly from those of the First Tablets. As *Rashi* notes (*Shemos* 34:3), while the first ones were given amidst great fanfare, Moshe received the second ones in total seclusion.

The absence of an audience witnessing the giving of the Second Tablets is hardly an insignificant detail, but rather reflects an essential facet of the Jews' mission in their first Elul as a nation. When the First Tablets were given in full public view, they carried with them the challenge not only to elevate ourselves spiritually but also to leave an impact on the rest of mankind, as Hashem told Moshe (*Shemos* 19:5), וִהְיִיתֶם לִי סְגֻלָּה מִכָּל הָעַמִּים כִּי לִי כָּל הָאָרֶץ, *you shall be to Me the most beloved treasure of all peoples, for Mine is the entire world.*

Tragically, that dream was dashed primarily as a result of Amalek's rejection of Hashem's sovereignty and subsequent skirmish with the Jewish people. This started a spiritual erosion that may well have contributed to the debacle of the Golden Calf. As a result of the Jewish people's decline and ultimate sin, their mission was sharply redefined to focus now on internal self-improvement rather than on perfecting mankind. It follows naturally that the Second Tablets should have a lower profile, reflecting the new inward-directed orientation. Consequently it was no longer necessary to subject them to an elaborate ceremony which would expose them to all mankind, therefore both sides — Hashem and His people — could focus on establishing a unique and direct covenant. (*Elul* 5647)

כי כל אדם יש לו חלק בתורה כמי"ש ותן חלקנו כו' כי באורייתא
ברא קוב"ה עלמא ולכך זה עיקר התשובה אף בלי חטא ממש . . .

Moshe's ascent to Mount Sinai to receive the Torah a second time, now at the helm of a nation of penitents, highlights a central objective of Elul — the return to Torah. Each and every Jew has his own unique contribution to make towards our national mission of studying and disseminating the Torah, as we ask thrice daily in our prayers, וְתֵן חֶלְקֵנוּ בְּתוֹרָתֶךָ, *Grant us our share in Your Torah.*

The origins of this concept reach back even before the Creation of the world, since the Sages teach (*Yalkut Shimoni, Bereishis* 2) that Hashem used the Torah as His blueprint in constructing the universe. Thus the world came into existence and continues to exist only for Torah; it follows that each individual being is sustained only because of his unique portion in Torah. Though a Jew may stray from his Torah roots during the year, when Elul comes he always finds his way back to them.

Indeed, precisely this process of reconnecting to one's Torah roots is the essence of *teshuvah* (repentance): to extricate ourselves from the morass of materialism which engulfs the world and cling to Hashem and His Torah once again. In this light, we can see that *teshuvah* is by no means reserved exclusively for sinners, since it actually involves no more nor less than turning away from our normal excessive preoccupation with the modalities of the material world and returning to (לָשׁוּב) Hashem (*Likutim*). Thus we pray three times every weekday, הֲשִׁיבֵנוּ אָבִינוּ לְתוֹרָתֶךָ, *Bring us back, our Father, to Your Torah.* (*Likutim*)

וכמו כן בדורות בימים אלו שנתקבלו תפלות אבותינו. יכולין לעלות תפלותינו דלים ורשים בהתדבקות באותן התפלות שהתפללו אבותינו ומשה רבינו ע"ה.

Finally, the Second Tablets are intimately associated with the theme of *tefillah*, the heartfelt prayers of the Jewish people. During the forty-day period between Rosh Chodesh Elul and Yom Kippur, Moshe's prayers, like those of the then contrite Jewish people, pierced through to open the gates of heaven not only for themselves but for all of posterity as well. As a result, even the far more feeble prayers of a spiritually impoverished generation such as our own can still find acceptance by attaching themselves to the earnest pleadings of our predecessors, especially those of Moshe's time. This theme can be derived from the renowned verse recited in *Ashrei* every day, קָרוֹב ה׳ לְכָל קֹרְאָיו לְכֹל אֲשֶׁר יִקְרָאֻהוּ בֶאֱמֶת — *HASHEM is close to all who call upon Him — to all who call upon Him sincerely* (*Tehillim* 145:18). In the merit of the righteous of our people of all ages and generations who have called upon Hashem in the deepest sincerity, He accepts the pleas of *all* those who seek Him out. (5647).

◄§ The Shofar of Elul

ויש להקשות למה לא תקעו גם במ' ימים אמצעים והרגישו נפשות בנ"י כי נפתחו למעלה מקורות הרחמים והמה ימי רצון שזה אמת שע"י שנתעורר למעלה עי"כ הרגישו למטה מ"מ גם זה אמת שע"י תקיעות שופר נתעורר עת רצון בשמים כמ"ש נתעלה באותו שופר . . .

The tradition of sounding the *shofar* throughout the month of Elul is derived from a Midrash (*Pirkei d'Rabbi Eliezer* 15) which states that the *shofar* was blown each day of Moshe's final sojourn on Mount Sinai, which began on Rosh Chodesh Elul, in order to remind the people that he was still alive, though temporarily absent. It will be remembered that during his first sojourn on the mountain, the people were induced to fashion the Golden Calf as a replacement for him when they were tricked into thinking he would never return to them.

If this was indeed the reason, however, we may ask why the *shofar* was not blown during his second stay on Mount Sinai as well, which lasted from the eighteenth of Tammuz (after the shattering of the First Tablets) until the twenty-ninth of Av, while he was pleading with Hashem to forgive the people and not destroy them.

One simple answer is that in their chastened state following the Sin of the Golden Calf, the people were unlikely to sin again so quickly. Later, however, after they were absolved from their sin on Rosh Chodesh Elul, Moshe had greater grounds for concern that in their newfound confidence the people might succumb once again to their passions and turn to idols during his absence.

On a more profound level, we can say that the Jewish people realized the futility of sounding the *shofar* at any other than the most opportune time. During Elul, Israel could sense that they were in the midst of a period of unique grace, a time when the gates of heaven were open to their prayers. Only at such a time could the *shofar* be effective in preventing any further straying.

In fact, the association between the Elul grace period and the *shofar* is symbiotic. By sounding the *shofar*, the Jewish people arouse Hashem's Attributes of Mercy perpetrating a period of grace. Israel, sensing that Elul had been designated a period of Divine kindness, determined that it is an opportune time to sound the *shofar*.   (*Likutim*)

Allusions to Elul

While the Torah makes no explicit reference to the month of Elul, numerous allusions can be found. The following section analyzes and explores the significance of some of them.

⋙ Constellation of Elul: A Virgin (בְּתוּלָה)

והנה מזל אלול בתולה. היינו שיש נקודה פנימית בנפש ישראל
שאין שולט שם מגע נכרי.

According to ancient Jewish tradition, the twelve heavenly constellations correspond to the twelve months of the year. Specifically, the month of Elul is represented by the constellation (מַזָּל) that resembles a virgin (בְּתוּלָה).

The association between the concept of a virgin and Elul may be appreciated in light of our previous assertion that no matter how far a Jew strays, a pure untouched spark of goodness that is not affected by the alien values of the Gentile world remains. This spark, the *"pintele yid,"* is aroused every Elul and propels and inspires the individual to repent. The בְּתוּלָה, a chaste young woman unfettered by ties to anyone, is the perfect symbol for depicting this inherent purity that resides in every Jewish soul. (5647)

ואיתא דמאן דכפות באחרא א״י לקבל עליו עומ״ש לכן צריכין
בחודש הזה לצאת משיעבוד הסט״א ויצה״ר להיות נקי לקבל
עומ״ש [לכן נקרא מזל חודש הזה בתולה]

The association between the בְּתוּלָה and Elul can be drawn even further if we perceive an unmarried young woman as being symbolic of purity and freedom, one who is not bound by marriage ties. This freedom is an essential prerequisite for one of Rosh Hashanah's central themes — the coronation of Hashem (מַלְכִיּוֹת). As the *Zohar* (*Behar* 108a) states, someone who is bound and attracted to the temptations of the Evil Inclination (יֵצֶר הָרָע) is incapable of proclaiming Hashem's sovereignty. By unshackling ourselves from evil, much as a virgin is uncommitted to any man, we will be free to accept Hashem's Kingship on Rosh Hashanah. (5640)

אֲנִי לְדוֹדִי וְדוֹדִי לִי

I Am for My Beloved and My Beloved Is for Me (*Shir HaShirim* 6:3)

Perhaps the most famous allusion to Elul in all of *Tanach* is that voiced by Shlomo *HaMelech* in *Shir HaShirim*, אֲנִי לְדוֹדִי וְדוֹדִי לִי, *I am for my Beloved and my Beloved is for me*. As it is well known, the first letters of each of these words, when combined, form the word אֱלוּל. In the following segment we will explore some of the implications of this apparent rapprochement between lovers (allegorically) occurring every Elul.

הרמז לאלול אני לדודי ודודי לי. כי בזמן הזה נתעוררו בנ״י בתשובה וזכו במעשיהם לעורר עת רצון בשמים

A primary factor necessary to effecting a reconciliation in a damaged relationship is *reciprocity*, a mutual exchange between both parties. That first Elul when Moshe ascended Mt. Sinai, the Jewish people took the first step repenting from their flirtation with idolatry. Hashem matched their initiative by accepting Israel's *teshuvah*. (5641)

כפי מה שמכין אדם עצמו להיות רק לדודי כן דודי לי

So too, every Elul, a direct association exists between Israel's return to Hashem (אֲנִי לְדוֹדִי, *I am for my Beloved*) and Hashem's subsequent rapprochement with the Jewish people (וְדוֹדִי לִי). The more effort expended by the Jewish people as it returns to Hashem, the greater will be the assistance rendered by Him towards facilitating our *teshuvah*. As the Jew takes the initiative — the first small steps towards reconciliation — he suddenly senses his latent potential for sanctity emerging.　　　　　　　　　　　　　　　　　　　　　(*Likutim*)

וזה הרמז אני לדודי ודי״ל שבני״י מכוונים לאותו מדה המתעוררת
למעלה והיא עדות שבני״י מיוחדים אליו ית׳ כמ״ש במי״א

A renewed relationship between former partners requires *sensitivity*, that innate ability of each partner to read the other's mind and sense his most intimate feelings. As stated previously, the Jewish people sounded the *shofar* that first Elul feeling intuitively that this was a period of Divine grace (עֵת רָצוֹן). This uncanny ability to sense Hashem's sublimest "emotions," to detect the Divine Will with such precision, is indicative of the closeness between Israel and Hashem.

Moreover, a relationship between lovers implies the ability of one partner to impact upon the other. At the time of Moshe's ascent, by blowing *shofar* the Jewish people aroused Hashem's innate Mercies. They helped open the floodgates of heaven to their prayer and they ensured that henceforth Elul became a time of Divine grace. Israel's ability to impact on the Divine Presence (*Pirkei d'Rabbi Eliezer* 15) may be the underlying intent of the Midrashic comment: נִתְעַלָּה הקב״ה בְּאוֹתוֹ שׁוֹפָר, *Hashem was elevated through the shofar [of Elul]*. This alludes to the great effect of Israel's action that compelled Hashem to reveal His Attributes of Mercy.　　　　　　　　　　　　　　　　　(*Likutim, Elul*)

ובחודש אלול (הזה) מתקיים אני לדודי. וע״י כן מתקיים בחודש
תשרי ודודי לי.

Perhaps, most profoundly, it is known that lovers are "obsessed" with each other, thinking of nothing but how to please one another. While all year long Israel is entrusted with a cosmic mission, a global goal to perfect the entire universe, every Elul the Jewish people abandon that global mandate in favor of a more restricted one — to return to its own spiritual roots. And for good reason! In our zeal to perfect this universe, we invariably develop connections with evildoers. Such tangential ties with the wicked may be acceptable all year long in the interest of expunging evil. However, every Elul the Talmudic dictum of חַיֶּיךָ קוֹדְמִין (*Bava Metzia* 62a) — your own spiritual and physical well-being takes precedence — requires us to come back exclusively to Hashem (our Beloved, אֲנִי לְדוֹדִי). At this time of the year we set aside our global mission. If we can find our way back in Elul, then Hashem reciprocates on Rosh Hashanah by bestowing upon us His blessing (וְדוֹדִי לִי).

(5640)

וביאור הענין שבנ״י צריכין להיות מוכנים בלתי לה׳ לבדו כדכ׳ עם זו יצרתי לי. וזה אני לדודי שיודעין שאין לנו צורך בעולם רק לעשות רצונו ית׳ ולהרבות כבודו בעולם. וכפי מה שמבורר כן אצלינו כן מתברר למעלה דודי לי שכל בריאות העולם והתגלות כל מיני הארות שנמצא מאתו ית׳ בעולם הכל רק בעבורינו. . . . ועיקר פי׳ אני לדודי להיות איש ישראל יודע שנברא רק לשמש את קונו ואין לו מציאות וצורך אחר כלל בעולם. . . . וז״ש וצאן מרעיתו. כדאיתא בתנא דבי אליהו יושב והוגה בתורה כבהמה החורשת בשדה. . . . שיודעין שאין להם מציאות אחר רק לדודי. וכן ודודי לי הפי׳ כן כי כל מה שצימצם הש״י כביכול להיות נודע בעולם ושיתגלה שם הוי׳ ב״ה בעולם הכל לי. כמ״ש בשביל ישראל שנק׳ ראשית.

עיקר התשובה צריך להיות ע״ז לזכור כי נשתלחנו בעוה״ז לעשות רצונו ית״ש בלבד.

I am for my Beloved and my Beloved is for me implies more than returning to the fold — it suggests a single-minded devotion to each other. *I am for my Beloved* — every Elul, Israel resolves that its sole *raison d'être* (reason for existing) is to serve Hashem. As Yeshayahu proclaims: עַם זוּ יָצַרְתִּי לִי, *The nation (Israel) which I have created for me* (43:21). This is no abstract ideology but rather a summons to the Jewish people every Elul to detach themselves from the material world and awaken from the spiritual slumber that overcomes them all year long and return now to their *Beloved*, Hashem.

The Talmudic sage captured the essence of Elul by suggesting אֲנִי נִבְרֵאתִי לְשַׁמֵּשׁ אֶת קוֹנִי, *I was created to serve my Master* (*Kiddushin* 82b). Israel is "obsessed" with its Creator and in turn, Hashem displays an equally single-minded devotion to the Jewish people, as the verse concludes, *my Beloved is for me*, וְדוֹדִי לִי.

G-d's presence in this world, His desire to somehow "compress" His Infinite Majesty to allow a few rays of His *Shechinah* to penetrate the earth so that His Presence can be felt in this finite universe (צָמְצֵם כִּבְיָכוֹל

הש"י אֶת אוֹר כְּבוֹדוֹ כְּדֵי לִהְיוֹת נוֹדַע בָּעוֹלָם), was all done for Israel's benefit. In fact, the creation of heaven and earth was intended to be a habitat for the Jewish people, בִּשְׁבִיל יִשְׂרָאֵל שֶׁנִּקְרְאוּ רֵאשִׁית. (5644, 5647, 5657)

שופטים תרנ"ח: אני לדודי הוא ביטול הטבעיות לבטל כל הכח אל הש"י וזה אינו בנמצא רק בב"י וכמו כן דודי לי שמה"ט יש התגלות אלקותו ית"ש לבנ"י מה שאין בנמצא לשום אומה.

The mutual obsession of Israel and Hashem with each other is unique and attests to their special relationship. No other nation ever developed such an intimacy with Hashem, and Hashem never displayed such affection to any other nation. (*Shoftim* 5658)

ונק' בתולה ועֵ"ז הנקודה נאמר אני לדודי שלעולם לא נתרחקה זו הנקודה מדביקות בשורשה. ושמורה לשמו ית'. אך לא בכל עת יכולין למצוא זו הנקודה. ועתה הזמן גורם שנתעוררו בנ"י בתשובה.
ג"כ שיש למעלה מדות מיוחדים רק לבנ"י. כמ"ש הנה אנכי כורת כו' נגד כל עמך כו' אשר לא נבראו כו'. א"כ יש מדות מיוחדים לבנ"י. והם י"ג מדות כמ"ש הורית לנו לומר שלש עשרה.

By using the metaphor of love to describe Israel's relationship with Hashem, Shlomo HaMelech is alluding to the inner spark latent in every Jew (נְקוּדָה הַפְּנִימִית) that never lost contact with his Creator. No matter how estranged a Jew may have become, something embedded in his innermost soul never stopped loving Hashem. Every Elul, that deep-seated love emerges, inspiring the Jew to repent. Similarly, Hashem has always felt a special attachment towards Israel (*and my Beloved is for me*), feelings that come to the forefront every Elul. In concrete terms, our "Beloved," Hashem, reasserts His covenant with us every Elul pledging to be guided by the Thirteen Attributes of Mercy. As the liturgist writes, אֵל הוֹרֵיתָ לָּנוּ לוֹמַר שְׁלֹשׁ עֶשְׂרֵה זְכֹר לָנוּ הַיּוֹם בְּרִית שְׁלֹשׁ עֶשְׂרֵה, O G-d, *You taught us to recite the Thirteen [Attributes of Mercy], so remember for us today the Covenant of these Thirteen [Attributes].* (5647)

✒ Total Indebtedness to Hashem

הוּא עָשָׂנוּ וְלֹא אֲנַחְנוּ

Who made us and not ourselves (Tehillim 100:3).

אני והוא יכולין לדור. מו״ז ז״ל אמר על אחד באלול לא אנחנו
הקרי והכתיב. ע״י שלא אנחנו ומבטלים עצמינו לכן לו אנחנו ר״ה
למעשר בהמה עב״ד ז״ל. ויש להוסיף על דבריו כי גם להיפוך כן
הוא שע״י שמתקרבים אליו ית׳. ממילא מתבטלים בעיני עצמם.
כמאמר בהמות הייתי עמך דכ׳ אדם ובהמה תושיע ה׳ דרשו חז״ל
שערומין בדעת כאדם ומשימין עצמן כבהמה. פי׳ שזה הסימן ע״י
שבהמות הייתי עמך חל עליהם צורת האדם. ודרשו אתם קרויין
אדם ולא האומות שאין להם בחי׳ ביטול הנ״ל כמ״ש אתם המעט
שממעטין עצמן.

A nother allusion for Elul is derived from this verse in *Tehillim*
acknowledging our total indebtedness to Hashem.
The verse is *written* (כְּתִיב: דְּעוּ כִּי ה׳ הוּא אֱלֹהִים הוּא עָשָׂנוּ וְלֹא אֲנַחְנוּ עַמּוֹ)
וְצֹאן מַרְעִיתוֹ, *Know that Hashem, He is God, it is He Who made us and*
not ourselves (i.e. we did not create ourselves), *His people and the sheep*
of His pasture.
However, the verse is *read* (קְרִי) with one significant difference as
לא אֲנַחְנוּ (with a ״ו״ replacing the ״א״ of לא), *we are His people.* The
Chiddushei HaRim (the *Sfas Emes'* grandfather) noted that by combining the written (כְּתִיב) text, לא, and the actual rendition of the verse,
לו, we derive the word אֱלוּל.
Upon analyzing the *Chiddushei HaRim's* assertion, we realize that he
was alluding to a critical prerequisite for *teshuvah* — self-negation. Only
if the *written* version of the text is fulfilled — וְלֹא אֲנַחְנוּ, we are totally
insignificant in our own estimation — can the actual *reading* — וְלוֹ אֲנַחְנוּ,
becoming His (God's people and flock) — also be true. As the Talmud
relates (*Sotah* 5a), Hashem can not dwell amongst haughty people.
In truth, the reverse effect may also be true, whereby the *kri* לו pre-
cedes the *K'siv* לא. By coming close to Him and proclaiming Him as our
God (וְלוֹ אֲנַחְנוּ, *we are His*), Israel acquires the capacity for self-negation
(וְלֹא אֲנַחְנוּ), feeling truly humble in the Presence of Hashem. As David
exclaimed (73:22): בְּהֵמוֹת הָיִיתִי עִמָּךְ, *I was like an animal with You* (i.e. I

perceived myself as being nothing more than an animal in the presence of the *Shechinah*). The relationship between self-negation and coming close to Hashem may also be the intent of the following Talmudic saying (*Chullin* 5b): אֵלּוּ בְּנֵי אָדָם שֶׁהֵן עֲרוּמִין בְּדַעַת כְּאָדָם וּמְשִׂימִין עַצְמָן כִּבְהֵמָה, *these are people who are wise as people but* (nonetheless) *consider themselves to be no more than animals.* Not only the association but also the sequence is indicated by the foregoing statement. First the individual attains wisdom and subsequently he achieves self-negation.

To extend the analysis we could argue that the designation of Israel as the Chosen People may be based on our capacity for self-negation. As the Talmud notes, שֶׁמְּמַעֲטִין עַצְמָן (cf. *Chullin* 89a), Israel was chosen because it diminishes itself.

The famed (often misunderstood) Rabbinic statement: אַתֶּם קְרוּיִין אָדָם וְאֵין הָעַכּוּ"ם קְרוּיִין אָדָם , *you are called "man" and the other nations are not called "man"* (*Yevamos* 61a), may be based on the same reasoning. Only Israel with its capacity for self-negation may truly be called "man." The verse itself from which this dictum is derived seems to suggest that this reason for Israel's designation as man, וְאַתֵּן צֹאנִי צֹאן מַרְעִיתִי אָדָם אַתֶּם, *you are My sheep, the sheep of My pasture, you are man* (*Yechezkel* 34:31), is only because the Jewish people view themselves as being little more than God's flock (צֹאן מַרְעִיתִי), therefore they deserve the title *man!*

(5632, 5642, 5647)

◈ Elul and Tithing

בְּאֶחָד בֶּאֱלוּל רֹאשׁ הַשָּׁנָה לְמַעֲשֵׂר בְּהֵמָה

On the first of Elul is the New Year for the tithe of animals
(*Mishnah Rosh Hashanah* 1:1).

אני והוא יכולין לדור. מו"ז ז"ל אמר על אחד באלול לא אנחנו
הקרי והכתיב. ע"י שלא אנחנו ומבטלים עצמינו לכן לו אנחנו ר"ה
למעשר בהמה עב"ד ז"ל. ויש להוסיף על דבריו כי גם להיפוך כן
הוא שע"י שמתקרבים אליו ית'. ממילא מתבטלים בעיני עצמם.
כמאמר בהמות הייתי עמך דכ' אדם ובהמה תושיע ה' דרשו חז"ל
שערומין בדעת כאדם ומשימין עצמן כבהמה. פי' שזה הסימן ע"י
שבהמות הייתי עמך חל עליהם צורת האדם. ודרשו אתם קרויין
אדם ולא האומות שאין להם בחי' ביטול הנ"ל כמ"ש אתם המעט
שממעטין עצמן.

While we generally perceive the month of Elul as a preparation period for Rosh Hashanah, in reality it is also a Rosh Hashanah for tithing animals. In addition to the Mishnah's halachic ramification [animals must be born in the same year for the purpose of tithing, and the year begins on the first of Elul] for this purpose, the Mishnah may be hinting at Elul's essence as well.

As the Kabbalists maintain, every individual possesses an animal soul, i.e. his baser instincts and drives.

Every Elul we focus on this material component of ourselves, and guided by this Mishnah determine to take action. Two options exist regarding the animal soul of man. The first is to disassociate oneself (at least during the annual period of *teshuvah*) from any contact with one's baser instincts. According to this approach, the Mishnah should be interpreted as follows: *The first of Elul*, it is a Rosh Hashanah to separate (i.e. in the same manner the tithe is ordinarily separated) oneself from one's animal instincts. As stated in the essay on אֲנִי לְדוֹדִי וְדוֹדִי לִי, every Elul the Jew detaches himself from the temporal world and returns to Hashem. This process occurs both externally and internally, the turning away from the animal component in oneself.

On the other hand, tithing also implies sanctity and spiritual elevation (for example, the animal that is tithed is offered as a sacrifice). Wherever possible the Jew prefers to consecrate and elevate his animal soul — to utilize it for a higher purpose — rather than to utterly destroy it.

The association between tithing and Elul may also be indicated in the verse analyzed in the previous essay: הוּא עָשָׂנוּ וְלֹא אֲנַחְנוּ עַמּוֹ וְצֹאן מַרְעִיתוֹ. By negating ourselves and proclaiming our fealty to Hashem we become His sheep — we attain the capacity to engage and contend with our animal soul. (5632, 5640, 5642)

Finally the analogy to an animal (צֹאן מַרְעִיתוֹ) may be understood in the light of the Midrash's depiction of the Torah scholar as יוֹשֵׁב וְהוֹגֶה בְּתוֹרָה כִּבְהֵמָה הַחוֹרֶשֶׁת בַּשָּׂדֶה, *meditating in Torah as an animal plowing in the field* (*Tanna d'vei Eliyahu*). Just as an animal knows instinctively that its sole purpose is to fulfill its master's bidding, so too the *talmid chacham* realizes that his sole function is to serve Hashem. As Yeshayahu laments (1:3): יָדַע שׁוֹר קֹנֵהוּ . . . יִשְׂרָאֵל לֹא יָדַע, *the ox knows its master*, and that its existence is contingent upon pleasing its master — *but Israel does not know Me!* (5647)

▄§ Preparation for the Spiritual Battles of Rosh Hashanah

כִּי ה' אֱלֹהֶיךָ מִתְהַלֵּךְ בְּקֶרֶב מַחֲנֶךָ לְהַצִּילְךָ וְלָתֵת אֹיְבֶיךָ לְפָנֶיךָ

For Hashem, your God, walks in the midst of your camp to rescue you and to deliver your enemies before you (Devarim 23:15).

This verse, ostensibly referring to battles against the foes of the Jewish nation, may also allude to Elul, the preparatory period for the battle against the Satan on Rosh Hashanah. This can be demonstrated by the first letters (רָאשֵׁי תֵּיבוֹת) of the final four words of this verse which spell אֱלוּל (albeit in scrambled order). Just as Hashem assists Israel in its struggle against the mortal foe, so every Elul and Rosh Hashanah, He shields us against all spiritual forces and heavenly angels that would condemn us. (*Ki Seitzei 5640*)

▄§ Removal of All Impediments to Teshuvah

אֲנִי ה' הוּא שְׁמִי וּכְבוֹדִי לְאַחֵר לֹא אֶתֵּן

For I am Hashem, this is My Name and My Honor I will give to no other (deity) (Yeshayahu 42:8).

This verse also contains on allusion to Elul. Again, the first letters of the final four words of this verse (in scrambled order) spell אֱלוּל. By promising that His glory will be given to no other forces, Hashem is assuring Israel that all external (i.e. other) forces that could impede Israel's return — all the threats of Satan — will be overcome every Elul. (*Ki Seitzei 5640*)

▄§ From One Generation to Another

וּמָל ה' אֱלֹהֶיךָ אֶת לְבָבְךָ וְאֶת לְבַב זַרְעֶךָ

And Hashem your God will circumcise your heart and the heart of your offering (Devarim 30:6).

It is commonly known that the first letter of the words אֶת לְבָבְךָ וְאֶת לְבַב spell אֱלוּל. By choosing this particular allusion the Torah may be subtly reminding us of the impact that the *teshuvah* of fathers has on their children. Our fathers who returned to Hashem that first Elul after worshiping the Calf merited that Hashem circumcised their hearts. We too enjoy this period of grace every Elul.   (*Nitzavim 5635*)

◆§ From the Beginning to the End

מֵרֵשִׁית הַשָּׁנָה וְעַד אַחֲרִית שָׁנָה

From the beginning of the year until the end of the year
(*Devarim* 11:12).

מכלל שדרשו חז״ל מראשית השנה על תשרי א״כ אחרית שנה
הוא אלול. ויתכן לומר כי אחרית הוא הסוף והתכלית שגלוי
לפניו ית׳ שבנ״י שבים אליו ית״ש בסוף השנה.

The Talmud interprets this verse to be referring to the relationship between Rosh Hashanah judgment and the events that occur as the year unfolds.

מֵרֵשִׁית הַשָּׁנָה נִדּוֹן מַה יְהֵא בְּסוֹפָה, *At the year's beginning, it is determined what will occur at the end* (*Rosh Hashanah* 16b). While it seems that this Rabbinic saying is emphasizing the pivotal role of the year's beginning, Rosh Hashanah, it is also introducing the concept of אַחֲרִית שָׁנָה, *the year's end*, (i.e. its final month) Elul. In fact, the term אַחֲרִית connotes not only the year's end but also its ultimate purpose, its *raison d'être*. Israel, looking retrospectively upon the year that it had just experienced, realizes its feeble spiritual position. It determines to not only repent but to also return to one of its own ultimate purposes, the propagation of Hashem's name. In the merit of our appreciating the significance of the year's end and purpose — Elul — Hashem renews the Jew's and the universe's lease on life in Tishrei. The relationship between the year's end (אַחֲרִית) and its renewal (רֵשִׁית) may be appreciated in light of the אֲנִי לְדוֹדִי וְדוֹדִי לִי relationship previously discussed. By coming back at the year's end (אַחֲרִית) to our Beloved (אֲנִי לְדוֹדִי), Hashem reciprocates and returns to us, at the beginning of the following year (וְדוֹדִי לִי).   (5644)

Rosh Hashanah

בַּכֶּסֶה לְיוֹם חַגֵּנוּ
The Hidden Yom Tov

תִּקְעוּ בַחֹדֶשׁ שׁוֹפָר בַּכֶּסֶה לְיוֹם חַגֵּנוּ. כִּי חֹק לְיִשְׂרָאֵל הוּא מִשְׁפָּט
לֵאלֹהֵי יַעֲקֹב

Blow the shofar at the moon's renewal (New Moon), at the time appointed (hidden) for our festive day. Because it is a decree for Israel, a judgment for the God of Yaakov (Tehillim 81:4-5).

The foregoing renowned verse (recited during the *Maariv* of Rosh Hashanah) emphasizes two aspects of the *Yom Tov*. On one hand, it is a *festival* akin to the *Shalosh Regalim* also called חַג; on the other hand, it is a hidden occasion, בַּכֶּסֶה.[1] The following remarks elaborate on both the festive and the hidden elements of Rosh Hashanah.

◄§ The Festival Joy Is Hidden

החגים יש התגלות . . . ובר״ה הוא באתכסיא . . . וכמו ברגלים
יש ראי׳. עתה יש מצות שמיעת קול שופר. ומתקיים ג׳״כ בב׳
אופנים שיכולין לשמוע התעוררות שבא משמים ביום זה. וכמו כן
מתעלה קול שופר לשמים ושומע קול תרועת עמו ברחמים.

Simply stated, the joy of Rosh Hashanah is muted though certainly present. Unlike the *Shalosh Regalim*, occasions of visible joy, on

---

1. כֶּסֶה — related to the word כִּיסוּי, *covering*. All the other Festivals occur when the moon is clearly visible. Rosh Hashanah occurs at the very beginning of the month when the moon is hidden (covered) (*Rosh Hashanah* 8a).

Rosh Hashanah Israel's rejoicing is veiled beneath an exterior of awe and judgment.

In fact, a major factor contributing to the Festival's joy, perceiving Hashem upon entering the *Beis HaMikdash* (cf. *Devarim* 16:16, יֵרָאֶה כָּל זְכוּרְךָ), is lacking on Rosh Hashanah, since the Jewish people were not required to travel to Yerushalayim. As a result of Rosh Hashanah's lack of overt joy, the *Hallel*, consisting of David's joyous Psalms, is not recited. The recitation of *Hallel* is limited to those occasions in which the Divine Presence was visibly felt by the Jewish people. The term *Hallel* itself is derived from בְּהִלּוֹ נֵרוֹ עֲלֵי רֹאשִׁי, *When His lamp would shine over my head* (*Iyov* 29:3) — Iyov's depiction of Hashem's light being revealed to man. [See our essay entitled "Hallel on Rosh Hashanah" for further discussion of this theme.]

Yet, despite the absence of the pilgrimage to Yerushalayim on Rosh Hashanah, the *shofar*, in its own inimitable fashion, "transports" the Jewish soul to the innermost sanctum of the *Beis HaMikdash*'s Holy of Holies (קֹדֶשׁ קֳדָשִׁים). As the Talmud relates (*Rosh Hashanah* 26a) שׁוֹפָר כֵּיוָן דִּלְזִכָּרוֹן קָאָתֵי כְּלִפְנִים דָּמֵי, the *shofar*, whose purpose is to bring Israel's merit before Hashem, enjoys the same status and significance as artifacts used in the innermost recesses of the *Beis HaMikdash*.

Consider some of the ramifications of the hidden joy of Rosh Hashanah. While it may appear to us that Hashem's Presence is obscured on this day, He certainly watches over and protects Israel. The *Zohar* suggests that the Attribute of Hashem of יָשֶׁת חֹשֶׁךְ סִתְרוֹ, *He made darkness His concealment* (cf. *Tehillim* 18:12), prevails on Rosh Hashanah. Though veiled in darkness, He is certainly present.

The changed ambiance of Rosh Hashanah calls for a different emotion to emerge — awe and fear of Hashem, יִרְאָה rather than overt joy. Accompanying this altered emotion comes a shift towards an entirely different preceptor — *listening* (שְׁמִיעָה) to the Divine Voice rather than perceiving Him. The attentive Jew listening to the *shofar*'s sound (לִשְׁמוֹעַ קוֹל שׁוֹפָר) also hears the voice of Hashem arousing him from his year-round torpor. Similarly, while on the Three Festivals Hashem *sees* Israel (יֵרָאֶה כָּל זְכוּרְךָ), on Rosh Hashanah He also *listens* to the sound of our *shofar* blasts and it evokes His mercy, as the liturgist concludes the זִכְרוֹנוֹת blessing, שׁוֹמֵעַ קוֹל תְּרוּעַת עַמּוֹ יִשְׂרָאֵל בְּרַחֲמִים.

An association exists between Rosh Hashanah's emphasis on *fear* (יִרְאָה) of Hashem and *listening*. One who listens to the Divine word is motivated to fear Hashem (cf. *Chabakuk* 3:2, שָׁמַעְתִּי שִׁמְעֲךָ יָרֵאתִי ה').

(5644)

ולכן רמזו שבר"'ה הוא בחי' מרחוק ה' נראה לי.... ולכן אפילו
בזמן הזה שאין לנו ביהמ"'ק ובכל רגל נחסר לנו מצות הראי'
ועתה בחג של ר'"'ה יש לנו גם עתה בחי' כלפנים דמי:

Upon further contemplation, one can draw an even closer parallel between Rosh Hashanah and the Three Festivals. In each instance the Jew *perceives* Hashem. Whereas on *Yom Tov* Israel detects its Creator from a particularly close vantage point — the *Beis HaMikdash* — on Rosh Hashanah, though remote from Yerushalayim, he is able to approach Hashem. The *shofar* enables us to perceive Hashem and to feel as if we were present at the site of the *Beis HaMikdash*. It transports the Jewish soul to the site of the Holy of Holies (כְּלִפְנִים דָּמִי).

This theme of perceiving Hashem from afar is voiced in the Rosh Hashanah liturgy. The story of the *Akeidah*, read on the second day, concludes with a promise to future generations of Jews — every Rosh Hashanah they will be able to perceive Hashem (בְּהַר ה' יֵרָאֶה).

Similarly, in the *Haftarah* reading for the second day, Yirmiyahu (31:2) comforts a grieving Israel by assuring them, מֵרָחוֹק ה' נִרְאָה לִי, *Hashem appears to me from afar*.[1]

While one might conceive that perceiving Hashem from afar is a less exalted position than feeling His presence in Yerushalayim, in contemporary times the reverse is true. Though we can no longer embark on the annual pilgrimage to Yerushalayim to perceive Hashem closely, we can just as effectively as ever be aware of Hashem from afar through the powerful intermediary, the *shofar*.

(5651)

---

1. The ability to perceive Hashem on Rosh Hashanah though distant from the *Beis HaMikdash* may be alluded to in the same rabbinic saying, "In the place where the *baalei teshuvah* stand, even the completely righteous are unable to stand." Only on Rosh Hashanah can we stand at a distance from the *Beis HaMikdash* and yet perceive the sanctity of the Temple. The ability of the Jew, on Rosh Hashanah, to surmount the barriers of time (see following paragraph on the significance of Rosh Hashanah today) may be based on Rosh Hashanah being an occasion that celebrates the Creation when barriers of time and place did not exist.

(5665)

◆§ The Hidden Divine Sparks and Yom Tov

ויש לבנ״י הארה מטוב הגנוז . . . כי יש בכל איש ישראל נקודה
טמונה בלב שיש לנקודה זו דביקות בהשי״ת ממש . . . אך נקודה
זו צריכה להיות נסתר באדם שלא יהי׳ קטרוג עליו שלא יהי׳
ניכר על פניו היתרון שיש לו על כל הנבראים.

As stated previously, Rosh Hashanah deserves a place among the
Festivals as a time of veiled joy if not overt rejoicing. Upon further
reflection, a more profound association exists between Rosh Hashanah
and the Festivals. This relationship can be deduced from the term
Yom Tov, literally *a good day*, a day in which (according to the
Kabbalists) rays of the first light of Creation described by the Torah
as being "good" (cf. *Bereishis* 1:4) permeate the earth. Though mankind was not deserving to bask in this Divine Light (cf. *Rashi* ibid.,
stating that Hashem reserved the light of creation for the righteous
and the World to Come), a few rays of this rarefied light descends
every *Yom Tov*. These rays of heavenly light infiltrate the earth, but
it is only Israel — described as a nation that is totally righteous
(cf. *Yeshayahu* 60:21, וְעַמֵּךְ כֻּלָּם צַדִּיקִים) — that can benefit from such
intense spirituality.

On Rosh Hashanah, as well as every *Yom Tov*, this light permeates
the Jewish soul, causing Israel to rejoice.

But where is this light lodged? Not visibly; you cannot read a Jew's
face and detect this shining countenance. Instead, as David sings, אוֹר
זָרֻעַ לַצַּדִּיק, *A light is implanted in* (the soul of) *the righteous* (*Tehillim*
97:11). It is as an inner spark, a "*pintele Yid*" (נְקוּדָה הַפְּנִימִית) that
burns in the Jewish soul and allows every Jew, no matter how
estranged, to return and cling again to Hashem. It is this spark of
good light, ensuring the Jew's successful *teshuvah*, that generates
such joy every Rosh Hashanah, reassuring him inscription in the
Book of the Righteous. However, it is this selfsame spark that must
be *hidden* (בַּכֶּסֶה) from mankind at large. While a special relationship exists between Israel and Hashem (cf. *Devarim* 14:1, *you are
children to Hashem, your God*), it is absolutely critical this not be
publicized. In this context, we can better appreciate why the angels
desired that Israel recite *Hallel* on Rosh Hashanah. A moment of such

inner enlightenment certainly deserves acknowledgment in the form of *Hallel* (see our essay entitled "Hallel on Rosh Hashanah" for further discussion). (5634)

וְאֶמֶת שֶׁבְּנֵי"י בְּטוּחִין שֶׁיֵּצְאוּ זַכָּאִין וְגֶמֶר הַשִּׂמְחָה הוּא נִיכָּר בְּסוּכּוֹת. וְזֶהוּ בַּכֶּסֶה לְיוֹם חַגֵּנוּ. כִּי בְּר"ה יֵשׁ קִטְרוּג עַל זֶה שֶׁבְּנֵי"י מוּבְטָחִין יוֹתֵר וּבָזֶה מוּבָן הַגְּמ' לָמָּה אֵין אוֹמְרִים הַלֵּל בְּר"ה

The joy latent in Rosh Hashanah felt in the inner recesses of every soul need not be stifled forever, for the verse states, לְיוֹם חַגֵּנוּ, *for our festive day*, a name that is generally associated with Succos. While Rosh Hashanah is a time of judgment for *all* men, Israel's special relationship with Hashem must be acknowledged only tacitly on Succos. Israel exuberantly proclaims its joy for its survival as it parades with the Four Species (5635) (*Yalkut Shimoni, Emor* 651). Additionally, Israel is granted another occasion in which it may celebrate its unique relationship — the Jewish New Year, Rosh Chodesh Nissan. This month, renowned for its supernatural miracles, is reserved for Israel. (5640,5643)

וּבְנֵי יִשְׂרָאֵל מִתְבַּטְּלִין אֶל הַקַּבָּ"ה וּצְרִיכִין לְהַכְנִיס כֹּחַ'ם בִּכְלָל כָּל הַבְּרִיאָה כְּדֵי לְהַחֲיוֹת כּוּלָם.

Another reason for suppressing Israel's special relationship with Hashem is to compel the Jewish people to present themselves in judgment alongside *all* mankind. This, in turn, enables the non-Jewish world to survive Hashem's awesome judgment by clinging to Israel's spiritual "coattails." Evaluated on their own merit, the world at large would surely not emerge unscathed. (5641)

כִּי צְרִיכִין בְּר"ה לְכַסּוֹת מַדְרֵיגוֹת בְּנֵי"י וּלְהִתְעָרֵב בְּתוֹךְ כָּל הַבְּרוּאִים לְבַקֵּשׁ רַחֲמִים. וְהָאֱמֶת כִּי עַ"יז מְקַבְּלִין בְּנֵי"י כָּל הַשֶּׁפַע גַּם הַשַּׁיָּיךְ לְהָאוּמוֹת עַ"יי שֶׁכּוּלָם נִיצּוֹלוּ בִּשְׁבִיל בְּנֵי"י

While it may seem to be an entirely altruistic act on Israel's part to subsume itself amongst all men on Rosh Hashanah, in reality, the Jewish people are well rewarded for their self-sacrifice. Not only is

Israel's lease on life renewed every Rosh Hashanah, not only do the Jewish people receive their portion of God's bounty, but as a result of commingling with mankind they share in the material blessings that were originally designated solely for the Gentile world. This outcome is justified inasmuch as mankind's survival is due to Israel's participation in their judgment. (5643)

והנה מעלת האבות גבוה מזה אך כדי לזכות בני ישראל מסר להם גם בחי' אלו.

Submerging Israel's destiny with that of mankind and then permitting the Jewish people to share in the Gentile world's largesse is hardly confined to Rosh Hashanah's judgment. The very beginning of the Torah dealing at length with Creation, a concept not of exclusive interest to Jewry, is justified on the basis of כֹּחַ מַעֲשָׂיו הִגִּיד לְעַמּוֹ לָתֵת לָהֶם נַחֲלַת גּוֹיִם, *The strength of His deeds* (i.e. Creation) *He declared to His nation to give them the heritage of the peoples* (*Tehillim* 111:6). By including the story of Creation, a universal theme in the Torah designated for Jewry (thus subsuming the Jewish people with all of mankind), Hashem ensured that Israel would receive the rewards originally destined exclusively for non-Jews. (5643)

◆§ Hiding the Jewish People

ראש השנה הוא בכסה. וכמו כן בכל שנה שמתחדש הבריאה. מתחדש ג''כ בחירת בנ''י. ולכן מתחלה נסתר חיבת בנ''י ואח''כ מתחדש בחירת בנ''י

Israel's special relationship with Hashem is not only hidden, but the Jewish people themselves are obscured, shielded from the public on Rosh Hashanah. This is based on the notion that Israel's "chosenness" is not permanent, but is rather reviewed every Rosh Hashanah. Hashem "hides" His preference and close association with Israel compelling them to be judged with all mankind. Once vindicated they are chosen again. (5647)

⋙ Seeking Our Hidden Roots

פי׳ שבני ישראל צריכין לראות בכל מיני התחדשות לקשר
ההשפעות במקור עליון דהוא שופרא דכולא. ...שבנ״י מקשרין
ההתחדשות בעלמא דאתכסיא.

Utilizing an entirely different approach, one may suggest that on
Rosh Hashanah the Jew, blessed with renewed life and with all of
God's abundant bounty, is exhorted to remember the hidden (בְּכֶסֶה)
Source of all this largesse, Hashem. Accordingly, this verse may be
interpreted as follows: תִּקְעוּ בַחֹדֶשׁ שׁוֹפָר בַּכֶּסֶה, at the time of annual
renewal [בַּחֹדֶשׁ] attach [the term תָּקַע related to וּתְקַעְתִּיו יָתֵד בְּמָקוֹם נֶאֱמָן,
(Yeshayahu 22:23)] all your blessings בַּכֶּסֶה — to the hidden source, the
root (שׁוֹרֶשׁ) of all, Hashem. In this context, the term שׁוֹפָר should be
interpreted as being derived from שֶׁפֶר, beauty. The ultimate source of
spiritual harmony, שׁוּפְרָא דְכֹלָּא, is הקב״ה. Israel is beseeched: "Connect"
your bounty accruing on Rosh Hashanah to its true — albeit hidden
source, Hashem.   (5637, 5641)

⋙ Our Hidden Potential — The Oral Law

ותרועת מלך שגם יהושע מריע ומפיל חומה. דע״י תקיעת שופר
בז׳ ימים הפילו חומות יריחו שהיתה סוגרת ומסוגרת והיא הי׳
יסוד של א״י. והוא ענין תורה שבע״פ. . .הוא בהסתר כמ״ש וחיי
עולם נטע בתוכנו. והפנימיות בכחה להפיל החומה. . .ועל זה
הענין כתיב הקול קול יעקב שנאמר זה כשהתלבש עצמו בבגדי
עשו ואעפ״כ הפנימיות קול יעקב הגביר הקדושה וביטל כחו של
עשו.

In order to appreciate the role of the shofar in eliciting man's hidden
potential especially through immersion in the Oral Law, it would be
appropriate to cite the following Midrash (Yalkut Shimoni, Bamidbar
768): "ה׳ אֱלֹהָיו עִמּוֹ וּתְרוּעַת מֶלֶךְ בּוֹ" אָמַר בָּלָק לְבִלְעָם אִם אֵין אַתָּה יָכוֹל לָהֶם
מִפְּנֵי מֹשֶׁה רַבָּם עֲשֵׂה לַדּוֹר שֶׁלְּאַחֲרָיו וְהֵשִׁיב "וּתְרוּעַת מֶלֶךְ בּוֹ" שֶׁגַּם יְהוֹשֻׁעַ מֵרִיעַ

וּמַפִּיל חוֹמָה, "Hashem his God is with him and the teruah (trumpet blast) of the King is with him" (Bamidbar 23:21). Balak said to Bilam, "If you are unable (to curse them) because of Moshe's good merit, do it (i.e. curse) to the following generation. He (Bilam) responded, "and the King's teruah is with him' — Yehoshua also will sound the teruah (sound of the shofar) and collapse the walls (of Jericho).

Careful analysis of this Midrash reveals an association between Yehoshua, the sound of the shofar and the collapse of barriers, such as Jericho's wall. This relationship can be developed further if we consider Yehoshua's mission as the propagator of the Oral Law (תּוֹרָה שֶׁבְּעַל פֶּה), disseminating orally the teaching of his mentor Moshe. When reciting the blessing after reading the Torah, we describe the Oral Law as חַיֵּי עוֹלָם נָטַע בְּתוֹכֵנוּ, the permanent life implanted in our midst. While the Written Law was visible, given by Hashem in full public view at Sinai, the transmission of the Oral Law was not quite as apparent or dramatic. Instead, it was an inner process by which the scholars of each generation learned Torah and transmitted it to their disciples. Based on the foregoing associations, we can derive the following formulation: The shofar wielded by the great teacher of the Oral Law, Yehoshua, was able to tear down and breach any barriers to the Jewish people's entry to the Promised Land. By blowing the shofar on Rosh Hashanah we are reminded of our "hidden" inner capacity (בַּכֶּסֶה) to raze barriers to our spiritual growth.

A classic example of a Jew's inner capacity is the triumph of Yaakov, depicted by his inner voice, הַקֹּל קוֹל יַעֲקֹב (Bereishis 27:22), over Esav, known for the brute strength of his hand, הַיָּדַיִם יְדֵי עֵשָׂו. Even when dressed as Esav (ibid. 27:15,16), Yaakov's voice still prevailed over his superficial resemblance to his brother.

The ultimate challenge for every Jew, his raison d'être, is to induce his outer personality to follow the lead of his inner voice. If he can succeed in this task of eliciting his hidden inner potential, he can breach the barrier erected by the Evil Inclination (יֵצֶר הָרָע) just as Yehoshua, assisted by the shofar, toppled Yericho's walls. (5646)

✥ The Gates of Rosh Chodesh Are Hidden

דכתיב וביום החודש יפתח. ובחודש הזה החודש מתכסה כמ״ש
חז״ל. והיינו שאין מתגלה זה הפתח שנפתח בכל החדשים וצריכין
לעורר ההתחדשות ע״י תקיעת שופר. . . כי גם בהסתלקות כח
המיוחד להם כמ״ש החודש הזה לכם. . . . . בהשתתפות כל
האומות יש להם כח לעורר התחדשות. . .ולכך מתכסה החודש
כנ״ל שיצטרכו בנ״י לבוא למדת הרחמים כדי לזכות בזה לכל
העולם כי במדה״ד אין העולם מתקיים.

The Talmud interprets the phrase בַּכֶּסֶה לְיוֹם חַגֵּנוּ (*Tehillim* 81:4) to be referring to the total negation of one aspect of Rosh Hashanah — its status as *Rosh Chodesh* (cf. *Rosh Hashanah* 8a אֵיזֶהוּ חַג שֶׁהַחֹדֶשׁ מִתְכַּסֶּה בּוֹ, *Tosafos* ibid.).

By noting the virtual absence of any mention of *Rosh Chodesh* in the Rosh Hashanah liturgy, the Talmud is not merely pointing out an aspect of the *Yom Tov* that is deliberately ignored, but is also noting that on this awesome day of judgment — precisely at the moment when the Jewish people require additional merits — a major source of merit is closed (not available). Whereas every *Rosh Chodesh* the gates of heaven open to the Jewish people, as depicted by Yechezkel, וּבְיוֹם הַחֹדֶשׁ יִפָּתֵחַ (46:1), this *Rosh Chodesh* the unique relationship between Israel and its Creator is subsumed in the larger process of the universe's renewal. However, the Jewish people are far from defenseless. To compensate for the loss of their "special monthly window," Israel turns to an equally potent weapon — the *shofar*. According to this approach, our verse should be interpreted thus: תִּקְעוּ בַחֹדֶשׁ שׁוֹפָר, Sound the *shofar* in order to renew your relationship (בַחֹדֶשׁ connoting renewal, חָדָשׁ) with Hashem; בַּכֶּסֶה, though the day of *Rosh Chodesh* and its merit may be hidden.

Why would Hashem remove a major source of merit for the Jewish people precisely when Israel desperately desires and needs His favor? Perhaps to demonstrate an even greater source of merit for the Jewish people — that Israel can survive Divine scrutiny even when deprived of its singular relationship with its Creator, even when it is compelled to be judged along with all of mankind. As the verse following ours continues: כִּי חֹק לְיִשְׂרָאֵל הוּא מִשְׁפָּט לֵאלֹהֵי יַעֲקֹב, *because it is a decree for*

Israel, a judgment for the God of Yaakov (Tehillim 81:5). This means that Israel is able to prevail even in the hidden, dark, labyrinthine sanctum of Divine Justice (חֹק is referring to the mysterious ways of Hashem, related to חוקים, mitzvos whose reason is unknown) at the time of the judgment rendered by the God of Yaakov, on Rosh Hashanah.

Moreover, Hashem obscured the "gates of Rosh Chodesh" in order to benefit mankind. Deprived of the unique meirt that it enjoys every Rosh Chodesh, Klal Yisrael evokes the Divine Attributes of Mercy (מִדַּת הָרַחֲמִים). It is the mercy — rather than strict justice — that ensures our survival.   (5645)

⏤§ The Hidden Merit of Yosef

עדות ביהוסף שמו. דכל החדשים נקראו ראשים . . . ובכולם יש
זכרון כמו שמתפללין יעלה ויבוא . . . הזכרון של ר״ה למעלה
מזכרון דראשי חדשים. . . . ובר״ה צריכין לעורר זכרון של יוסף
שהוא למעלה מזכרון השבטים שמדריגת יוסף למעלה ממדריגת
השבטים . . . ולכן מצינו דזכרון ר״ח של תשרי בכסה וצריכין
לעורר הזכרון מעולם שלמעלה והוא זכרון דיוסף.

Although a major source of merit — the monthly renewal of Rosh Chodesh — is not available, an even greater merit — albeit one that is veiled, shrouded in obscurity (בַּכֶּסֶה) and far too sacred for Israel to generally partake of — can be exploited on Rosh Hashanah — the merit of Yosef. The existence of a relationship between Yosef and Rosh Hashanah is alluded to by the juxtaposition of the verse עֵדוּת בִּיהוֹסֵף שָׂמוֹ, He appointed it as a testimony for Yosef (Tehillim 81:6), dealing with Yosef's liberation, to תִּקְעוּ בַחֹדֶשׁ שׁוֹפָר.

To appreciate the association between Yosef and Rosh Hashanah, it would be instructive to first explore the relationship between Rosh Hashanah and the monthly New Moon (Rosh Chodesh). Many similarities exist. The concept of being "the head of" (ראש) is by no means confined to Rosh Hashanah. Every New Moon is called ראש חֹדֶשׁ (cf. Bamidbar 10:10, וּבְרָאשֵׁי חָדְשֵׁכֶם) — literally, the head of the month. Likewise, the designation of Rosh Hashanah as a day of remembrance (יוֹם הַזִּכָּרוֹן) — in which all men are remembered and judged by Hashem — is shared with every Rosh Chodesh. As the Rosh Chodesh liturgy reads: יַעֲלֶה וְיָבֹא . . . וְיִזָּכֵר זִכְרוֹנֵנוּ, May our remembrance *be elevated and be brought before Hashem.* In fact, the similarities between Rosh Hashanah and *Rosh Chodesh* is so great that the Talmud (40b) rules that no explicit mention of *Rosh Chodesh* need be made on Rosh Hashanah (זִכְרוֹן אֶחָד עוֹלֶה לְכָאן וּלְכָאן).

The difference between *Rosh Chodesh* and Rosh Hashanah is clearly one of degree, Rosh Hashanah being the most elevated and exalted of all the New Moons.

So too is the relationship between Yosef and the other tribes, the שְׁבָטִים.[1]

The memory of each of the tribes has served as an eternal source of merit for the Jewish people. In particular, when the High Priest would enter the *Beis HaMikdash* wearing the breastplate (חוֹשֶׁן) which bore the names of the Tribes, Hashem would remember their merit and forgive Israel. In the same manner that Rosh Hashanah is elevated and exalted above the monthly New Moon, so too Yosef's merit exceeds that of his brothers.[2]

As Yaakov blesses him (*Bereishis* 49:26), בִּרְכֹת אָבִיךָ גָּבְרוּ ... תִּהְיֶין לְרֹאשׁ יוֹסֵף, *the blessings of your father surpassed ... Let them be* (i.e. bestowed) *on the head of Yosef.* On Rosh Hashanah, the day that is described as בַּכֶּסֶה, a day that is hidden, we invoke the most mysterious and esoteric source of merit, that of Yosef *HaTzaddik.* (5660)

◄§ The Joy of Subtle Renewal

בנ"י צריכין לשמוח בר"ה שמתחדש העולם. ולכן יש קצת חירות
כי הטבע משכח הפנימיות. והוא מטובת הבורא ית"ש שמתחדש
החיות בכל ר"ה שלא להיות נטבע בחומר הגשמיות.

Just as the shift from day to night reminds Israel of God's role in creating this universe,[3] so too the change from year to year prevents

---

1. The emphasis in this discussion is on the eternal merit of Yosef and his brothers, not on their personal relationship during their lifetime.

2. The analogy between Rosh Hashanah, *Rosh Chodesh*, and Yosef and his brothers is illustrated vividly in the famous scene dreamt by Yosef in which their sheaves bowed down to his sheaf (i.e. they were nurtured by Yosef). In a similar vein, all the months of the year are "nurtured" by Rosh Hashanah.

3. Consequently, we thank Hashem every morning and evening in the בִּרְכוֹת of יוֹצֵר הַמְּאוֹרוֹת, *Who fashions the luminaries,* and הַמַּעֲרִיב עֲרָבִים, *Who brings on evening.*

us from being entrapped by materialism. No greater reason for rejoicing exists than the advent of Rosh Hashanah with its renewal of the universe, propelling Israel away from the humdrum routine of daily life and the material world with its many pitfalls, and bringing us back to our Creator. (5664)

כי האלקים עשה האדם ישר. ובכל ר״ה מתחדש זה הדרך הישר. אבל עיקר הנהגת הטבע מאתו ית״ש נעלם ואין הכל זוכין לזה רק הצדיקים.

If so, why obscure Rosh Hashanah's joy? Why is it a holiday muted by בַּכֶּסֶה, a hidden joy rather than overt celebration?

The answer to this question demonstrates graphically the difference between the *universal* New Year — Rosh Hashanah in Tishrei — and the *Jewish* New Year in Nissan. Whereas every Spring the sensitive Jewish soul is stimulated by the miracles that occurred and feels a sense of sweeping miraculous change leading to festive joy, on Rosh Hashanah a far more subtle change occurs.[1] The natural world is renewed. Only the most finely calibrated souls of Israel's righteous, however, can detect this subtle shift from year to year. They rejoice, knowing that in a new year even the most wayward individual who strayed from the "straight path" (cf. *Koheles* 7:29, *God has made man straight*) can return. But this shift is not clearly evident and is subsumed with a day of judgment for all mankind. Thus, the festival's joy is muted.

(ד״ה והנה 5662; ד״ה החיים 5662)

הנביא צוה לשמוח בר״ה אכלו משמנים כו׳ חדות ה׳ היא מעוזכם. עיקר העוז לבנ״י לשמוח בחלק אלקות המיוחד לנפשות בנ״י. ובר״ה מתחדש זה הכח שבו נברא האדם ויפח באפיו נשמת חיים.

Just as the Jewish nation rejoices as the universe is renewed, every individual Jew delights in his personal renewal on Rosh Hashanah. Israel's entreaty for life should not be confused with an appeal for

---

1. Perhaps for that reason the Talmud (*Rosh Hashanah* 9b) describes the month of Nissan as שָׁנָה שֶׁיֵּשׁ עִמָּהּ חֲדָשִׁים, *a year with sense of renewal.*

material abundance; instead, we are really pleading for the restoration of "the soul of life" infused by Hashem into the first man, the נְשָׁמָה (cf. *Bereishis* 2:7, וַיִּפַּח בְּאַפָּיו נִשְׁמַת חַיִּים, *He blew into his nostrils the soul of life*).[1] There can be no better reason to rejoice on Rosh Hashanah than the restoration of every Jew's inner core, his נְשָׁמָה. When Nechemiah proclaimed on his first Rosh Hashanah upon returning to *Eretz Yisrael*, אִכְלוּ מַשְׁמַנִּים וּשְׁתוּ מַמְתַקִּים . . . כִּי חֶדְוַת ה׳ הִיא מָעֻזְּכֶם, *eat rich (fatty) foods, drink sweet beverages . . . because the delight of Hashem is your strength* (*Nechemiah* 8:10), he was referring to Israel's true strength, the return of the soul emanating from Hashem (i.e. the delight of Hashem).

(5661)

◆§ Joy as a Prerequisite for Acceptance of Hashem's Kingdom

וצריך להיות בשמחה כמ״ש כל [מצוה] שקיבלו עליהם בשמחה
עדיין עושין בשמחה. וכפי השמחה בר״ה בקבלת מלכותו ית״ש
כן מתקיים כל ימי השנה.

Alternatively, the joy of Rosh Hashanah may be not so much a reflection of the events of that day but rather a *prerequisite* for a vital part of Jewish life — acceptance of Hashem's sovereignty (קַבָּלַת עוֹל מַלְכוּת שָׁמַיִם). While the *Yom Tov* of Rosh Hashanah is dedicated to the theme of renewed commitment to Hashem's kingdom (see our essay on *Malchios* for expanded discussion), in reality such a commitment to God's sovereignty is a central theme of Jewish life all *year* long. However, the manner in which we accept this commitment upon ourselves on Rosh Hashanah is critical. By joyously proclaiming God's kingdom at the year's commencement, we are assured of joyously fulfilling this commitment all year long. As the Talmud relates (*Shabbos* 130a): Any *mitzvos* joyously accepted by Israel are happily performed as well.

(5661)

---

1. See our essay entitled "Life" for an expanded version of this theme.

כִּי חֹק לְיִשְׂרָאֵל הוּא מִשְׁפָּט לֵאלֹהֵי יַעֲקֹב

*Because it is a decree for Israel, a judgment for the God of
Yaakov (Tehillim 81:3).*

כי הנה נקרא ראש השנה שבו יורד מוחין ובינה על כל השנה
כמ"ש . . . בפ' בינו שנות דור ודור שיש בינה מיוחדת בכל שנה
. . . . וממילא יש משפט מי שיזכה לקבל הבינה והמוחין היורדים
בר"ה לעולם . . . כי חוק לישראל שמתחוקק בו חוקים ודרכים
חדשים.

This verse poses various difficulties. Firstly, the seeming emphasis
and double theme of *a decree for Israel* and *a judgment for the God of
Yaakov*. Moreover, the relationship between the first verse (תִּקְעוּ
. . . בַּחֹדֶשׁ, 81:4) and this one needs clarification. As the opening term כִּי,
because, implies, this verse serves as the rationale for sounding the
shofar.

Refer to our previous remarks where it was suggested that this verse
explains why on this *Rosh Chodesh* we require the *shofar* and cannot
subsist on the basis of the gates of heaven that open every *Rosh
Chodesh*. David responds to this: "Because it is a decree to Israel" — to
demonstrate that even when Israel operates in the dark, where things
are obscured and hidden as the statutes (laws whose reason is unknown
to us) and are judged alongside mankind, even then they emerge
successfully by blowing the *shofar*.

Alternatively, this verse may be explaining why Rosh Hashanah is
described in the previous verse as a Festival (יוֹם חַגֵּנוּ). The response — כִּי
חֹק לְיִשְׂרָאֵל הוּא — states this is a day in which Hashem grants intuition
and understanding of His ways to the deserving. Certainly, obtaining
even a glimpse of the inscrutable Divine Will is an occasion of joy.

To further appreciate why man can acquire an enhanced understanding of Hashem's ways on Rosh Hashanah, consider Moshe's admoni-
tion in his farewell song of *Haazinu*, בִּינוּ שְׁנוֹת דֹּר וָדֹר, *understand the
years of generation after generation (Devarim 32:7)*. According to the
Chiddushei HaRim's interpretation, this verse is implying that every
year (שָׁנוֹת) Israel, if found worthy, acquires new understanding of
Hashem's Will. Likewise, the verse הַמֵּבִין אֶל כָּל מַעֲשֵׂיהֶם, *Who com-
prehends all their deeds (Tehillim 33:15)* — interpreted by the Talmud

(*Rosh Hashanah* 16a) to refer to Rosh Hashanah — is suggesting the same theme, God grants understanding (בִּינָה) to all His beings (מַעֲשִׂים).

Yet, not everyone is worthy of grasping the inscrutable Divine will, of gaining insight into Hashem's ways. As our verse concludes מִשְׁפָּט לֵאלֹהֵי יַעֲקֹב, *it is a* (time of) *judgment for the God of Yaakov* determining who among His subjects will prove worthy of being granted additional intention in His ways. (5648)

וכתיב חק לישראל הוא משפט לאלקי יעקב. בחי' ישראל כח
הנשמה עלמא דחירות ושם אין מגע נכרי ופסולת והיא חקיקה
רשומה שא''א להמחק. רק בבחי' הגוף משפט לאלקי יעקב
להמשיך חיות ואלקות גם בבחי' הגוף.

But why the double, seemingly contrary expression of יַעֲקֹב and יִשְׂרָאֵל? Perhaps the Psalmist is suggesting that the impact of the *shofar* is *not* required for the spiritual core, "the pintele Yid," — כִּי חֹק לְיִשְׂרָאֵל — Godliness is inherent, it is "engraved" (חֹק related to חֲקִיקָה) in every soul. As the name יִשְׂרָאֵל implies, the Jewish people's spiritual core will remain essential (cf. *Bereishis* 32:29, this name being derived from the Patriarch's ability to triumph over all obstacles). However, the *shofar* is required to help ensure a successful outcome to Rosh Hashanah's central issue: Will the Jewish *body* as well as its soul be imbued with sanctity — or will it succumb to the temptations of the Evil Inclination (יֵצֶר הָרָע)? The name יַעֲקֹב always refers to the Patriarch's *physical* struggles with Esav and Lavan. This is the essential judgment of Rosh Hashanah, infusing spirituality in the physical side of man. This task is enhanced through the *shofar*. (5662)

Omission of Hallel on Rosh Hashanah

אָמְרוּ מַלְאֲכֵי הַשָּׁרֵת לִפְנֵי הקב״ה, רִבּוֹנוֹ שֶׁל עוֹלָם מִפְּנֵי מָה אֵין יִשְׂרָאֵל אוֹמְרִים שִׁירָה לְפָנֶיךָ בְּר״ה וּבְיוֹם הַכִּפּוּרִים אָמַר לָהֶן אֶפְשָׁר מֶלֶךְ יוֹשֵׁב עַל כִּסֵּא הַדִּין וְסִפְרֵי חַיִּים וְסִפְרֵי מֵתִים פְּתוּחִין לְפָנָיו וְיִשְׂרָאֵל אוֹמְרִים שִׁירָה לְפָנָי (ערכין י:).

The Ministering Angels in the Presence of Hashem asked, "Master of the Universe, why doesn't Israel sing the Song (i.e. Hallel) on Rosh Hashanah and Yom Kippur?" Hashem answered, "Is it possible that the King sits on the throne of judgment and the Books of Life and Death are opened before Him and Israel recites the Song?"

אבל מרוב התשוקה נבראו מלאכים ג״כ. ואפשר מלאכים אלו המה למעלה מבחי׳ המלאכים שנבראו מאמירת ההלל כידוע שמדריגת המחשבה למעלה מהדיבור.

Who were these angels? Quite simply, they are the angels that were created from Israel's desire to say *Hallel* (cf. *Avos* 4:13, הָעוֹשֶׂה מִצְוָה אַחַת קוֹנֶה לוֹ פְּרַקְלִיט אֶחָד, *he who fulfills even a single mitzvah gains himself a single advocate*).

Though the Jewish people do not actually recite *Hallel*, since they must suppress their joy and confidence of achieving a good verdict, in their hearts Israel wishes it could have recited *Hallel*.

Not only the actual performance of a *mitzvah*, but even the *desire* to do so creates angels who act as advocates on behalf of the Jewish people. In fact, these angels may be more exalted than those that were created

from an actual recitation of *Hallel* inasmuch as thoughts are always
loftier than the spoken word.   (5647)

שצריך האדם להיות מוכן לומר ההלל בר״ה כי הוא בכלל
המועדות רק שהוא נסתר . . . והוא בחי׳ רצוא ושוב שיש לבנ״י
מדרגה זו למעלה ממה״ש והוא כמ״ש במקום שבע״ת עומדין
כו׳.

In truth, not only the angels but also the Jewish people were (and
even today should be) prepared to recite *Hallel*. The *intention* to sing
Hallel on Rosh Hashanah is certainly appropriate though the deed may
not be. Israel, however, retracts its original intention and does not recite
Hallel. Changing one's plans upon further contemplation is hardly an
admission of weakness but rather an integral part of the Jewish nation's
thought process. As Yechezkel (1:14) notes, וְהַחַיּוֹת רָצוֹא וָשׁוֹב, life
consists of desire (to do a *mitzvah*) and then returns (retracting that
desire).

By withdrawing its original intention, Israel correctly arrived at the
same conclusion as Hashem, that it would be inappropriate to recite
Hallel on Rosh Hashanah.[1]

By opting *not* to recite *Hallel*, Israel correctly assessed Hashem's Will,
something that the angels were incapable of. This illustrates the
renowned saying (cf. *Berachos* 34b), discussed at length in the section of
teshuvah, that the *baalei teshuvah* "stand at a place" that the righteous
are unable to attain. Israel, as *baalei teshuvah* on Rosh Hashanah, stood
closer to Hashem, correctly gauging His intentions. The angels,
righteous as they were, could not fathom the Divine Will.   (5636)

ועפ״י זה מובן דברי הגמ׳ אמרו מלאכי השרת מפני מה אין בנ״י
אומרים הלל כו׳.

Israel desired to recite *Hallel*, but eventually did not. Why? There are
several reasons, many detailed in the essay entitled "The Hidden
Festival." First is the need to "hide" (בַּכֶּסֶה) Israel's special status from the

---

1. A parallel may be drawn between the angels' desire that *Hallel* be recited on Rosh
Hashanah and their wish to chant a song upon the drowning of the Egyptian armies at the
Red Sea. In each instance they were overruled by Hashem.

Gentile world. Moreover, *Hallel* is reserved for those occasions in which Hashem's presence is *visibly* felt such as the Three Festivals during the times of the *Beis HaMikdash*, and not during occasions of subtle and muted joy as is Rosh Hashanah.   (5634, 5635, 5644)

ולכן בימים אלו שהחיים ניתן במשפט ותלויין ועומדין לדין. על זה
לא שייך הלל.

Finally, let us explore further Hashem's response to the angels' question. Perhaps we can appreciate Hashem's response by considering the verse in *Hallel*, לֹא הַמֵּתִים יְהַלְלוּ יָ-הּ, *the dead will not praise God* (*Tehillim* 115:17), referring not only to the deceased but also to the wicked who are "spiritually" dead.

Hallel may not be recited every day (cf. *Shabbos* 118b) but instead is confined to those occasions when Israel *perceives* renewed spirituality, occasioned either by a supernatural miracle or at those festive times when the Jewish people perceive an extraordinary spiritual stimulus. However, *Hallel* is not recited when the natural world is renewed, a process occurring every day, as we pray, הַמְחַדֵּשׁ בְּטוּבוֹ בְּכָל יוֹם תָּמִיד מַעֲשֵׂה בְרֵאשִׁית, *He renews daily, perpetually, the work of creation*.[1]

Rosh Hashanah, when the very issue is being determined whether Israel's spirituality will be renewed, is not an appropriate occasion to recite *Hallel*. Only when a favorable verdict is already assured, on Succos, may Israel recite *Hallel*.   (5653)

---

1. In this light, the Talmudic ruling אֵין קוֹרִין הַלֵּל לְמַפְרֵעַ, (*Megillah* 17a) usually understood as *not to read the Hallel in reverse form*, may also be construed not to read *Hallel* if we are celebrating the renewal of the material world.

The Head of the Year

The term רֹאשׁ הַשָּׁנָה translated literally means *the head of the year*. The following remarks consider why this *Yom Tov* is called the Head of the Year.

◄§ Purest Form of Divine Blessing

ראש השנה פי' קודם התחלקות השפע להיות נשתנה. כי כשבא
חיות השי"ת לעוה"ז תחת הזמן והטבע משתנה מרוחניות
לגשמיות. ור"ה הוא המקור וההתחלה קודם ההשתנות כי
במקורו הוא בלי ציור גשמיי:

The *Yom Tov's* name may be related to the fact that on this day God's bounty is still not yet tainted by materialism. As the year proceeds, Hashem's blessing, decreed on Rosh Hashanah and bestowed upon man, becomes tinged with materialism as it is utilized by man for his mundane needs. When the Heavenly Tribunal showers blessings upon mankind on the Day of Judgment, those blessings are still pure and pristine as they were in heaven. Upon entering the natural world, with its limitations of time and space, God's blessings are transformed from pure spirituality to a material form. According to this approach the term רֹאשׁ הַשָּׁנָה suggests the *beginning* of all the year's blessings unalloyed and unadulterated — in its purest form.[1]   (5632)

---

1. Perhaps the term שָׁנָה, according to this interpretation, is derived from שִׁנָּה, *change*. It refers to the beginning of Hashem's largesse prior to its being modified and changed by man to serve his material needs.   (5632)

◆§ A Humbling Moment

שנה שרשה בתחלתה מתעשרת בסופה כו' מראשית מרשית
כו'. פי' שעיקר התחדשות בר''ה כפי הביטול שמבטלין הכל אל
השורש.

The Talmud (*Rosh Hashanah* 16b) interprets the phrase מֵרֵשִׁית הַשָּׁנָה, *the year's beginning*, as being related to רָשׁ (cf. *Devarim* 11:12). It suggests that a year that begins poorly (i.e. humbly) will eventually end on a more affluent note.

Thus, the term רֹאשׁ הַשָּׁנָה may also be understood as the moment of utter humility. This refers to the feeling of complete self-negation that grips the Jew every Rosh Hashanah. While Rosh Hashanah is generally associated with renewal, such renewal is almost impossible without first negating oneself, without first returning to one's heavenly roots.

The comment of the Talmud (*Rosh Hashanah* 17b) that Hashem is closest to one who makes himself into a *remnant* (לְמִי שֶׁמֵּשִׂים עַצְמוֹ כְּשִׁירַיִם) is not preaching self-negation as a goal, but rather as a means to enable the Jew to soar back to his heavenly roots. (For further discussion of *teshuvah* as a return to one's heavenly roots, refer to our discussion on *Shuvah Yisrael* and *Shabbos Shuvah*.)   (5648)

◆§ The Microcosm of the Jewish Year and World History

ויום ראש השנה כולל כל השנה כמו שהראש כולל כל הגוף. . . .
הי' ב' אלפים תהו. אח''כ זכו בנ''י לב' אלפים תורה. ואח''כ ב'
אלפים ימות המשיח. וכ''ז מתחדש בכל שנה. וכ''ז מתחדש ג''כ
ביום ר''ה מתחלה בכסה וצריכין לעורר ע''י תקיעת שופר זכות
התורה. ובסוף היום אכלו משמנים חדות ה' היא מעוזכם.

Just as the head serves as a microcosm of the entire body (containing the sensory components that control most bodily functions), so too the day of Rosh Hashanah, in itself, represents the entire Jewish calendar year in miniature, and by extension, all world history.

The festival season transports the sensitive Jew through the full cycle of human emotions from the abject slavery of Egypt prior to the Exodus occurring on Pesach, to the Giving of the Torah on Shevuos, culminating in the pure joy of Succos. The Talmud (*Avodah Zarah* 9a) trisects world history in a similar fashion commencing with the millennia of chaos (שְׁנֵי אֲלָפִים תֹּהוּ) prior to Avraham's emergence followed by two thousand years dominated by תּוֹרָה, and concluding with two thousand years anticipating *Mashiach*'s arrival. Examining Rosh Hashanah's "itinerary" we see evidence of the same pattern. The day begins in veiled obscurity (בַּכֶּסֶה) reminiscent of Egypt's slavery and the universe's first two millennia, followed by the sound of the *shofar* reminding us of the *shofar* heard at Sinai, and concludes with the *mitzvah* of rejoicing and partaking of a festive meal (cf. *Nechemiah* 8:10 who urges the Jewish people to rejoice on Rosh Hashanah).

(5650)

◂§ The Year's Eyes

הֶחָכָם עֵינָיו בְּרֹאשׁוֹ

The wise man's eyes are in his head (Koheles 2:14).

ראש בנפש והוא משגיח על כל הגוף ובו הנשמה ועיקר ראיות
העין מתוך החושך והשחור שבו כמ״ש חז״ל. כמו כן בזמן זה
היום הראשון בו ההשגחה על כל השנה והחכם מבין שכל השנה
תלוי׳ בראש השנה. ולכן בכסה כתיב בי׳.

This verse may allude to Rosh Hashanah. The wise man realizes that just as a person's eyes monitor and control the entire body (all sights and sounds enter through it), so too the year's "head," Rosh Hashanah, affects the entire year. Though the day is veiled in obscurity (בַּכֶּסֶה), he peels away the layers of darkness and sees that Rosh Hashanah is the pivot, the "head" and "eyes" of the entire year.

How ironic and yet how appropriate that the day shrouded in darkness is also the day in which the wise man can gain insight regarding the Divine Will for the coming year. While paradoxical, this relationship resembles that of the human eye, whose main capacity for sight is in the pupil, its blackest component. Hashem too often veils His majesty in darkness. As we read in *Tehillim* 18:12, יָשֶׁת חֹשֶׁךְ סִתְרוֹ, *He made dark-ness His concealment.* (5653, 5664)

ᴥᵇ The Patriarchs — Israel's Heads

צריכין בנ"י לשוב בו להתחזק בראשיתן והוא התורה . . . והוא
בחי' אשא דעי למרחוק לזכור השורש שלנו. כענין שאמרו מתי
יגיעו מעשי למעשי אבותי.

On this day, "the Head of the Year," Israel derives strength from its "head" — its earliest luminaries, the Patriarchs (אָבוֹת), and the Torah itself, the source of all Jewish learning. As Iyov proclaims (36:3): אֶשָּׂא דֵעִי לְמֵרָחוֹק, *I lift my knowledge* (i.e. my aspirations), *to the distance* (i.e. I turn my thoughts to my ancestors). The Midrash (*Talmud D'Bei Eliyohu*) exhorts the Jew to always consider, מָתַי יַגִּיעוּ מַעֲשַׂי לְמַעֲשֵׂי אֲבוֹתַי, *when will my actions reach the level of my forefathers* (the Patriarchs), a lofty aspiration at all times and especially on Rosh Hashanah. Likewise, the verse cited previously, הֶחָכָם עֵינָיו בְּרֹאשׁוֹ, *the wise man's eyes are in his head*, may refer to his gazing back (i.e. his eyes) to Israel's head — the Patriarchs. (5653)

ᴥᵇ The Year's Soul

וע"ז מבקשין זכרנו לחיים. ונקרא ראש השנה שבו התחדשות
הנשמה שהיא בראש.

In Rabbinic literature (as well as in common speech) the term "head" often connotes the soul, the intellectual and emotional center of the human body. When Jews appeal for life, they are really pleading for the restoration of the soul. (Refer to our essay entitled "Life.") While on other occasions the soul may be inspired and affected by the events that we commemorate, on Rosh Hashanah the soul's very existence — its head — is being determined. By extension, survival itself is contingent on the soul. On the "year's head" the soul and all that revolves about it are granted a new lease of life. (5663)

⋖§ Renewal of Israel — Hashem's "Head"

ראש השנה מיוחד באמת לבני ישראל שנק׳ ראשית. ישראל לי
ראש. ונקראו ראשית ולא ראש. שראשית הוא לעולם סמוך.
שאין לבנ׳׳י ראש בפ׳׳ע אלא שהם למי שאין לו ראשית ותכלית.
. . . ולכן כ׳ תהי׳ לראש ולא לזנב. ולא כ׳ תהי׳ ראש. רק לראש.
שיהיו דבוקים אל הראש ולא אל הזנב שהוא ההנהגה הטבעיות
(תרס׳׳ג). צריכין להמשך חיים מן השורש כמו שחיות כל הגוף
נמשך מן הנשמה שבראש (תרס׳׳ד).

Finally, the concept of the "year's head" may allude to the renewal of
the Jewish people. In fact the very name יִשְׂרָאֵל (Israel) spells out
(albeit in scrambled form) לי ראש, *Israel is my head*. Every Rosh
Hashanah, Israel — designated by Hashem to head and lead mankind
— renews its relationship with Hashem.

Our concept of leading (of being "the head") is not achieved by living
an independent existence. Rather we must be the first, the head of
mankind, to cling to Hashem Who is the true ראש. This very theme is
reflected in the Rosh Hashanah prayer, שֶׁנִּהְיֶה לְרֹאשׁ וְלֹא לְזָנָב, that we
should be "attached" to (ל) the head, Hashem, rather than be ראש, our
own head. The renewal of Israel, mankind's head, may be closely related
to the previous suggestion that Rosh Hashanah is the time of the
restoration of the soul. Israel's mission in the universe is similar to that of
the soul in the body — to infuse a lifeless void with spiritual life. Just as
the soul brings vitality to the entire body, so the Jewish people infuse the
universe with true life — the Torah depicted as the Tree of Life.

(5663, 5664)[1]

---

1. It is noteworthy that generally the Jewish people are called רֵאשִׁית, *the beginning*, rather
than ראש, *the head*. שֶׁנִּהְיֶה לְרֹאשׁ וְלֹא לְזָנָב, *that we should be as the head and not as the tail*,
is based on *Devarim* 28:13 — Hashem *shall place you as a head and not as a tail*... as a
mighty one and not as a weakling.

Life

וְכָתְבֵנוּ בְּסֵפֶר הַחַיִּים

Inscribe us in the Book of Life.

This entreaty along with others for sustenance (פַּרְנָסָה), healing (רְפוּאָה), and forgiveness (מְחִילָה וּסְלִיחָה) form an essential part, if not the core of the Rosh Hashanah services.

Yet, the *Zohar* criticizes those who present Hashem with a "laundry list" of requests comparing them to "barking dogs." How does one reconcile these seemingly contradictory views of Rosh Hashanah? More fundamentally, the Jewish people's annual plea for life needs further clarification. What exactly are we requesting?

✥ Life of the Soul

ובר״ה שמתחדש הבריאה נתחדש ג״כ כח הנשמה. וזה עיקר
התיקון לחדש כח הנשמה שנטבע בחומר הגוף.
והם ג׳ בחי׳. והם ג׳ ספרים הנפתחים בר״ה שבו נברא האדם
ונתחדש אלה הג׳ בחי׳. עפר מן האדמה הוא הגוף שעומד למיתה
ואין בו חיים וזה מדת הרשעים . . . ויפח באפיו נשמת חיים הוא
בחי׳ הצדיקים שאפילו במיתתן קרוין חיים. . . . ויהי האדם לנפש
חי׳ הם הבינונים שזה וזה שופטן.

In order to appreciate Israel's plea for life we need to return on the anniversary of man's creation to the origin of Adam. וַיִּיצֶר ה׳ אֱלֹהִים אֶת הָאָדָם עָפָר מִן הָאֲדָמָה וַיִּפַּח בְּאַפָּיו נִשְׁמַת חַיִּים וַיְהִי הָאָדָם לְנֶפֶשׁ חַיָּה, *And Hashem God formed the man of dust from the ground, and He blew into his nostrils the soul of life; and man became a living being (Bereishis*

2:7). Careful analysis of this verse reveals three distinct personalities of man that emerged from God's creation.

We began with עָפָר מִן הָאֲדָמָה, *dust from the ground*, in which the material side of man prevails dimming the soul. Such a lifestyle is associated with the wicked who are considered spiritually dead even while they are physically alive. (Cf. *Berachos* 18b רשעים שבחייהם קרויין מתים).

וַיִּפַּח בְּאַפָּיו נִשְׁמַת חַיִּים, *and He blew into his nostrils the soul of life*, refers to the righteous whose entire existence — body and soul — was infused with the soul of life emanating from Hashem. As Chizkiyahu proclaims (*Yeshayahu* 38:19), חַי חַי הוּא יוֹדֶךָ, *those who are doubly alive praise You* (i.e. the righteous whose body as well as soul is infused with spiritual life).

And finally, וַיְהִי הָאָדָם לְנֶפֶשׁ חַיָּה, *and man became a living being* that desired (spiritual) life.[1] This refers to the בֵּינוֹנִים, the intermediate category of Jews, whose fate is being determined between Rosh Hashanah and Yom Kippur. At times they desire to cling to the soul and become totally infused with spirituality. While they may not have succeeded in becoming completely spiritual beings, there remains an intense desire to do so. The entreaty, *remember us for life*, זָכְרֵנוּ לְחַיִּים, is a plea to return to the life of the soul, the original נִשְׁמַת חַיִּים infused by Hashem into the first man. Help us liberate our soul from virtual imprisonment by the physical passions demanded by the body is their supplication.

Upon analyzing world and Jewish history we detect an element of tragedy. Opportunities presented themselves to lead such a rarefied spiritual life, the life of the soul, and were unfortunately forfeited.

Adam, created by Hashem to be נִשְׁמַת חַיִּים, the ideal being, fails to exploit his potential and instead succumbs to his physical desires by eating the Forbidden Fruit. As a result he is condemned to die. The famous pronouncement, כִּי עָפָר אַתָּה וְאֶל עָפָר תָּשׁוּב, *for you are dust and to dust shall you return* (*Bereishis* 3:19), may be reinterpreted in this light. Since you opted to follow your physical inclination created from the dust, you will be condemned to return to the dust.

At the time of the Giving of the Torah, Israel once again forfeited its golden opportunity to achieve eternal life by following its material instincts. (5659, 5663)

✑ Return of the Inner Spark

צריך האדם לבקש רחמים מהקב״ה לחדש זאת הרשימה בלבו
בר״ה וע״ז מבקשין כתבנו לחיים.

One of the consequences of the restoration of the Jewish soul every
Rosh Hashanah is the return of that inner spark (נְקוּדָּה הַפְּנִימִית) of
sanctity that somehow has lain dormant all year. Liberated from his
material impulses, every Rosh Hashanah the Jew pleads for and
achieves the renewal of the inner spiritual drive.

In truth, this spiritual drive is hardly new. When the First Tablets
(לוּחוֹת רִאשׁוֹנוֹת) were given, a spark was implanted in every Jewish soul,
a spark of the Divine and a permanent reminder of the Tablets. God's
Word was written not only on the Tablets but also engraved in every
Jewish soul. As it says (*Shemos* 32:16): וְהַמִּכְתָּב מִכְתַּב אֱלֹהִים הוּא חָרוּת עַל
הַלֻּחֹת, *and the script was God's script engraved on the Tablets* — of
every Jewish soul!

Along with that permanent impression of the Divine embedded in
the Jewish psyche came the promise of eternal life and freedom from the
Evil Inclination (יֵצֶר הָרָע). Though this spark was lost when Israel
sinned and worshiped the Golden Calf, it can be and is restored every
Rosh Hashanah as we pray כָּתְבֵנוּ לְחַיִּים — restore that spark of life!

(5636)

✑ Restoring the Universe to Its Beginnings

פי׳ כי כל הבריאה של מעשה בראשית הוא צמצום אלקות
בהתלבשות הטבע. . . . ברא האדם ויפח באפיו נשמת חיים ויהי
האדם לנפש חיה פי׳ שהוא הכלי שיחזור ויתמשך החיים מחי
החיים אל כל מעשה בראשית.

By pleading for life, Israel is also referring to a return to the universe's
purely spiritual origins. Every year on the anniversary of creation, we
return to the universe's beginning, the time when nothing existed but
רוּחַ אֱלֹהִים מְרַחֶפֶת, *the spirit of God hovering* over the emptiness and
void that engulfed the world. As Hashem proceeded to create the

universe, He in His infinite Wisdom commenced to veil His Presence in the natural world now unfolding. The renowned concept of יֵשׁ מֵאַיִן, "something from nothing" (*ex nihilo*), is the succinct form chosen by the Rabbis to describe this process — a universe in which there had been nothing but His Presence now yielding to a material world made possible by Hashem obscuring His Majesty.

However, as magnificent as Creation was, Hashem still was not completely satisfied. For as the universe emerged during the Six Days of Creation in its material form, the danger lurked that all of Hashem's Creation would lose contact and perhaps forget their Creator. Instead of a "something from nothing," the *something* (יֵשׁ) would obscure any mention of the *nothing* (אַיִן); the universe would lose touch with its origins.

At this point man came to the rescue as the apex of creation and blessed with intellect far superior to any of God's other creations. Man was destined to restore the אַיִן, the primeval universe in which there was nothing but Hashem. Man was ordained to remind the universe of its true origins. Consider how man was uniquely endowed to fulfill his mission: וַיִּפַּח בְּאַפָּיו נִשְׁמַת חַיִּים וַיְהִי הָאָדָם לְנֶפֶשׁ חַיָּה, Hashem *blew into his nostrils the soul of life; and man became a living being* (soul).

By infusing man with this soul, man became a direct link to the Source of Life, Hashem. Whereas while creating lower forms of life, Hashem shrouded His Presence, in this instance His Presence was transparent as He breathed the soul of life into man.

To fully appreciate man's role in restoring the universe to its original form, we need to delve further into the significance of נֶפֶשׁ חַיָּה, *a living soul*. By infusing His soul into man, Hashem endowed Adam with the unique ability to bring Godliness into all His creations. נֶפֶשׁ חַיָּה, *a living soul*, should be interpreted thus: a soul which will infuse all beings with true life (כְּלִי שֶׁיַּחֲזוֹר וְיִתְמַשֵׁךְ הָרַחֲמִים מֵחֵי הַחַיִּים אֶל כָּל מַעֲשֵׂה בְרֵאשִׁית). To appreciate even further why man's ability to inspire nature is characterized as life, consider the impact of the Six Days of Creation. As the earth developed and God's creation became increasingly more remote from Him, the universe experienced a form of death, being cut off from the Source of life. Now, reconnecting all of creation to its Source, man restores true life.

In perceiving man as a link between nature and the Divine Presence, we can better appreciate why Adam was entrusted with naming all Hashem's creations (cf. *Bereishis* 2:20, וַיִּקְרָא הָאָדָם שֵׁמוֹת, *And the man assigned names*). As the link between the created and the Creator, only man could understand the true nature and consequently the name of any living thing.

On the anniversary of man's creation, Rosh Hashanah, we plead זָכְרֵנוּ לְחַיִּים — Grant us again the capacity to cleanse ourselves from the materialism which is tantamount to death and to link the entire universe with the true Source of life. In so doing, all Hashem's beings shall acclaim along with Nechemiah (9:6), אַתָּה מְחַיֶּה . . . אַתָּה עָשִׂיתָ אֶת הַשָּׁמַיִם אֶת כֻּלָּם, [not only did] *You create heaven . . . and You are constantly sustaining them.* (5657)

והנה התמשכות חיות הנ״ל תליא ברמ״ח מ״ע ושס״ה ל״ת. ולכן הדין בר״ה לפי שיקול רוב הזכיות או רוב עונות.

In this context we can also better understand why on Rosh Hashanah the verdict of life or, God forbid, death is contingent upon the evaluation of man's merit and especially his observance of the 248 positive commandments and 365 negative commandments. As it is well known, these commandments correspond to the number of limbs (248) and sinews (365) of the human body. Each *mitzvah* that is observed (each transgression not being violated) brings life to a distinct component of the human being.

By weighing man's merits and demerits, Hashem is evaluating whether the individual deserves true life — the ability to be connected to the source of all life, Hashem. Each *mitzvah* observed allows a significant part of the human body (corresponding to the particular commandment) to be linked with Hashem. The individual whose merits outweigh his demerits is rewarded with life, a renewed link with his Creator. (5657)

רך חיים תוכחות מוסר ע״י יסורים . . . והתורה נותנת עצה לבנ״י להמשיך החיים ע״י התורה. ולא ע״י יסורים.

While in theory all men, Jew or Gentile alike, could merit to become the link between God and His creation, to serve as the conduit for spirituality in a material world, Israel's claim to that distinguished task was enhanced by accepting the Torah. By affirming that אָנֹכִי ה׳ אֱלֹהֶיךָ,

Hashem is our God, the Jewish people forged the link between creation and the Creator in explicit terms. Thus, every Rosh Hashanah they are particularly well positioned to fulfill their historical mission.   (5662)

◄§ Life — Clinging to Hashem (דְּבֵקוּת)

ולכן איתא בזוה״ק תרעומות על אותן שצווחין ככלבים הב לנו
מזוני סליחה מחילה. וחז״ל התקינו כל אלו הבקשות. . . . אבל
עיקר בקשתינו הוא להיפוך להיות כל צרכינו בדביקות.

Perhaps the clearest definition of life, (perhaps the clearest statement of) every Rosh Hashanah is articulated by the verse, וְאַתֶּם הַדְּבֵקִים בַּה' אֱלֹהֵיכֶם חַיִּים כֻּלְּכֶם הַיּוֹם, *but you who cling to Hashem, your God, you are all alive today (Devarim 4:4).*

Our entreaty for life is simply a fervent heartfelt request for דְּבֵקוּת, clinging to Hashem.

With this in mind, we can resolve the opening question of this essay. On one hand, the *Zohar* criticizes those who present Hashem with a long list of personal requests comparing them to "barking dogs." Yet, Israel's many needs comprise a major part of the Rosh Hashanah service. In truth, no contradiction need exist. Undoubtedly, the Jewish people beseech Hashem for His fulfillment of their personal requests. But that is not enough. It is critical that we pray for דְּבֵקוּת so we are able to continue to cling to Hashem even after our physical needs have been met and that living a comfortable life need not sever our links with our Creator. In fact, Israel's goal every Rosh Hashanah is to achieve that exalted state in which it constantly realizes that *all* of its blessings are from the Source of life, Hashem.   (5653)

◄§ Life for Hashem's Sake

אבל מבקשין שיהי' כתיבתנו לחיים למענו. דכ' עם זו יצרתי לי
לשמי. ורצון בנ״י לקבל החיים לשמו ית' כי הכל לכבודו ברא.

The concluding words of the זָכְרֵנוּ לְחַיִּים insertion help define Israel's request for life: לְמַעַנְךָ אֱלֹהִים חַיִּים, *for Your sake, the God of life,* not for our own personal gain. This concept that Israel's survival "benefits" God as well is eloquently stated by Yeshayahu, עַם זוּ יָצַרְתִּי לִי תְּהִלָּתִי יְסַפֵּרוּ, *this nation I have created for Me (so that) they will speak My praise* (43:21).

As *Avos* (6:11) states: כָּל מַה שֶּׁבָּרָא הקב״ה בָּעוֹלָמוֹ לֹא בְרָאוֹ אֶלָּא לִכְבוֹדוֹ, *Whatever Hashem created in His universe, He created solely for His glory.*

Israel's survival then is an integral part of Hashem's glory. By praying for life we are seeking the greater sanctification of Hashem's name as well. (5654)

◄§ Hints but no Explicit Requests

כי בר״׳ה אין מבקשין על עניני עוה״׳ז. . . . רק לבקש על מ׳׳ש תן
פחדך . . . דלכך מרמזין על צורכי עוה״׳ז שהם באמת רק רמזים
להוציא מכל ענין רמיזא דחכמתא

An additional insight into our requests for life can be derived from the Talmud's (*Horayos* 12a) recommendation that one partake of various foods on Rosh Hashanah that allude to our wishes (e.g. when eating כַּרְתִּי, *leek*, we plead שֶׁיִּכָּרְתוּ שׂוֹנְאֵינוּ, *that our foe be eradicated*).

It is significant that we do not explicate our requests but merely hint at them. In fact, throughout the Rosh Hashanah service emphasis is placed on God's kingdom being accepted by all mankind rather than our personal needs.

If so, why even hint at physical requirements? Perhaps to suggest that the entire material world only exists for a higher purpose to serve Hashem. Every material entity that exists (e.g. a house, a vehicle, an animal) is, in effect, hinting to us that it should be utilized for a higher purpose. In fact, all of Israel's prayers for life — and all material things — are really pleas for all the prerequisites so that we may better serve Hashem. (5632)

◦§ Life — Clinging to the Tree of Life — The Torah

רק בשביל התורה ומבקשים כתבנו בספר החיים שהוא להתדבק בתורה שנק' עץ החיים.
אבל צריכין לראות שלא להיות יראה רק מעונש. אך יראת ה' לחיים. פי' שיהי' עיקר היראה שלא יהיו נדחין מעץ החיים שהיא התורה. וע"ז עיקר הבקשה להיות נדבקין בתורה.

Upon further contemplation we may say that by entreating Hashem for life, Israel is actually pleading to return to its close association with Torah described as the Tree of Life (cf. *Mishlei* 3:18, עֵץ חַיִּים הִיא לַמַּחֲזִיקִים בָּהּ, *It is a Tree of Life for those who grasp it*).

Israel's very exalted desire — seeking Torah rather than material possessions — serves as a source of merit for the Jewish people and "reminds" Hashem of our greatest day, the Giving of the Torah. Additionally, the *shofar* itself, which played so prominent a role at Sinai (refer to our discussion of the *shofar*), helps to accentuate Israel's merit for receiving the Torah.

Likewise, our plea כָּתְבֵנוּ בְּסֵפֶר הַחַיִּים, *write us in the Book of Life*, may be interpreted thus: Allow us to cling to the Torah which is called the Book of Life (cf. *Shemos* 32:32, מְחֵנִי נָא מִסִּפְרְךָ, *erase me now from this book*, and *Ramban's* commentary).

In fact, the entire concept of יִרְאַת ה', *fear of Hashem*, may be reinterpreted in this light. Not merely does it connote a dread of being punished (יִרְאַת הָעוֹנֶשׁ) but rather fear of being cast adrift from the Torah, of being cut off from the Tree of Life. (5648, 5651)

◦§ How Does One Obtain Life?

דכ' באור פני מלך חיים. ובראי' זו דבאי עולם עוברין לפניו מזה ניתן לכל אחד חיות.

We have just considered some of the ramifications of Israel's entreaty for life. But how does one obtain our most coveted goal — life on Rosh Hashanah? Firstly, by appearing in Hashem's Presence.

Typically, one assumes that standing before Hashem in judgment and being rewarded with life are two distinct processes (i.e. one who stands before the Heavenly tribunal is judged and then awarded his verdict).

In fact, merely *appearing before* Hashem in itself helps Israel to be inscribed in the Book of Life. As Shlomo notes, בְּאוֹר פְּנֵי מֶלֶךְ חַיִּים, *The light of the King's countenance (gives forth) life (Mishlei* 16:15).

Ample precedent exists for this concept, if we only hearken back to the first Rosh Hashanah ever, the day of man's creation.

Upon completing the process of creation with man as the apex and hub, Hashem beholds all of His creation and proclaims it *very good,* וַיַּרְא אֱלֹהִים אֶת כָּל אֲשֶׁר עָשָׂה וְהִנֵּה טוֹב מְאֹד (*Bereishis* 1:31). With this "seal of Divine approval" the world received its initial burst of life; every year, upon the anniversary of man's creation, Hashem beholds His creations and renews their lease on life. (5644)

וּבָחַרְתָּ בַּחַיִּים / Choose Life

וכמו במעשה בראשית איתא לדעתן נבראו שכל הברואים בחרו
כל אחד ציור המיוחד לו.

As the Torah makes abundantly clear, man can choose life — וּבָחַרְתָּ בַּחַיִּים (cf. *Devarim* 30:19). Evidently, the quality of life, especially spiritual life that man attains in the coming year, is dependent upon his wishes. One who desires a highly spiritual life can obtain it.

Again, ample precedent exists for this association between man's desire and his achievements on the Day of Judgment.

The Talmud (*Chullin* 60a) relates that all beings were created according to their desires (i.e. in the form that they wished). One may assume that Adam, who is depicted as a נֶפֶשׁ חַיָּה, a soul infused with spiritual life, chose this particular lifestyle and mission. Likewise, every Rosh Hashanah, on the anniversary of man's creation, all of us — by opting for a life based on Torah — merit such a life. The more intense one's desire for spirituality, the greater his reward. (5661)

איתא כל מעשה בראשית לדעתן נבראו כו'. לכן כפי הכנת האדם
ובחירת רצונו בימים אלו כך ניתן לו התחדשות החיות שבכל
ר"ה מתחדש מעשה בראשית. ובכלל עיקר הדעת בעולם הם
בנ"י אדם אתם קרוין אדם כו'.

Moreover, the very notion of Divine Judgment (מִשְׁפָּט) can be described as the occasion in which all men upon presenting themselves before Hashem — כָּל בָּאֵי עוֹלָם יַעַבְרוּן לְפָנֶיךָ כִּבְנֵי מָרוֹן, *All mankind will pass before You like members of the flock* — are granted life, spiritual, in direct correlation to the wishes for such an illuminating lifestyle.

This is especially true for the Jewish people. All men were created — and on Rosh Hashanah renewed — לְדַעְתָּן, *according to their aspirations*. While all men could have spiritual objectives, Israel is the epitome of דַּעַת, of great aspiration. As the Talmud (*Yevamos* 61a) notes, אַתֶּם קְרוּיִין אָדָם, *You*, Israel, *are called man*; you possess that lofty aspiration that no other can enjoy, thus meriting the name אָדָם.   (5644)

יוֹם הַדִּין
Judgment

◄§ Kindness — Imperative for Judgment

In this section, we will offer a few insights, culled from the *Sfas Emes*, about Hashem's Judgment of the universe on Rosh Hashanah.

וּלְךָ ה׳ חָסֶד כִּי אַתָּה תְשַׁלֵּם לְאִישׁ כְּמַעֲשֵׂהוּ

And Yours, my Lord, is kindness, for You reward each man in accordance with his deeds (Tehillim 62:13).

כשהקב״ה שופט העולם הוא מתלבש בחסד. כי בוודאי השופט כל הארץ צריך להיות מלא חסד ורחמים. ורמז לזה מה שאמרו חכמים כי הדיינים מתעטפין בטליתות כמ״ש מאימתי התחלת דין משיתעטפו הדיינים.

With these words, David defines the essence of Divine Justice. Even when practicing justice by compensating an individual for his deeds, Hashem is cloaked in the Attribute of Kindness. It is imperative that the Judge of all Mankind be suffused with compassion. The requirement that judges (during Talmudic times) cloak themselves in a *tallis* alludes to the outer wrapping (of kindness) that envelops the judge. In fact, the Talmud (*Shabbos* 10a) implies that a court proceeding could not begin until the jurists had donned their *talleisim*, suggesting that justice only commences when the outer cloak of kindness is present.

The essential prerequisite for kindness in the administration of justice can be proven from a different perspective as well. It is well known that an enemy (of any of the litigants) may not serve as a judge in any proceeding regarding his foe. Hashem's annual review and judgment of Israel is predicated on His love for us. The Midrash points out the relationship between His love for us and Hashem's capacity for judging us by noting: הי יִתְבָּרֵךְ אוֹהֵב אֶת יִשְׂרָאֵל וְאוֹהֵב אֶת הַמִּשְׁפָּט לָכֵן נוֹתֵן לָהֶם מִשְׁפָּט, *Hashem loves Israel and loves justice, therefore [because of His love for Israel] He gave them justice [i.e. He sits in judgment].*

In light of these remarks, the verse quoted may be interpreted thus: וּלְךָ הי חָסֶד, *and to You, Hashem, kindness is [the appropriate Attribute] when You judge every person according to his deeds.*

Alternatively, we may suggest the following interpretation: Since You do judge every individual, this alone is indicative of Your Kindness. The Judge of all Mankind would never have assumed that role had He not been laden with compassion.

The *Zohar's* assertion that Tishrei, the month of Rosh Hashanah, is a period of Divine Kindness also supports our contention that only if the Judge and the time of judgment are associated with kindness can justice take place. (5640)

◄§ Granting Understanding

הַיּוֹצֵר יַחַד לִבָּם הַמֵּבִין אֶל כָּל מַעֲשֵׂיהֶם

He Who fashions their hearts together, Who understands all their deeds (Tehillim 33:15).

כי הנה נקרא ראש השנה שבו יורד מוחין ובינה על כל השנה . . . בינו שנות דור ודור שיש בינה מיוחדת בכל שנה ושנה. וז״ש המבין אל כל מעשיהם פי׳ שהשי״ת נותן בינה לכל המעשים.

This renowned verse associated with Hashem's Judgment on Rosh Hashanah (cf. *Rosh Hashanah* 16b) also introduces us to another aspect of Divine Justice, Hashem's annual granting of בִּינָה, *intuition*, into His ways of governing the universe. The very name Rosh Hashanah, the *head of the year*, implies that at this time Hashem bestows intellect (associated with the head) and wisdom for the coming year (see our essay on Rosh Hashanah). In this sense, הַמֵּבִין אֶל כָּל מַעֲשֵׂיהֶם should be interpreted: *He gives understanding to all of His creations.* (5648)

◄§ The Common Source of all Mankind

היוצר יחד לבם הוא ע״י כ״ב אותיות התורה גי׳ יח״ד שזה הוא
השורש של כל הברואים ושורש זה מייחד ומחבר הכל ובזה כולן
נסקרין בסקירה אחת.

The first segment of the verse הַיּצֵר יַחַד לִבָּם helps explain why Hashem judges everyone simultaneously. All things emanate from the same source — the twenty-two letters of the *aleph beis* through which Hashem created the universe. (Note that the numerical equivalent [גִּימַטְרִיָא] of יַחַד is 22.) Since our roots are identical, we can all stand united before Hashem on the Judgment Day, Rosh Hashanah. He in turn perceives us with one glance as the Talmud (*Rosh Hashanah* 18a) says: וְכוּלָן נִסְקָרִין בִּסְקִירָה אַחַת, *And all are scanned with one scan*. [Please refer to our remarks on וְכָל בָּאֵי עוֹלָם יַעַבְרוּן לְפָנֶיךָ כִּבְנֵי מָרוֹן for additional insights on the judgment process.] (5648)

חֵרוּת
Freedom

While we ordinarily associate freedom with Pesach, known as זְמַן חֵרוּתֵנוּ, *the time of our freedom*, in the following section we will demonstrate that Rosh Hashanah is also intimately related to the theme of freedom.

✍ The Name Tishrei

מאמרם ז״ל תשרי ותשבוק. כי בר״ה נעשו בנ״י בני חורין וכל
מה שנתלכלכו כל השנה ונקשרו הנפשות בהבלי עולם נעשו בני
חורין בר״ה

The very name of the month in which Rosh Hashanah occurs, Tishrei (תִּשְׁרֵי), implies freedom, related to the Aramaic term שָׁרֵי, *permissible*. Every Rosh Hashanah, the Jewish soul is released from the clutches of materialism polluting it all year. (5648)

✍ Shemittah of the Soul

וכענין זה רמזו במשנה ר״ה לשמיטין ויובלות. עי״ז ולנטיעה.
שלאשר בר״ה צריכין לקבל מלכות שמים. ומאן דכפית באחרא
אינו יכול לקבל מלכות שמים כדאיתא בזוה״ק בהר. ולכן נעשין
מקודם בני חורין משעבודא וסט״א שיהיו מוכנים לקבל מלכות
שמים מחדש.

The Mishnah (*Rosh Hashanah* 1:1) notes that Rosh Hashanah marks the beginning of the *Shemittah* year (the Shabbos of the land, observed every seventh year) as well as the beginning of a new year for purposes of reckoning saplings (נְטִיעָה and *orlah*). [The fruit of the first three years is prohibited. However, if the tree took root more than forty-five days prior to Rosh Hashanah, then that short period is considered as if it were a full year and Rosh Hashanah marks the beginning of another year.] A beautiful homiletic comparison may be drawn between the literal translation of *shemittah* and *netiah*. שְׁמִיטָה, *release* (just as a farmer releases his grip on the land), from the clutches of evil is a necessary prerequisite for נְטִיעָה, for *planting* oneself firmly, for committing oneself and accepting Hashem's Sovereignty.   (5648)

◆§ The Shofar

וְהוּא בכח תקיעות שופר שנק' יובל על שם החירות. והתקיעה רמז שמצפין לצאת לחירות ולהתיר אגודות מוטה ונעשין כבריּ חדשה.

The *shofar* itself is called יוֹבֵל (cf. *Yehoshua* 6:5, וְהָיָה בִּמְשֹׁךְ בְּקֶרֶן הַיּוֹבֵל) recalling the *Yovel* year in which slaves were released from bondage. (In fact, many of the details of *shofar* blowing are derived from the sounding of the *shofar* during the *Yovel*.) So too, every Rosh Hashanah, inspired by the *shofar*, the Jewish soul is released from its imprisonment within the confines of the body. Just as the *shofar* sounded on Yom Kippur of the *Yovel* year marked the release of the Jewish slave, so too, upon hearing the *shofar* we determine to unshackle ourselves from the יֵצֶר הָרָע and to start a new life on Rosh Hashanah.   (5656)

◆§ Renewal and Freedom

כי שינוי מעשה בראשית גולל אור מפני חושך וחושך מפני אור הכל עדות על הבורא שהוא מנהיג העולם, ובנּיּ משבחים על זה כי הוא מסייע לעבודת הבורא. ובר"ה מתחדש ביותר כל ההנהגה של ימי השנה החדשה

Ezra urges the Jewish people to rejoice on Rosh Hashanah (cf. *Nechemiah* 8:10, כִּי חֶדְוַת ה' הִיא מָעֻזְּכֶם, *for the delight of* HASHEM, *that is your strength*). This joy may be based on the sense of renewal that we all experience on the anniversary of Creation. While the natural progression of daily life causes us to forget our true inner personalities and our spiritual potential, the fresh new start that we enjoy on Rosh Hashanah causes us to turn again to our פְּנִימִיוּת, *our inner self*. Just as Hashem renews the universe every day, rotating day and night, which prevents us from slipping totally into the grip of the natural world, so too, every year, Hashem renews the universe with far greater vigor. Daily or annual renewal, the realization that the universe is not on an automatic cycle but that every day and every year, Hashem conducts the universe in a unique fashion, is a powerful stimulus to shake us from our lethargy to help us earn our freedom from the יֵצֶר הָרָע. We express our gratitude for Hashem's constant reinvigoration by reciting the blessings of יוֹצֵר אוֹר every morning and הַמַּעֲרִיב עֲרָבִים every evening. These blessings describing the daily re-creation of light and darkness not only attest to Hashem's guidance of the universe but also allude to its impact on us — the daily renewal of spiritual life that accompanies the shift from day to night and vice versa.

(5664)

◆§ Freedom as Experienced by the Avos

והוא המשכות החירות. ולכן הם שלש תר״ת להזכיר זכות
שלשה אבות. שהם היו דביקים בעלמא דחירות. כדאיתא בגמ׳
שלשה הטעימן הקב״ה מעין עולם הבא. שלשה לא שלט בהם
יצה״ר בכל מכל כל ע״ש.

As previously mentioned, the *shofar* of Rosh Hashanah symbolizes freedom of the souls from the יֵצֶר הָרָע. There could be no better exemplar of such freedom than the *Avos* who sampled the World to Come already in this world (cf. *Bava Basra* 16b, שְׁלֹשָׁה הִטְעִימָן הקב״ה מֵעֵין עוֹלָם הַבָּא). This other-wordly perception, feeling unfettered from the shackles of the יֵצֶר הָרָע, was experienced by the three *Avos* and is preserved through the three distinct sounds of the *shofar* (the initial תְּקִיעָה followed by a תְּרוּעָה and the concluding תְּקִיעָה). While it may seem farfetched for us to aspire to the singular levels of spiritual freedom attained by the *Avos*, in truth any Jew

who decides to follow in their footsteps will merit freedom from the
יֵצֶר הָרָע.

Just as the *Avos* mastered their יֵצֶר הָרָע, so too can we triumph over
the Evil Inclination, assisted by the sound of the *shofar*. Even
temptation to commit the most severe of all sins — idolatry, prohibited
marriages, murder and evil talk (לָשׁוֹן הָרָע) — can be curbed as we attain
renewed freedom on Rosh Hashanah.   (5664)

◆§ Yosef Released from Imprisonment

כי נקודת יוסף מתגלה בר״ה. דיש לבחי׳ יוסף ג׳ מחיצות
מפסיקות. ערלה פריעה אטופי דדמא.

The Talmud (*Rosh Hashanah* 11a) relates that Yosef was released
from Potiphar's prison on Rosh Hashanah. While his actual release
is of great significance (marking the beginning of the Egyptian Exile),
this may be interpreted homiletically to allude to the release of the
Divine spark of every Jew on Rosh Hashanah. This kernel of goodness, called יוֹסֵף, *to add*, because of our sincere wish that it be *enhanced*,
is bound all year long to the body and its physical passions but is
released on Rosh Hashanah (see our remarks on מַלְכִיּוֹת, בַּכֶּסֶה, and
שׁוֹפָר).[1]

An analogy may be drawn between the release of this pure inner
spark and the בְּרִית מִילָה. Just as this sacred ritual always associated with
attaining moral purity involves three phases — הֲסָרַת עָרְלָה, *removal of
the outer flesh*; פְּרִיעָה, *retraction of a membrane*; and הַטָּפַת דַּם בְּרִית,
extricating [some of] *the blood of the bris* [milah] — so too, releasing the
soul from its own עָרְלָה, the limitations imposed by the body, involves
three phases — מַלְכִיּוֹת, זִכְרוֹנוֹת, שׁוֹפָרוֹת. Just as the consummation of the
בְּרִית מִילָה enables the inner light inherent in every Jew to radiate, so too
the combined effect of these תְּפִילוֹת and the שׁוֹפָר dismantle all barriers
to our spiritual and moral growth.   (*Likutim 5663*)

---

1. The designation of the Divine Spark as *Yosef* may also be related to the high standards of
moral purity maintained by Yosef as he ignored Potiphar's wife's repeated importuning.

⇜ Impact of Freedom —
The Soul Judges the Body

הנשמה נדמית להקב״ה מה הקב״ה יושב בחדרי חדרים כו׳ מה
הקב״ה זן עולם כולו כן הנשמה זנה הגוף. ובילקוט גורס הקב״ה
דן העולם והנשמה הגוף. לכן בימים האלו כמו שהקב״ה דן
העולם. כך צריך כל בעל נפש להשגיח ולדון את הגוף ביותר מכל
ימי השנה.

On Rosh Hashanah the soul is not only released but also dominates the body. In fact, a parallel may be drawn between the role of Hashem and the soul (cf. *Berachos* 10a drawing many parallels between the soul and Hashem) that is particularly pertinent to Rosh Hashanah. Just as Hashem during this period judges the universe, so too, the soul judges and evaluates the body (cf. *Yalkut Tehillim* 857, הקב״ה דָּן הָעוֹלָם וְהַנְּשָׁמָה וְהַגּוּף). While only Hashem can judge the universe, we should at least follow the Midrash's suggestion and encourage our soul to be dominant. We should permit our soul to judge our body. We should evaluate whether our body does, in fact, meet the criterion and standards of the soul.

Let us draw the parallel between the soul and Hashem even tighter. When Hashem pronounced at Sinai: אָנֹכִי ה׳ אֱלֹהֶיךָ, *I am Hashem, your God*, He, in effect, was saying that an element of Godliness (חֵלֶק אֱלֹהוּת) is contained and embedded within every Jew. The ideal repository for this Divine spark is the soul. An extraordinary symbiotic relationship exists between the soul containing an element of Godliness and Hashem Himself. The soul perceives and senses the Divine Will. Likewise, whatever occurs to the Jewish people, bearers of Divinity, is acutely sensed and has an impact in Heaven. (5652)

The Tefillos of Rosh Hashanah

The following section will discuss selected passages of the *tefillos* of Rosh Hashanah.

וּבְכֵן תֵּן פַּחְדְּךָ ה׳ אֱלֹהֵינוּ עַל כָּל מַעֲשֶׂיךָ

And so too, HASHEM, our God, instill Your awe upon all Your works.

ועתה בעונותינו הרבים בגוים אין תורה צריכין לבקש מקודם על תיקון מלכות שמים

In our essay on the Verses of Kingship, we noted that we first pray for the spiritual welfare of all mankind, and only afterwards do we think of our own needs, as we say in the following paragraph, וּבְכֵן תֵּן כָּבוֹד לְעַמֶּךָ, *And so too, grant honor . . . to Your people*. Although under ideal circumstances our first prayers should be directed to the glory of the Torah itself, the reality is that in the world we actually inhabit we must give greater emphasis to the needs of the rest of the universe. Living as we do amidst a host of nations who are totally unaware of the Torah and its blessings, we pray that at the very least Hashem's Sovereignty should be accepted by humanity.[1]   (5651)

---

1. Please refer to that essay for a discussion of the benefits that accrue from our prayers on behalf of mankind.

כי בר״ה צריכין להיות טוב עין אפילו לאומות . . . וכמו הטוב עין
שיש לבנ״י בר״ה כך מתראין לפניו לטובה.

We can say also that placing other people's welfare before our own reflects an innate collective altruism on our part, which the Sages referred to as *a good eye*, by which they meant generosity and a sincere wish for others to enjoy as much success as we do ourselves.[1]

Furthermore, this selflessness rebounds to our own benefit as well. It is known that Hashem treats people in accordance with the standards they apply to others, and since we put the well-being of others before our own, Hashem in turn blesses us before them, as the wise Shlomo HaMelech noted, טוֹב עַיִן הוּא יְבֹרָךְ, *It is the generous one who will be blessed* (Mishlei 22:9).

Chiddushei HaRim notes an interesting allusion to the importance of showing a generous spirit at the beginning of any new time-cycle. The Talmud (*Rosh Hashanah* 25a) relates that Rabbi Yehudah HaNasi instructed his student Rabbi Chiya to sanctify the New Moon in a place called *Ayin Tav* (literally, "good eye"), implying that not only was he to proclaim the new month in that location but also that he was to make sure that the month began with a "good eye," i.e. on a note of selfless generosity, so that that tone would continue throughout the month to come. (5654)

שכ׳ האריז״ל כ׳ כל בכן עולה חסד וג׳ בכן גבורה.

Elsewhere, in our discussion of the verse אַשְׁרֵי הָעָם יוֹדְעֵי תְרוּעָה, *Praiseworthy is the people who knows the shofar blast*, we emphasize the theme that underneath the outer layer of harsh justice with which Hashem appears to conduct the world lies an inner core of kindness. In this light we can appreciate the significance of an interesting *gematria* which emerges from this prayer. Each of the first three sections begins with the word וּבְכֵן(1), *and so too*, whose combined *gematria* equals that of the word גְּבוּרָה, *strength* (216), a reference to Divine Justice, while the

---

1. Cf. *Avos* 5:22: *Whoever has the following three traits is among the disciples of our forefather Abraham . . . a good eye, a humble spirit and a meek soul.*

gematria of each individual occurrence of the word בְּכֵן (72) is equal to that of the word חֶסֶד, *kindness*.[1]

Finally, in praying for the whole world to repent, we are only following the example of Hashem, Who looks forward to the time when His ultimate plan for the creation — a world in which all mankind is righteous — will be realized, as the prophet Yeshayahu (46:10) proclaims: מַגִּיד מֵרֵאשִׁית אַחֲרִית . . . וְכָל חֶפְצִי אֶעֱשֶׂה, *I foresee the end from the beginning . . . My entire wish [for all mankind to be righteous] will be fulfilled.*

(5659)

יוֹם [זִכְרוֹן] תְּרוּעָה
A day of [remembrance of] shofar blowing.

וּפִ׳ תרועה רצון כמ״ש ותרועת מלך בו

While this phrase is usually understood to say that we blow the *shofar* on Rosh Hashanah, perhaps it is also meant to indicate that this is a day of "goodwill."[2] While on the surface Rosh Hashanah is a day of judgment, it is also a day of goodwill for the Jewish people, since on this day Hashem's will that Israel accept His Sovereignty is fulfilled.

In this vein, we may note that when Ezra urged his followers who had returned from the Babylonian exile *not* to weep on Rosh Hashanah in spite of the overwhelming remorse they felt over their numerous sins, he comforted them with the words, כִּי חֶדְוַת ה׳ הִיא מָעֻזְּכֶם, *for the delight of Hashem, that is your strength* (*Nechemiah* 8:10). From this we see that Hashem takes delight in Israel's renewed vitality on Rosh Hashanah.

(5654)

זֵכֶר לִיצִיאַת מִצְרָיִם
A memorial of the Exodus from Egypt.

שבכל מצרים שיש לפעמים לטוב הוא כדי לצאת אח״כ ביתר שאת
לצרף ולזכך

The inclusion of this phrase in the Rosh Hashanah liturgy raises

---

1. *Editor's Note:* This equation comes out properly only if we ignore the letter *vav* at the beginning of the word וּבְכֵן.
2. See our comments below (p. 179) on the use of the word *teruah* in *Bamidbar* 23:21, וּתְרוּעַת מֶלֶךְ בּוֹ, *The friendship of the King is in him.*

questions, since this Festival is not generally thought to have a connection with the Exodus from Egypt. Perhaps, however, we can understand the word מִצְרַיִם in a different sense, as an allusion to the "narrow straits" in which the Jewish soul finds itself as the judgment of Rosh Hashanah approaches. All the awe and dread which fill us on this day is for our benefit, causing us to repent and consequently be purified. The sensation of purity and spiritual rebirth which follows the catharsis of Rosh Hashanah is truly a redemption from servitude, a release of the soul from the dire straits in which it had been confined by its sins.   (*Likutim*)

מְלוֹךְ עַל כָּל הָעוֹלָם כֻּלּוֹ

Reign over the Entire Universe

וכאשר מבקשין מלוך על כל העולם וכו, צריך להיות עיקר הבקשה על עצמינו שכל אדם מישראל נקרא עולם בפני עצמו

While this appears to be a simple plea for Hashem to cause His Sovereignty to be accepted by all mankind, it can be interpreted on an individual level as well. The Sages have said that every Jew is an entire world in his own right (cf. *Sanhedrin* 37a). Thus in this phrase each of us is pleading for Hashem to reign over every aspect of his personal world — and this in turn will bring about the fulfillment of the cosmic goal of Hashem's acceptance by all of mankind.   (5646)

Conversely, perhaps the reason we plead for Hashem's rule to be accepted by all of mankind is to make our own commitment to His service as complete as possible. As long as any one of Hashem's creations — even the least significant or the most wicked of them — does not accept His Will, then all of us — even the most righteous — are incapable of reaching our full potential.   (5646)

וְיֵדַע כָּל פָּעוּל כִּי אַתָּה פְעַלְתּוֹ

Let everything that has been made know that You are its Maker.

וע׳׳ז מבקשין . . . וידע כל פעול וכו׳ היינו לבטל הבחירה

This request that all creatures be made aware Who created them is, in a way, tantamount to a request that Hashem take away our free will. While evildoers revel in the ability to act in whatever selfish and abhorrent fashion they please, our sole desire is to serve Hashem with all the faculties He has given us, and therefore plead for Him not to allow us to do anything contrary to His will.

(5647)

וּדְבָרְךָ אֱמֶת וְקַיָּם לָעַד

And Your word is true and endures forever.

כי עיקר המשפט הוא בבחי' אמת ושלום . . . והקב"ה זוכה את
בנ"י באלה ה"ב'

Although this phrase, which concludes the blessing of the Sanctification of the Day, is said only on Rosh Hashanah, it does not appear to have any specific connection to the Festival. Perhaps, however, a well-known Midrash (*Bereishis Rabbah* 8:5) about the creation of the universe can shed some light on its relevance to this day:

אָמַר אֱמֶת אַל יִבָּרֵא עוֹלָם דְּכוּלָא שִׁיקְרָא וְשָׁלוֹם אָמַר אַל יִבָּרֵא דְּכוּלָּא קְטָטָה,

Said Truth, "Do not create a world because it will be all falsehood," and Peace said, "Do not create because it will be all conflict."

In spite of the protests raised by Truth and Peace, Hashem did create the universe, and each year on the anniversary of that creation Israel is judged anew on its performance in upholding these two qualities. In His great kindness, however, Hashem assists us in meeting the exacting standards which Truth and Peace demand for the universe to continue to exist.[1]

Actually, truth is one of the main themes of Rosh Hashanah. As we have explained at length elsewhere,[2] the *shofar* we blow on Rosh Hashanah reminds of the giving of the Torah, the ultimate truth. Moreover, the *wordless shofar* represents the pure unadulterated sound which always remains truthful, even if *words* are often used to mislead.

Therefore, in concluding the Sanctification of the Day we remind Hashem of Torah — His "word [which] is true and established forever."

(5655)

---

1. See *Avos* 1:18: עַל הַדִּין וְעַל הָאֱמֶת וְעַל הַשָּׁלוֹם — עַל שְׁלשָׁה דְבָרִים הָעוֹלָם קַיָּם, *the world endures on three things — justice, truth and peace.*

2. See our essay on the *shofar*.

The Torah Reading
of the First Day

וַיַּעַשׂ ה' לְשָׂרָה כַּאֲשֶׁר דִּבֵּר . . . וַתַּהַר וַתֵּלֶד שָׂרָה לְאַבְרָהָם בֶּן לִזְקֻנָיו

And HASHEM did for Sarah as He had spoken . . . Sarah conceived and bore a son unto Avraham in his old age (Bereishis 21:1,2).

ובמדרש הוסיפה על המאורות דכתיב הכא עשי' וכתיב ויעש
המאורות ע"ש. . . . כן שרה בצדקתה הוסיפה על המאורות
והמשיכה אור הגנוז למעלה מן המזלות

The Midrash (*Bereishis Rabbah* 53:1), commenting on this verse, recalls Yechezkel's prophecy: וְיָדְעוּ. . . כִּי אֲנִי ה' הִשְׁפַּלְתִּי עֵץ גָּבֹהַּ הִגְבַּהְתִּי עֵץ שָׁפָל. . . וְהִפְרַחְתִּי עֵץ יָבֵשׁ אֲנִי ה' דִּבַּרְתִּי וְעָשִׂיתִי, *And they shall know. . . that I Hashem lowered a high tree and raised a low tree. . . I have made a dry tree blossom. I am Hashem, I spoke and did* (Yechezkel 17:24).

This Midrash may be suggesting that the birth of Yitzchak had to occur through supernatural means. Sarah giving birth to Yitzchak at the ripe old age of ninety after having previously been barren demonstrates the power of the righteous to overcome all natural limitations. As the *Chiddushei HaRim* noted, it is entirely fitting that the birth of the first native Jew occurred supernaturally. This demonstrates graphically that our very existence — our very souls — is rooted in heaven and we are only sent to this earth temporarily, to perfect this world.

In a similar vein, the Midrash (*Bereishis Rabbah* 53:12), noting the similarity between the expression used to describe Sarah's miracle (וַיַּעַשׂ)

and the term describing Hashem's creation of the luminaries on the fourth day of creation (also with the word וַיַּעַשׂ), suggests that Sarah enhanced the light of creation.

To comprehend the Midrash's intention let us recall that Hashem hid the primeval light of creation. Determining that this light was too rarefied for mankind to enjoy, Hashem reserved this treasure for the souls of the righteous in the World to Come.

If mankind's unworthiness and especially Adam's sin caused Hashem to remove this primeval light, it follows that the exemplary good deeds of the righteous, such as Sarah, would enhance this light sufficiently to shine again on earth.

Perhaps this is also the in-depth meaning of the renowned Midrash (Bereishis Rabbah 44:14) that Hashem caused Avraham to gaze *above* the stars, when assuring him that he will have children. True, in the natural world (below the stars) it is ordained that Sarah cannot conceive. However, in the supernatural world, above the stars — in the ambiance of the primeval hidden light — natural law may be overridden. In *that* world no obstacles exist to Yitzchak's birth.   (*Vayeira 5658*)

וַיִּקְרָא אַבְרָהָם אֶת שֵׁם בְּנוֹ הַנּוֹלַד לוֹ אֲשֶׁר יָלְדָה לוֹ שָׂרָה יִצְחָק

Avraham named his son who was born to him — whom Sarah had borne him — Yitzchak (v. 3).

אך להיפוך בהצדיק יצחק אבינו ע״ה הי׳ כל תחבולי היצה״ר כשחוק מה שלאדם אחר הר גבוה . . . שלא הי׳ ניכר על פניו רק שמחה וחדוה . . . ויתכן לומר שישמעאל רצה להדמות אליו בבכי׳ השמחה. אבל שרה הנביאה ידעה להפריש שלשמחה זו מה עושה

The *Chiddushei HaRim* suggests that the term יִצְחָק, connoting laughter (צְחֹק), refers not only to Sarah's scoffing at the angel's prophecy of Yitzchak's birth but especially emphasizes Yitzchak's uncanny ability to tackle the יֵצֶר הָרָע. From his perspective, all of the Evil Impulse's attempts to lure him to sin were but a laughing, trivial matter. Temptations that appeared to others — even to the righteous — to be as weighty as a great mountain (cf. *Succah* 52a stating that the יֵצֶר הָרָע appears to the righteous as a lofty mountain) were insignificant to Yitzchak. He could *laugh off* evil.

This approach can be deduced from the Torah's description of Yishmael as מְצַחֵק, understood by *Rashi* to be referring to his violation of grave prohibitions (i.e. idolatry, prohibited relationship, murder; v. 9).

If מְצַחֵק connotes a sense of indifference to and even mockery of serious transgression, it follows that the similar term יִצְחָק also should be understood in the context of good and evil.

Alternatively, the term יִצְחָק recalls the joy that was present on the Patriarch's face. Though Yitzchak personified the characteristic of fear of Hashem (cf. *Bereishis* 31:42, פַּחַד יִצְחָק, *the Dread of Yitzchak*), his external countenance was always one of joy. It is perfectly logical that the truly God-fearing man, such as Yitzchak, is immune from any other source of fear and thus understandably could display a happy countenance. This is especially true of Yitzchak who lived on such an exalted level that God deemed him to be fit to be sacrificed.

It is entirely possible that Yishmael observing his brother's outer joy determined to emulate him and also displayed an outer veneer of joy. Sarah, blessed with Divinely-inspired wisdom, was able to discern between Yishmael's insincere, superficial joy and that of Yitzchak which reflected fear of Hashem. Armed with this knowledge, Sarah insists that כִּי לֹא יִירַשׁ בֶּן הָאָמָה הַזֹּאת עִם בְּנִי עִם יִצְחָק, *for the son of that slavewoman shall not inherit with my son, with Yitzchak* (ibid. 21:10). Sarah knows that her heir would have to be an individual suffused with true joy emanating from piety as the name יִצְחָק suggests. (ibid. 5643)

ראה כי עיקר השמחה על ידי המילה . . . ויצחק ראשון הנימול
לשמונה והיה מלא שמחה.

Alternatively, the joy manifested by the name יִצְחָק may be derived from the *bris milah* mentioned in the following verse: וַיָּמָל אַבְרָהָם אֶת יִצְחָק בְּנוֹ בֶּן שְׁמֹנַת יָמִים, *Avraham circumcised his son Yitzchak at the age of eight days* (ibid. 21:4).

It is well known that sadness stems from the blurring (confusion) of good and evil resulting from Adam's Sin. For example, the pain and sadness often associated with childbirth (cf. *Bereishis* 3:16, בְּעֶצֶב תֵּלְדִי בָנִים) stems from the First Couple's tragic error. By participating in the בְּרִית מִילָה, which represents extinction of evil, Avraham was able to retrieve some of the joy Adam and Chavah experienced in Eden. Even more so, Yitzchak, who was the first individual to be circumcised eight

days after birth, could truly rejoice. As David sings: וּלְיִשְׁרֵי לֵב שִׂמְחָה,
those who enjoy an upright heart (purged from evil) may truly rejoice
(Tehillim 97:11). (ibid. 5663)

וַיִּפְקַח אֱלֹהִים אֶת עֵינֶיהָ וַתֵּרֶא בְּאֵר מָיִם וַתֵּלֶךְ וַתְּמַלֵּא אֶת הַחֵמֶת
מַיִם וַתַּשְׁקְ אֶת הַנָּעַר

Then God opened her eyes and she perceived a well of
water; she went and filled the skin with water and gave
the youth to drink (v. 19).

אמר המדרש מה שמלאה החמת מים הוא חסרון אמונה והרמז
בתורת ה׳ שהמאמין כראוי התורה נגלה אצלו בכל עת ואין
צריך למלא בטנו מים.

On this verse the Midrash (*Bereishis Rabbah* 53:14) deduces that we
are all considered to be "blind" (i.e. oblivious), even of our immediate
environment, until Hashem opens up our eyes. The Midrash (ibid.)
continues by criticizing Hagar for filling an entire flask with water.

Perhaps these two Midrashic comments are related. The true מַאֲמִין,
believer, in Hashem realizes that all of his needs are present in his
immediate environment. He need only plead, as David does, גַּל עֵינַי,
Reveal to my eyes (Tehillim 119:18), the site, the exact location where
the solution to my problem lies. The resolution to Hagar's dilemma —
not finding adequate water — was right beside her. But it took an act of
Hashem to open her eyes so that she finally realized that the resolution
to her cries was at hand.

By filling the flask with water — with far more water than Yishmael
required — Hagar demonstrates a lack of faith in Hashem. The truly
devout believer knows with absolute conviction that the answer to his
problems is before him. By immersing himself in Torah, he can be sure
that Hashem will open his eyes and reveal the answer to his dilemma, as
He did for Hagar.

By filling the flask with far more water than necessary, Hagar is
displaying an apparent lack of faith in Hashem. (5655)

The Akeidah —
The Reading of the Second Day

This section will explore many aspects of Yitzchak's near sacrifice, the *Akeidah*. (Much of this material is culled from the *Sfas Emes's* commentary on *Vayeira*.)

וְהָאֱלֹהִים נִסָּה אֶת אַבְרָהָם

That God tested Avraham (Bereishis 22:1).

The following is a free translation of those excerpts from *Midrash Rabbah* on וְהָאֱלֹהִים נִסָּה אֶת אַבְרָהָם.

כתיב נתתה ליראיך נס להתנוסס מפני קושט סלה נסיון ... כנס הזה של ספינה וכל כל למה מפני קושט בשביל שתתקשט מדת הדין בעולם. שאם יאמר לך אדם למי שהוא רוצה להעשיר מעשיר למי שהוא רוצה מעני ולמי שהוא רוצה הוא עושה מלך ... יכול את להשיבו ולומר לו יכול את לעשות כמו שעשה אברהם אבינו ...

It is written, You gave those who fear You a miracle to absorb (לְהִתְנוֹסֵס) for the sake of the truth (קֹשֶׁט) ... this is compared to the sail of a boat and why is all this necessary for the truth? So that the Attribute of Justice (מִדַּת הַדִּין) should be appreciated (תִּתְקַשֵּׁט, literally: adorned) in the universe. If someone would say to you that Hashem enriches or impoverishes or coronates whomever He desires [without any justification], you may respond [to such a questioner]: Could you accomplish what Avraham did?

L et us begin our analysis of this opening verse of the *Akeidah* by asking why the test (נָסָיוֹן) of the *Akeidah* is attributed to Avraham more than Yitzchak, who was after all prepared to sacrifice his very life to fulfill Hashem's Will.

The answer may lie in the fundamental personality difference between father and son. Avraham epitomized the attribute of love of Hashem (אַהֲבַת ה׳) and Yitzchak personified fear of Hashem (יִרְאַת ה׳). From the perspective of Yitzchak, it was perfectly reasonable to give up his life to fulfill Hashem's Will. However, from Avraham's vantage point, whose entire focus had been to sway mankind to love Hashem as he did, the act of sacrificing his son was contrary to his usual nature. The true test of any Jew is his willingness to fulfill the Divine Will even if it involves behavior that is the antithesis of his entire nature.

(cf. *Vayeira* 5643)

Avraham's trial was made considerably more difficult by the fact that he did not perceive the same surge of love, the same attachment (דְּבֵקוּת) to Hashem that he ordinarily experienced when performing Hashem's Will. Avraham, as the ultimate עוֹבֵד מֵאַהֲבָה, *one who serves [Hashem] with love*, had so developed his sense of devotion that all the 248 limbs of his body — nurtured by the 248 positive commandments (מִצְוֹת עֲשֵׂה) — would naturally, almost instinctively, follow Hashem's bidding. In this instance, inasmuch as Hashem did not actually intend to take Yitzchak's life — since the *Akeidah* was not a *mitzvah* that Hashem desired Avraham to fulfill — Avraham did not feel the same intense love and attachment that he normally experienced. Thus, the Patriarch was exposed to the ultimate test — performing Hashem's Will even when his natural instincts did not propel him to do so. (*Vayeira* 5641)

Let us focus on the various explanations of the term נִסָּה offered by the Midrash.

אבל עכשיו נתעלה אע״ה בכח עצמותו. וזהו פי׳ הנסיון כמ״ש
במד׳ נתת ליריאיך נס להתנוסס. פי׳ בעצמו.

Firstly, הֵרִים אוֹתוֹ, [Hashem] elevated him [Avraham]. This may refer
to the supernatural status attained by Avraham as a result of successfully "passing" the trial of the Akeidah. While Avraham had already
been elevated — lifted above the stars when he was informed of the
birth of Yitzchak — at the Akeidah he attains this status on the basis of
his own merit. (Rosh Hashanah 5664)

והענין הוא דכ׳ והאלקים נסה את אברהם. דרשו חז״ל הרים
אותו. כי באמת מדת אברהם החסד. ויצחק הגבורה. . . . אך
אברהם אע״ה זכה במעשה העקידה שיגבור החסד על הגבורה.

Alternatively, this Midrash may be alluding to the dominance of
Avraham's attribute of kindness (חֶסֶד) and love of Hashem (אַהֲבַת ה׳)
that as a result of the Akeidah prevailed over Yitzchak's attribute, fear
and reverence of Hashem (פַּחַד יִצְחָק). While under ordinary circum-
stance, the attribute of fear of Hashem — described as יָד חֲזָקָה, the
Mighty Hand — prevails over חֶסֶד, kindness, as a result of the Akeidah, Avraham's attribute was elevated over all other characteristics.
(Rosh Hashanah 5654)[1]

מסר הקב״ה את יצחק תחת יד אברהם להיות מדת החסד גובר
על מדת הדין. והנה לאברהם נאמר לך לך כו׳ התהלך בארץ
לארכה ורחבה כי מדת החסד הוא צריך להתפשט . . . ועתה
בעוה״ז צריכין להשען במדת אברהם אבינו. ולעתיד נאמר על
יצחק אתה אבינו כמ״ש בגמ׳.

Reflecting further on the relationship between kindness and justice
we realize that their functions are entirely different, though both are
virtually important. Avraham's characteristic of kindness was hardly
intended to be confined to the Patriarch himself. Instead, he was told:

---

1. This theme, prevalence of kindness over the Attribute of Justice, is reflected in Hallel: כִּי
גָבַר עָלֵינוּ חַסְדּוֹ, for His [Hashem's] Attribute of Kindness has become mighty (i.e. prevailed
over the Attribute of Justice.)

קוּם הִתְהַלֵּךְ בָּאָרֶץ לְאָרְכָּהּ וּלְרָחְבָּהּ, *Go through the length and breadth of the land* disseminating and propagating your message (*Bereishis* 13:7). By contrast, the Attribute of justice, while critical to the preservation of the universe, needs to be "diluted" and tempered with mercy. By bringing Yitzchak, the personification of Justice, to the very edge of the heavens (though not actually taking his life), the source of Divine Mercy — Hashem — blended justice with mercy. While in this world, we are nurtured by Avraham's trait of kindness, as David sings: עוֹלָם חֶסֶד יִבָּנֶה, *forever will [Your] kindness be built* (*Tehillim* 89:3), in the World to Come, we will be sustained through the Attribute of Justice, as personified by Yitzchak (cf. *Shabbos* 89b). In that future world, in which a higher standard will prevail, we will merit to live up to the sterling example of Yitzchak.   (Cf. *Vayeira* 5656)

וכן חשבון המשנה עשרה מאמרות כו' אח"כ עשרה נסיונות כו'
עשרה ניסים כו' כי כמו שעשרה מאמרות הם קיום עולם הטבע
בכלל. כן עשרה נסיונות הכנה וקיום הנהגת בני ישראל. . . . ע"י
אמצעות מעשה אבות מנהיג הבורא ית' בנ"י במדריגת הנסים
כנ"ל. נס להתנוסס כי יש נס לשעה ויש נס שעושה תולדות
ומתפשט ממנו נסים תמיד.

The Midrash continues to describe the *Akeidah* as a miracle to personally experience (לְהִתְנוֹסֵס, utilizing the הִתְפָּעֵל form in which the individual personally identifies with the action that is being performed).

While some events were primarily intended for a short duration, the trials of the *Akeidah* radically transformed the very nature of the Jewish people and their survival in this world. This was a נֵס לְהִתְנוֹסֵס, *a trial to be absorbed into the very fiber of the Jewish people* — to change their entire lifestyle from an entirely natural one to one governed by miracles. If Hashem subjected Avraham to the ultimate trial of sacrificing his son, it was because Hashem knew that Avraham and his descendants — the Jewish people — lived a supernatural existence. By passing this test, Avraham merited that his children also would deserve נִסִים, *great, supernatural events.*

The sequence of Mishnayos in *Avos* (5:1,4,5) confirms this approach beginning with the Ten Divine Statements (עֲשָׂרָה מַאֲמָרוֹת) through which the universe was created, followed by the Ten Trials (עֲשָׂרָה נִסְיוֹנוֹת) and finally the Ten Miracles occurring to the Jewish people in

Egypt and on the Sea. This sequence implies that just as the Ten Statements are essential for the continued existence of the natural world, so too the Ten Trials — and especially the greatest trial, the *Akeidah* of Avraham — were crucial for the miraculous survival of Israel, through the Ten Miracles.   (*Vayeira* 5639)

מדרש על העקידה נתת ליריאיך נס להתנוסס כו׳. דכמו דיש
עשרה מאמרות שמזה נבראו כל הברואים ע״י הרבה מיני
התפשטות. . . . ע״כ דרשו חז״ל נא עמוד לי בנסיון הזה כו׳ ע״י
שתלוי בזה כל בית ישראל.

In this light, we can appreciate why Hashem pleads with Avraham to pass this trial (עֲמוֹד לִי בַּנִּסָּיוֹן הַזֶּה, cf. *Sanhedrin* 89b). Had Avraham not risen to the challenge and failed the formidable test of the *Akeidah*, we would be "doomed" to the same natural challenge as the world at large. It is only in the merit of the *Akeidah* that individual Jews as well as the Jewish nation are able to overcome all the temptations of the natural world.   (*Vayeira* 5642)

וזה הרמז כנס של ספינה שיש עבודה בהשתוקקת אהבה. הגם
שאין לו יסוד בעולם העשי׳ כמי שפורח באויר וספינה המשוטה
ע״פ המים.

The Midrash continues by interpreting נֵסָה as the נֵס שֶׁל סְפִינָה (in some versions כְּתוֹרֶן), *the sail of a boat*, which flutters very visibly above the vessel.

The analogy to the sail of a boat may be appreciated by considering the uniqueness of the trial of the *Akeidah*. By contrast to all of the other trails which Avraham actually was required to perform (e.g. leaving his ancestral home), Avraham never actually sacrificed Yitzchak. Instead, this test was fulfilled purely in the realm of thought (עוֹלָם הַמַּחֲשָׁבָה). (Refer to our essay on the *shofar* for further discussion of this theme.) With each trial, Avraham rose to a higher level, rising from the world of deed (עוֹלָם הָעֲשִׂיָּה) in which he was required to actually *perform* Hashem's Will to the final test of the *Akeidah*, which only existed in the realm of thought (Hashem never intending for Avraham to actually sacrifice Yitzchak).[1]

---

1. This characteristic, being able to serve Hashem through the rarefied world of thought, as well as deed, is unique to the Jewish people for whom Hashem considers their intentions to perform a *mitzvah* to be as significant as the performance of the deed itself (*Kiddushin* 40a).

There is no more pithy and beautiful way to convey the idea of a world — very different from our mundane world — than a boat floating on the water, in an ambiance removed from our earth, in the sea, not on land. (*Vayeira* 5645)

ואומרים ז״ל כתורן של ספינה שרואין אותו מרחוק היינו שהי' צריך להיות הכנה לכל הדורות.

The analogy to the sail of a boat — fluttering above the vessel and often seen at a distance — was also intended to emphasize the *permanent* impact of the *Akeidah*.

While Avraham prior to this great trial was primarily noted for his love of Hashem, the world at large could not appreciate the uniqueness of this attribute. As the Midrash cited at the onset of this essay states, there were indeed those who wondered about Avraham's extraordinary relationship with Hashem, contending that Hashem simply chose Avraham on the basis of His whim, without much justification. To counter this misconception, Hashem subjected Avraham to these difficult trials, which accentuated his fear as well as his love of Hashem.

Appropriately, the Midrash cites the verse נָתַתָּה לִּירֵאֶיךָ נֵּס, *You granted trials to those who fear You* (*Tehillim* 60:6) for it was through the trial of the *Akeidah* that Avraham's fear of Hashem could be appreciated. The analogy to the sail of a boat now becomes apparent. Just as the sail identifies the vessel at a distance, so too distant generations will benefit from the combination of fear and love that Avraham now personified. (*Vayeira* 5649)

שיוכל אאע״ה למצוא לו הנהגה שלמעלה מן הטבע והוא להתנוסס כתורן של ספינה להיות נודע לנו.

The sail also stands above the actual physical framework of the vessel. So too, Avraham's descendants will merit to a supernatural existence. (Refer to our previous remarks.) (5651)

אבל התחיל להתפשט להתפשט החסד יותר מדאי לכן אחר שכרת ברת עד אבימלך האלקים נסה

The above-cited Midrash concludes: וְכָל כָּךְ לָמָה מִפְּנֵי קֹשֶׁט בִּשְׁבִיל שֶׁתִּתְקַשֵׁט מִדַּת הַדִּין בָּעוֹלָם נָתַתָּה לִירֵאֶיךָ נֵּס לְהִתְנוֹסֵס מִפְּנֵי קֹשֶׁט סֶלָה, *And what was the purpose of all this* (i.e. the *Akeidah*)? *For the sake of truth so that the Attribute of Justice should be made truthful.*

This baffling Midrash should be understood in its immediate context — the covenant that Avraham had arranged with Avimelech, the Philistine monarch, ceding him much of *Eretz Yisrael* for four generations. While this was certainly a well-intentioned act of kindness (חֶסֶד) on the Patriarch's part, kindness has its limits. As the Midrash notes, this treaty, yielding effective control of the land that Hashem had promised to Avraham's progeny, was an error and misapplication of the trait of kindness. To curb Avraham's natural (and usually correct) instincts toward the attribute of kindness, Hashem subjects him to the *Akeidah* in which he is required to subsume his tending toward kindness in favor of the requirement of obeying the strict, unyielding interpretation of Hashem's Will — even at the expense of his beloved son. As David sings: נָתַתָּה לִירֵאֶיךָ נֵּס, *You lifted up Avraham who feared You* — מִפְּנֵי קֹשֶׁט סֶלָה, *for truth's sake,* so that the Attribute of Justice can be appreciated. As the Midrash concludes: שֶׁתִּתְקַשֵׁט מִדַּת הַדִּין בָּעוֹלָם. Delving deeper, we can say that the *Akeidah* was hardly meant as a rejection of Avraham's attribute of kindness but rather a means of its purification, by blending it subtly with the unyielding submission to Hashem that Avraham displayed. Just as Hashem's Attribute of Kindness is integrated with His Attribute of Truth (וְרַב חֶסֶד וֶאֱמֶת), ensuring that His Kindness is reserved for the deserving, so too as a result of the *Akeidah*, Avraham's kindness is purified and is given appropriate parameters.

The true fruits of the *Akeidah*, the ideal synthesis of kindness and justice, was Yaakov who personified the Attribute of Truth, אֱמֶת (cf. *Michah* 7:20, תִּתֵּן אֱמֶת לְיַעֲקֹב). Avraham grieves over Sarah's insistence that Yishmael be sent away, and he is only consoled when Hashem tells him: כִּי בְיִצְחָק יִקָּרֵא לְךָ זָרַע, *that it is through Yitzchak that your true offspring will emerge* (21:12). In light of the above remarks, this may refer to Yaakov, who personifies the true combination of Avraham and Yitzchak's virtues. The Midrash's suggestion that the *Akeidah* was intended to bring to the forefront the virtue of truth (קֹשֶׁט) may refer to Yaakov, who exemplified the Attribute of Truth, the epitome of all that Avraham and Yitzchak had striven for. (5658)

ולפי שאברהם אבינו נתנסה ב׳׳י נסיונות וביטול כל הטבע זכה
שינתן עשרת הדברות לבני ישראל ולעשות להם עשרה הנסים

Alternatively, the Midrash may be extolling Avraham's virtue. He demonstrated his loyalty throughout the Ten Trials (עֲשָׂרָה נְסִיוֹנוֹת) never wavering in his *emunah* despite the supernatural sacrifices required. Therefore, Avraham merited that his children would enjoy a supernatural and miraculous lifestyle. In the merit of the עֲשָׂרָה נְסִיוֹנוֹת, *Ten Trials*, Avraham's descendants would enjoy the Ten Commandments (עֲשֶׂרֶת הַדִּבְּרוֹת) as well as the Ten Miracles (עֲשָׂרָה נִסִּים) occurring in Egypt. Avraham's loyalty was particularly remarkable since it was accomplished in a universe *prior* to the dissemination of the Torah, a universe that is often called a false world (עָלְמָא דְּשִׁיקְרָא). This may be the intention of the verse מִפְּנֵי קֶשֶׁט סֶלָה — before (מִפְּנֵי) the truth (קֶשֶׁט) of the Torah was revealed to Yaakov, You gave the Patriarch who feared You (נָתַתָּה לִירֵאֶיךָ), an opportunity to be elevated in a supernatural fashion — prior to the giving of the Torah to Yaakov and his children.   (5659)

קַח נָא אֶת בִּנְךָ
Please take your son (Bereishis 22:2).

וזה שבח בגדול בנסיון הזה שלא נאמר לו בלשון ציווי רק אם חפץ
בדבר זה.

The term "please" implies that Hashem did *not demand* that Avraham sacrifice Yitzchak but instead requested that Avraham surrender Hashem's greatest gift to him, his son, Yitzchak. This approach magnifies Avraham's incredible act — he was prepared to sacrifice his only son on the basis of a Divine *plea*, not even a command! Avraham, who loved Hashem, understood though that his mission was not merely to obey Divine edicts, but also to fulfill Hashem's Will.   (5634)

אֶת יְחִידְךָ
Your only one (v. 2).

אבל אמר לי כי אין לו עוד בן רק יצחק ושיעלהו לעולה באופן
שנותן את כל זרע ישראל.

Hashem made no attempt to hide from Avraham the full implications of the *Akeidah*. Lest Avraham console himself that he would be granted another son as worthy as Yitzchak, Hashem made it abundantly clear that Yitzchak was Avraham's *one* and *only* child, now and evermore. His martyrdom would signal a death sentence to the Jewish people's future. Despite the realization that his entire posterity — all of the would-be descendants — were also participating in the *Akeidah*, Avraham, nevertheless, still pursues his mission joyously.   (ibid.)

אֶת בִּנְךָ אֶת יְחִידְךָ אֲשֶׁר אָהַבְתָּ
Your son, your only one, whom you love (v. 2).

ולכן נכתב בנך יחידך כן נגד כל המדריגות שנמצא במס״נ של
בנ״י וכולם ע״י הכנת האבות.

Rashi notes that the Divine request was communicated to Avraham in piecemeal fashion (i.e. first *your son*, then *your only son*, and finally *whom you love*) in order to reward him for acquiescing to each Divine statement.

This raises the following question. Surely, Avraham himself would have acquiesced to the Divine request even if it had been presented to him as *one* entity. Why was his reward greater for having being subjected to *three* distinct statements?

Apparently, Hashem "broke down" His request into three distinct segments not for Avraham's sake who would have obeyed the Divine edict in any form, but for the benefit of future generations of Jews, Avraham's descendants who would be called upon to render great sacrifices of their own.[1]

They too would sacrifice everything, if necessary, to fulfill Hashem's commandment. To facilitate the ability of future generations of Jews to be מוֹסֵר נֶפֶשׁ, *sacrifice for Hashem's Will*, Hashem "broke the news" to Avraham in phases. This would signify to future generations that they could attain Avraham's exalted level but only through a sequential process. First they would render lesser sacrifices, and then gradually progress to the point where they could give up everything.

---

1. In this instance, we see how Avraham's actions were motivated by their impact on future generations of Jews. This is consistent with the overall behavior of the *Avos*, who were given that name (Fathers) because their every action was performed with the interests of their children, the Jewish people, in mind.

How does this process of incremental מְסִירוּת נֶפֶשׁ occur, whereby the individual "graduates" from sacrificing smaller things to a far more encompassing sacrifice, culminating in martyrdom, if necessary? *Rashi* supplies the answer to this question, as well, noting לְחַבֵּב עָלָיו אֶת הַמִּצְוָה. In "breaking the news" of Yitzchak's sacrifice in piecemeal fashion, Hashem caused Avraham *to love the mitzvah*. By taking small but significant steps along the path of מְסִירוּת נֶפֶשׁ, the Jew develops a heightened sense of אַהֲבַת ה', *love of Hashem*. Reinforced with this new-found awareness of his relationship with Hashem, he is now ready for greater sacrifices.   (5637)

אֲשֶׁר אָהַבְתָּ

whom you love (v. 2)

בעוצם אהבתו אליו יעלנו לעולה ולא ינוח האהבה . . . אשר
אהבת יישר כחך שאהבת.

The *Chiddushei HaRim* offers a powerful compelling thought on this pithy expression. Sacrifice your son as *you love him* — with your full love. It would have been relatively simple for Avraham to have superseded his love of Yitzchak in favor of fulfilling the Divine Commandment, but Hashem called upon Avraham to perform a far more daunting task — to sacrifice Yitzchak, if necessary, while simultaneously retaining his love for his son.

Alternatively, Hashem is emphasizing the intimacy and extra-ordinary relationship between Avraham and Yitzchak despite the vastly different personalities of father and son. Sacrifice your son as you love him — not ח"ו because of any differences with him. On the contrary, though Avraham and Yitzchak exemplified the extensively different traits of kindness and strength (חֶסֶד וּגְבוּרָה), their relationship was not only harmonious but one of complete unity in service to Hashem.

While in the natural world it is virtually impossible to harmoniously blend such disparate traits as kindness and justice, as a result of the *Akeidah* (as discussed in our remarks on הָאֱלֹהִים נִסָּה אַבְרָהָם) not only Avraham but his descendants, the Jewish people, were elevated to a higher, more supernatural existence. Just as in heaven, Hashem regulates the characteristics of various angels (e.g. Gavriel epitomizing the force of fire and Michoel epitomizing water) and blends them in a balanced whole, so too on earth, as a result of the sacrifice of the *Akeidah*, His children, the Jewish people, can unite despite their differences.

The theme of unity — despite differing personalities — is particularly appropriate in the case of the *Avos* who are depicted as the מֶרְכָּבָה, *the Bearers of the Shechinah*. United completely as they are in heaven — championing their common cause — through the *Akeidah*, the *Avos* attained the capacity to be totally united on earth as well[1] overcoming their differences for the common objective of performing Hashem's Will.

In fact, the expression אֲשֶׁר אָהַבְתָּ may be interpreted as יִישַׁר כֹּחֲךָ שֶׁאָהַבְתָּ, in which Hashem congratulates Avraham for maintaining his love for Yitzchak despite the vast difference in their approach to Divine Service.[2]

(5652)

עַל אַחַד הֶהָרִים אֲשֶׁר אֹמַר אֵלֶיךָ

Upon one of the mountains which I shall tell you (v. 2).

אחד ההרים יעקב המיוחד שבאבות.

If we assume that the term הָרִים, *mountains*, alludes to the Patriarchs (cf. *Bamidbar* 23:9, כִּי מֵרֹאשׁ צֻרִים אֶרְאֶנּוּ in which *Rashi* interprets the term צֻרִים, *peaks*, to refer to the *Avos*), then אַחַד הֶהָרִים, the most distinguished of the mountains, refers to Yaakov (cf. Midrash identifying Yaakov as the בְּחִיר שֶׁבָּאָבוֹת, *the chosen one amongst the Avos*). Refer to our previous remarks describing how the kindness symbolized by Avraham and the strict justice of Yitzchak were melded together at the *Akeidah*, resulting in the emergence of the sterling personality of Yaakov, who personified truth, the ideal amalgam of kindness and justice.

But truth does not come easily. It requires מְסִירוּת נֶפֶשׁ, *self-sacrifice*. Avraham prevails over his natural instinct of kindness which could have led him to spare his son, while Yitzchak was willing to give up his very life, so as a result, Yaakov, the personification of truth (cf. *Michah* 7:20, תִּתֵּן אֱמֶת לְיַעֲקֹב), emerged. We can learn from here the supreme

---

1. In this light, we can appreciate the repetition of Avraham's name, referring to his heavenly roots as well as his role on earth. Just as in heaven complete unity was achieved, so too on earth. (5652)

2. Cf. *Rashi*, *Devarim* (34:12) who interprets אֲשֶׁר שִׁבַּרְתָּ referring to Moshe's shattering of the Tablets as being congratulatory — יִישַׁר כֹּחֲךָ שֶׁשִּׁבַּרְתָּ.

significance of this virtue, which is so valuable in fact that, if necessary, one may even be willing to sacrifice one's life or one's natural kindly instincts so that the bearer of truth may emerge.   (5662)

וַיַּשְׁכֵּם אַבְרָהָם בַּבֹּקֶר
So Avraham woke up early in the morning (v. 3).

ולא זז אהבתו כמלא נימא מכל הנסיונות וזה דבר גדול מאד

The Midrash comments: אַהֲבָה מְקַלְקֶלֶת הַשּׁוּרָה, *love supersedes the natural order.* While ordinarily, esteemed individuals such as Avraham would not saddle their own donkey, in this event the Patriarch does, thereby demonstrating his boundless love for Hashem.

By tending to such mundane and seemingly degrading details, Avraham is demonstrating not only his willingness to remain loyal throughout all of his trials but also his unadulterated and total love of Hashem that never wavered even one iota despite all the trials to which he was subjected. As *Avos* (5:4) states: עֲשָׂרָה נִסְיוֹנוֹת נִתְנַסָּה אַבְרָהָם אָבִינוּ וְעָמַד בְּכֻלָּם, *[throughout] the Ten Trials that Avraham was subjected he perseveres* [i.e. his love of Hashem remained intact].

In the spirit of מִדָּה כְּנֶגֶד מִדָּה, *a measure for a measure* (cf. *Sotah* 8b), Hashem's love for Avraham's descendants, the Jewish people, remains intact despite our own unworthiness. As we say in the *Shemoneh Esrei*: וּמֵבִיא גוֹאֵל לִבְנֵי בְנֵיהֶם לְמַעַן שְׁמוֹ בְּאַהֲבָה, *Hashem brings the redeemer to the descendants (of the Patriarchs) for the sake of His Name, with love.* (Please refer to our commentary on אֲשֶׁר אָהַבְתָּ for a similar theme.)
(5660)

וַיַּרְא אֶת הַמָּקוֹם מֵרָחֹק
And perceived the place from afar (v. 4).

כי הקב"ה ניסה אותו במדת היראה כי עיקר מדתו הי' אהבה

The term *from afar* may be interpreted homiletically as referring to the trait of יִרְאַת ה', *fear of Hashem.* As discussed in our commentary on וְהָאֱלֹהִים נִסָּה אֶת אַבְרָהָם, Avraham's love of Hashem was tempered at the *Akeidah* and melded with יִרְאַת ה', *fear of Hashem.* (See also our commentary on עַתָּה יָדַעְתִּי כִּי יְרֵא אֱלֹהִים.) Prior to the *Akeidah,* the trait of *fear of Hashem*, critical though it is in enabling one to reach his potential greatness, was not a primary characteristic of Avraham. As such, he is described as perceiving Hashem *from afar*, recognizing Hashem through an attitude to which he was not ordinarily accustomed. (5643)

ולבו של אברהם לא הרגיש דביקות ואהבה בזו העובדא ע״י שבאמת לא הי׳ כן רצונו של השי״ת

In a somewhat similar vein, inasmuch as Hashem did not actually intend to take Yitzchak's life, Avraham could not experience the same complete devotion in which every fiber of his body would feel naturally propelled to perform the *mitzvos*, as he ordinarily did. Unlike any other occasion in his splendid career of Divine service, on his way to the *Akeidah* Avraham experienced difficulty in performing the Divine commandment. He felt as if the Word of Hashem was *distant*. Nonetheless, despite the lack of a natural attraction to perform Hashem's command, Avraham remains steadfastly loyal throughout this last and greatest of his trials. (5641)

דרשו על יעקב דכתיב ויפגע במקום

Finally, the term מֵרָחוֹק may allude to the *distant* descendant of Avraham and Yitzchak who would eventually emerge from the *Akeidah* — Yaakov, who combined his grandfather's kindness and father's justice. In fact, the term הַמָּקוֹם may also allude to Yaakov of whom it says: וַיִּפְגַּע בַּמָּקוֹם, *he encountered the place* (*Bereishis* (28:11). (5658)

וַאֲנִי וְהַנַּעַר נֵלְכָה עַד כֹּה
I and the lad will go yonder (v. 5).

נכנס עחה אברהם אע״ה לתקן במעשה זו כל מה שעתידין בנ״י לתקן עד סוף כל הדורות.

Rashi comments: אֶרְאֶה הֵיכָן הוּא מַה שֶׁאָמַר לִי הַמָּקוֹם כֹּה יִהְיֶה זַרְעֶךָ, *I will see where is [the promise] that [Hashem] said to me: "So will be your children."*

It seems at first, that Avraham, despite having agreed to sacrifice Yitzchak, now questions the validity of Hashem's promise that *your children will be numerous as the stars of the heaven*, a promise that was also expressed using the term כֹּה. Upon further analysis, however, we see that Avraham was alluding to a particularly ambitious plan that he had recently devised. The Patriarch realized that along with Yitzchak's sacrifice would come the crushing blow to his lifelong dream of building a great nation. This ideal, first conveyed to Avraham at the time of his pilgrimage to *Eretz Yisrael*, וְאֶעֶשְׂךָ לְגוֹי גָּדוֹל (ibid. 12:2), *I will make you into a great nation*, seemingly would come to naught as Yitzchak, his sole heir, is brought to the Altar. Yet, none of these considerations caused Avraham to flinch even one iota from his priority to fulfill Hashem's Will — even at the risk of forfeiting the Jewish people's future. Avraham's sense of priorities was in accordance with the well-established rule of חֲבִיבָה מִצְוָה בְּשַׁעְתָּה, (*Pesachim* 68b) a *timely mitzvah* takes precedence and *is preferred* over a *mitzvah*, no matter how significant, that would not be pertinent until a later time. Hashem's request to sacrifice Yitzchak immediately took priority over the *eventual* destiny of the Jewish people. His behavior also reflected the Mishnaic rule, וֶהֱוֵי זָהִיר בְּמִצְוָה קַלָּה כְּבַחֲמוּרָה, (*Avos* 2:1) *be as scrupulous in performing a "minor" mitzvah as in a "major" one*. Preserving the future of Jewry may be of greater significance than any particular *mitzvah*, yet a "lesser" *mitzvah* is given priority over a greater one.

Having determined to surrender Israel's entire future to fulfill the Divine Will, Avraham now resolves to *fulfill* in one stroke what he had envisioned would take many generations. The Divine promise of כֹּה יִהְיֶה זַרְעֶךָ implied not only that Avraham's children would be numerous as the stars, but they would brighten the darkest reaches of the universe as stars do. Avraham originally contemplated that this lofty goal would be accomplished through the *cumulative* effect of generations of his descendants, but now, with Yitzchak's sacrifice imminent, Avraham determines that the *Akeidah* itself will be the fulfillment of that Divine promise. He wishes that the sanctification of Hashem's Name emanating from Yitzchak's sacrifice be equivalent to the actions of countless generations of would-be successors.[1]　　　　(5639)

---

1. The term כֹּה used to introduce Hashem's promise to Avraham connotes the diffusion of the heavenly light into the darkest reaches of this world; cf. *Rashi Bamidbar* (30:2) regarding the difference between כֹּה אָמַר ה' and זֶה הַדָּבָר.

וַיִּשְׁלַח אַבְרָהָם אֶת יָדוֹ

Avraham stretched out his hand (v. 10).

ובכח התשובה יכולין לאחוז בעץ החיים. ועתה הוא בחי' תשובה.
ישלח ידו הוא הכח ומקומו. והוא עשרת ימי התשובה. ידו. יוד.
ובאברהם אע״ה כתיב וישלח אברהם את ידו שמסר נפשו בזה
הנסיון ונתעלה למעלה מן הטבע ונתאחז בעץ החיים.

Avraham, poised to slaughter his son to fulfill the request of Hashem, lifts up his hand. The phrase וַיִּשְׁלַח אֶת יָדוֹ evokes memories of a similar phrase at the beginning of history. Adam is driven out of Eden: וְעַתָּה פֶּן יִשְׁלַח יָדוֹ וְלָקַח גַּם מֵעֵץ הַחַיִּים, *and now, lest he stretch out his hand and take also from the Tree of Life (Bereishis 3:22).* This Divine statement was not only an expression of fear that Adam would partake of the Tree of Life, but a pronouncement that one day, in a moment of *teshuvah* (cf. *Midrash Bereishis Rabbah* 21:6 stating that וְעַתָּה, *now*, also implies תְּשׁוּבָה, *repenting*, for the past and focusing on the present) — when Avraham would personally atone for Adam's sin through his sacrifice — man would actually be able to partake of the Tree of Life again. Avraham not only stretches out his hand seeking a knife for the *Akeidah*, but simultaneously is lifted from the narrow confines of this world and thrust into Eden again.

In a sense, we emulate the Patriarch's behavior every year during the Ten Days of Repentance. In the spirit of וְעַתָּה, we too put aside the past and focus on perfecting the present and future. Even the duration of this period — ten days — is alluded to in פֶּן יִשְׁלַח יָדוֹ; the term יָדוֹ in scrambled order spells out יו״ד, *ten*, Ten Days of Repentance.

(*Rosh Hashanah 5664*)

וַיִּקַּח אֶת הַמַּאֲכֶלֶת

And took the knife (v. 10).

ידע שכל מעשיו הם עצות עבור כלל ישראל . . . כה האבות הי'
ע״י שכל שורש בנ״י היו בתוכם.

Rashi (v. 6) notes that the knife of the *Akeidah* is called מַאֲכֶלֶת עַל שֵׁם (אוֹכֵל), *because the Jewish people consumed* שֶׁיִּשְׂרָאֵל אוֹכְלִים מַתַּן שְׂכָרָהּ, *its reward.*

In what sense did the Jewish people benefit from the *Akeidah*? We also wonder why Israel did merit to benefit from the *Akeidah*'s lingering impact.

From the opening term וַיִּקַּח, *[Avraham] took*, it is apparent that the Patriarch was well aware of the lasting impact of his actions. He *took* every action mindful of the ramifications and effect it would have on his children. As the father of his people, it was only natural and totally appropriate for him to contemplate the impact on his descendants. We too should be vigilant to the future consequences on forthcoming generations of every action that we take.

Why do the Jewish people deserve to profit from Avraham's courageous sacrifice? Quite simply, because without us as his children, Avraham could never have accomplished as much as he did. The awesome power of the *Avos* was, at least in part, based on the fact that they were the forebears of the Jewish people. As individuals alone, they could never have achieved the heights that they attained as fathers of our people. (5634)

ע״י אמצעות מעשה אבות מנהיג את בנ״י במדרגות הנסים . . . וכי״ש המאכלת שבבנ״י אוכלין מתן שכרה.

As we stated previously, the greatest and most lasting impact of the *Akeidah* (and all of Avraham's traits) was the ability of Israel to surmount the confines of the natural world and live a miraculous existence. As a result of Avraham's resolve to leap above his natural instincts to spare his son, we the Jewish people reap the benefit of the *Akeidah*, and we too merit a supernatural lifestyle. (5639,5645)

שכל מעשה אבות נשתתפו עם כל הדורות

While future generations of Jews would frequently take the correct course of action (מַעֲשֶׂה), rarefied thoughts are also critical. In the merit of the *Akeidah*, Hashem merges the noble thoughts of Avraham with the pious deeds of his children (cf. *Kiddushin* 40a, מַחֲשָׁבָה טוֹבָה מְצָרְפָה לְמַעֲשֶׂה, *a good thought is regarded as a [good] deed*).

It is also possible that the reward envisioned by Avraham accruing to his children was not some type of material blessing, but simply the capacity to perform *mitzvos*. As *Avos* states (4:2): שְׂכַר מִצְוָה מִצְוָה, *the [greatest] reward of a mitzvah is [the opportunity to perform more]* *mitzvos*. In fact, every act of Divine service (עֲבוֹדַה ה') performed by Jews in contemporary times stems from the *Akeidah*. (5645)

וזהו שרמזו חז״ל בעקידה ויקח כו׳ המאכלת שישראל אוכלין
מתן שכרה. והיינו ע״י מעשה העקידה יכול כל איש ישראל
למסור נפשו בעבור קדושת שמו ית׳.

Most fundamentally, the ability of Jews throughout history to sacrifice everything — their very lives if necessary — to sanctify Hashem's Name is directly derived from Avraham's willingness to sacrifice. By following in their footsteps we are able to emulate their ways and sacrifice as they did. The prayer concluding the *Zichronos*, וְעֲקֵדַת יִצְחָק לְזַרְעוֹ הַיּוֹם בְּרַחֲמִים תִּזְכּוֹר, *and may You mercifully remember today the Akeidah of Isaac for the sake of his offspring*, may refer to us, the progeny of the *Avos*. By choosing to follow in their footsteps we deserve the title לְזַרְעוֹ, *the offspring*, of the *Avos*.

(*Rosh Hashanah 5653*)

אַבְרָהָם אַבְרָהָם
Avraham, Avraham (v. 11).

דע״י העקידה נתקן חלקו שלמטה להיות ממש כמו למעלה.

The *Zohar* (*Bereishis* 120a), noting the apparent repetition of Avraham's name, suggests קַדְמָאָה לֹא שְׁלִים בַּתְרָאָה שְׁלִים (he had not yet attained perfection). While at the first mention of Avraham's name the Patriarch was not yet "complete," when his name was repeated he attained שְׁלֵמוּת, *completion*. This abstruse *Zohar* may be understood by recalling that every individual not only enjoys a presence on earth but also benefits from his roots in heaven. The first mention of his name, referring to Avraham's physical presence on earth, was but a beginning. The true consummation of the *tzaddik's* personality required a second mention of his name, drawing upon his heavenly roots as well.

While other righteous individuals are graced with the Divine repetition of their name (cf. *Bereishis* 6:9, נֹחַ נֹחַ), in Avraham's case the implication is that while on earth the Patriarch was able to attain a status commensurate with his heavenly roots and this is particularly significant. The *Avos*, known as the מֶרְכָּבָה, *the Bearers of the Shechinah* (Divine Presence) on earth, must have possessed spiritual roots in heaven well beyond those of other individuals. Nonetheless, Avraham was able to attain through the *Akeidah* and the other trials a status on earth appropriate to his heavenly roots.

In this light, we can derive additional meaning from a renowned Mishnah in *Avos* (5:4): עֲשָׂרָה נִסְיוֹנוֹת נִתְנַסָּה אַבְרָהָם אָבִינוּ וְעָמַד בְּכֻלָּם לְהוֹדִיעַ כַּמָּה חִבָּתוֹ שֶׁל אַבְרָהָם אָבִינוּ, *Avraham Avinu was given ten tests, and he withstood them all. This shows how great was Avraham Avinu's love [for Hashem].*

While this Mishnah is usually interpreted to refer to Avraham's love of Hashem proven by his steadfast loyalty through the Ten Trials, it may also refer to the *necessity* for those trials. Whereas other individuals could "match" (i.e. attach a status on earth commensurate to their heavenly roots) their heavenly roots through a few trials, Avraham so beloved by Hashem (לְהוֹדִיעַ כַּמָּה חִבָּתוֹ שֶׁל אַבְרָהָם) — and possessing such sacred roots — could only achieve such perfection through ten trials. (5652)

כי החסד נתברר ונתאמת ובעקידה אז נתאמת החסד של אברהם בשלימות

In light of the above assertion that Avraham's kindness (חֶסֶד) was "tempered" with justice, we may derive additional meaning from the *Zohar's* comment. The first Divine Call, אַבְרָהָם, alluded to Avraham's personality *before* the *Akeidah* — he was the epitome of kindness. Great as he was, the Patriarch did not achieve perfection (שְׁלֵמוּת) without the additional dimension to his personality revealed at the *Akeidah*. The repetition of his name thus confirms the enhanced level of sanctity that Avraham attained at the *Akeidah*. (5658)

עַתָּה יָדַעְתִּי כִּי יְרֵא אֱלֹהִים אַתָּה
For now I know that you are a God-fearing man (v. 12).

The obvious question occurs. Was Hashem not aware previously of Avraham's fear of God?

◄§ Avraham's Potential Realized

מקודם הי' היראה בכחו ולא בפועל

Perhaps a distinction should be made between one who possesses the
potential for fear of Hashem (יִרְאַת ה') and the individual whose fear
of Hashem has been proven through difficult trials. Prior to the
Akeidah, Avraham certainly enjoyed the capacity to fear Hashem.
However, this potential only came to fruition at the *Akeidah*.

Upon carefully examining this verse, we notice that Hashem does not
merely extol Avraham's fear of God but instead depicts him as a יְרֵא
אֱלֹהִים, one whose *entire* personality is defined by יִרְאַת שָׁמַיִם. Attaining
so exalted a level whereby one's entire being manifests יִרְאַת אֱלֹהִים is
only possible after performing deeds that demonstrate יִרְאַת שָׁמַיִם. A
potential יְרֵא שָׁמַיִם could never attain the status of a יְרֵא אֱלֹהִים.

(5636)

◄§ Realm of Thought

פ' אף כי לא בא לידי מעשה כן ניתקן בדעת העליון

Conversely, the verse may be emphasizing that though Yitzchak was
never actually sacrificed and the *Akeidah* was only realized in the
realm of *thought* (מַחֲשָׁבָה) [see our previous remark on וְהָאֱלֹהִים נִסָּה אֶת
אַבְרָהָם], Hashem considered the Patriarch's fear of God to be as
complete as if he had actually sacrificed his son (מַעֲשֶׂה).

This somewhat surprising statement can be appreciated by recalling
that the *Akeidah* was never intended to be performed, but rather was a
mitzvah that existed solely in the realm of thought. Avraham's
readiness to sacrifice his son — his pure thought — was all that Hashem
desired. By joyously consenting to the *Akeidah*, the Patriarch already
attained the status of a יְרֵא אֱלֹהִים.

While it may appear that the *Akeidah* has been relegated to an
inferior status as a *mitzvah* performed only in thought and not in deed,
in reality, Yitzchak's near sacrifice belongs to the most exalted class of
mitzvos — those that are only required to be performed in the realm of
thought. As we have mentioned repeatedly, all *mitzvos* are rooted in

heaven. In most instances, the *mitzvah* cannot be consummated without a physical base (מַעֲשֶׂה גַּשְׁמִי). Other *mitzvos*, such as the supreme sacrifice of the *Akeidah*, are so exalted that they need no physical base but instead are completed through the thought alone.

It is fitting that this tenth and final trial of Avraham should be observed in this rarefied form, in the realm of thought.

Inasmuch as the Ten Trials correspond to the Ten Divine Statements (עֲשָׂרָה מַאֲמָרוֹת) through which the universe was created, it follows then that the final trial, the *Akeidah*, corresponds to the most exalted Statement — the Creation of Man (נַעֲשֶׂה אָדָם).   (cf. 5641)

◆§ Out of Character

אברהם לא הרגיש דביקות ואהבה בעובדא זו

Additionally, Hashem is praising Avraham for having excelled in a trait that was not his usual means of Divine service (יִרְאַת אֱלֹהִים). Avraham, known as אוֹהֲבִי (cf. *Yeshayahu* 41:8), the lover of Hashem, had already attained the extraordinary high level of אַהֲבַת ה'. For him, in certain respects, the *Akeidah* with its emphasis on fear of Hashem elicited personality traits that were inferior to the spiritual levels that he had already attained through love of Hashem. Moreover, as discussed previously, when performing the *Akeidah*, Avraham did not experience the same pull that normally gravitated his entire body to perform *mitzvos*. Although out of character, by drawing upon untapped reservoirs of strength, Avraham acted as a יְרֵא אֱלֹהִים, *God-fearing man*, and did not question His Will.

Mindful of the extreme difficulty that he had experienced performing a *mitzvah* on the basis of יִרְאַת ה' alone, Avraham in the aftermath of the *Akeidah* pleads to be subjected to no more such trials.   (5641)

◆§ Love Based on Fear

בודאי היא ירא ה' לאמתו ובזה זכה לעלות לבחי' אהבה

We have discussed earlier in this essay that Avraham only earned the respect of a skeptical mankind through his behavior at the

Akeidah. The outside world could not properly appreciate the attribute of אַהֲבַת ה', asserting (wrongly) that *anyone* could attain such a level. Having shown his resolve to sacrifice his son if necessary, Avraham clearly demonstrated that his love of Hashem is based on fear of Hashem. Contrary to the erroneous claims of mankind at large, not anyone can attain אַהֲבַת ה'. Only those who have demonstrated the mettle and steadfast fear of Hashem as Avraham did may eventually deserve the accolade of being designated as an אוֹהֵב ה'.   (5649)

⧉ Permanent Merit of Avraham

לא שייך ידיעת הבורא עד כי נגמר הדבר עד סוף כל הדורות

To properly evaluate the meaning of this phrase and to appreciate the concept of יְדִיעַת ה', let us turn to the first chapter of *Tehillim* in which David contrasts the path of the righteous and those of the wicked: כִּי יוֹדֵעַ ה' דֶּרֶךְ צַדִּיקִים וְדֶרֶךְ רְשָׁעִים תֹּאבֵד, *Because Hashem knows the ways of the righteous while the ways of the wicked will perish* (1:6).

While Hashem was certainly aware of Avraham's יִרְאַת אֱלֹהִים , the concept of יְדִיעַת ה' (knowledge of Hashem) implies far more — a path of life based on righteousness (דֶּרֶךְ צַדִּיקִים) bequeathed to countless generations of descendants. It is only this path that Hashem knows (יוֹדֵעַ ה'). By contrast, the road of life traveled by evildoers (דֶּרֶךְ רְשָׁעִים) is for naught. Only at the *Akeidah* — when it became apparent that Avraham's merit was sufficient to sustain Israel's entire posterity to enable them to live a supernatural lifestyle while on earth — could it be truly said that Hashem *knew* Avraham.   (5635, 5642)

וְלֹא חָשַׂכְתָּ אֶת בִּנְךָ אֶת יְחִידְךָ מִמֶּנִּי

since you have not withheld your son, your only one, from Me (v. 12).

כי הי' התגברות החושך לולי מעשה העקידה

The term חָשַׂכְתָּ is related to חֹשֶׁךְ , *darkness,* also associated with מִדַּת הַדִּין , *the Attribute of strict Justice ,* as personified by Yitzchak. Were it not for the harmonious blending of the מִדַּת הַדִּין of Yitzchak and the

מִדַּת הָרַחֲמִים of Avraham as they travel together to the *Akeidah* (cf. vs. 6,8, וַיֵּלְכוּ שְׁנֵיהֶם יַחְדָּו). Israel might have been confronted with the Attribute of Justice existing *alone*. Already at the Creation, when Hashem, realizing that the universe could not exist on the basis of strict justice alone (cf. *Rashi, Bereishis* 1:1), tempered justice with mercy, so too, Israel could never survive in an atmosphere of justice alone. In the aftermath of the *Akeidah*, Hashem extols Avraham for not withholding (וְלֹא חָשַׂכְתָּ) Yitzchak, for not allowing Yitzchak's characteristic of justice (מִדַּת הַדִּין) to exist alone.

Consider how different a course the *Akeidah* might have taken had Yitzchak's attribute of justice not been melded with Avraham's kindness. On the basis of strict justice *alone*, Yitzchak might actually have been sacrificed on the Altar. Only through the combination of justice and mercy would the animal surrogate, the ram, be acceptable as an alternative sacrifice. In a world dominated by מִדַּת הַדִּין, only an actual sacrifice would suffice. In an ambiance of דִּין diluted with רַחֲמִים, Avraham's readiness, his מַחֲשָׁבָה, combined with the offering of the ram, was sufficient. (5648)

ה׳ יִרְאֶה
"Hashem Yireh," (v. 14).

וכ״כ ה׳ יראה שבא עתה למדת היראה

As discussed previously, at the *Akeidah*, Avraham emerged as the ultimate יְרֵא אֱלֹהִים, *God-fearing man*, as well as the lover of Hashem. To commemorate his newfound status, Avraham names the site of the *Akeidah*, ה׳ יִרְאֶה. (5643)

בִּי נִשְׁבַּעְתִּי נְאֻם ה׳
By Myself I swear — the word of Hashem (v. 16).

הוא הכנה לדורות השפלים שתמו זכות האבות . . . ע״ז נשבע שלא יעזוב אותן

The purpose of this oath, after Hashem had already extolled Avraham's יִרְאַת אֱלֹהִים, is to assure future generations of Jews that even if the merit of Avraham had ceased to exist (cf. *Shabbos* 55a stating that the merit of the *Avos* no longer exists), still Hashem had sworn never to forsake Israel (cf. *Tosafos* ibid. that the covenant of Hashem is still in force). An oath — invoking Hashem's Name — is irrevocable. It evokes such intense spiritual force that it is no way contingent upon the behavior of mortals.

An analogy may be drawn between this oath and the giving of the Torah at Sinai. The Talmud refers to the "oath of Sinai" (cf. *Shevuos* 21b, נִשְׁבַּע וְעוֹמֵד מֵהַר סִינַי). While we find no explicit indication that our forefathers swore at Sinai, perhaps this refers to Hashem's oath at the *Akeidah*. This oath (already sworn by Hashem prior to the giving of the Torah and thus designated as נִשְׁבַּע וְעוֹמֵד, *the oath was already standing*) enabled the Jewish people to undergo a radical personality change at Sinai, as their previous personality exposed to the mores of the Gentile world yielded to the spiritual core implanted in every Jew at Sinai (cf. *Shabbos* 88b, יָצְאָה נִשְׁמָתָן). It was through this oath that the Jews acquired the inner resolve to cling to Hashem at Sinai no matter how trying the circumstances.   (5661)

כִּי בָרֵךְ אֲבָרֶכְךָ וְהַרְבָּה אַרְבֶּה אֶת זַרְעֶךָ

That I shall surely bless you and greatly increase your offspring (v. 17).

זה השכר שיהי׳ לו כל אלה הברכות בזכות מעשיו

It seems that these blessings had already been bestowed upon Avraham, well before the *Akeidah*. However, a crucial distinction exists between those earlier *berachos* and those granted at the *Akeidah*. Whereas all of Avraham's previous blessings were unearned gifts from Hashem (cf. ibid. 15:6, וַיַּחְשְׁבֶהָ לּוֹ צְדָקָה, *and He reckoned it to him as righteousness*, Hashem considered His blessings to be an act of charity towards Avraham), now at the *Akeidah* he earns those blessings. As verse 16 states: כִּי יַעַן אֲשֶׁר עָשִׂיתָ אֶת הַדָּבָר הַזֶּה, these blessings are yours *because you have done this thing* (i.e. because of the *Akeidah*). (5636)

כי אין זה נתינת שכר בלבד רק שמעשה זו הי׳ הכנה שיוכלו בנ״י לתקן הכל עד סוף הדורות

Moreover, Hashem's oath was not merely a means of compensating Avraham for his heroic sacrifice but rather a statement of *fact*, attesting to the new circumstances engendered by the *Akeidah*. As a result of the new supernatural order ushered in by the *Akeidah* (refer to our remarks on וְהָאֱלֹהִים נִסָּה אֶת אַבְרָהָם), the Jewish people now possess the capacity to do great things — to be numerous as *the stars of the heavens and like the sand on the seashore*; to *inherit the gate of its enemy* and to be the source of blessing for all mankind. (5645)

כי ברך אברכך והרבה ארבה. לשונות כפולים. שהבטיח לו שיהיו זרעו מבורכים מעולם העליון.

The apparently redundant and repetitive language, בָּרֵךְ אֲבָרֶכְךָ וְהַרְבָּה אַרְבֶּה, alludes to the double blessing of the *Akeidah*, not only our physical presence on earth but also that Israel's heavenly roots, their souls lodged in the World to Come, should also be blessed. (Refer to our commentary on אַבְרָהָם אַבְרָהָם.) (*Rosh Hashanah 5664*)

וְיִרַשׁ זַרְעֲךָ אֵת שַׁעַר אֹיְבָיו

And your offspring shall inherit the gate of its enemy (v. 17).

שכל השפע לאומות ע״י ישראל. וכל השערים שבא מהם שפע לכל ע׳ אומות הם נפתחים לבנ״י.

This blessing refers not primarily to Israel's conquest of the lands of its foes but rather that the gates of prosperity (שֶׁפַע) through which Hashem channels blessings to all mankind will be directed through the Jewish people. All the blessings that Hashem will bestow upon mankind will be funneled through the Jewish people, who will be the first to benefit from Hashem's munificence. (*Rosh Hashanah 5635, 5636*)

ויש ללמוד ק״ו מאדה״ר ע״י חטא אחד הביא המות לכל באי עולם. מדה טובה המרובה אברהם אע״ה וכל האבות שמסרו נפשם על קדושת המקום. מביאים חיים לכל הבוחר בדרכיהם.

In conclusion, let us refer to our previous remarks (on וַיִּשְׁלַח אַבְרָהָם אֶת יָדוֹ) in which Avraham's sacrifice allows the Patriarch to vault into *Gan Eden*, partaking of the Tree of Life denied Adam. Compare the tragic consequences of Adam's sin and the noble impact of Avraham's sacrifice. If the first man's sin brought death to the world, Avraham's great *mitzvos* brought life to all of his disciples. (*Rosh Hashanah 5664*)

תְּקִיעַת שׁוֹפָר
Tefillos Accompanying

In the following essay we shall discuss selected *tefillos* recited immediately preceding and following the sounding of the *shofar*.

‎לַמְנַצֵּחַ‎ / Prelude to Shofar-Blowing

יִבְחַר לָנוּ אֶת נַחֲלָתֵנוּ אֶת גְּאוֹן יַעֲקֹב אֲשֶׁר אָהֵב סֶלָה

He will choose our heritage for us, the pride of Yaakov that He loves eternally (*Tehillim* 47:5).

מדה״ד עצמו שופט כי יהי׳ נשמע קול יעקב ולכן יצחק שהוא
מדה״ד הנחיל ליעקב הקול

To appreciate the significance of the concepts "heritage" and "the pride of Yaakov," and why they are beloved to Hashem, let us consider a Midrash which sheds light on the matter (*Shemos Rabbah* 21).

הָדָא דִּכְתִיב ״צָעֲקוּ וַה׳ שָׁמֵעַ״ מַהוּ כֵן אֶלָּא שְׁתֵּי יְרוּשׁוֹת הִנְחִיל יִצְחָק
לִשְׁנֵי בָּנָיו הִנְחִיל לְיַעֲקֹב הַקּוֹל וְכֵן הוּא אוֹמֵר ״הַקּל קוֹל יַעֲקֹב״
וְהִנְחִיל לְעֵשָׂו הַיָּדַיִם . . . וְעֵשָׂו הָיָה מִתְגָּאֶה בִּירוּשָׁתוֹ וְיַעֲקֹב הָיָה
מִתְגָּאֶה בִּירוּשָׁתוֹ

This is as it is written (Tehillim 34:18), "Call and Hashem will hear." Why should this be so [that Hashem should hear]? However Yitzchak gave two legacies to his two

children: To Yaakov he gave the "voice" [i.e. the ability to pray], as the Torah says,[1] *"The voice is Yaakov's voice"; and to Esav he gave "the hands" [i.e. military prowess] . . . Esav was proud of his legacy and Yaakov was proud of his legacy . . .*

The expression וַה', *And* HASHEM, is normally understood as an allusion to Hashem's Attribute of Justice.[2] In this light, perhaps the Midrash has concluded from the Psalmist's use of this word that even Hashem's Attribute of Justice hears our cries. If so, perhaps it was the strict Yitzchak who was suited among the Patriarchs to bestow the power of prayer as a legacy. This inner voice, with its ability to appeal directly to Hashem, was given to Yaakov and his descendants not merely as a gift but rather as a permanent and immutable heritage.

Words are an unreliable medium of expression, constantly changing under the pressure of circumstances and capable of total insincerity, as we see from the way Esav camouflaged his evil core beneath a veneer of pious rhetoric. In consequence Yitzchak was able to recognize Yaakov's wordless but honest voice as his true legacy, with the result that however far and wide Yaakov's descendants may have strayed since then, they have never lost the legacy of their inner voice, as expressed by the wordless *shofar*.

Indeed, perhaps it is for this very reason that we give ourselves the following reminder before sounding the *shofar*: *He will choose our heritage for us, the pride of Yaakov that He loves eternally.* Undoubtedly it is our pride in this inner voice which is never spurned by Hashem — the *pride of Yaakov*, in the Psalmist's expression — over which Yaakov prided himself. *Tosafos* observed (*Rosh Hashanah* 26a, s.v. חוטא) that those who blow the *shofar* generally take pride in this activity; in light of the above, we can suggest that this refers not just to the satisfaction of producing a sharp and clear sound, but also to the pride we take in being the sole nation to possess such a potent weapon as the *shofar*, Yaakov's wordless voice.

What is more, this legacy lasts forever, as the Psalmist concludes: אֲשֶׁר אָהֵב סֶלָה, *that He loved eternally*. Whereas Esav's wily importunings could evoke Yitzchak's love only temporarily, Yaakov's legacy, the voice in which he had such pride, is capable of engendering an everlasting love.

---

1. *Bereishis* 27:22.
2. Cf. *Bereishis*, *Rashi* 19:24, s.v. וה'.

The Torah expresses this quality in an otherwise unexplainable change in tense in the verse: וַיֶּאֱהַב יִצְחָק אֶת עֵשָׂו כִּי צַיִד בְּפִיו וְרִבְקָה אֹהֶבֶת אֶת יַעֲקֹב, *Yitzchak loved Esav for game was in his mouth; but Rivkah loves Yaakov* (*Bereishis* 25:28). Indeed, every time Rivkah heard Yaakov's voice, her love for him would increase (cf. *Yalkut Bereishis* 110).

Still another distinction is the fact that Yitzchak's love for Esav depended on the latter's ability to provide him with game, while Rivkah's love for Yaakov was purely altruistic. The Mishnah expresses the contrast between these two kinds of love most succinctly: *Any love that depends on a specific cause, when that cause is gone, the love is gone; but if it does not depend on a specific cause, it will never cease* (*Avos* 5:19). Since Yitzchak's love for Esav depended on Esav's game (as well as Esav's deviousness, as we discuss above), it could endure only as long as its source remained in existence. In contrast, Rivkah's love for Yaakov, since it depended on his eternal soul rather than any specific cause, is equally eternal. Just as Rivkah's love for Yaakov continues to grow with increased exposure, so too Hashem's love for Israel knows no bounds and He always receives the voice of His people with favor.

In blowing the *shofar* on Rosh Hashanah we are just following the example of our forefathers who, not knowing how to pray at the Sea of Reeds, simply cried out to Hashem (cf. *Shemos* 14:10). Although the cries of our ancestors at the Sea were loud and vocal, the Psalmist prescribes that our service on Rosh Hashanah be בַּכֶּסֶה, "covert," so we naturally turn to the *shofar* as a wordless vehicle to convey our prayers. The Sages described blowing the *shofar* as a חָכְמָה, *an act of wisdom*, referring to Israel's capacity every year to resort to the proven weapon of the Jewish people — the voice of Yaakov, for there is no greater wisdom than rediscovering one's ancestral weapon. (See our essay on תְּקִיעַת שׁוֹפָר for additional explanations of this concept.) (5652)

עָלָה אֱלֹהִים בִּתְרוּעָה ה' בְּקוֹל שׁוֹפָר

God has ascended with a blast, HASHEM, with the sound of the shofar (Tehillim 47:6).

ולכן מצד הברית מוחל עונותיהם . . . אז עיקר הברית שיתעלו ויתדבקו בו יתברך.

Sounding the *shofar* also evokes Hashem's memory of the covenant and the oath He swore to Avraham after the *Akeidah*.[1] Thus the Midrash (*Yalkut Vayikra* 645) suggests that Tishrei is called הַחֹדֶשׁ הַשְּׁבִיעִי, *the seventh month*, not only because of its position as the seventh in the count of months (beginning with Nissan, the month of the Exodus from Egypt), but also because it is the month of the שְׁבוּעָה, the *oath* Hashem swore to preserve and nurture Avraham's descendants.

This oath contains two components. While the beginning of our verse alludes to forgiveness of Israel's sins — עָלָה אֱלֹהִים בִּתְרוּעָה, *God has ascended with a blast* — because Israel has been vindicated in Hashem's Judgment (אֱלֹהִים — מִדַּת הַדִּין), far more profound is Hashem's oath after the *Akeidah*. At that time He promised never to allow the bond between Himself and His people to erode. However far we have strayed, we are always able to return and cling to Him again, as Moshe assures us: וְאַתֶּם הַדְּבֵקִים בַּה׳ אֱלֹהֵיכֶם חַיִּים כֻּלְּכֶם הַיּוֹם, *You who cling to* H*ASHEM, your God, you are all alive today* (*Devarim* 4:4).

This never-ceasing ability to reattach ourselves to the Creator is truly the primary function of the *shofar*, as the verse concludes ה׳ בְּקוֹל שׁוֹפָר, we cling again to Hashem through the *shofar*.

(5665)

⋙ After Shofar-Blowing

אַשְׁרֵי הָעָם יוֹדְעֵי תְרוּעָה ה׳ בְּאוֹר פָּנֶיךָ יְהַלֵּכוּן

Praiseworthy is the people who knows the shofar blast; O HASHEM, *in the light of Your countenance will they walk* (*Tehillim* 89:16).

אַשְׁרֵי הָעָם שֶׁיּוֹדְעִים לְפַתּוֹת אֶת בּוֹרְאָם בִּתְרוּעָה

Praiseworthy is the people that knows how to conciliate its Creator through the shofar blast (*Yalkut Shimoni, Tehillim* 840).

Numerous interpretations have been given to this verse, which is normally recited immediately after the first round of *shofar* blasts. Every explanation, however, addresses the obvious question of what is unique about Israel's ability to sound the *shofar*, when surely any other nation could also learn to produce the same sound. In the following section we shall consider several approaches to resolving this problem.

---

1. Cf. *Bereishis* 22:16-18; a more complete discussion of this oath is to be found in our essay on the *Akeidah*, p. 92.

⊰ The Function of Divine Justice

וזהו יודעי תרועה שמבינים המבוקש ממדת הדין . . . שליח המלך
שבא אל האדם שא״צ להשגיח עליו רק לרוץ אל המלך עצמו.

Perhaps the simplest understanding of this verse is as a praise of Israel's ability to grasp the purpose of the *teruah* sound, and thereby to avert the consequences that often are associated with it.

Although it is well known that the *teruah* sound represents Divine Justice (cf. *Ramban*, *Vayikra* 23:24), we must understand that this form of justice is not connected with punishment, but is simply a reminder of our pressing need for self-improvement. As Shlomo HaMelech says, וְהָאֱלֹהִים עָשָׂה שֶׁיִּרְאוּ מִלְּפָנָיו, *God has acted so that man should stand in awe of Him* (*Koheles* 3:14). Once this purpose has been fulfilled and we have demonstrated that we are a nation of יוֹדְעֵי תְרוּעָה, of people who have grasped the message of the *teruah* sound, then the harsh justice of that sound is mitigated. As the Midrash (cited in the section of *shofar*) says, עוֹמֵד מִכִּסֵּא הַדִּין וְיוֹשֵׁב עַל כִּסֵּא הָרַחֲמִים, *Hashem rises from the Throne of Justice and sits on the Throne of Mercy* (refer to our commentary there).

The conclusion of our verse, ה׳ בְּאוֹר פָּנֶיךָ יְהַלֵּכוּן, *O HASHEM, in the light of Your countenance will they walk*, is illuminated by a beautiful and compelling insight of the *Baal Shem Tov*. Whenever we experience difficulties (Heaven forbid), we should remind ourselves that they are only messengers from Hashem, and rather than attempt to resolve our problems by dealing with the messengers (e.g. attempting to treat just physical afflictions), we should turn to Hashem Himself and ask ourselves what message He wishes to send us with these particular emissaries.

So too, the Psalmist assures us that if we would only hearken to the *shofar's* true message of abandoning our errant ways and returning to Hashem rather than allowing ourselves to be obsessed with surface phenomena of affliction and other messengers, we could walk in the light of Hashem's Countenance.[1]   (5658)

---

1. In this light we can offer a homiletic interpretation of a verse in *Koheles*: חָכְמַת אָדָם תָּאִיר פָּנָיו וְעֹז פָּנָיו יְשֻׁנֶּא, *A man's wisdom lights up His face, and the boldness of His face is transformed* (8:1). By sounding the *shofar*, which is described as an act of wisdom, Hashem's countenance is enlightened (*in the light of Your countenance will they walk*), and the strength (i.e. Hashem's harsh justice) will be *transformed*.

◆§ Through the Teruah, Israel Becomes Aware of Hashem's Love

ומכלל דכ' יודעי תרועה משמע שהשופר נותן דעת לבנ"י . . .
והוא שזוכין לקבל הנשמה יתירה . . . שנמשך הארת הנשמה
והדעת ע"י הקול שופר

Perhaps the phrase יוֹדְעֵי תְרוּעָה, *who knows the shofar blast*, also refers to the knowledge of Hashem's ways Israel acquires through sounding the *shofar*. The Mishnah in *Avos* (3:18) speaks of Hashem's special love for man in order to teach us that humanity — and especially Israel[1] — not only was created in Hashem's image but also acquires a special sense of love through the sounding of the *shofar*. Hearing the *shofar* makes a Jew aware of the enormous spiritual potential latent inside him, the "extra soul" with which Hashem has favored him above and beyond the rest of mankind. This is suggested by the very word *shofar* (seemingly derived from the same root as שׁוּפְרָא, "beauty"), intimating that listening to the *shofar* strengthens and solidifies the sublimely beautiful Divine Soul within us. Thus the Psalmist concludes, *in the light of Your countenance will they walk* — hearing the *shofar* makes us more acutely aware of our unique soul. (5646)

◆§ Shattering the Teruah!

וזוה"ק דמתברין ההיא תרועה כי באמת הדין הוא רק מכסה אבל
לפנים משורת הדין נמצא הרחמים.

The Zohar (cf. *Emor* 99b) suggests that the phrase יוֹדְעֵי תְרוּעָה, *who knows the shofar blast*, refers to Israel's ability to fragment and shatter the harsh *teruah* sound.[2] Unlike the *tekiah*, which is a continuous

---

1. Cf. *Yevamos* 61a: *You are called man, but the other nations are not called man.*

2. This approach interprets the word יוֹדְעֵי according to its use in the verse וַיֹּדַע בָּהֶם אֵת אַנְשֵׁי סֻכּוֹת (*Shoftim* 8:16), in the account of how Gideon chastised and shattered the people of Succoth.

sound, *shevarim* and *teruah* both consist of series of fragmented sounds symbolizing our attempts to shatter harsh judgments into small pieces.[1]

In this light it is noteworthy that the *gematria* of the word גְּבוּרָה, *strength* (216), can be divided evenly into three "segments," each equal to the *gematria* of the word חֶסֶד, *kindness* (216 ÷ 3 = 72).   (5658)

In a somewhat similar vein, the phrase יוֹדְעֵי תְרוּעָה, *who knows the shofar blast*, may suggest that Israel knows how to break through the outer layer which appears as harsh justice to reveal the Divine Mercy hidden beneath. Hashem created the world with a blend of Justice tempered by Mercy, and while the universe may seem on the surface to be governed by the strict dictates of harsh Justice, when we strip away this outer shell we find that even those events which appear to result from harsh judgments are really based entirely on Hashem's compassion.

This holds especially true if we can appreciate on our own that the purpose of Hashem's justice is to make an often recalcitrant mankind accept His Sovereignty. When we, Hashem's chosen nation, voluntarily accept His Kingship upon ourselves — as we say in the evening prayer, וּמַלְכוּתוֹ בְּרָצוֹן קִבְּלוּ עֲלֵיהֶם, *His Kingship they accepted upon themselves willingly* — we avert the consequences of Hashem's Justice and can instead reveal the underlying wellspring of Divine Mercy, as our verse concludes: *O HASHEM, in the light of Your countenance will they walk.*
(5663)

◈§ Shattering Hearts Through Torah

והרמז שמשברין לכם ע״י התרועה . . . ועי״ז נשבר כל הדינים גם
כן

The *teruah* sound also has the power to shatter our hearts and fill them with contrition, which in turn shatters any harsh decrees that may have been issued.

A precedent for *teshuvah* resulting from the mere act of hearing can be found in Yisro's decision to return to Hashem after hearing of the

---

1. This approach is reminiscent of the one employed by Yaakov in the face of the enormous strength Shimon and Levi deployed against Shechem; cf. *Bereishis* 49:7, אֲחַלְּקֵם בְּיַעֲקֹב וַאֲפִיצֵם בְּיִשְׂרָאֵל, *I will separate them within Yaakov, and I will disperse them in Israel.*

miracles Hashem had done for Israel.[1] The *Zohar* notes that the rest of mankind also heard the very same events which so moved Yisro as we read, שָׁמְעוּ עַמִּים יִרְגָּזוּן, *Peoples heard — they were agitated*,[2] and yet it was only Yisro who "heard and was shattered and submitted himself to Hashem's Will," as the *Zohar* (*Yisro* 68a) relates. So too, by listening to the *shofar* and allowing it to "shatter" our hearts, we will merit to bask in Hashem's light, to *walk in the light of His countenance*.

(*Shabbos Shuvah* 5662)

✥ Understanding Hashem's True Desires

והנה באמת רצונו ית' הוא רק רצון לרחמים טובה . . . וזהו יודעי
תרועה שיש להם דעת להבין פנימיות הרצון

The word *teruah* also has overtones of "will" or "desire," as *Rashi* comments on the verse וּתְרוּעַת מֶלֶךְ בּוֹ, *The friendship of the King is in him* (*Bamidbar* 23:21). (This verse is discussed elsewhere in this essay.) Thus, to say that Israel is יוֹדְעֵי תְרוּעָה implies that only Israel among the nations is capable of comprehending Hashem's true wishes, of realizing that in spite of the facade of harsh justice with which Hashem appears to rule His world, even the judgment process is really only a means of showering Divine mercy and goodness on His creatures. Only we can fathom Hashem's inner workings (to the extent that any mortals can) and know that the *shofar* has the power to call Hashem's infinite mercy to the surface, and to transform justice into compassion.

The conclusion of our verse also hints at this power: בְּאוֹר פָּנֶיךָ יְהַלֵּכוּן — because we understand Hashem's true purpose, we are privileged to bask in Hashem's *inner* (in Hebrew פְּנִימִי, related to the word פָּנֶיךָ) light in the knowledge that that His Justice is truly merciful. (5652)

✥ Conciliating Hashem

The expression a nation that is able to "reconcile" its Creator with the *teruah* may also refer to Israel's ability to convert the awesome *teruah* sound into a means of reconciliation with Hashem. (5658)

---

1. Cf. *Shemos* 18:1, אֵת כָּל אֲשֶׁר עָשָׂה אֱלֹהִים . . . אֶת יִתְרוֹ, וַיִּשְׁמַע, *Yisro . . . heard everything that God did*.
2. *Shemos* 15:4.

⊷§ Appearing as Servants, Not as Children

וזה התפארת שהגם שהם בנים יודעים הם כי אינם כדאי אף
להיות עבדים

Perhaps the simplest way of grasping what it means to conciliate
Hashem is to realize that in sounding the *shofar*, we are presenting
ourselves before Hashem merely as servants wishing only to coronate
their King, but do not presume to call ourselves His children, even
though the Torah gives us full right to use that exalted title.[1] This
approach "appeases" Hashem, Who takes pride in our humility and lack
of presumptuousness, as the prophet Yeshayahu proclaims: עַבְדִּי אַתָּה
יִשְׂרָאֵל אֲשֶׁר בְּךָ אֶתְפָּאָר, *You are My servant, Israel, in whom I take pride*
(*Yeshayahu* 49:3). (See our commentary on the prayer אִם כְּבָנִים אִם
כַּעֲבָדִים on page 188 for further discussion of this contrast.)

The Sages appreciated that humility is often a sign of wisdom, and
praised those people who have the wisdom of humans and yet the
humility of animals (cf. *Chullin* 5b).   (5646)

⊷§ Israel Learns to Talk

ובאמת כחן של ישראל בפה . . . שע״י השופר נתעורר כח הפה

Alternatively, we can suggest an almost literal interpretation of this
Midrash: Praiseworthy is the people which learns how to conciliate
its Creator through sounding a *teruah* blast! As we discuss at length
elsewhere, the *shofar* is an extension of the "voice of Yaakov" which
Yitzchak recognized in his righteous son even in disguise as his wicked
older sibling. By sounding the *shofar*, we reawaken this facility of
speech, the ability to communicate our pleas directly and effectively to
Hashem.   (5662)

---

1. Cf. *Devarim* 14:1:, בָּנִים אַתֶּם לַה' אֱלֹהֵיכֶם, *You are children to* HASHEM, *your God*.

✑ Clinging to Hashem Through Torah

השתוקקות אל התורה . . . להיות מדובק בתורה

Finally, on this topic, let us note an intriguing thought offered by the Kotzker Rebbe.[1] He notes that *Onkelos* renders the word יְפַתֶּה (to *seduce* or *conciliate*) as וִישַׁדֵּל,[2] suggesting the obvious role of strenuous efforts at Torah study in conciliating Hashem. By immersing ourselves in Torah and plumbing its depths with our whole heart — for the Torah's sake rather than out of desire for personal gain — we will surely merit not only to reconcile ourselves to Hashem but also to cling to Him.

(5662)

קוֹל שׁוֹפָר

Sounds, not Words

While the *shofar* may be the most effective vehicle for conveying Israel's prayers to Hashem, the prayers it expresses are unlike any others in that they are wordless, consisting simply of the sounds *tekiah*, *shevarim*, *teruah* and *tekiah*, without a single word enunciated. What is the significance of this wordless *mitzvah* described as *kol shofar*, "the *voice* of the *shofar*"?

---

1. A great Chassidic leader, mentor of the *Chiddushei HaRim*, grandfather of the *Sfas Emes*.
2. Cf. *Shemos* 22:15, וְכִי יְפַתֶּה אִישׁ בְּתוּלָה, *If a man shall seduce a virgin*, which *Onkelos* translates as וַאֲרֵי יְשַׁדֵּל גְּבַר בְּתֻלְתָּא.

~§ The Origins of the Universe

וזהו התקיעות שהוא קול בלי דיבור. שדיבור הוא התחלקות
הקול לתנועות נפרדים ושונים. אבל הקול אחד מיוחד דבוק
במקורו והיום בר״ה החיות דבוק בשורשו כנ״ל קודם התחלקות
והשתנות.

The Torah's choice of a wordless medium for Israel's prayers may
stem from the simple fact that all speech is based on sound. However
varied the fashions in which people verbalize their thoughts, they all
originate in the human capacity to emit sound.

By producing sounds on this day, the anniversary of Creation, we
return to the source of all articulate speech, and indeed, to the source of
all life and existence — the Divine Utterances through which the
universe that we know came into being.

The *Baal Shem Tov* noted that these Ten Utterances not only set into
motion the various forms of life with which we are familiar, but they
actually became the sole source of life-giving power for every facet of
creation, and continue to fill this role until this very day. Thus, the
heavens are still sustaining themselves — thousands of years later —
from the original Divine pronouncement, יְהִי רָקִיעַ בְּתוֹךְ הַמָּיִם, *Let there
be a firmament in the midst of the waters (Bereishis* 1:6).

Throughout the year we are taken up with the physical nature of the
universe, but when Rosh Hashanah comes, the *shofar* allows us to peel
away the surface layers of our existence and to return to the source and
continuing sustainer of all life, the Word of Hashem.   (5632)

~§ The Hidden Force Behind the Universe

ענין תקיעת שופר לאחוז בקול תורה שהוא פנימיות כל הבריאה
כדכ׳ בראשית בשביל התורה שנקראת ראשית

Just as sounds are the true source of words, by blowing the *shofar* we
are reminded of the true inner motivation of Creation — the Torah.
In the unforgettable words of the Midrash, בִּשְׁבִיל הַתּוֹרָה שֶׁנִּקְרָאת רֵאשִׁית,

the universe was created in the merit of the Torah, which is called
רֵאשִׁית, the beginning.

In this light we can postulate that the single Divine Utterance with
which the Sages said the universe could have been created (cf. *Avos* 5:1)
refers to the Torah itself, which was the source of all of Creation. (5656)

⋑ The Intuitive Cry of Every Jew

יש וזה ענין התקיעות שצועקין בלי טעם רק לדבק בחלקנו קול קול
יעקב

In sounding the wordless *shofar*, Israel is actually returning to one of
its oldest and most enduring weapons — the *voice of Yaakov*, the
inner voice of the Jew who, although he may have a superficial
resemblance to Esav, uses the *shofar* to appeal wordlessly to Hashem.
When Yitzchak was confronted with a composite person who appeared
to possess the *hand of Esav*, he sensed that the voice which emerged
from beneath that rough exterior was really that of Yaakov.

This voice was to prove a most formidable weapon in the service of
Yaakov's descendants. In all times of trial — and especially on the annual Day of Judgment — the Jewish people know that the inarticulate
cry conveyed by the wordless *shofar* will stand in their stead.

It should be emphasized that resorting to this ancient source of merit
is to be used only as a last resort, but it is by no means the preferred
means of returning to Hashem's good graces. Only when absolutely
necessary do we make an appeal on the basis of the merits of the
Patriarchs. Otherwise, we would greatly prefer to be judged favorably
on the basis of our own merit.

This preference of ours not to rely on the merit of our forefathers but
rather to benefit from a verdict we deserve is voiced subtly in a moving
Midrash which describes Yaakov's prophetic dream:

> *"Behold a ladder was set earthward" [Bereishis 28:12]* ...
> *This teaches us that Hashem showed Yaakov the guard-*
> *ian angel of Babylonia ascending and descending [on the*
> *ladder], the guardian angel of Media ascending and*
> *descending, the guardian angel of Greece ascending and*
> *descending, and the guardian angel of Edom [Rome]*

ascending and descending. Said Hashem to Yaakov: "You too should ascend." At that moment, Yaakov was afraid and said, "Just as they [the other nations] have their downfall, so I too [the Jewish people] will have a downfall." So Hashem said, "Do not be afraid. If you rise, you will never descend." Yaakov did not believe this and did not ascend (Midrash Rabbah Emor 29:2).

Why did Yaakov not want to ascend the ladder? We can answer quite simply that Yaakov recognized that were he to ascend any number of rungs on the ladder as the other nations did, it would place finite limits to his descendants' potential. By refusing to ascend, on the other hand, he expressed his conviction that there are no limits to the spiritual heights his children can attain. From this we see that if we prove ourselves deserving, we can reach heights beyond description and reap rewards no other nation can dream of. (5632)

✑ Tapping Our Own Heavenly Roots

הקול מעורר כח שורשו שלמעלה מהקול . . . ולכן הקול בלי
דיבור כדי לרמוז שאין הסמיכה על הקול רק לעורר השורש
שלמעלה מהקול ע״י שהקול יש בו מעין שופרי׳ דלמעלה. וזה קול
שופר.

The sound of the *shofar* is reminiscent of another important occasion when the Jews were told not to cry: At the Sea of Reeds, surrounded by the Egyptian army, the raging Sea, and the Wilderness, the Jews cried out, and Hashem responded, *"Why do you cry out to Me?"* (*Shemos* 14:15).

Crying is a way of arousing our heavenly roots. Whenever we cry out and utilize the *shofar* to convey our wishes and aspirations, we receive the same answer, "Why do you cry out to Me? Your cries are not the solution to your problem, but rather a way of tapping a source of merit greater even than your wordless prayer, of reaching up to the uppermost sanctum in heaven, to the spiritual roots of every Jew." While the spiritual sources of the Jewish soul are located in heaven, our cries can help tap those latent sources of merit, and can remind Hashem that no matter how much we may have strayed in our pursuit of the material goals of this world, our true goals retain their heavenly character, untainted and pure as ever.

This ability of the *shofar*'s unarticulated sound to evoke the heavenly roots of the Jew has been an essential part of our heritage ever since Yitzchak's proclamation, *the voice is the voice of Yaakov.* Only Yaakov and his descendants have the power to evoke the heavenly components of the Jewish soul, only we are capable of utilizing the *shofar* in addition to our own wordless pleas.

The similarity of the word שׁוֹפָר to a similar word שַׁפִּיר, *beautiful,* may also allude to the association between the *shofar* and our roots in heaven, since true beauty can exist only in the ethereal, sublime atmosphere of the World to Come. In this light, the Sages' suggestion that Yaakov's beautiful countenance resembled that of Adam[1] may be seen as an allusion to the ability of the *shofar* (which we have called "the voice of Yaakov") to transport us out of the confines of this world into the beautiful environment of *Gan Eden*, where Adam lived. It seemed for a while — at the giving of the Torah — that the Jewish people would be able to recapture the ambiance of Eden. But alas, by venerating the Golden Calf we forfeited that status. Now, on Rosh Hashanah, we plead to be restored to that exalted lifestyle.   (cf. 5637)

~§ Hashem's Absolute Covenant with Israel and the Universe

והנה יש שפע לעולם כפי צורך קיום העולם שאינו תלוי במעשה
התחתונים. וזה הי' כריתות ברית עם נח שלא יהי' חרוב העולם
בכל אופן. . . . וכעין זה ממש הי' כריתות בריתו ית"ש עם בנ"י
להיות פנימיות החיות לעולם. חלק ה' עמו. ולא תשכח מפי זרעו.
רק אם זוכין בנ"י מתרבה ומתפשט כח התורה בהם ביותר. וברית
הזה מתחדש בכל ר"ה ע"י תקיעות שופר. כמ"ש זוכר הברית.

 One of the distinctive characteristics of sound as the foundation of speech is its immutability (the basic sounds do not change). While man can formulate numerous words — combinations from basic sounds — those sounds are never altered.

---

1. Cf. שׁוּפְרֵיהּ דְּיַעֲקֹב מֵעֵין שׁוּפְרֵיהּ דְּאָדָם, *Yaakov's beauty was similar to that of Adam.*

By invoking the voice of the *shofar*, we affirm our conviction that certain essentials never change. Whatever precise fate may be decreed for the universe and its inhabitants of the mineral, vegetable, animal and human kingdoms in the coming year, we can be assured that Hashem will fulfill the covenant He made with Noah after the Flood never again to destroy the world. Similarly, whatever specific verdict may be rendered for Israel, we may also be assured that we shall continue to be Hashem's Chosen people and that Torah will never be forgotten from our children, as we read כִּי לֹא תִשָּׁכַח מִפִּי זַרְעוֹ, *It shall not be forgotten from the mouth of its [Israel's] offspring (Devarim 31:21).*[1] It is certainly true that the exact quantity of material blessings that Hashem will grant humanity during the coming year is directly proportional to their worthiness or lack thereof, and that the degree of association Israel will be privileged to have with the Torah will depend upon its efforts in studying and upholding the Torah. It is also certain, however, that these twin pillars — the universe's permanence and Israel's special relationship to Torah — will never falter.

(Nitzavim, 5656; Rosh Hashanah 5657)

✑ Dedicating Our First Sounds to Torah

ולכן בתחלה צריכין לשעבד הקול והדיבור לשמים. והוא קול שופר.

R osh Hashanah commemorates not only the rededication of the universe to Hashem's service but also the renewal of man's numerous talents, especially his unique gift of speech. Just as the first words learned by every Jewish child consist of verses from the Torah, so too our first speech of the New Year is dedicated to the sacred sounds of the *shofar*.[2]   (5647)

---

1. *Editor's Note*: Nonetheless, as the Steipler Gaon, *zatzal*, points out in *Sefer Chayei Olam*, this promise applies only to the nation as a whole and assures only that there will continue to be observers of the Torah in each generation; on the individual level, however, each of us has to act as if there were no such promise and must therefore do everything in his power to ensure that his children and descendants continue in the path of Torah and *mitzvos*.

2. Please refer to our remarks on *Malchiyos, Zichronos, Shofaros*. See page 169 for a similar thought.

⊰ Expressing Our Inarticulate Unspoken Wishes

אפשר זה עצמו בחי' השופר כדאיתא בזוה"ק שיש צעקה בלב
שא"י לפרש בפה ע"ש שמות כ' ע"א. וכמו כן קול שופר הוא
סתום

While many of our requests and aspirations for the forthcoming year can be clearly articulated, others are so deeply and subtly embedded in our psyche that no words can express them. As the *Zohar* notes (*Shemos* 20a), certain cries find their voice only in the heart of the Jew.

There can exist no better vehicle to express these inarticulate, subconscious cries than the wordless *shofar*. In this light, the *psalm* we read on Rosh Hashanah describes the *shofar* as a "hidden storm" through which Hashem answers our pleas: אֶעֶנְךָ בְּסֵתֶר רַעַם, *I answered you when you called privately with a thunderous reply* (81:8). Earlier in the same *psalm* (v. 4) we are exhorted to "sound the *shofar* בַּכֶּסֶה, *in hiding*," since the *Shofar* has the power to convey our hidden wishes.

The prayer recited between the various phases of the *shofar*-sounding mentions various angels who emerge together with the sounds of the *shofar*. Perhaps these are the angels who are stimulated by the *shofar* to convey Israel's unexpressed wishes.   (5647)

⊰ The Voice of Sinai

זהו רמז תקיעת שופר שמשתוקקין לאותו הקול ששמענו בהר
סיני כמ"ש ישקני מנשיקות פיהו.

By recognizing that all of our pleas on Rosh Hashanah are for renewal of our spiritual life,[1] a life of Torah rather than a life dominated by our physical desires, we can better appreciate the significance of the voice of the *shofar*. In sounding the *shofar*, are we not actually clamoring to hear once again Hashem's voice as He gave us the Torah

---

1. See our essay "Life" for further discussion of this theme.

at Mount Sinai, the Voice which the Torah describes as קוֹל גָּדוֹל וְלֹא יָסָף, *a great voice, never to be repeated* (Devarim 5:19)? Isn't the *shofar* a cry from Israel, depicted in *Shir HaShirim* (1:2) as Hashem's "bride" yearning for the halcyon days when Hashem kissed her with the "kisses of His mouth"? And even now, the voice of the *shofar* continues to cry out on Rosh Hashanah for a return to the intimacy which once existed between Hashem and Israel, the intimacy whose renewal is our greatest wish in the world. (5662)

◆§ The Divine Breath of Life

היינו שקודם החטא היי הבריאה היי הבריאה שיהיי בו ההבל של ויפח שהוא רוח הקודש ממש וזהו שופר וזהו בכסא שהוא מעולם המחשבה. ולע״ד מה שלא מצינו בספרים הקדושים לומר לשם יחוד קודם תקיעות שופר כמו בכל המצות כי כל מצות הם במעשה

The sound of the *shofar* is not the only significant feature of this mitzvah, even the specific actions required to produce that sound have meaning. Just as the *shofar*'s sounds are produced by a human being breathing into it, its sound reminds us of another breathing, the "breath" of Hashem with which He infused life into the first man: וַיִּפַּח בְּאַפָּיו נִשְׁמַת חַיִּים וַיְהִי הָאָדָם לְנֶפֶשׁ חַיָּה, *He blew into his nostrils the soul of life; and man became a living being* (Bereishis 2:7).

Let us attempt to grasp some small measure of this most esoteric concept — "Divine Breath." While it is well known that Hashem manifests Himself through actions, words, and thoughts, the term "thought," as it is applied to Hashem, actually describes the sublime and rarefied processes through which He manages His universe. Thus He formed man, the apex of creation, not only with physical actions and speech, but also, and especially, by means of His most ethereal process, that of "thought," which the Torah describes with the closest word comprehensible to humans as "breathing."[1]

---

1. *Editor's Note:* Cf. *Rambam, Hilchos Yesodei HaTorah* 1:9, who writes that although Hashem has no physical existence and does not resemble any physical being, the Torah nonetheless ascribes physical features to Him simply in order to depict Him in terms to which humans can understand and relate.

Every time we sound the *shofar*, then, we are reminded of the Divine Breath, and of the thoughts which created the first human.

The description of Rosh Hashanah as בַּכֶּסֶה לְיוֹם חַגֵּנוּ, *the hidden festival* (see our essay on this topic), may be closely related to this theme. While other occasions are primarily associated with Hashem's "Deeds" and "Words," Rosh Hashanah, the annual commemoration of the infusion of the Divine Breath into the first man, allows us to soar to the *hidden* realm of Divine Thought.

This insight can perhaps help us appreciate why we do not preface sounding the *shofar* with the Kabbalistic prayer לְשֵׁם יְחוּד, recited before performing many other *mitzvos*. The purpose of this prayer is to unify the realm of thought with the actual performance of the *mitzvah* we are about to do. However, in the case of *shofar* this would obviously be superfluous since this *mitzvah* in itself is so closely associated with the realm of thought.

The *Chiddushei HaRim* proved this insight by noting the juxtaposition of these two rulings in the Mishnah.

הַתּוֹקֵעַ לְתוֹךְ הַבּוֹר אוֹ לְתוֹךְ הַדּוּת אוֹ לְתוֹךְ הַפִּטָם אִם קוֹל שׁוֹפָר שָׁמַע יָצָא; וְאִם קוֹל הֲבָרָה שָׁמַע לֹא יָצָא. וְכֵן, מִי שֶׁהָיָה עוֹבֵר אֲחוֹרֵי בֵית הַכְּנֶסֶת אוֹ בֵיתוֹ סָמוּךְ לְבֵית הַכְּנֶסֶת, וְשָׁמַע קוֹל שׁוֹפָר . . . אִם כִּוֵּן לִבּוֹ יָצָא, וְאִם לָאו לֹא יָצָא, אַף עַל פִּי שֶׁזֶּה שָׁמַע וְזֶה שָׁמַע, זֶה כִּוֵּן לִבּוֹ וְזֶה לֹא כִּוֵּן לִבּוֹ, *If a person blows into a pit or into a cistern or into a cask: if one heard the sound of the shofar, he has fulfilled his obligation; but if he heard the sound of an echo, he has not fulfilled his obligation. Similarly, if one were passing behind a synagogue, or if his house was close to a synagogue, and he heard the sound of the shofar ... if he concentrated — he has fulfilled his obligation, but if not — he has not fulfilled his obligation, even though both he and someone else listened, this one concentrated but the other did not concentrate (Rosh Hashanah 3:7).*

The term וְכֵן — *similarly, and in the same manner* — is used to link together these two cases and implies that one who hears the *shofar* without any premeditated intent (כַּוָּנָה) has accomplished no more than one who would listen to an echo (קוֹל הֲבָרָה) emanating from a pit (הַבּוֹר). Whereas כַּוָּנָה, *premeditated intent*, is welcome, even preferable for the complete performance of most *mitzvos*, in this instance, it is absolutely critical. (*Likutim*)

✦ Total Self-Negation

והענין ע״י שבנ״י מבינים שהכל מהקב״ה ואין לנו שכל לכוון
מעצמנו את לבנו לאבינו שבשמים ובאין בבחי׳ קול שופר שהוא
קול בלי חיתוך האותיות

The use of a wordless medium to convey our prayers reflects total self-negation. The *shofar's* sound expresses the innate emotions embedded deep in every Jewish heart and its cries, which emanate from the very lifeblood of the Jew, soar to the heavens. If this cry were accompanied by words, it would imply that we are somehow able to initiate our return to Hashem. But when we resort to the sound of the *shofar*, which is really Jewry's collective inner cry, we demonstrate our total and absolute reliance on Hashem to bring us back to Him.

(*Likutim*)

✦ The Pintele Yid

כפי הצעקה במרירות כ״כ עד שנתבטל כל הדברים החיצונים וכל
רצונו לעורר זאת הנקודה ובפרט בתקיעות של כלל ישראל ע״י
זאת הכוונה עי״ז מתעורר גם בחי׳ עומק למעלה דהיינו ג״כ בחי׳
שומר ישראל אשר נשאר תמיד רק בריחוק לפעמים

To appreciate even further the significance of the sound of the *shofar*, let us recall the famous insight that an inner spark of goodness (known in the Chassidic milieu as *"der pintele Yid"*) exists in every Jew. No matter how far a Jew may stray from his Torah roots, Hashem guards that spark zealously and protects it from further decay. On Rosh Hashanah, the day characterized by the Psalmist as *secret* (בַּכֶּסֶה), that inner spark comes alive. The wordless *shofar*, and the heartfelt remorse it evokes in the *"pintele Yid,"* shatters all the obstacles that inhibit Israel's return to Hashem.

For this resurgence of its inner spark of goodness, Israel enjoys ample reward. A particular characteristic of Hashem which is always present, but sometimes remote, surfaces. David recalls that the שׁוֹמֵר יִשְׂרָאֵל, *the*

Guardian of Israel, never slumbers nor sleeps: הִנֵּה לֹא יָנוּם וְלֹא יִישָׁן שׁוֹמֵר יִשְׂרָאֵל (*Tehillim* 121:4).

At times, however, our sins may appear to cause the Guardian of Israel, associated with the Attribute of Mercy, to distance Himself from His People. However, as soon as the *shofar* sounds, it evokes that inner spark and causes us to draw closer to Hashem; He in turn moves closer to His people.[1] (*Likutim;* ibid.)

Listening to the Shofar

Shofar is one of the very few *mitzvos* that emphasize listening (לִשְׁמוֹעַ קוֹל) rather than *performance* of the *mitzvah.* We shall now consider the various aspects of the significance of *listening* to the *shofar:*

⋖§ Remnants of Sinai

עיקר המצוה השמיעה . . . ויי״ל ע״פ המדרש קלקלתם נעשה
הזהרו בנשמע כו׳.

When Hashem hears the *shofar*, it "reminds" Him of one of the high points in His relationship with Israel: the pledge of *na'aseh v'nishma, We will do and we will hear.* Tragically, with the Sin of the Golden Calf we forfeited our claim to the *doing* part of this commitment (because we *did* the antithesis of Hashem's Will), and ever since, the road to Israel's restoration lies in *listening,* the *nishma,* as the Midrash states (*Shemos Rabbah* 27), קִלְקַלְתֶּם נַעֲשֶׂה הִזָּהֲרוּ בְּנִשְׁמָע, *you have failed in your pledge to do; be careful to observe your pledge to listen.*

---

1. For a still more profound analysis of the relationship between the sound of the *shofar* and speech, the reader is referred to the *Likutim* on Rosh Hashanah, especially the segment dealing with the relationship between פְּרָט וּכְלָל and קוֹל וְדִבּוּר.

Probing further, we can draw a parallel between the significant role played by *listening* to the *shofar* and the equal emphasis placed on the *voice* of the *shofar* (קוֹל שׁוֹפָר). Even if a Jew strays (ח״ו) from fulfilling the Torah (נַעֲשֶׂה), he will at least always be willing to listen to its teachings. And even if our actions and speech have been corrupted, our *sound* — the innermost feelings of a Jewish soul throbbing with life (refer to our previous remarks on קוֹל שׁוֹפָר) — remains pure. The two elements of the Jewish character that are incorruptible are juxtaposed in the blessing recited before sounding the *shofar*: לִשְׁמוֹעַ קוֹל שׁוֹפָר, *to listen to the voice of the shofar*.

The association between the voice and listening is emphasized by David: עֹשֵׂי דְבָרוֹ לִשְׁמֹעַ בְּקוֹל דְּבָרוֹ, *who do His bidding [word], to obey the voice of His word* (*Tehillim* 103:20).

Whereas listening (to Hashem's Voice permits us to hear the *voice* of His Word (קוֹל דְּבָרוֹ), only by performing *mitzvos* can we fulfill His Word, עֹשֵׂי דְבָרוֹ. Every Rosh Hashanah we pray for and eagerly anticipate the time when, in the merit of listening to (שׁוֹמֵעַ) Hashem's Voice, we will be privileged to fulfill (עוֹשֶׂה) His Word as well. (5633)

≈§ Going into Battle with the Merit of Shema

ויתכן שזה עצמו רמז שמיעת קול שופר שאפילו אין לישראל רק
זכות שמע ישראל כדאי הם להנצל כמ״ש רש״י בפ׳ שופטים
במאמר משוח מלחמה. וכמו כן בר״ה יום מלחמה מזכירין קולן
של בנ״י.

This Judgment Day, when we combat all those forces which seek to harm Israel, is a good time to recall other battles against our enemies. Israel has always preferred not to rely on military might alone but rather to confront the foe fortified by the inspiration given by a specially appointed priest מְשׁוּחַ מִלְחָמָה, *anointed for war*, who would charge them with an exhortation commencing with the *Shema*. As *Rashi* notes (*Devarim* 20:3), the merit of reciting the *Shema* every day was by itself enough to ensure triumph.

Here too, as we prepare to do battle against our spiritual foes by pronouncing the blessing, לִשְׁמוֹעַ קוֹל שׁוֹפָר, *to hear the sound of the shofar*, we recall that Israel's merits are based on its capacity for *listening*, be it our daily recitation of the *Shema*, or listening to the Word of Hashem [as revealed in the Torah], or at least to the innate impulse ingrained in every Jew which seeks to listen to the Torah.

(5646)

⊷ Hastening the Redemption

וע״ז נאמר היום אם בקולי תשמעו שהוא מצות שמיעת קול
שופר. וכדאיתא בזוהר כי אם יזכו בני ישראל יהי׳ הגאולה
בתשרי לכן אמר משיח היום אם בקולו תשמעו.

I n our essay on the verses of מַלְכִיּוֹת, זִכְרוֹנוֹת, and שׁוֹפָרוֹת, we interpreted the verse (*Tehillim* 95:7), הַיּוֹם אִם בְּקֹלוֹ תִשְׁמָעוּ, *Even today, if we but heed His call*, as a reference to the day of Rosh Hashanah. If Israel would only *hearken* to the sound of the *shofar today* — on Rosh Hashanah — and absorb its message of faith and repentance, then *Mashiach* would arrive shortly. In this light we can suggest a new understanding of the *Zohar's* assertion that the redemption could occur in Tishrei if Israel has the requisite merits: Perhaps this actually refers to the merit of listening to the *shofar*.   (5639)

⊷ The Tree of Life

ובפה יש קנה וושט והם רמוזים לעץ החיים ועץ הדעת. וקודם
החטא הי׳ לנו דעת טוב בלי תערובות. ואחר החטא צריכין לקול
שופר שהוא מן הקנה בלבד דאין קטיגור נעשה סניגור.

W hen we refer to the sound of the *shofar*, we are speaking not just of the sound itself but also of the organs which produce the sound, particularly the trachea (windpipe). Unlike the esophagus which serves as a conduit for food matter, the trachea contains only air and thus is always void of foreign substances.

Symbolically, those two adjacent tubes correspond to two "vital organs" in *Gan Eden*, the Tree of Life and the Tree of Knowledge of Good and Evil. When Adam sinned by partaking from the latter tree, he blurred the distinction between good and evil, as indicated by the tree's

very name: עֵץ הַדַּעַת טוֹב וָרָע, *The Tree of Knowledge of Good and Evil.*
This corresponds to the esophagus which contains foreign food substances as well as the flesh of the organ itself. On Rosh Hashanah, by
devoting our concentration to the sound of the *shofar*, whose origin is
the uncontaminated trachea, which is also free of impurities, we invoke
the merit of the Tree of Life as it was before Adam's sin tainted it.

(5662)

◄§ Active Listening and Thinking

שצריכין להטות אוזן לשמוע לא בשמיעה ע״י גבורת הקול רם
שהוא מעשה חמריות רק לעשות פעולה לשמוע והוא במחשבה
מוכנת לשמוע

Listening to the *shofar* is by no means intended to be a passive
mitzvah; even though simply waiting to hear its sound and hoping
that it will penetrate into our souls may suffice to fulfill the technical
requirements of the *mitzvah*, to do so would be to relegate the listener to
the status of a spectator, a passive observer of another person's act. As
we discussed above, however, the *mitzvah* of *shofar* originates in the
rarefied realm of thought, and therefore listening to the *shofar* requires
an active effort to concentrate on the sound, on its significance and
impact, to the exclusion of all other stimuli and extraneous thoughts.

The Sages alluded to this demand for active participation on the
listener's part in their discussion of the requirement that one concentrate
on listening to the *shofar* (*Rosh Hashanah* 3:7). They ask why
premeditated intent (כַּוָּנָה) to hear the *shofar* is necessary to fulfill the
mitzvah, since one in any case hears the *shofar*, whatever his intent is.
The answer is given that hearing the *shofar* passively is no better than
hearing a donkey bray.

Homiletically, we can connect the word חֲמוֹר, *donkey*, with the
similar word חָמְרִיּוּת, *material actions*. This suggests that if one fulfills
the *mitzvah* of *shofar* as a passive spectator to someone else's
performance, the *mitzvah* becomes relegated to the sphere of the
material world. How much more inspiring and effective will the
mitzvah be in accomplishing its purpose if a person prepares himself to
hear the sound of the *shofar* in thought as well as in deed.   (*Likutim*)

⊷ Sitting on the Throne of Mercy

בְּשָׁעָה שֶׁבְּנֵי יִשְׂרָאֵל תּוֹקְעִין בְּשׁוֹפָר הַקַבְּ״ה עוֹמֵד מִכִּסֵּא הַדִּין וְיוֹשֵׁב
עַל כִּסֵּא הָרַחֲמִים

When the Jews sound the shofar, Hashem arises from His
Throne of Judgment, and sits on His Throne of Mercy
(Yalkut Shimoni, Vayikra 645).

עיקר המכוון כדי שישב המלך על כסא רחמים. כי אין טוב
שיגרמו בני אדם שיהי׳ המלך במדת הדין

W hile this Midrash seems to be making a statement about the effect
of blowing the *shofar*, we can also extract from it an insight
concerning the purpose of this *mitzvah*, namely that our primary
objective in sounding the *shofar* should be to arouse Hashem's mercies
for Israel. If this objective were to go unrealized, Heaven forbid, our loss
would be twofold: Not only would we be subject to a harsh verdict, but
we would also be responsible for causing Hashem to remain "seated" on
His Throne of Justice, since failing to use every means at our disposal to
ensure a good judgment for ourselves is itself a sin.

Simply being aware of this objective brings us rich rewards. The fear
that Hashem might not move from His Throne of Justice is sufficient to
arouse His mercies for us, and indeed this by itself causes Him to move
to His Throne of Mercy. (5636)

⊷ Having Mercy on the Soul

הקב״ה עומד מכסא דין ויושב על כסא רחמים. כי עיקר הרחמים
למעלה על הנשמה שהם מעשה ידיו של הקב״ה כמ״ש ונשמות
אני עשיתי כמ״ש בס׳ שערי תשובה מר״יי ז״ל. וכמ״ש כרחם אב
על בנים

I n appealing for Divine Mercy, we frequently cite the Psalmist's plea,
כְּרַחֵם אָב עַל בָּנִים רִחַם ה׳ עַל יְרֵאָיו, *As a father is merciful towards his
children, so has* HASHEM *shown mercy to those who fear Him* (Tehillim

103:13). Really, this is far more than a plea for Hashem to show us the pity of a father for his child; rather, we ask Hashem to be merciful to us for similar reasons that a father would pity a child. Just as a parent feels an attachment to his child who is immersed in the greatest spiritual treasure, the Torah, so we too plead with Hashem to spare our most spiritual component — our soul, as the prophet Yeshayahu says, וּנְשָׁמוֹת אֲנִי עָשִׂיתִי, *souls I have made* (57:16).

But how can a mortal creature overcome all the demands of the material world and become aware of the awesome potential of his soul? The *shofar* is one of the more powerful instruments to enable us to come to grips with our souls, as we say immediately after the first set of *shofar* blasts (*Tehillim* 89:16): אַשְׁרֵי הָעָם יוֹדְעֵי תְרוּעָה, *Happy is the people who know the teruah* — who acquire understanding of the potential of his soul through the *teruah* sound.

Upon hearing the *shofar* on Rosh Hashanah, Hashem has pity on the soul as a parent would have on a child and, as the Midrash concludes, "arises from His Throne of Judgment, and sits on His Throne of Mercy." (cf. 5646)

⋙ Sparing Israel in the Merit of Torah

עיקר השופר לעורר רחמים בזכות התורה . . . וראה שאין העולם מתקיים ושיתף עמה מדה''ר. זה התורה דאיתא מי שאין בו דעת אסור לרחם עליו.

One last task accomplished by the *shofar* is to "remind" Hashem of the Torah, which He gave to His people against the backdrop of the sound of the *shofar*. Perhaps it is the merit of Torah which the *shofar* evokes that causes Hashem to arise from His Throne of Justice and "sit" on His Throne of Mercy.

What is more, any appeal to Hashem's Mercy can be understood in the context of Torah. A well-known Midrash states that Hashem overrode His original intention to create the universe on the basis of strict justice and instead blended mercy with justice. In light of the above, perhaps this Midrash can also be interpreted as an allusion to the power of Torah.

Perceiving that the universe could not exist on the basis of strict justice, Hashem determined to give Israel the Torah, the greatest source of mercy. The Rabbinic statement, *Berachos 33a,* מִי שֶׁאֵין בּוֹ דַּעַת אָסוּר לְרַחֵם עָלָיו, *one may not display mercy to an individual lacking knowledge*, should be understood in the same vein. One who lacks even a rudimentary appreciation for Torah is not worthy of our mercy. Yirmiyahu's fond remembrance of the Jewish people, כִּי מִדֵּי דַבְּרִי בּוֹ ... רַחֵם אֲרַחֲמֶנּוּ, *whenever I speak about him [i.e. Israel] I have mercy on him [i.e. Israel]*, also refers to the Torah (31:19). By gracing us with His commandments — by speaking to us at Sinai — Hashem also made it possible for Him to have mercy on Israel. Instead, the Talmud frequently refers to the Torah as רַחֲמָנָא, *The Merciful One*, since the Torah is the catalyst causing Hashem to be merciful.

The *shofar*, which enhances the Jewish people's commitment to Torah,[1] evokes the eternal merit of the Torah causing Hashem to sit on the Throne of Mercy. (5664)

←§ Revisiting Eden

הנה עיקר השופר הוא לעורר ולתקן המדרגה הראשונה שהי׳
קודם חטא הראשון

The name שׁוֹפָר connotes (שׁוּפְרָא) *beauty*. This implies that the *shofar* transports us from the narrow confines of this world to the splendid realm of the World to Come (cf. *Tehillim* 27:4 where David describes עוֹלָם הַבָּא as לַחֲזוֹת בְּנֹעַם ה׳).

In fact, there was a time when the sublime beauty of the World to Come graced this universe — in Eden. Tragically, this period was short-lived. But there was another attempt to create the ambiance of the World to Come on earth, at the giving of the Torah. Alas, when Israel venerated the Golden Calf this plan was foiled. Our dream, our fond wish as conveyed by the *shofar*, is to return to the halcyon days of Eden. (5637)

---

1. As we say immediately after listening to the *shofar*: אַשְׁרֵי הָעָם יוֹדְעֵי תְרוּעָה. *Happy is the nation that acquires knowledge* (דַּעַת) *of Torah through the shofar.*

והנה בחג השבועות הוא בחי׳ עץ החיים. אמנם ר״ה בחי׳ תיקון
עץ הדעת טו״ר והוא בחי׳ המשפט והדין.

The analogy to Eden may be extended even further by considering
the nature of the two trees that stood in the Garden of Eden's center. The
Tree of Life, symbolizing the Torah (described by Shlomo as a *Tree of
Life*), is commemorated annually on Shavuos with the giving of the
Torah.

However, the far more complex Tree of Knowledge, which after
Adam's sin became symbolic of our confused world in which good and
evil are often blurred or intermingled (refer to our previous remarks in
this essay about the effect of the First Sin), enjoys a *Yom Tov* of its own
— Rosh Hashanah. On this day, all of man's deeds, good and evil
together, are weighed by the Creator. Scales, מאזְנַים , the constellation
for the month of Tishrei, symbolize weighing and selecting between
these two extremes. Standing before Hashem, concerned that we will
still suffer from the repercussions of Adam's original act, we blow the
shofar, through which we recall the memories of Eden before the First
Sin (cf. *Rosh Hashanah* 26a, in which parallels are implied between the
shofar and the first sacrifices brought by Adam while still in Eden). The
shofar pleads our case: "Allow us to soar above our miseries; allow us to
return to the Tree of Life, to the purity of Eden before the sin."

In this light, we can better appreciate the insight of *Zohar* that one
who observes Shavuos properly need not fear the judgment of Rosh
Hashanah. Those who observed Shavuos meticulously have already
lifted themselves from the petty vanities of this world. They reside
beneath Eden's Tree of Life. Rosh Hashanah, on the other hand,
corresponds to the Tree of Knowledge of Good and Bad — to the
lifestyle of those who still reside in this world — in which the
parameters of good and evil are often blurred. (5638)

תְּקִיעָה תְּרוּעָה תְּקִיעָה
Symbolism and Significance

⋖§ Recognizing Hashem
Before, During, and After צָרוֹת

ג׳ ענינים אלו עשרה מאמרות ועשר מכות ונסים במצרים ועשרת
הדברות הכל אחד .. זה עצמו תקיעה שברים תרועה תקיעה
. . . והוא נגד ג׳ אבות שאברהם אע״ה הי׳ בחי׳ ראשונה שהקנה
להקב״ה שמים וארץ כמ״ש שקראך אדון תחלה. ויצחק אע״ה
העקיד עצמו להקב״ה והוא ביטול עצמותו. . . . ויעקב אבינו הוא
שלימות הראוי התגלות האמת

The sequence of sounds, תְּקִיעָה, תְּרוּעָה, תְּקִיעָה,[1] an opening unbroken sound followed by a broken sound, and then another continuous unbroken sound in conclusion, alludes to the ability of the Jew to cling to Hashem in good times, during times of distress, and finally during the liberation that follows our suffering.[2] The first תְּקִיעָה reminds us of creation when all of His Creations immediately honored the Creator by harmoniously following His Will.

---

1. At this point, we will assume that only three distinct sounds exist. The שְׁבָרִים, a variation of the תְּרוּעָה sound instituted by Rabbi Abahu during a later period, will be subsequently discussed.

2. In this approach, we assume this תְּקִיעָה means to cling or insert one object into another. It is not uncommon for תּוֹקֵעַ to be used in that sense (cf. תקיעת כף, a handshake, or גזירה שמא יתקע).

This era of bliss was eventually followed by the dark period of the Egyptian exile. Yet, even then, when others may have thought that Hashem was no longer present, Israel cleaved to its Creator — this time by crying, as symbolized by the shattered תְּרוּעָה sound. Our loyalty to Hashem during the bitterness of the Egyptian exile was amply rewarded at Sinai, when we experienced Divine Revelation. Such closeness, the personal "intimacy" between Israel and Hashem, is represented by the final and most magnificent "clinging," the final תְּקִיעָה. As we preface the שׁוֹפָרוֹת prayer, אַתָּה נִגְלֵיתָ בַּעֲנַן כְּבוֹדֶךָ עַל עַם קָדְשֶׁךָ, *You were revealed in Your cloud of glory to Your holy people*. Only at Sinai could we experience with such clarity, felt by every fiber of the body, the Presence of Hashem. While we always maintained our belief (אֱמוּנָה) in Hashem even during the most difficult of times, only at Sinai did we *feel* and *experience* with certainty what we always believed. This is the תְּקִיעָה אַחֲרוֹנָה — the final and most glorious link between Israel and Hashem. (Refer to our remarks on מַלְכִיּוֹת, זִכְרוֹנוֹת, שׁוֹפָרוֹת for a similar presentation.)   (5633)

◄§ The Patriarchs

This pattern of clinging to Hashem in good times, in the worst of times, and in the best of times, as symbolized by the תְּקִיעָה, תְּרוּעָה, תְּקִיעָה is strikingly similar to the life and times of the Patriarchs. Avraham was the first to teach a disbelieving mankind about the Creator of Heaven and Earth. He initiated the contact between mankind and Hashem, and was truly the first תְּקִיעָה. Yitzchak, at the *Akeidah*, embodies the תְּרוּעָה by cheerfully accepting the Divine Will and clinging to Hashem at a most trying time. His sterling example of self-negation and total submission set the tone for his descendants during all of Israel's troubled times. They would seek out Hashem and cry the shattered תְּרוּעָה sound while simultaneously subsuming all of their reservations and questions in the form of total acceptance of the Divine Will. Yaakov, known as the most complete of the Patriarchs, combining the virtues of Avraham and Yitzchak, merited through his immersion in Torah to experience the same clinging to Hashem that our forefathers did at Sinai, the final תְּקִיעָה.   (ibid.)

⊰ Connecting to Our Heavenly Roots

וזהו תקיעה לתקוע הכל בשורש העליון המכוסה

As discussed in the essay on "בַּכֶּסֶה", Rosh Hashanah enjoys the unique capacity of enabling the Jew to "connect" all the events of this world with their heavenly antecedents. As David sings (*Tehillim* 81:4), תִּקְעוּ בַחֹדֶשׁ שׁוֹפָר בַּכֶּסֶה לְיוֹם חַגֵּנוּ, On the day of the *shofar* sounding, connect (תִּקְעוּ) everything new (חָדָשׁ) to the hidden world above (בַּכֶּסֶה).

The תְּקִיעָה, תְּרוּעָה, תְּקִיעָה sequence may convey the same message. Under ideal circumstances, we relate everything (connect, תָּקַע) to its heavenly roots. However, as mortals, we may slacken, and not live up to so lofty a challenge. Though we may be shattered, as indicated by the תְּרוּעָה, we can repent and restore the full effect of the first תְּקִיעָה.

(5637)

⊰ Introductory, Intermediate, and Concluding Blessings of the Shemoneh Esrei

לכן יש תקיעה לפני' ולאחרי' הוא כמ"ש בג' ראשונות כעבד שמסדר שבחו. ואחרונות כמקבל פרס והולך. ותרועה באמצע הוא בקשת צרכיו.

A striking parallel may be drawn between the sequence of the *shofar* sounds and the order of the *Shemoneh Esrei*. The Torah stipulates that we sound three תְּקִיעוֹת, followed by three תְּרוּעוֹת, and another three תְּקִיעוֹת. The association between those requirements and the arrangement of the *Shemoneh Esrei* is intriguing. Just as the first three blessings of the *Shemoneh Esrei* preface the *tefillah* with praise of Hashem, so too the first תְּקִיעוֹת. Likewise, in the same manner that the final three blessings actually acknowledge the receipt of Divine Blessings (such as peace and life) as a servant hands His master a gift before leaving him, so too the final three תְּקִיעוֹת are intended to express our gratitude to Hashem. The relationship between the תְּרוּעוֹת and the intermediate blessings of the *Shemoneh Esrei*, which consist of many specific requests appealing for Divine assistance, is particularly interesting. They too are equivalent. The תר״ת, תש״ת, תשר״ת (consisting of the three instances in which the תְּרוּעָה is sounded alone, the three שְׁבָרִים sounds, and the three instances in which *both* the שְׁבָרִים and the תְּרוּעָה are sounded) correspond to the twelve intermediate blessings of the *Shemoneh Esrei*. Just as those blessings voice our request for Divine assistance for virtually every situation in life, so too the תְּרוּעוֹת in various configurations help convey Israel's pleas to be spared from all the vicissitudes (צָרוֹת) that life may bring.

The renowned tradition that the *shofar* conveys Israel's prayers to Hashem now assumes additional significance. The various components to the *Shemoneh Esrei* are virtually identical with and serve the same purpose as the various *shofar* sounds.   (5648)

ﻭ§ Nullification of Israel's Sins — Jewish People Are Overwhelmingly Good

---

שע״י התשובה מתבשרין כל הקולות . . . ראשיתן ואחריתן של
בנ״י הוא טוב. . . . ולעתיד ג״כ טוב אחרית דבר מראשיתו.
והזמן שבנתים. אעפ״י שחטאנו. ע״י תשובה מתקנים החטאים
ומתבטל קול נשבר שבאמצע לקול פשוט שלפני׳ ואחרי׳. והרמז
איסורא ברובא בטל.

As discussed previously, the voice of the *shofar* symbolizes the inner voice of Torah embedded in every Jewish soul. Even the Jew who has gone astray can return on Rosh Hashanah. The ruling that any type of pitch is acceptable to fulfill the *mitzvah* of *shofar* (כָּל הַקּוֹלוֹת כְּשֵׁרִין בְּשׁוֹפָר, *Rosh Hashanah* 27b)) may be understood homiletically — that the voice of every Jew (his *inner workings*), **no matter how far he may have drifted from his heritage,** is essentially good and is purified through repentance.

The sequence of the sounds beginning and concluding with a continuous sound also emphasizes the innate goodness of the Jewish people whose historical *beginning* and *end* were great, even if there were periods of decline in between. The annals of Jewish history commence with the giving of the Torah and conclude with *Mashiach* described by *Koheles* (7:8) as "an end even better than the beginning"

(טוֹב אַחֲרִית דָּבָר מֵרֵאשִׁיתוֹ). Undoubtedly there were many tragic moments in which Israel veered from the straight path, moments represented by the shattered תְּרוּעָה sound. However, the broken sound of the תְּרוּעָה is nullified by the presence of a majority of תְּקִיעוֹת. Israel's sins are also negated by the overwhelming majority of merits it enjoys.

There is a great *halachic* dictum: אִיסוּרָא בְּרוּבָּא בָּטֵל (cf. *Chullin* 100a), A prohibited substance is nullified in the presence of a greater amount of permissible material. So too the broken תְּרוּעָה hinting a period of drift is rectified and negated amidst the unbroken sounds of תְּקִיעָה.   (5651)

⋖§ Before and After Sinning

שתקיעה על הטוב שקודם החטא. . .ואח״כ תרועה ותקיעה
אחרונה שהוא תשובה

I n a similar vein, we may suggest that the תְּקִיעָה, תְּרוּעָה, תְּקִיעָה sequence reminds us of a Jew's odyssey to תְּשׁוּבָה. The first תְּקִיעָה represents the individual prior to sinning, the תְּרוּעָה the shattering spectacle of sinning, and the final תְּקִיעָה representing the returnee (בַּעַל תְּשׁוּבָה) whose position is even greater than that of the totally righteous individual.   (*Likutim*)

⋖§ The שברים Sound

אבן זה הגלות האחרון כולל כל הגליות לכן יש בו כל הגניחות
ויללות.

T he Talmud (*Rosh Hashanah* 34a) relates that Rabbi Abahu instituted that the תְּרוּעָה resound both in the form of a sound simulating a sigh (גְּנוּחֵי גָּנַח) known as the שְׁבָרִים and as a series of short sobs, the תְּרוּעָה. In accordance with the symbolism of the *shofar* sounds, we suggest that the broken תְּרוּעָה and שְׁבָרִים represent the sighs and sobs of the *Galus* Jew. Each of the many exiles undergone by the Jewish people can be depicted by a sigh or sob alone. However, this long contemporary exile, combining the most difficult aspects of each of the previous exiles, is represented by both the sigh and sob.   (5648)

~ Crying About Past Sins

ולע״ד מה שלא מצינו בספרים הקדושים לומר לשם יחוד קודם
תקיעות שופר כמו בכל המצות כי כל מצות הם במעשה . . . אבל
שופר מחשבה לחוד לשם הוי׳ ב״ה בלבד . . . והתרועה גנח ויליל
ניכר בו יותר תנועת התוקע והיינו שהתרועה היא הצעקה ויללה
על מה שקלקלנו במעשינו

The sigh and sob of the שְׁבָרִים and תְּרוּעָה symbolize the anguish and bitter regrets of the individual Jew as well. The process of return begins when the sinner realizes that everything — even the capacity to sin — is derived from Hashem. Contemplating the terrible abuse of Hashem's gifts that occurs every time we sin and the sheer folly and the ultimate ingratitude of using our God-given talent to foil His Will, the Jew bitterly regrets his past sins. There can be no better antidote for the pleasure derived from sinning than the bitterness and sobbing exuded by the *baal teshuvah*.[1]

As the very name שְׁבָרִים (to break) implies, the sighs accompanying the שְׁבָרִים sound as well as the sound itself help shatter any evil deeds. Likewise, the תְּרוּעָה sounds and its accompanying cries effectively shatter and destroy sins that may have been committed. The term תְּרוּעָה also connotes shattering (cf. *Tehillim* 2:9, תְּרֹעֵם בְּשֵׁבֶט בַּרְזֶל, *You will smash them with a rod of iron*).

We have previously emphasized the role played by מַחֲשָׁבָה, *thought*, in the *mitzvah* of shofar. This is primarily true in the case of the תְּקִיעָה. The שְׁבָרִים and the תְּרוּעָה, on the other hand, while certainly being derived from the realm of thought, are only possible through a major effort on the part of the one who sounds the *shofar* (בַּעַל תּוֹקֵעַ). Action as well as thought are critical in the formation of these sounds. To rectify past misdeeds, our action as well as thought are essential.

(*Likutim*)

---

1. While generally joy is the primary means of Divine Service, the *Tanya* (noted philosophical work of Rabbi Schneir Zalman of Liadi) states that the יֵצֶר הָרָע which causes man to sin by depressing and frustrating him is most effectively foiled through his own weapons. Sadness, bitter regrets and remorse are the most effective means of destroying the יצה״ר.

❧ "The Bent Horn" — Humbling Oneself

אכן המצוה בכפופין כדי שיזכו כל העולם ע״י התעוררות
הרחמים שבני״י מתעוררין וכופפין עצמם ומבקשין לעורר
מדה״ר בעולם.

The Gemara relates that it is preferable that the *shofar* be bent (as is typical of a ram's horn). However, this preference is hardly essential. If necessary, any type of horn — even a straight one — may be utilized.

In light of the underlying thesis of this essay that the laws and customs of the *shofar* enjoy a great deal of symbolic importance, let us attempt to explain this apparent "dual standard," a preference for a bent *shofar* coupled with acceptance of any שׁוֹפָר.

A bent *shofar* symbolizes Israel's selfless act of contrition, humbling itself on Rosh Hashanah, as it beseeches Hashem for His Mercy. As cited previously, the bent *shofar* "reminds Hashem of Israel's contrition and causes Him to rise up from the Throne of Justice and sit on the Throne of Mercy." But this contrition is a selfless act — and thus not absolutely mandatory. Israel itself would merit survival — it would be vindicated — on the basis of strict justice alone.   (5643)

כי כמו שאין בכח בו״ד להגיד גדולתו של הקב״ה כן אין בכח
בו״ד להגיד זכותן של בני״י המקדשין שמו ית׳ בעולם בגלוי
ובסתר

Just as no mortal can begin to describe the greatness of Hashem, so too no one can even imagine the merit of the Jewish people who are constantly sanctifying Hashem's Name both publicly and privately. Israel is not required to humble — to "bend" itself — but rather does so, in order that mankind, lacking Israel's merits, will be spared a harsh verdict. Furthermore, as discussed in the essay on בַּכֶּסֶה, Israel benefits from subsuming itself among mankind and hiding its unique status on Rosh Hashanah. By opting to use a bent *shofar*, to precipitate an outpouring of Divine Mercy on behalf of mankind, rather than assert its uniqueness, Israel is truly disguising itself on the Day of Judgment.   (5643)

✍ Remembering the Giving of the Torah

כי בנ״י זכו להוציא מכח אל הפועל זה היום של קבלת התורה.
וזה היום אינו יכול להתגלות תמיד ובר״ה שמתחדש הבריאה
מכש״כ שמתחדש כוחן של בנ״י. . . . א״כ בזה היום מתחדש יום
מתן תורה וע״י קול שופר יכולין להתדבק ביום הזה.

Perhaps the primary purpose of sounding the *shofar* is to remember the day of the giving of the Torah which was given amidst the background of the *shofar* sound. In reality, this commandment is hardly confined to Rosh Hashanah. The Torah insists that we never forget the day that we stood before Hashem at Sinai (cf. *Deuteronomy* 4:10, יוֹם אֲשֶׁר עָמַדְתָּ לִפְנֵי ה׳ אֱלֹהֶיךָ בְּחֹרֵב). However, Rosh Hashanah is the most propitious time to fulfill this *mitzvah*. While all year long we can fulfill this *mitzvah* in an abstract sense remembering the concept of the giving of the Torah, on Rosh Hashanah we can actually *experience* and feel once again as if we are at Sinai. The reason for this phenomenon may be quite clear. On this day when all mankind derives renewed strength, when the universe itself is renewed, certainly the Jewish people's ability to relate to Torah is enhanced.

Even more profoundly, heaven and earth's continued viability is at stake every Rosh Hashanah. Just as at the time of the original creation, Hashem stipulated that their existence was contingent upon Israel's eventual acceptance of the Torah (refer to our essay in *The Three Festivals* entitled "The Universe's First Day" [p. 189] for further discussion of this theme), so too every year the earth's viability is only renewed because of Israel's continued acceptance of Torah. Every time we sound the *shofar*, we demonstrate our personal commitment to Torah. Our plea וְכָתְבֵנוּ בְּסֵפֶר הַחַיִּים, *and inscribe us in the Book of Life*, is really a request to renew our ties to Torah which is described as the Tree of Life. Upon seeing Israel's renewed dedication to Torah and continued remembrance of Sinai, Hashem evokes the merit of the giving of the Torah and renews His special ties with Israel.   (5648)

⇨ To Prevent Any Deviation

כמו כן תוקעין בר״ה לעמוד בזה ההתחדשות שלא לנטות עוד
מדרך הישר.

The commandment of sounding the *shofar* on Rosh Hashanah may serve to promote the same objective as the custom of blowing it during Elul (refer to our commentary on this topic) — preventing any further deviation from the proper path. Just as the *shofar* was sounded when Moshe ascended Mt. Sinai on *Rosh Chodesh Elul*, to warn Israel not to flirt again with idolatry (as they had just done when worshiping the Golden Calf), so too the *shofar* of Tishrei prevents us from straying from the straight path of life. Every Rosh Hashanah, Hashem renews our lease on life and in effect, "recreates" man. As *Koheles* states, עָשָׂה הָאֱלֹהִים אֶת הָאָדָם יָשָׁר וְהֵמָּה בִקְשׁוּ חִשְׁבֹנוֹת רַבִּים, *God has made man simple, but they sought many intrigues* (7:29).

We blow the *shofar* to ensure that we never deviate from that straight path. The famed verse תִּקְעוּ בַחֹדֶשׁ שׁוֹפָר may be interpreted in a similar fashion: When adopting a *new* path (חָדָשׁ — בַחֹדֶשׁ), use the *shofar* as the mechanism to ensure that you remain *ensconced* on that path (interpreting תִּקְעוּ as to fasten). (5662)

⇨ חָכְמָה וְאֵינָה מְלָאכָה / Wisdom but not Work

The Gemara (*Rosh Hashanah* 29b), while discussing why the *shofar* is not blown on Rosh Hashanah coinciding with Shabbos (see the essay on that topic), notes that sounding the *shofar* is an act requiring wisdom (חָכְמָה) and not a form of work (מְלָאכָה) which would be Biblically prohibited. Let us consider the homiletic significance of this expression "Wisdom but not work."

⇨ Seeking the Source of Creation

שהחכם מעיין על מהות הדברים . . . ובכח התורה שמלמדת לנו
החכמה לעמוד על מהות הפנימיות הבריאה

The term חָכְמָה may be construed as an acronym for כֹּחַ מָה, *wherein lies the strength* (of the universe). The first Jew, Avraham, came to recognize Hashem by wondering how could this infinitely perfect universe exist without a guiding force. As a result of his probing search for the truth, Hashem revealed Himself to Avraham and said, "I am the Guiding Force of the universe." We who are his descendants seek to coronate Hashem by reciting מַלְכִיּוֹת every Rosh Hashanah. But such a lofty objective can only be achieved if we too delve into the source of every creation. Unlike the Patriarch who discovered Hashem in a vacuum, who was compelled to seek the כֹּחַ מָה, the source of all, we can achieve this aim through Torah. The role of the Torah in helping us find and coronate Hashem can be deduced from the juxtaposition of תּוֹרָה צִוָּה לָנוּ מֹשֶׁה, *the Torah that Moshe commanded us* (*Devarim* 33:4), the verse describing the transmission of Torah from generation to generation and וַיְהִי בִישֻׁרוּן מֶלֶךְ, *He became King over Jeshurun* (v. 5), discussing the coronation of Hashem.

As a rule, Hashem only reveals His kingdom to those who seek Him out, whether it be through an intensive self-search as Avraham did, or as we do, through Torah. (5662)

◆§ Self-Negation in Favor of Hashem

עיקר החכמה היא הביטול אל השורש . . . שיודע ומבין שאינו
מצד זכות לו רק שירשנו מבוא מאבותינו

In another approach, we also assume that the term חָכְמָה is derived from כֹּחַ מָה. However, here the emphasis is placed on self-negation. What strength do I enjoy, in the Presence of Hashem? As we have previously discussed, the wordless sound of the *shofar* was intended to spur us to seek the source of life — Hashem. By denoting the *shofar* as חָכְמָה, our rabbis were suggesting that the wordless sound of the *shofar* was the ideal mechanism through which self-negation is achieved. The Talmud (*Chullin* 5b) praises those people who are as wise as men but had (nonetheless) acted as if they were merely animals. This refers to those worthy individuals who realize that on the basis of their own merit they are no better than animals. As *Koheles* states, וּמוֹתַר הָאָדָם מִן הַבְּהֵמָה אָיִן כִּי הַכֹּל הָבֶל, *man has no superiority over beast, for all is futile* (3:19). Such self-negation helps to reverse the basic sin of Adam, who by partaking of the Tree of Knowledge of Good and Evil (עֵץ הַדַּעַת) sought to develop himself into an independent source of wisdom. The true חָכָם, however, realizes מָה כֹּחַ, what his wisdom is in comparison to Hashem's. The famed verse, פִּיהָ פָּתְחָה בְחָכְמָה וְתוֹרַת חֶסֶד עַל לְשׁוֹנָה, *She opens her mouth with wisdom, and a lesson in kindness is on her tongue* (Mishlei 31:26), may be reinterpreted in this light. פִּיהָ פָּתְחָה בְחָכְמָה, the Jewish people opened their mouth — they pray to Hashem through self-negation, כֹּחַ מָה. Rather than issue elaborate verbose appeals, they simply cry — using the ancient Jewish weapon of הַקּוֹל קוֹל יַעֲקֹב, Yaakov's inner voice, realizing their total lack of worth and placing their trust in Hashem.

The verse concludes וְתוֹרַת חֶסֶד עַל לְשׁוֹנָה. Israel realizes that the Torah is also a gift (תּוֹרַת חֶסֶד) from Hashem and not a result of our own initiative.[1]   (5660)

◄§ The Inner Workings of Creation

עניין תקיעת שופר לאחוז בקול תורה שהוא פנימיות כל הבריאה
כדכ׳ בראשית בשביל התורה שנקראת ראשית

By describing *the shofar* as חָכְמָה, our Rabbis may have been hearkening to the very beginning of creation. The Aramaic translation of the Torah known as *Targum Yerushalmi* interprets בְּרֵאשִׁית בָּרָא אֱלֹהִים as בְּחָכְמָתָא, *through wisdom*, the Torah. Hashem created the universe with one *statement* may refer to the creation of the Torah from which the universe emerged. The *shofar*, reminding us of Sinai and the giving of the Torah, is the perfect vehicle through which we can feel attached to the Creator of Heaven and Earth.   (5656)

---

1. For another homiletical explanation of פִּיהָ פָּתְחָה בְחָכְמָה, see our commentary on אָז יָשִׁיר in *The Three Festivals*.

ৰ্ঙ Restoring to Life

דאיתא תקיעת שופר חכמה דכ׳ החכמה תחי׳ בעלי׳. תחי׳ הוא
אפילו כשהאדם בשעת הסכנה. דכ׳ ימותו ולא בחכמה. וע״י
החכמה יכולין להחיות א׳׳ע.

Perhaps the *shofar* is called wisdom because of its ability to maintain and restore life. *Koheles* (7:2) praises the wise man, הַחָכְמָה תְחַיֶּה בְעָלֶיהָ, *wisdom enlivens its master* (one who knows to use wisdom properly). On the other hand, Iyov notes, יָמוּתוּ וְלֹא בְחָכְמָה, *those who are not wise will perish* (4:21). On the day of judgment when all our lives are at stake, the *shofar*, symbolizing wisdom, keeps us alive. (For a discussion of the association between שׁוֹפָר and חָכְמָה utilizing this approach, see the section of אַשְׁרֵי הָעָם יוֹדְעֵי תְרוּעָה. (5658)

ৰ্ঙ Confusing the Satan

לָמָה תוֹקְעִין וּמְרִיעִין כְּשֶׁהֵן יוֹשְׁבִין, וְתוֹקְעִין וּמְרִיעִין כְּשֶׁהֵן עוֹמְדִין,
כְּדֵי לְעַרְבֵּב אֶת הַשָּׂטָן

Why do we sound the תְּקִיעָה *and* תְּרוּעָה *when we sit* (i.e. during the first *shofar* blowing before *Shemoneh Esrei* when one may sit) *and also sound the* תְּקִיעָה *and* תְּרוּעָה *when we stand* (i.e. during the repetition of the *Shemoneh Esrei*)? *In order to confuse Satan* (*Rosh Hashanah* 16a).

ונמצא שמערבין הרע שיהא נכלל בהטוב ובטל אל הטוב . . . זה
ענין שמערבין השטן . . שיש ב׳ מיני תפלות ובקשות א׳ לעורר
מדה״ר יב׳ לעורר הרחמים תוך מדה״ד

Rashi explains that when the *Satan* (cf. *Rashi, Shabbos* [89a], who notes that the *Satan* is identical with the Evil Inclination who entices Israel to sin and the Angel of Death) learns how much Israel loves *mitzvos* to the extent that they repeat the same *mitzvah*, he loses his ability to prosecute the Jewish people.

The question, however, remains. Why didn't the Gemara state simply that we repeat the *shofar* blowing because of our love for *mitzvos*?

Moreover, the concept of confusing — or more literally *mixing up* the Satan — requires clarification. While it is clear that *Satan* is silenced as a result of our effort, in what manner is he "mixed up"?[1]

To appreciate this concept, let us return to Adam's sin. As mentioned repeatedly, Adam, endowed with pristine spiritual existence in Eden, forfeited everything by partaking of the Tree of Knowledge of Good and Evil. The struggle of man in general and Israel in particular has been to sift the good from evil, to undo what Adam had wrongly done. As we have also mentioned, Rosh Hashanah — and especially at the time of *shofar* blowing — is a particularly propitious time to rectify or at least mitigate Adam's sin. As stated previously, the wordless *shofar* represents the inner voice of Yaakov (קוֹל יַעֲקֹב) that has never become tainted. Even if on the surface the Jewish people have strayed from Torah and *mitzvos*, the inner spark, the voice of Jacob, has never dimmed Yaakov's luster. In turn, it reminds us of Adam prior to the sin (cf. *Bava Basra* 58a, שׁוּפְרֵיהּ דְּיַעֲקֹב מֵעֵין שׁוּפְרֵיהּ דְּאָדָם). Thus, when sounding the *shofar*, Israel links itself to the realm of the righteous of Yaakov, and to the pure Adam, prior to their sinning. While it may not be possible to totally reverse Adam's sin, to eradicate evil while existing in this world, at the very least we can blend good with evil in such great proportions that evil becomes subservient to good. In this light, the Gemara's statement may be understood quite literally. We mix up the *Satan* by blending evil, by diluting its effect as we sound the *shofar*. The Talmud's (cf. *Rosh Hashanah* 26a) implication that the sacrifice brought by Adam upon repenting was similar in effect to the *shofar* may be understood in this light. Just as Adam attempted to at least blur the effect of his sin — to at least subdue, if not totally destroy the evil forces he had unleashed — so too, every time we sound the *shofar* we begin to remedy man's first error.

Probing further, let us consider the significance of blowing *shofar* when they are sitting (כְּשֶׁהֵן יוֹשְׁבִין) and when they are standing (כְּשֶׁהֵן עוֹמְדִין).[2]

Upon examining closely the nature of Israel's pleas for Divine mercy (רַחֲמִים), we find two distinct types of requests, the first — and most

---

1. The following approach is based on selected excerpts from the *Sfas Emes'* commentary. Due to the particularly esoteric nature of the material, replete with Kabbalistic implication, much of the commentary was deleted.

2. While this Gemara is typically understood to be referring to the sounding of the *shofar* before and during the *Shemoneh Esrei*, *Sfas Emes* interprets this statement homiletically.

familiar one — to arouse Hashem's Attribute of Mercy (מִדַּת הָרַחֲמִים). Though Israel is totally undeserving of His Mercy, we nonetheless beseech Him to spare us. However, there is another, perhaps more subtle plea — asking Hashem to invoke His Mercy because the Jewish people deserve it on the basis of their deeds. In other words, we are not requesting that Hashem "deviate" from His Attribute of Justice in favor of Mercy, but rather on *the basis of Justice* He should have mercy upon us.

A precedent for such a plan — invoking deserved kindness — can be found in the entreaties of Yitzchak that Rivkah conceive (וַיֶּעְתַּר יִצְחָק); described by the Midrash (*Bereishis Rabbah* 63:5) as compared to that of a *pitchfork* (עֶתֶר). Much as a pitchfork turns over the grain, so too the prayers of the righteous transform the Divine Attribute of Justice into Mercy. Yitzchak, in particular, embodying Divine Justice (דִּין), had no alternative but to pray that Justice *itself* be transmuted into Mercy; he could not request an undeserved outpouring of Divine Mercy. Likewise, the prayer of Moshe to enter *Eretz Yisrael* in which he appeals to 'ה אֱלֹהִים, Hashem — invoking the Attribute of Mercy — and *Elokim* — Justice — must be understood in this light. Entering the Promised Land could only be accomplished on the basis of *deserved* kindnesses.[1]

So too the repeated sounding of the *shofar* contains a double plea. Firstly, that Hashem should invoke those kindnesses that are deserved (לְעוֹרֵר רַחֲמִים תּוֹךְ הַדִּין) and then, that He should rise from the Throne of Justice and sit on the Throne of Mercy (refer to our previous discussion of these concepts). While the *shofar* blowing during the *Shemoneh Esrei* — when we are required to *rise* — seeks to invoke Hashem's Mercy granted while He is still *standing* on the Throne of Justice, "these kindnesses" are dispensed only to the deserving. On the other hand, the *shofar* sounded while the congregation may *sit* evokes a different plea, beseeching Hashem that He spare even the undeserving, as He rises from the Throne of Justice and *sits* on the Throne of Mercy.[2]

---

1. This is also the intent of *Rashi* (*Devarim* 3:24) commenting that though the righteous could rely upon their good deeds, they chose to plead with Hashem. Clearly, *Rashi* is referring to a plea for *deserved* kindnesses.

2. This concept may also be implied in *Rashi*'s comment that sounding the *shofar* twice is indicative of Israel's love for *mitzvos*. Based on the above discussion, we suggest that this refers not only to the repetition of the *mitzvah* of *shofar* but also the the relatively "risky" strategy of invoking the Divine Attribute of Justice — through the "standing" תְּקִיעוֹת — while simultaneously pleading for Mercy. Better to risk invoking the Attribute of Justice if at the same time we give Hashem the *"nachas"* of seeing our *worthiness* of His kindness.   (*Likutim*)

Mussaf —
מַלְכֻיּוֹת זִכְרוֹנוֹת שׁוֹפָרוֹת

אָמַר הקב״ה . . . אִמְרוּ לְפָנַי בְּרֹאשׁ הַשָּׁנָה מַלְכֻיּוֹת זִכְרוֹנוֹת
וְשׁוֹפָרוֹת: מַלְכֻיּוֹת כְּדֵי שֶׁתַּמְלִיכוּנִי עֲלֵיכֶם, זִכְרוֹנוֹת כְּדֵי שֶׁיַּעֲלֶה
זִכְרוֹנְכֶם לְפָנַי לְטוֹבָה, וּבַמֶּה? בַּשּׁוֹפָר.

The Holy One, Blessed is He, said, "... on Rosh Hashanah
recite before Me [verses that speak of God's] Sovereignty,
Remembrance [of all events] and Shofar blasts: Sover-
eignty, in order to make Me your King; Remembrance, in
order for your remembrance to rise up before Me for [your]
benefit; and through what? — through the shofar" (Rosh
Hashanah 16a). {translation adapted from ArtScroll Rosh
Hashanah Machzor}

וּבְכֵן תֵּן פַּחְדְּךָ, ה׳ אֱלֹהֵינוּ, עַל כָּל מַעֲשֶׂיךָ, וְאֵימָתְךָ עַל כָּל מַה
שֶּׁבָּרָאתָ, וְיִרָאוּךָ כָּל הַמַּעֲשִׂים, וְיִשְׁתַּחֲווּ לְפָנֶיךָ כָּל הַבְּרוּאִים

And so too, O HASHEM, our God, instill Your awe upon all
Your works, and Your dread upon all that You have cre-
ated. Let all works revere You and all creatures prostrate
themselves before You (Rosh Hashanah Prayer Service).

⋖§ Nobility Coronating the King

תהיו לי ממלכת כהנים הוא בר״ה זמן המלוכה וגוי קדוש הוא
ביום הכפורים שנמשלו בנ״י למלאכים

Although it may appear brazen for ordinary mortals to presume to
coronate Hashem, this is precisely the mission Israel was given just
prior to receiving the Torah: וְעַתָּה אִם שָׁמוֹעַ תִּשְׁמְעוּ בְּקֹלִי . . . וְאַתֶּם תִּהְיוּ לִי

וְעַתָּה אִם שָׁמוֹעַ תִּשְׁמְעוּ בְּקֹלִי... מַמְלֶכֶת כֹּהֲנִים וְגוֹי קָדוֹשׁ, *And now, if you hearken well to Me ... You shall be to Me a kingdom of ministers and a holy nation* (*Shemos* 19:5-6).

In this passage Hashem assures Israel that by listening to His voice — the voice of the *shofar* on Rosh Hashanah — they will become a nation of nobility[1] who coronate their King, and a sacred nation — on Yom Kippur when Israel has attained the status of angels. (5647)

◆§ Appear Voluntarily

חיבת בנ״י בין האומות כשושנה בין החוחים כו׳. וע״ז נאמר
הראיני את מראיך. כי כל באי עולם עוברים בע״כ. אבל בנ״י
מבקשין להתראות לזכרון לפניו לטובה בלא״ה מי לא נפקד
כהיום הזה... אבל ע״י שבנ״י מבקשין הזכירה שיעלה זכרוננו
לפניו ית׳ אעפ״י שיודעין שזו הזכירה הוא למשפט... וכדאי
להיות נשפט רק שיעלה זכרוננו לפניו ב״ה... ועי״ז עצמו
הופך הקב״ה מכסא דין ויושב על כסא רחמים.

Hashem asks Israel to recite Verses of Remembrance to evoke His memory of His people on the Day of Judgment. While all mortals must stand before the Heavenly Tribunal on Rosh Hashanah, whatever their wishes concerning the matter, Hashem desires that Israel present themselves of their own free will. This voluntary submission to judgment is a great source of merit for the Jewish people, especially in contrast to the compulsion required to bring the rest of mankind to appear.

Shlomo *HaMelech* alludes to this contrast in the following depiction of the Jewish people: כְּשׁוֹשַׁנָּה בֵּין הַחוֹחִים כֵּן רַעְיָתִי בֵּין הַבָּנוֹת, *As a rose among the thorns, so is My beloved among the maidens* (*Shir HaShirim* 2:2). We stand before Hashem on Rosh Hashanah out of love, even as the rest of humanity comes before Him with such reluctance. Hashem's plea to us also alludes to this contrast: הַרְאִינִי אֶת מַרְאַיִךְ הַשְׁמִיעִנִי אֶת קוֹלֵךְ כִּי קוֹלֵךְ עָרֵב וּמַרְאֵיךְ נָאוֶה, *Show Me your countenance, let Me hear your voice, for your voice is sweet and your countenance comely* (ibid. v. 14). How different is our deportment from that of the rest of mankind! By reciting the Verses of Remembrance and appearing voluntarily, totally without duress, we *show our comely countenance*. By sounding the

---

1. Cf. *Rashi's* interpretation of the word כֹּהֲנִים (which normally means *priests*) as meaning here *ministers* or *nobility*.

shofar and reciting the Verses of the *Shofar* blasts, again of our own free will, we allow Hashem to *hear our voice — for our voice is sweet and our countenance is comely*. How fortunate we are to have these two great sources of merit on this Judgment Day. (5648)

In this light, we can appreciate the precise meaning of Hashem's plea, *Recite before Me ... [verses of ...] Remembrance ... in order for your remembrance to rise up before Me for [your] benefit*. While the rest of humanity, on the community as well as the individual level, is also subject to the scrutiny of Hashem's memory on this Judgment Day, this occurs regardless of their wishes, as we say: מִי לֹא נִפְקָד כְּהַיּוֹם הַזֶּה, *Who is not recalled on this day?*[1] Nonetheless, Hashem still addresses a special plea to us, His people: "Recite before Me Verses of Remembrance, which show Me that you come to Me of your own free will, and that you realize how important it is to you to be remembered on Rosh Hashanah regardless of the outcome. In reward for your eagerness to be judged by Me, I will remember you only to your benefit."

The Midrash (*Yalkut Vayikra* 645) states that on Rosh Hashanah, Hashem arises from His throne of strict justice and moves to His throne of mercy. Surely this change of attitude and perspective occurs in the merit of Israel's insistence of facing up to its judgment on this day rather than evading responsibility for its actions. (5639)

◆§ In My Presence — In the Merit of the Torah

והנה ר"'ה ועשי"'ת הוא מימות עולם. אבל לבנ"'י נעשה הכל עפ"'י
התורה ומקודם הי' בכח עשרה מאמרות. ולבנ"'י הוא בכח עשרת
הדברות והתורה.... כלומר שיהי' נעשה כל התקונים ביום הזה
עפ"'י התורה.

It is noteworthy that Hashem requests not merely that we recite Verses of Sovereignty, Remembrance and *Shofar* sounding, but also that we do so in His presence, *before Me*. Although the events which Rosh Hashanah and the Ten Days of Repentance commemorate *predate* the Giving of the Torah and Israel's selection as the Chosen People, nevertheless they are especially significant from a Torah perspective. Thus, *prior* to Sinai, the Ten Days of Repentance simply corresponded to the

---

1. From the beginning of the Remembrance prayer of *Mussaf*.

Ten Divine Statements. *After* the Giving of the Torah, these days attained additional meaning corresponding to the Ten Commandments.(5641)

◄§ The Role of the Shofar

קשה הלא אמרו באמירה א''כ מאי הקושיא ובמה. רק דקאי על
מ''ש לפני. ואיך יכולין להתקרב לפניו. רק בשופר דאיתא בגמ'
שופר דלזכרון קאתי כלפנים דמי. . . . על ידי השופר נכנסים
הדיבורים לפניו ית'. . . . ולכן אינו בדיבור ממש שהוא
בהשתתפות שכל האדם רק קול פשוט.

The Talmud concludes with a question: "With what [do we evoke Hashem's remembrance]? With the *shofar*." This is a surprising question in that the Sages had earlier suggested that we recite passages of *Malchiyos, Zichronos* and *Shofaros* implying that we are remembered merely by *reciting* these verses. In light of our previous discussion, however, the Gemara's question takes on a new understanding.

How can someone draw close to Hashem? Simply reciting words, while helpful, will not permit a mere mortal to penetrate Hashem's inner sanctum, to stand "before Him." To achieve such a lofty objective, the medium of the *shofar* is required, since not only does the *shofar* remind Hashem of His special bond with Israel, it actually penetrates the innermost recesses of the heavens (cf. *Rosh Hashanah* 26a, שׁוֹפָר כֵּיוָן דְלְזִכָּרוֹן קָאָתֵי כְּלִפְנִים דָמִי).

While all of mankind could possibly *speak* Hashem's praises, the *wordless shofar* reminds Hashem of Israel's special relationship with Him. It is reminiscent of the *voice* of Yaakov (קוֹל יַעֲקֹב) and the *shofar* of Sinai. Through the *shofar*, Israel's prayers penetrate the innermost recesses of the heaven. (5648)

The *shofar's* ability to convey our prayers directly to Hashem may lie in the very nature of its "voice," which consists of wordless sounds. Human speech always results from a premeditated thought process, while sounds are innate. Thus the fact that we offer our prayers to Hashem through the inchoate sound of the *shofar*, rather than through articulate speech of humans, expresses our recognition that even our ability to speak is a Divine gift.

In fact, all of Israel's efforts are directly due to Hashem's blessings and are in no way the result of our own efforts. Upon hearing Israel's *shofar*

— with its implicit message that we owe everything we have to Him —
Hashem's mercies are aroused to spare His children.   (5648)

⋙ Coronate Me over You and over All Your Works

ולכן עליהם לקבל מלכות שמים שהם נקראי' ראשית. ובכח זה
נמשך מלכות שמים גם על כל העולם.

The two passages we cited at the beginning of this essay reflect two
seemingly different approaches to Hashem's Sovereignty: On the one
hand, Hashem's request of us to coronate Him over ourselves (כְּדֵי
שֶׁתַּמְלִיכוּנִי עֲלֵיכֶם) suggests the unique relationship between the Jewish
people and Hashem. At the same time, the request we make in the prayers
of Rosh Hashanah for mankind to fear and pay homage to Hashem
implies that we want to coronate Hashem as Sovereign over *all* mankind
(and over all of creation, as we say, תֵּן פַּחְדְּךָ . . . עַל כָּל מַעֲשֶׂיךָ).

⋙ An Example for Mankind

One way to resolve this apparent contradiction is by noting that Israel
was the first nation to coronate Hashem. Thus it is entirely appropriate
that we, who are known as the first amongst nations (*Yirmiyahu* 2:3,
רֵאשִׁית תְּבוּאָתֹה), should serve as a model to the rest of humanity by taking
the initiative to coronate Hashem on the first day of the New Year.
                                                                      (5661)

מצינו בדוד המע"ה כאשר מרדו בו בימי אבשלום אח"כ השלימו
עמו שלח לזקני יהודה למה תהיו אחרונים להשיב את המלך אח"כ
אמרו שאר השבטים עשר ידות לי במלך כו' ויקש דבר איש יהודה
לפי שהראו להם כתב מהמלך ע"ש סוף שמואל. בכל הדבר הזה
יהי' לעתיד כשיבואו כל האומות והשרים ויקבלו עול מלכותו ויודו
לשמו. ואעפ"י שהם ע' אומות יהי' יד בנ"י בראשונה. . . . ולא
תהיו אחרונים להשיב את המלך.

An interesting illustration of the significance of being the first to
coronate Hashem is contained in David's impassioned plea to his
fellow members of the tribe of Yehudah in the aftermath of Absalom's

revolt: *Why should you be the last to restore the king?* (*II Shmuel* 19:11). Although the remaining ten tribes argued that because of their numerical superiority they deserved a greater role in restoring David's monarchy and should have escorted him on his return from exile after Absalom's revolt was suppressed, the two tribes of Judah and Benjamin were given preference simply because David wrote a letter requesting that they coronate him first.

So too, in the future Messianic era when all mankind will acknowledge Hashem's sovereignty and claim Him as their own, Israel will maintain its unique status with Hashem, despite the Gentile world's numerical superiority. When paganism prevailed and no one was even aware of Hashem's existence, it was Abraham who taught the universe to know Him; when the Sea of Reeds split, it was Israel who sang, *HASHEM will reign forever and ever* (*Shemos* 15:18); and every year on Rosh Hashanah, it is Israel to whom Hashem knows He can plead with confidence: "Be the first to coronate Me." (5662)

◆§ Coronate Me —
Teach Humanity About Me

פי׳ שעל ידכם יהי׳ נגלה מלכותי בעולם. כל העולם ומלואו אינו
כדאי שיתגלה מלכותו ית״ש עליהם. רק באמצעיות בנ״י בכח
האבות ובכח התורה שמלמדת לנו החכמה

Israel is not only the first among nations, it is also a catalyst which enables all of humanity to accept Hashem's Sovereignty upon themselves.

In truth, it is almost inconceivable that mortals could have the ability to coronate Hashem, just as it is beyond belief that this world, with all its frailties, could be the ideal place for Him to be coronated. Indeed the whole universe, which seems so enormous from our minuscule perspective, is inadequate as a dwelling place for Hashem's Presence. If Hashem nonetheless insists that we proclaim His sovereignty to an unbelieving mankind, it must be because of certain unique gifts with which He has endowed us.

Specifically, perhaps it is the merit of the Patriarchs together with that of the Torah itself which enables Israel to proclaim Hashem's

Sovereignty to a reluctant humanity. We can find an allusion to the role of the Torah proclaiming Hashem's Sovereignty in the juxtaposition of two well-known, significant verses at the beginning of *Parashas VeZos HaBerachah:* תּוֹרָה צִוָּה לָנוּ מֹשֶׁה מוֹרָשָׁה קְהִלַּת יַעֲקֹב, *The Torah that Moshe commanded us is the heritage of the Congregation of Yaakov,* and וַיְהִי בִישֻׁרוּן מֶלֶךְ בְּהִתְאַסֵּף רָאשֵׁי עָם יַחַד שִׁבְטֵי יִשְׂרָאֵל, *He became king over Jeshurun when the numbers of the nation gathered — the tribes of Israel in unity (Devarim 33:4-5).* The first verse teaches us about the importance of transmitting Torah across all the generations, while the second describes Hashem's coronation.   (5662)

⋟ Teaching Mankind About Hashem — Coronating Him over Ourselves

---

ובגמ׳ איתא כדי שתמליכוני עליכם. הפי׳ כי העבד הנאמן צריך לבקש מלכות האדון על כל. רק ע״י שמבקש זה בכל לבו ממילא מתפשט המלכות עליו מקודם.

The objective of teaching humanity about Hashem's Sovereignty as proclaimed in the וּבְכֵן תֵּן פַּחְדְּךָ prayer is not dichotomous with Hashem's plea, "Coronate Me over yourselves." On the contrary, it is the fervent wish of every loyal subject of Hashem that all mankind come to accept His Sovereignty. Moreover, by praying for mankind to come to a wholehearted recognition of Hashem, we can ensure a fuller appreciation of His kingdom and His Sovereignty for ourselves as well.

By praying that Hashem's Sovereignty be accepted by all mankind Israel emulates Hashem's own behavior during Creation. Even though Hashem created the universe primarily for Israel's benefit,[1] He created the rest of mankind as well. In His infinite wisdom He realized that Israel would be able to accomplish its role as an exemplar to mankind only in such a complex and multifaceted context as a world made up of Jews and Gentiles. On Rosh Hashanah we emulate Hashem in praying that all His subjects accept the yoke of Heaven. By doing so, our own awareness of Hashem's Sovereignty is enhanced.   (cf. 5634)

---

1. Cf. *Rashi* on *Bereishis* 1:1: בִּשְׁבִיל יִשְׂרָאֵל שֶׁנִּקְרְאוּ רֵאשִׁית, *For the sake of Israel, who are called the **first.***

By praying for the rest of mankind, Israel emerges not only as the
primary beneficiary but also becomes the *first* to accept Hashem's
Sovereignty. This is because we are the first to appreciate and be fully
aware of Hashem's Sovereignty. In this light we can appreciate the
aptness of the famed Rabbinic dictum that if someone prays for another
person's needs when he himself needs the same thing, he will be
answered first. By praying for the other nations to be favored with an
awareness of Hashem's greatness and sovereignty, we make it possible
for our own awareness to flourish. (5651)

Just as Avraham's prayers for Sarah to be blessed with a child were
answered when he prayed for the recovery of Avimelech, so too when
we pray that the rest of mankind come to accept Hashem, we are almost
immediately granted a fuller appreciation of His Majesty (cf. *Bava
Kamma* 92a). (5651)

◄§ Israel Fears It May Have Dislodged the Gentile World

Perhaps our prayers for the Gentile world on Rosh Hashanah are also
based on a fear that we may have indirectly contributed to the
Godlessness that pervades the non-Jewish world. Since we have
preempted the rest of the world by accepting the Torah, we have
grounds to fear that we may have deterred the Gentiles from the
universally desired goal of accepting Hashem's Sovereignty. Therefore
on this annual reenactment of Hashem's coronation, we attempt to

assuage our feelings of guilt by praying for the spiritual needs of the other nations first.[1]   (5651)

⋖§ Israel's Unique Proclamation of Sovereignty

באמת מלכות שמים הוא לכלל כל הבריאה ולבנ״י מיוחד ענין
יצ״מ . . . וחודש ניסן . . . אבן גם חודש תשרי שהוא כלל
הבריאה זה היום תחילת מעשיך נתן השי״ת לבנ״י . . . וזה הוא
ר״ה.

As the foregoing discussion makes clear, the right to accept and proclaim Hashem's Sovereignty is by no means the exclusive province of the Jewish people. Indeed, we have seen that just the opposite is true, and requests that the Gentile world also accept Hashem and proclaim His control over the world are an important, recurring theme in our prayers.

Nonetheless there are significant distinctions between our concept of Hashem's Sovereignty and that of the non-Jewish world. For one thing, our understanding of Hashem's Kingdom derives primarily from the Exodus from Egypt, the central event in our emergence as a nation, while the Creation of the world plays at best a secondary role.[2] From the Gentiles' perspective, however, the Exodus has no significance, and their attention focuses entirely on the Creation as the foundation of Hashem's rulership.

This difference in perspective expresses itself also in the yearly festival cycle. Only Israel celebrates its national renewal during Nissan, the month of the Exodus, as ordered by Hashem in the first commandment He gave us as a nation: הַחֹדֶשׁ הַזֶּה לָכֶם, *This month shall be for you* (Shemos 12:2). This is also the month from which Jewish kings date their reign, while the reign of non-Jewish kings begins in Tishrei, when the world was created.

---

1. In this light, the analogy we cited above to Avraham's prayers for Avimelech emerges as particularly apt: Just as Avraham prayed for Avimelech's recovery out of concern that the monarch's punishment on Avraham's account might have propelled him to return to paganism, our prayers on behalf of the nations are motivated by similar concerns.

2. *Editor's Note:* This explains also why the Exodus receives so much attention in the daily prayer service, while the Creation is barely mentioned at all.

In spite of this unique status reflected in the fact that we have a unique, Divinely commanded New Year, and in our enhanced understanding of Hashem's Sovereignty, we are nonetheless required to participate in the general, world-wide New Year as well.

Although the observance of two New Years may seem like a redundancy, really this practice is not just for our own benefit but also for the benefit of the entire world, since the world's lease on life is renewed only because of our participation in the general New Year. As the Psalmist sings, כֹּחַ מַעֲשָׂיו הִגִּיד לְעַמּוֹ לָתֵת לָהֶם נַחֲלַת גּוֹיִם, *The strength of His works He declared to His nation, to give them the heritage of the nations* (111:6). This can be interpreted as an allusion to the requirement to celebrate the general New Year — the "heritage of the nations" — as well as our own.

What is more, we can rest assured that our participation will be amply rewarded. If the renewal of the universe depends upon our observance of the world-wide New Year, it is only fitting that we come ultimately to claim the "heritage of the nations," the spiritual treasures originally destined for the rest of humanity. (5640)

ובנ״י נקראו בנים למקום ב״ה. אבן צריכין להיות גם בבחי׳
עבדים . . . שגם בבחי׳ מלכותו יהי׳ מיוחד רק לבנ״י

There are also more direct benefits to be gained from our participation in the universal Rosh Hashanah. While our primary relationship to Hashem is likened to that of children to a Father, as the Torah says, בָּנִים אַתֶּם לַה׳ אֱלֹהֵיכֶם, *You are children to HASHEM, your God* (Devarim 14:1), it is also critical that we relate to Him as servants as well. In Nissan we return to Hashem as children returning to their Father; in Tishrei we are also servants renewing their contract with their Master. Hashem's plea to say in His Presence the Verses of Sovereignty is directed at us: Come back to Me, not just as children, but also as loyal servants. (5640)

◆§ Coronating Hashem for the Year Ahead

ראש השנה צריך כל אחד לקבל מלכות שמים על כל השנה . . .
ובכל יום צריך להיות כחדשים והיום הוא חדש באמת. . . . לכן
אמר משיח היום אם בקולו תשמעו.

While it may appear that our coronation of Hashem on Rosh Hashanah applies only to *this day*, now is actually the most propitious time to coronate Hashem for the *entire year*. Each year, inspired and reinvigorated by the start of the New Year, we accept Hashem's Kingdom for the entire year ahead.

The unique ability of this day to inspire us to year-long devotion is based largely on its very novelty — its status as the beginning of the New Year. Although we are supposed to treat the Torah and *mitzvos* as if they were new in our eyes each and every day,[1] on Rosh Hashanah this is not just a mode of perception but an absolute reality: The beginning of the New Year is an occasion for Hashem to renew His bond with us, to grant us His Torah and *mitzvos* anew. On this day the Torah and its commandments *are* new. Infused as we are with this vivid sense of renewal, our ability to accept and proclaim Hashem's Sovereignty for the coming year is enhanced as well.

Many of the references in *Tanach* to "this day" (הַיּוֹם) can be seen as allusions to the renewal which occurs on Rosh Hashanah. For example, in the *Shema* we speak of the *mitzvos* אֲשֶׁר אָנֹכִי מְצַוְּךָ הַיּוֹם (*Devarim* 6:6), *that I command you* **today.** On this extraordinary day Hashem commands us anew to observe Torah and its *mitzvos*. Similarly a verse we recite in the *Kabbalas Shabbos* service is really an eloquent plea from Hashem: הַיּוֹם אִם בְּקֹלוֹ תִשְׁמָעוּ, *Even* **today,** *if we but heed His call!*[2] — renew your bond to Me today on Rosh Hashanah, just as I renew for you My Torah and *mitzvos*.

The Sages relate (*Sanhedrin* 98a) that when the prophet Elijah was asked once when *Mashiach* would arrive, he answered by citing this verse: *Even today, if you but listen to My voice.* If, as we said above, this verse is intended as an allusion to Rosh Hashanah, then the Sages' story provides additional support for the Sages' dictum that Tishrei, the month in which Rosh Hashanah falls, is the most propitious time for the redemption.[3] The very phrase, *Today, if you but listen to My voice*, gives credence to this notion. By listening to Hashem's voice on this most special day — by heeding the *shofar's* call to repent and return to Hashem — we can accelerate the arrival of *Mashiach.* (5639)

---

1. Cf. *Rashi* on 11:13 s.v. מצוה.
2. *Tehillim* 95:7.
3. Cf. Rabbi Eliezer's opinion in *Rosh Hashanah* 11a.

✎§ Removal of Man's Free Will

עניין אמרו לפני מלכיות שתמליכוני הוא כי באמת קודם חטא
האדם לא הי' הבחירה. והי' מבורר מלכות שמים בעולם. ורק ע''י
עץ הדעת טו''ר ניתן הבחירה לאדם. וכשבנ''י מקבלין בשלימות
מלכותו ית' יכולין לצאת מזה ולהנטל מהם הבחירה

One of the most potent effects of our recitation of the Verses of
Sovereignty on this day, and of our acceptance of Hashem's
Sovereignty of our own free will, is the voluntary renunciation of our
ability to exercise that free will. After all, is it not primarily the wicked,
who seek only to gratify their base desires rather than to do Hashem's
bidding, who crave free will? For us, however, since our sole desire is to
fulfill Hashem's commands, our fondest dream is only to lose the ability
to make decisions on our own. We would like the universe to be restored
to the pristine purity which prevailed before Adam's sin, when Adam
and Eve were totally incapable of doing wrong and were therefore able
to perceive Hashem's Presence and to accept His Sovereignty with total
clarity.

Alas, when they partook of the Tree of Knowledge of Good and Evil,
the primeval parents of all life were confronted with the ability to sin,
for the first time in the history of the world. By praying on Rosh
Hashanah for Hashem's Sovereignty to be restored and acknowledged
in the world, we are in effect pleading for mankind to be returned to
that blessed time before the First Sin, when all of humanity accepted
Hashem's Will with the same total submission as any of His other
creations.[1] This is the intention of the Gemara שֶׁתַּמְלִיכוּנִי עֲלֵיכֶם: By
coronating Me, you are bringing the universe full circle, to its status
before Adam's sin when Hashem's Sovereignty was accepted by all.

(5647)

(See our discussion of the prayer וּבְכֵן תֵּן פַּחְדְּךָ.)

---

1. As a sidelight, we will note that there exists a precedent for the viability of prayers to
negate free will in the successful plea of the Men of the Great Assembly to eradicate the
Jewish people's craving to worship idols (cf. *Sanhedrin* 64a).

⋖§ Dedicating Our First Speech to Hashem

בר״ה נברא אדם. ועיקר מעלת האדם שהוא מדבר. ולכן בתחלה
צריכין לשעבד הקול והדיבור לשמים. והוא קול שופר. ופסוקי
מלכיות זכרונות שופרות.

On Rosh Hashanah we celebrate not only the original creation of man, but also our own spiritual revival. Given that man's uniqueness lies in his power of speech, it is entirely appropriate that each year on the anniversary of our creation and the celebration of our renewal we should rededicate our unique gift of speech to Hashem. This we accomplish through the sound of the *shofar,* as well as by reciting the Verses of Sovereignty, Remembrance and *Shofar*-sounding. Just as the first thing we teach a small child when he begins to speak is the words of Torah (cf. *Succah* 42a), so too our first speech of the year should be dedicated to Hashem in these prayers.   (5647)

⋖§ The Significance and Symbolism of Malchiyos, Zichronos and Shofaros

מלכיות זכרונות שופרות לאחוז בדרכי האבות. מלכיות בחי׳
אברהם . . . זכרונות בחי׳ יצחק . . ושופרות בחי׳ יעקב

One of the primary purposes of reciting the Verses of Sovereignty, Remembrance and *Shofar*-sounding is to inspire us to emulate the lifestyles of the Patriarchs. The Verses of Sovereignty (*Malchiyos*) remind us of Avraham, who was the first to proclaim Hashem's Sovereignty to humanity. By invoking his merit, we are only following the precedent set by the prophet Daniel's entreaty that the *Beis HaMikdash* be rebuilt: וְהָאֵר פָּנֶיךָ עַל מִקְדָּשְׁךָ הַשָּׁמֵם לְמַעַן אֲדֹנָי, *Let Your countenance shine upon Your desolate Sanctuary for my Lord's sake* (9:17). The Sages (*Berachos* 7b) saw these words as an allusion to Avraham, who was the first to proclaim the sovereignty of "my Lord."

The Verses of Remembrance (*Zichronos*) serve to "remind" Hashem of Yitzchak, who was willing to offer his very life for the God he loved. This near sacrifice has never been forgotten, as we see from the Midrash's (*Yalkut Vayikra* 675) depiction of his ashes piled upon the altar before Hashem as a perpetual source of merit for Israel. We pray that in the merit of Yitzchak, who did not lose sight of Hashem for even an instant, Hashem will remember him and his descendants. We too should make an effort to emulate the Patriarch and constantly remember Hashem, confident that in Yitzchak's merit, Hashem will remember us for good — on Rosh Hashanah.

Finally, the term *Shofaros* can be understood in terms of the related word שׁוּפְרָא (*beauty*) as an allusion to Yaakov, whose features resembled those of Adam (cf. *Bava Basra* 58a), who was created directly by Hashem to be the most beautiful mortal that ever lived. In order to invoke the merit of Yaakov, whose life was characterized by unceasing Torah study, we must also return to the Torah on Rosh Hashanah. No better vehicle exists to accomplish this goal than the *shofar* which reminds us — and Hashem — of the Giving of the Torah.

(5662)

⊷§ Dedicating Every Aspect of Our Lives

עול מלכות שמים . והיא למסור נפשו בג' עבירות ע"ז ג"ע וש"ד.
והם בחי' בכל לבבך נפשך מאודך.

These three topics we recall before Hashem also correspond to the three ways in which we commit ourselves to serve Him each day in the *Shema* — *with all your heart, with all your soul and with all your resources.* These in turn can be correlated to the three cardinal sins we are forbidden to commit, even at the cost of our lives.

Specifically, acceptance of Hashem's Sovereignty is the best counterweight to *avodah zarah* (literally "strange service"), which in its broadest sense refers to any desires or motivations for any end result apart from Hashem's service. By renouncing even the thought of serving anything other than Hashem (which would be tantamount to actually paying homage to idols), we fulfill the commandment to love Hashem *with all your heart.*

By extending the parallel between בְּכָל לְבָבְךָ and עֲבוֹדָה זָרָה, we arrive at an expanded definition of עֲבוֹדָה זָרָה, not merely idolatry but also any behavior that is inappropriate for someone of such stature. The greater one's עֲבוֹדָה שֶׁבַּלֵב (his capacity to serve Hashem not only by performing *mitzvos* but also in the realm of thought), the more that is expected of such an individual. Failure to fulfill such expectations is truly a form of עֲבוֹדָה זָרָה.

The Verses of Remembrance reflect the natural awe of the Jewish soul as its stands before Hashem on this Day of Judgment, the epitome of serving Hashem *with all your soul*. This in turn corresponds to the sin of prohibited relations, which erodes the very foundation of the soul.

Finally, by demonstrating our willingness to dedicate *all our resources* to do Hashem's bidding, we in a sense "inoculate" ourselves against the mortal sin of murder, which is usually motivated by jealousy and greed. If we can truly recognize that all our resources, any possessions and talents we might possibly have, are given to us by Hashem for the purpose of fulfilling His will, then we become a truly integral part of the Jewish people. In turn, we will surely be protected from jealousy, which is the root cause of murder, and will never even come to think of committing murder or any of its equivalents, such as anger, arrogance or humiliating others in public.

⋘ Ten Statements, Ten Plagues and Ten Commandments

עשר מכות ונסים במצרים ועשרת הדברות הכל אחד. ונראה שזה מלכיות זכרונות שופרות. וזהו עצמו תקיעה ש״ת תקיעה.

W e can also draw a correspondence between each of the ten verses of *Malchiyos*, *Zichronos* and *Shofaros* and three seminal historical events, each of which had a tenfold nature: the Ten Utterances with which the universe was created, the Ten Plagues inflicted upon the Egyptians, and the Ten Commandments.

The Verses of Sovereignty, which emphasize universal acceptance of Hashem's rulership, remind us that the sole purpose of Creation was to make it possible for the creatures to recognize and serve their King.

While all of Hashem's creations implicitly acknowledge His sovereignty by loyally performing their respective missions with total loyalty, we have been charged with the unique mission of recognizing and publicizing Hashem's often imperceptible role in the seeming void of the material world we occupy.

Never have we performed this mission more splendidly than during the dark days of Egyptian servitude, when we remembered Hashem amidst the darkness and cried out to be remembered by Him. In reward for our remembrance, He unleashed His fury in the form of the Ten Plagues — and we in turn continue to express our gratitude to Him each year on Rosh Hashanah by reciting the ten Verses of Remembrance.

Finally the ten Verses of *Shofar*-blasts, which open by mentioning the Divine Revelation that occurred at Sinai, reveal a clear and unequivocal awareness of Hashem's Presence to a degree which could never have been attained at the time of the Ten Utterances of Creation, nor even during the unfolding of the Ten Plagues. It was only at Sinai — after having seen Hashem's Presence even in the midst of our searing catharsis in Egypt — that we merited to perceive Hashem "face-to-face."

This intimate spiritual unification we achieved with the Creator, when He opened the Ten Commandments with the pronouncement *I am HASHEM, your God,* is beautifully and succinctly captured by the first words of the *Shofar*-blasts section: אַתָּה נִגְלֵיתָ, *You revealed Yourself.* Such a revelation of unsurpassed power and clarity — which we celebrate in the Verses of *Shofaros* — was the fitting finale of a process which began with the Ten Utterances and continued through the Ten Plagues.

⋖§ Parallels with The Patriarchs

Earlier we drew parallels between the Patriarchs and the concepts of Sovereignty, Remembrance and *Shofar*-blasts. Now we can expand on the role of the Patriarchs in light of the historical context we have just given for these three sequences of readings. Avraham was the first to proclaim that if there exists a world, there must also exist a Creator Who brought the world into being corresponding to the concept of the Ten Utterances.

Yitzchak, who showed himself to be so totally prepared to do Hashem's bidding that he was even willing to sacrifice his life on the Altar, taught his descendants that the only way to survive in exile (not just in the exile of Egypt but in all subsequent exiles as well) is to subordinate our desires and aspirations totally to Hashem's will. Only by doing so can we have the right to witness the downfall of our enemies, just as our ancestors witnessed the affliction and eventual destruction of their Egyptian oppressors with the Ten Plagues.

Finally Yaakov, who combined the virtues of his progenitors and devoted himself totally to studying and upholding the Torah, embodied the perfection and clarity attained by his descendants when Hashem revealed Himself at Mount Sinai and bestowed the Ten Commandments on His people. (adapted from 5633)

⊰§ Restoration of the Divine Spark

וי״ל אלו אלו הב׳ הם מלכיות וזכרונות כי מקודם צריך האדם לקבל הנקודה זו שבא מחדש בכל ר״ה ועשי״ת וקבלה זו נק׳ מלכיות שתמליכוני עליכם . . . וכמו שיוצא החיות מהקב״ה לאדם נקודה בלולה מכל כן נתעורר גם באדם פנימיות החיות שבו שנק׳ זכרון לקבל הנקודה הזו

To appreciate the relationship between *Malchiyos* and *Zichronos* on a more profound level, let us return to the creation of man on that first Rosh Hashanah. Although his body originated in the earth, it was only after he was infused with a Divine soul that Adam became a viable person, as the Torah relates, וַיִּפַּח בְּאַפָּיו נִשְׁמַת חַיִּים וַיְהִי הָאָדָם לְנֶפֶשׁ חַיָּה, *And He blew into his nostrils the soul of life* (*Bereishis* 2:7).

According to tradition, this spark is revitalized every year on Rosh Hashanah. In this light, the fact that Yosef's release by Pharaoh from his twelve-year imprisonment took place on Rosh Hashanah can be seen as an allusion to the liberation of our Divine soul on Rosh Hashanah from the physical passions that enslave it the rest of the year. This spark is referred to by the name *Yoseif*[1] which means to add (cf. *Bereishis* 30:24)

---

1. Cf. *Tehillim* 81:6: עֵדוּת בִּיהוֹסֵף שָׂמוֹ בְּצֵאתוֹ עַל אֶרֶץ מִצְרָיִם, *He set it for a testimony to Yoseif when he went out over the land of Egypt.*

because of our intense desire that its influence on our personalities —
and even on our bodies — be increased on this day.

In a similar vein, the *Arizal*[1] interpreted the prayer, הַיּוֹם הֲרַת עוֹלָם,
*today is the **conception** of the world,*[2] as a reference to the renewal of
the inner spark which is embedded deeply in the Jewish soul, much as
a fetus is embedded in its mother's womb.

The Verses of Sovereignty express the fervent wish we discussed at
the beginning of this essay, שֶׁתַּמְלִיכוּנִי עֲלֵיכֶם, *in order for you to make
Me your King*, not just to make Hashem our King but also that we be
privileged to dedicate all our forces, and in particular the Divine spark
which has just been revitalized within us, solely to the magnification of
Hashem's honor in the world, rather than to our selfish or material
purposes. This is also the point of the prayer we say every day, בָּרוּךְ
אֱלֹהֵינוּ שֶׁבְּרָאָנוּ לִכְבוֹדוֹ, *Blessed is He our God, Who created us for His
Glory* — to remind ourselves that everything we have, and our very
existence, was given to us for the sole purpose of furthering Hashem's
glory in the world.

The Verses of Remembrance describe the rewards we can reap for
fulfilling the lofty ideals we have just voiced in the Verses of
Sovereignty. In reward for dedicating our renewed Divine spark to the
supreme goal of publicizing Hashem's Sovereignty, Hashem brings to
the surface the innate potential which has lain latent for years in the
Jewish soul. Just as we seek out Hashem to dedicate our "gifts" to Him,
He also "reaches out" to us, lifting our souls from the abyss. Similarly,
Shlomo *HaMelech* describes the prisoner that greets the monarch (מִבֵּית
הָסוּרִים יָצָא לִמְלֹךְ) (*Koheles* 4:14) alluding to the human potential long
imprisoned with the soul, on the day of the king's coronation, Rosh
Hashanah.

The Verses of *Shofaros* represent the culmination of the development
of the emerging potential of the Jewish soul. In this, the final phase of
the process, the soul comes to the full flourishing that was achieved at
the Giving of the Torah to the accompaniment of the sound of the
shofar on Mount Sinai   (*Likutim*)

---

1. A saintly mystical scholar who lived in Safed approximately four hundred years ago.

2. This prayer is recited in the silent *Amidah* of *Mussaf* after the Verses of Sovereignty,
Remembrance and *Shofar*-blasts.

✑ Release of a Jew's Inner Devotion

ע״י קבלת מלכותו ית״ש נפדין בנ״י . . . תרועה היא הרצון . . . .
והוא מתגלה בפועל בזה היום.

By reciting the Verses of Sovereignty, not only do we accept Hashem's rulership but also, in return for having shown our loyalty as faithful subjects of the Monarch, we actually become His servants. As such, we are privileged to experience the most precious benefit of being servants of the King — the emergence and fulfillment of our intense, long-hidden inner desire to serve Hashem. As the Psalmist sings: פּוֹדֶה ה' נֶפֶשׁ עֲבָדָיו, *Hashem redeems the soul of His servants (Tehillim 34:23)* — Hashem reawakens the intense desire of His servants to serve Him, a desire which has lain so long hidden deep in their souls. As Hashem says, *Recite before Me Verses of Sovereignty so that your memory* — the deep-seated will of every Jew to serve Me — *may surface in My Presence* to be a source of merit.

In this light we can suggest a new interpretation of another renowned verse read in the *Maftir* of Rosh Hashanah: יוֹם תְּרוּעָה יִהְיֶה לָכֶם *(Bamidbar 29:1).* While normally translated *It shall be a day of shofar-sounding for you,* this phrase can also be understood according to a variant meaning of the word תְּרוּעָה as related to the word רָצוֹן, *will: It shall be a day of desire for you.* It is only after proclaiming Hashem's Sovereignty on Rosh Hashanah that the Jew's intense inner desire to serve Hashem comes to the forefront.

(5659)

✑ Does Hashem Forget?

כי הנה בהש״י נאמר אין שכחה לפני כסא כבודך ומה הבקשה על
זכרונות. אך כי לפי דבקות האדם כן יוכל להיות נזכר לפניו

One final question remains: Throughout the Prayer of Remembrance we plead for Hashem to remember us. Why, however, do we need to make such requests since, in the midst of that prayer itself, we say, "there is no forgetfulness before Your Throne of Glory"? What need is there to remind Hashem, Who never forgets anything?

The key to answering this question may lie in distinguishing between two different ways in which Hashem remembers us. The first is mere awareness of our actions, which is not so much remembrance as the simple absence of forgetting. It is of this kind of remembrance that we say, "There is no forgetfulness before Your Throne of Glory, and nothing is hidden from before Your eyes."

The second way, on the other hand, involves a positive remembrance of our merits, of the spark of Divinity within us, in order to bestow kindness and mercy on us for it. It is this remembrance for which we plead: "Remember us with a favorable remembrance before You, recall us with a recollection of salvation and mercy." In this sense it is possible to be effectively forgotten, to be practically deceased while still physically alive.[1]

Above we defined the life we pray for on Rosh Hashanah as the renewal of the Divine spark within us. In this sense, the wicked, who deny this spark and do not seek to be close to Hashem, are deemed to be forgotten because they have detached themselves from the source of life. Only through attaching the very core of the soul to its heavenly roots is it possible to remember, and be remembered by, Hashem.

It is appropriate that the Prayers of Remembrance, which call for the the soul to be reattached to its Creator, are followed by Prayers of *Shofar*-sounding, which recall and invoke the merit of the convocation on Mount Sinai. Never was there a moment of greater intimacy and closeness between the Jewish soul and its Creator than at the Giving of the Torah, which the Torah describes with the words, פָּנִים בְּפָנִים דִּבֶּר, *face-to-face* HASHEM *spoke with you* (*Devarim* 5:4).

The *shofar* itself, which consists of wordless sounds as we said above, is the ideal vehicle to express our inner attachment to Hashem. Although words are usually necessary for communication and even for prayer, sometimes they only hinder our attempts to express our innermost feelings. The *shofar* reminds Hashem of the latent inner feelings of the Jew — feelings which are too genuine and too deeply felt to be expressed in words (*Likutim* ר״ה זכרונות).

עָלֵינוּ לְשַׁבֵּחַ . . . לְהַעֲבִיר גִּלּוּלִים מִן הָאָרֶץ . . . לְתַקֵּן עוֹלָם בְּמַלְכוּת שַׁדַּי

It is our duty to praise ... to remove detestable idolatry

---

1. Cf. the Sages' saying *Berachos* 18b to the effect that the wicked are considered as if dead even though they are still alive.

from the earth ... to perfect the universe through the Almighty's sovereignty.

ובכח זה אנו שבין בתשובה על החטא שהשארנו מהם עכו"ז
מעוררין ג"כ זכות מחשבה טובה ראשונה שהי' לנו להעביר
גלולים

This passage, which introduces the *Malchiyos* segment, is said to have been composed by Yehoshua bin Nun as he led the Jews into *Eretz Yisrael*. In these words, we voice our grand eternal dream of eliminating idolatry from the face of Hashem's holy land.

Tragically this goal has never yet been realized, and it was precisely because we tolerated paganism in the territory under our control that we have been required to endure such a lengthy exile in atonement for this critical error. Therefore, dispersed as we are throughout the world, we plead for the non-Jewish nations to unite to serve Hashem so that our exile can end, as we say, וְיֵעָשׂוּ כֻלָּם אֲגֻדָּה אֶחָת, *Let them all become a single society.*

Recalling Yehoshua's grand design in this prayer accomplishes two purposes: First, by praying for mankind's salvation, we demonstrate that we have finally in our exile rectified the sins of our ancestors, who forfeited the opportunity to convert their homeland — and the whole world as well — into a bastion of faith in Hashem. Instead, we pray that all mankind, even the non-Jewish nations that currently dominate us, should accept Hashem's sovereignty.

Secondly, apart from recalling our ancestors' errors, our pleas also invoke their many merits. Although they failed to implement their grand dream of a pure land, their very desire to eliminate paganism, the fact that they even had such a dream, is by itself a source of merit to us on this Day of Judgment. So also is our faith that however long this dream may be forestalled, eventually — at the time of the Great Redemption — it will finally be realized.

(5644)

שֶׁלֹּא עָשָׂנוּ כְּגוֹיֵי הָאֲרָצוֹת וְלֹא שָׂמָנוּ כְּמִשְׁפְּחוֹת הָאֲדָמָה שֶׁלֹּא שָׂם
חֶלְקֵנוּ כָּהֶם וְגוֹרָלֵנוּ כְּכָל הֲמוֹנָם

For He has not made us like the nations of the lands, and has not emplaced us like the families of the earth; for He has not assigned our portion like theirs nor our lot like all their multitudes.

The liturgist uses these four expressions to emphasize our distinctiveness from the Gentile world in every respect. They in turn correspond to four aspects of the Jewish personality — the body and the three parts of the soul, *nefesh*, *ruach* and *neshamah* — each of which takes a unique form in a Jew which is clearly distinct from those of the rest of mankind.[1] (5650)

כִּי הַמַּלְכוּת שֶׁלְךָ הִיא וּלְעוֹלְמֵי עַד תִּמְלוֹךְ

For the Kingdom is Yours and You will reign for all eternity.

שגם קבלת מלכות שמים אינו בכח המקבלים רק הכל שלך

While the phrase, *For the Kingdom is Yours*, seems on the surface redundant, we may suggest that its true message is that even our ability to make Hashem into our King is itself a gift from Him. Although we sometimes feel that we have the capacity to proclaim Hashem's Sovereignty over ourselves as an independent power, really such a formidable mission would be totally impossible without Hashem's help.

This unique ability to coronate Hashem was first acquired at the moment He proclaimed to us, *I am Hashem, Your God*. By making ourselves into loyal subjects at that time, we acquired the ability to proclaim His Kingdom. But we did not receive this as a simple gift; our ancestors had previously earned the right to proclaim Hashem's Sovereignty when they took the initiative to announce at the Red Sea, ה׳ יִמְלוֹךְ לְעוֹלָם וָעֶד, *Hashem will reign for ever and ever*.

Once we have asserted on our own that Hashem grants the ability to proclaim His Kingdom to those who are worthy (as we say כִּי הַמַּלְכוּת שֶׁלְךָ הִיא, *For the Kingdom is Yours*), we conclude by pleading for Him to reveal His Majesty to all of mankind — וּלְעוֹלְמֵי עַד תִּמְלוֹךְ, *And You will reign for all eternity*.[2] (5661)

---

1. The Four Kingdoms which have always opposed the Jewish people — Egypt, Persia, Greece, and Rome — may also correspond to the four levels of the Jewish personality. In this conception, each of these tyrannies seeks to thwart a particular aspect of the Jew from reaching his potential.

2. For a similar thought, see our comments in the *Sfas Emes Haggadah* page 230 on the phrase לְךָ כִּי לְךָ, *Yours, for it is Yours*.

לֹא הִבִּיט אָוֶן בְּיַעֲקֹב וְלֹא רָאָה עָמָל בְּיִשְׂרָאֵל ה׳ אֱלֹהָיו עִמּוֹ וּתְרוּעַת
מֶלֶךְ בּוֹ

*He perceived no iniquity in Yaakov, and saw no perversity in Israel. H*ASHEM *his God is with him, and the friendship of the King is in him.*

כי באמת בנ׳׳י חפצים לקבל עול מלכות שמים ורחמנא לבא בעי
. . . אבל בנ׳׳י עושין כל תחבולות לקבל עליהם שעבוד מלכות
שמים.

The concluding phrase of this verse, which we say as part of the *Malchiyos* prayer, seems to explain its opening words. Unlike other mortals, who attempt to evade serving their rulers, Israel avidly desires to accept Hashem's Sovereignty upon itself, as the Torah says, וּתְרוּעַת מֶלֶךְ בּוֹ,[1] in reward for which Hashem overlooks our sins. Although we sometimes fall prey to the *yetzer hara* and do not succeed fully in our sacred mission of coronating Hashem, He in His mercy focuses on the contents of our hearts (as the Sages said, רַחֲמָנָא לִבָּא בָּעֵי, *Sanhedrin* 106b, H*ASHEM* *desires people's hearts*), and the desire of the Jewish heart to serve Hashem never slackens, however far one may stray from the observance of Torah and *mitzvos*. Thus the Torah proclaims, וּתְרוּעַת מֶלֶךְ בּוֹ: The wish — the inner longing of the Jewish heart — remains firm in its desire to accept Hashem's Sovereignty.

The Sages observe (*Bereishis Rabbah* 63:1) that when parents see their child deeply immersed in Torah, they are filled with compassion for him. Likewise, when Hashem sees how much Israel toils to comprehend every aspect of His Torah, He has compassion on us and overlooks our faults.

(5665)

פרש׳׳י הרצון של המלך הוא בהם . . . דכל מה שברא הקב׳׳ה
לכבודו ברא וזה ע׳׳י בני ישראל

Alternatively, the phrase וּתְרוּעַת מֶלֶךְ בּוֹ can be understood to mean that Hashem's desire is focused on Israel. To understand the implications of this, let us note the Sages' assertion (*Avos* 6:11) that everything

---

1. Cf. *Rashi*, who interprets תְּרוּעָה here as an expression of love and friendship, from the word רֵעוּת, *loving companionship*.

Hashem created in this world was intended for His Glory. Since, however, only Israel acknowledges its Creator, the entirety of creation is justified only by our eventual emergence onto the stage of world history.

Thus we read, וּתְרוּעַת מֶלֶךְ בּוֹ, HASHEM's Will [in creating the universe] is in him, in Israel's emergence. This is why before creating man Hashem consulted with the souls of the righteous (*Bereishis Rabbah* 8:6) since they are the ones who justify the universe's existence.   (5646)

שיש להם דעת להבין פנימיות הרצון

In closing we can suggest that the phrase וּתְרוּעַת מֶלֶךְ בּוֹ alludes to the intimate relationship which exists between Hashem and the Jewish people. *The King's desire is in him* — amongst mankind Israel alone possesses the ability to consistently perceive Hashem's wishes and desires. (This theme is developed further in the essay on freedom).   (5652)

כִּי מִדֵּי דַבְּרִי בּוֹ זָכֹר אֶזְכְּרֶנּוּ עוֹד

For whenever I speak of him I remember him more and more (Yirmiyahu 31:19).

ובפסוק זה נכלל מלכיות זכרונות שופרות דברי בו בח'
מלכות . . . זכור אזכרנו עוד זכרונות רחם ארחמנו הוא שופרות

Although this verse is placed at the end of the *Zichronos* section, it contains allusions to all of the three additional prayers of the Rosh Hashanah *Mussaf*. Firstly, מִדֵּי דַבְּרִי בּוֹ, *whenever I speak of him*, recalls Hashem's coronation as King, since there can surely be no greater manifestation of Hashem's Sovereignty — and of our acceptance of His will — than the fact that He reveals Himself directly to us. Then זָכֹר אֶזְכְּרֶנּוּ, *I remember him more and more*, relates clearly to the central theme of *Zichronos*, Hashem's remembrance of Israel on Rosh Hashanah. Finally רַחֵם אֲרַחֲמֶנּוּ, *I will surely take pity on him*, alludes to the *shofar*-blasts, which recall the voice of Yaakov (as we discuss extensively in our essay on the *shofar*) and arouse Hashem to have pity on us and spare us.   (5648)

וְכָל הָעָם רֹאִים אֶת הַקּוֹלֹת

And the entire people saw the sounds.

Chiddushei HaRim offers a homiletical interpretation of this verse, the first of the ten Verses of *Shofar-b*lasts. The entire people "saw" Hashem (i.e. attained a new level of perceiving His greatness) through the sounds they heard proclaiming, אָנֹכִי ה׳ אֱלֹהֶיךָ, *I am HASHEM, your God*. While the Jews had always retained their faith in Hashem, at Mount Sinai they achieved a new awareness of His Presence and Power which filled every fiber of their being.[1] (See also our commentary on *Shofaros* for a similar interpretation of the phrase אַתָּה נִגְלֵיתָ, *You were revealed*.)

On Rosh Hashanah the entire Jewish nation passes before Hashem[2] in judgment, to the accompaniment of the eternally powerful voice of the *shofar*. Just as Hashem's *shofar*-blasts that we heard at Mount Sinai stimulated an intuitive awareness of His Presence, so also when Hashem hears our *shofar*-blasts on Rosh Hashanah, He feels an intuitive closeness of us, His people.

(5652)

פִּיּוּטִים / Additional Tefillos

וְכָל בָּאֵי עוֹלָם יַעַבְרוּן לְפָנֶיךָ כִּבְנֵי מָרוֹן
All mankind will pass before You like members of the flock.

The phrase וְכָל בָּאֵי עוֹלָם in this segment is to be interpreted in its most literal sense, to say that not only humanity but *all* of Hashem's creations pass before Him on this Judgment Day.

---

1. This intuitive feel (in Hebrew, טְבִיעַת עָיִן) for the truth has *halachic* significance as well since, for example, a blind person is assumed to be capable of recognizing his wife by her voice; cf. *Chullin* 96a.

2. In this interpretation the word רוֹאִים, *seeing*, is to be read as מִתְרָאִים, *appearing*.

To appreciate the implications of this, let us return to the creation of man. Coming into the world at the culmination of the world's first six days, man was almost immediately given the daunting task of giving names to all of Hashem's other creatures (cf. *Bereishis* 2:19). In charging Adam with this mission, Hashem was in effect entrusting him with the fulfillment of His plan for all forms of life, making him a steward to implement His directives concerning the lower life-forms.

This formidable mission is implied by the unusual instruction Adam was given, to *see* all of Hashem's creations (וַיָּבֵא אֶל הָאָדָם לִרְאוֹת, *He brought them to the man **to see**)* before assigning them names. Why was Adam directed specifically to *look* at the lower forms of life? In light of our earlier interpretation, we can say that Hashem wanted to use Adam as His intermediary to see that His plans for all the many forms of life He had created would be realized.

The centrality of man's role in implementing the Divine blueprint may explain why Hashem could proclaim full satisfaction with His handiwork — וְהִנֵּה טוֹב מְאֹד, *Behold, it was very good!* — only after Adam had been created. Only then could He "look back" on His creations (as the Torah says, וַיַּרְא אֱלֹהִים אֶת כָּל אֲשֶׁר עָשָׂה, *God saw all that He had made*) in the knowledge that man would be the central instrument in implementing His Plan for them and say, וְהִנֵּה טוֹב מְאֹד. Indeed, the word מְאֹד, *very*, contains the exact same letters as אָדָם, *man*, the apex of all creation who embodies in complete form faculties and abilities which other life-forms attain only partially.

On this the annual anniversary of the Creation, then, all Hashem's creations, — Jews, Gentiles, and all the lower life-forms — are given new life and strength from Hashem, but without the need to appear directly before Him in judgment, for man — and especially the Jewish people who uniquely deserve the title "Man"[1] — acts as their agent. As the Sages said, וְכֻלָּם נִסְקָרִין בִּסְקִירָה אַחַת, (*Rosh Hashanah* 18a) *All of Hashem's creations are scrutinized in one glance.* Hashem can evaluate all His creatures and determine their fate using man as His standard of judgment. (5641)

וּתְשׁוּבָה וּתְפִלָּה וּצְדָקָה מַעֲבִירִין אֶת רֹעַ הַגְּזֵרָה

But repentance, prayer and charity remove the evil of the decree!

---

1. Cf. *Yevamos* 61a, אַתֶּם קְרוּיִין אָדָם וְאֵין אֻמּוֹת הָעוֹלָם קְרוּיִין אָדָם, *You [Israel] are called man but the other nations are not called man.*

The Midrash points out that while the gates of prayer may be closed some of the time, the gates of repentance always remain open. The difference may be caused by the fact that prayer involves pleas for individual needs, so that if the petitioner is found to be undeserving, his unrectified sins will actually prevent his request from being granted. In this vein the prophet Yeshayahu writes, עֲוֹנֹתֵיכֶם הָיוּ מַבְדִּלִים בֵּינֵכֶם לְבֵין אֱלֹהֵיכֶם, *Your iniquities separate you from your God* (59:2).

Repentance, on the other hand, is far more fundamental in scope, involving as it does the total subordination of the personality to Hashem's Will. When a person achieves such a complete return and commitment to Hashem, all the barriers are dismantled. Thus any time one sincerely desires to return to Hashem, he will find the gates of repentance are open for him. (*Shabbos Teshuvah 5652*)

הַפּוֹתֵחַ שַׁעַר לְדוֹפְקֵי בִתְשׁוּבָה
Who opens a gate to those who knock in repentance.

This phrase from the *piyut* וְכֹל מַאֲמִינִים arouses several questions. In the previous section we said that the gates of repentance are always open. Why, then, is it necessary to knock on the gates of *teshuvah*?

We may suggest, however, that the gate alluded to here is the same one which was described by the prophet Yechezkel (46:1), שַׁעַר הֶחָצֵר הַפְּנִימִית הַפֹּנֶה קָדִים, *The gate of the inner courtyard that faces eastward*, i.e. the innermost and holiest gate of the *Beis HaMikdash*. To the true penitent, Hashem opens even that gate, which the prophet describes as being closed during the week.

How can someone merit to have even the innermost sanctum be opened before him, to receive an answer to his knocking on that holiest of gates? This can come only through total self-negation, through the realization that genuine *teshuvah* involves far more than simply regretting past mistakes and sins, that *teshuvah* requires making a fresh start in life and becoming a totally new person. Just as תֹהוּ וָבֹהוּ... וְחֹשֶׁךְ, the *chaos, emptiness ... and darkness*, which existed at the time of creation were necessary prerequisites for the magnificent light Hashem created on the first day (יְהִי אוֹר, *Let there be light*), so too are total self-negation and a feeling of worthlessness essential requirements for the light of *teshuvah* to prevail.

(Indeed, we can find an allusion to these prerequisites in the word תְּשׁוּבָה itself, which contains the *tav* of תֹהוּ, the *beis* and *hei* of בֹהוּ, and the *shin* of חֹשֶׁךְ.)

If we can totally break down our all-consuming absorption with pride and ego, Hashem will open the gates of *teshuvah* for us. Especially on *Shabbos Teshuvah*, our sincere and determined *teshuvah* can have this power, as the prophet concludes: יִהְיֶה סָגוּר שֵׁשֶׁת יְמֵי הַמַּעֲשֶׂה וּבְיוֹם הַשַּׁבָּת יִפָּתֵחַ, *They shall be closed during the six days of labor, but on the Sabbath day it shall be opened.* (Shabbos Teshuvah 5635)

פותת שַׁעַר לדופקי בתשובה כי הם אבות

The term דּוֹפְקֵי בִּתְשׁוּבָה may also allude to the Patriarchs, who pleaded constantly with Hashem to forgive the wicked. In their merit (and especially if we follow in their ways), may we also be privileged to have our knocking on the gates of repentance answered.

(Shabbos Teshuvah 5636)

א׳׳כ זהו עיקר חשובה כשיהיו ישראל מתוקנים להשווות לבותם ללב האבות

To elaborate on this theme, it can be contended that true *teshuvah* can only be achieved when Israel is able to reach the high levels once attained by the Patriarchs. These bearers of the Divine Presence on earth[1] set for us, their descendants, a high standard of clinging to Hashem by emulating His ways. The prophet Malachi has bequeathed to us a renowned vision of the return of the prophet Elijah (*Malachi* 3:24): וְהֵשִׁיב לֵב אָבוֹת עַל בָּנִים, *He will restore the hearts of the fathers to the children* — only when the hearts of the Jewish people are reunited

---

1. Cf. *Rashi Bereishis* 17:22 s.v. מעל who described the Patriarchs as a מֶרְכָּבָה, a *vehicle* to bear Hashem's greatness in the world.

with those of their ancestors, when we can again go in the ways of Hashem with pure and joyous hearts as our holy fathers did, will we be able to achieve true *teshuvah*.

Perhaps these insights can help us answer an intriguing question. If, as the Sages said (*Shabbos* 55a), the merit of our ancestors has finally been exhausted over the millennia, why do we constantly call upon this merit in our prayers, both the daily ones and those of Rosh Hashanah?

In light of the above, however, we can say quite simply that even if the merit of the fathers has been depleted over the generations, it can still be revived through *teshuvah*. Although the sins of past generations may have extinguished the great light first kindled by our ancestors, our sincere *teshuvah* unquestionably has the power to re-ignite it.

(*Shabbos Teshuvah* 5652)

ועי"י הדפיקה הקב"ה פותח להם שער בשבת

But in truth, every Jew is constantly knocking on the gates of *teshuvah*, as the wise Shlomo *HaMelech* extols, אַשְׁרֵי אָדָם שֹׁמֵעַ לִי לִשְׁקֹד עַל דַּלְתֹתַי יוֹם יוֹם, *Happy is a man that listens to Me, to stand by My doors day after day* (*Mishlei* 8:34).

As we repent day after day, week after week, are we not knocking on the closed gates, eagerly seeking to penetrate inward, to dismantle any and all barriers to our *teshuvah*? The pleas we offer so persistently during the week, our knocking on the gates, will surely be answered on Shabbos, as the prophet Yechezkel promises (46:1), וּבְיוֹם הַשַּׁבָּת יִפָּתֵחַ, *on the Sabbath day [the inner gate of repentance] will be opened.* Thereafter, however, even during the week the gates we first opened on Shabbos with our repentance will remain open.[1]

(*Shabbos Teshuvah* 5637)

והם שערים בנפש . . . שיש חמשים שערי בינה

Perhaps also, the liturgist is referring here to the gates of the Jewish heart, the *Shaarei Binah* — gates of comprehension of Hashem — which can be opened only through *teshuvah*. In this light, the *Zohar* (*Vayeira* 225) interprets a famous verse in *Mishlei* (31:23),

---

1. Please see our essay on *Shabbos Teshuvah* for further discussion of this theme.

נוֹדָע בִּשְׁעָרִים בַּעְלָה, *Distinctive in the councils is her husband*, as a reference to the Fifty Gates of Comprehension which every Jewish heart has the potential to open through repentance, and through them to realize his full potential. *(Shabbos Teshuvah 5653)*

וְכֹל מַאֲמִינִים שֶׁהוּא פְּתוּחָה יָדוֹ

All believe that His hand is open.

ובכל השנה מבקשין פותח את ידך רק היא עולם התשובה . . . אבל ימים אלו שפתח התשובה מתגלה.

This phrase immediately follows our declaration that Hashem *opens a gate to those who knock in repentance*, and seemingly affirms our belief that Hashem's hand is always open to our pleas. If so, however, it seems to contradict an implied request we voice three times each and every day of the year: פּוֹתֵחַ אֶת יָדֶךָ וּמַשְׂבִּיעַ לְכָל חַי רָצוֹן, *Open Your hand and satisfy the desire of every living thing*. How can we in one place assert that Hashem's hand is constantly open and in another request Him to open it?

To resolve this contradiction, we can posit the existence of another universe higher than our own, the pure world of *teshuvah*,[1] in which no repentant's pleas are ever spurned. All year long, we require an intermediate stage between the lofty heights of the world of *teshuvah* and our mundane physical existence, and therefore request Hashem to "open" His hand, to cause his outpouring of abundance to "descend" to our material world.

During the Ten Days of Repentance, however, the gates of repentance remain wide open and the world of *teshuvah* is revealed even to us in the material world. During these days we have no need to request Hashem to "reach out" to us, to extend His hand to our mundane world, but instead need simply to affirm our belief that *His hand is open*. *(Shabbos Shuvah 5648)*

דיתכן לפרש על השבת . . . ובנ״י שהם דופקי בתשובה נותן להם השבת שהיא פותחת שערי תשובה.

---

1. Noteworthy in this context is the Sage's statement (*Pesachim* 54a) that *teshuvah* was one of the creations which existed before the material world came into being.

Alternatively, perhaps the gates of *teshuvah* mentioned here are actually one of Hashem's greatest gifts to Israel — the Sabbath Day itself. The Sabbath, which emanates directly from Hashem's treasure-house,[1] and which is compared to the World to Come, is a powerful "key" to open the gates of *teshuvah*. As the prophet Yechezkel says (46:1), *On the Sabbath day it will be opened*. By knocking on the gates of *teshuvah* and taking the first steps toward repentance, we are granted the Sabbath, the most opportune time for *teshuvah*.

(*Rosh Hashanah 5657*)

◌§ Two Great Shofaros

אִם כְּבָנִים אִם כַּעֲבָדִים

Whether as children [of God] or as servants.

כי השופר רומז לקבלת התורה וזה כבנים. ורומז ג׳׳כ לעבודת
בהמ׳׳ק שהיו שם שופרות

This section, which we recite after the *shofar*-soundings during the repetition of the *Mussaf Shemoneh Esrei*, can be seen as an allusion to two supremely critical phases of Jewish history. The description of Israel as Hashem's children recalls the Giving of the Torah, when we attained the status of children of the King, as Moshe said (*Devarim* 14:1), *You are children to HASHEM, your God*. Afterwards, when we performed the service of the *Beis HaMikdash*, we fulfilled the role of Hashem's loyal servants.

It is particularly appropriate that these allusions are juxtaposed to the *shofar*-sounding, since each of the events they represent was accompanied by the sounding of a *shofar*. As we know, the supernatural sound of the *shofar* (as well as other Heavenly phenomena) formed an awe-inspiring backdrop for the Giving of the Torah. Similarly, the *shofar* was sounded daily in the *Beis HaMikdash* as an integral part of the Divine Service.

Indeed, we can extend this analogy even further by suggesting that the *shofar*-soundings which accompanied the service of the *Beis*

---

1. Cf. *Beitzah* 16a מַתָּנָה טוֹבָה יֵשׁ לִי בְּבֵית גְּנָזַי, *I have a goodly gift in My treasure-house*.

HaMikdash served as a conduit to enable the people to relive each day the overwhelming power of the *shofar* they had first experienced at Mount Sinai.

Alas, no longer can we directly experience either the *shofar* of Sinai or its equivalent in the *Beis HaMikdash*, until Hashem has mercy on His people and restores to us the service of the *Beis HaMikdash*, may it be rebuilt speedily in our days. Nonetheless, once each year, on Rosh Hashanah, we are privileged to recapture a glimmering of the great spiritual light which that sound drew into our world.

In this light, we can suggest still another interpretation of the verse we recite immediately following the first soundings of the *shofar* before *Mussaf*:[1] *Praises to the people who know the teruah; HASHEM, in the light of Your countenance shall they walk* — Praises to the people who know and appreciate this greatest gift it receives from Hashem, the annual "glimpse" of the two great *shofaros* of Jewish history, the *shofar* of Mount Sinai and that of the *Beis HaMikdash*.

(*Rosh Hashanah 5648*)

⋖ Though Children, We Are Yet Servants

וזהו הנוסח שתקנו אם כבנים אם כעבדים . . . כי יש להם בחינת
בנים על כל זה עבדיו הם

A lternatively, recalling the dichotomy between children and servants may be intended to point out Israel's overwhelming humility. Though we are truly Hashem's children, we have no wish to exploit that elevated status, and instead content ourselves with petitioning Hashem humbly, as befits servants, while at the same time realizing that we may not deserve even that distinction. This is indeed the essence of *Malchiyos*, to accept Hashem's sovereignty lovingly, wishing for no more than to be the King's loyal subjects. Hashem, in turn, prides Himself in our humility as the prophet Yeshayahu proclaims (49:3): עַבְדִּי אַתָּה יִשְׂרָאֵל אֲשֶׁר בְּךָ אֶתְפָּאָר, *You are My servant, Israel, in whom I take pride.* (5646)

---

1. *Tehillim* 89:16.

אִם כַּעֲבָדִים עֵינֵינוּ לְךָ תְּלֻיּוֹת

If as servants, our eyes [look toward and] depend upon You.

כן עינינו אל ה׳ ולא נאמר אל יד ה׳ . . . כל עבדיו ושפחות כל
עבודתם בעבור הַפְּרָס אבל אנו עינינו אלה להיות טפלים ודבוקים
בו

This phrase offers another illustration of how our service of Hashem is sincerely altruistic. Not only have we no wish to exploit our unique status as Hashem's children, even in relating to Him as servants we do not serve Him for the sake of the reward He can give us. Instead, we seek nothing more than to cling to Him and to receive only those blessings which He wishes to give us, since He knows far better than we what our needs are and what is good for us.

This attitude is perhaps most eloquently expressed by the Psalmist הִנֵּה כְעֵינֵי עֲבָדִים אֶל יַד אֲדוֹנֵיהֶם כְּעֵינֵי שִׁפְחָה אֶל יַד גְּבִרְתָּהּ; כֵּן עֵינֵינוּ (123:2) אֶל ה׳ אֱלֹהֵינוּ, *Behold! Like the eyes of servants unto their masters' hand, like the eyes of a maid unto her mistress' hand, so are our eyes unto* HASHEM, *our God.* It is noteworthy that the Psalmist does not say that our eyes are fixed on Hashem's hand, but rather that they are unto Hashem Himself (so to speak), since we are seeking not material handouts, but rather the supreme fulfillment of clinging to Hashem Himself and gazing at His Presence. (*Rosh Hashanah 5653*)

⇜§ Tashlich

נֹשֵׂא עָוֹן וְעֹבֵר עַל פֶּשַׁע לִשְׁאֵרִית נַחֲלָתוֹ

Who pardons iniquity and overlooks transgression for the remnant of His heritage.

כי אעפ״י שחטא כשמכיר את מקומו ומבטל עצמו אל השורש
ע״י התשובה יש לו מקום באותו הראשית

The Sages (*Rosh Hashanah 17a*) interpreted this verse, which forms the core of the *Tashlich* ceremony, with a vivid metaphor: אֵלְיָה וְקוֹץ

בָּה ... לְמִי שֶׁמֵּשִׂים עַצְמוֹ כְּשִׁירַיִם, *This is a fat tail [i.e. a great gift] with a thorn embedded in it. Only for those who act as if they are remnants [i.e. insignificant] [will I forgive their sins].*

This interpretation seems to work to the disadvantage of *baalei teshuvah*. Even though they have already repented and, as the beginning of the verse assures us, their iniquity has already been pardoned and their transgression overlooked, Hashem now appears to be imposing an additional condition for His forgiveness, that they achieve a feeling of being totally insignificant and no better than a worthless remnant.

Upon further contemplation, however, we can see that the Sages were actually setting the stage for the *baal teshuvah's* road back to Hashem. The Jewish people have frequently been called *Reishis* (the "first" i.e. Hashem's premier nation); when a Jew sins, however, he is demoted from that elevated status to being little more than a worthless "remnant."

But this does not mean that all hope is lost. Once he becomes aware of the low station to which his sins have brought him, that he has become a mere remnant, the Jew yearns to find his way back to his people's time-honored status as a *Reishis*, the first and best, to reverse his decline.

In this light, the Sages' metaphor of a fat tail with an embedded thorn becomes particularly apt, especially in view of the *Zohar's* depiction of Torah as a tree with leaves, branches and bark. We also, if we realize our current lowly status as a mere remnant of our former pure selves, as a thorn on the periphery of the tree, and if we make prodigious efforts to improve ourselves, we can eventually reinstate ourselves in the center of the tree, in the core of Torah itself.

There is another sense in which the description "remnant of His heritage" is particularly relevant to our generations, the furthest removed to date from the original *Reishis*, the "first" generation which accepted the Torah and, along with it, nationhood. If we can only admit to our shortcomings, to admit to our lowly status as a "remnant," we could also reassume our status as *Reishis*, Hashem's first and foremost possession. (*Rosh Hashanah 5648*)

זְכוֹר רַחֲמֶיךָ ה' וַחֲסָדֶיךָ כִּי מֵעוֹלָם הֵמָּה

Remember Your mercies, O HASHEM, and Your kind-nesses, for they are from the beginning of the world.

פ׳ כי הקב״ה ברא עולמו כדי להטיב ולגמול חסד להצריכים לו

Although the concluding phrase of this plea, כִּי מֵעוֹלָם הֵמָּה, is usually understood as an affirmation that Hashem's kindness is eternal, it also allows a quite literal interpretation: "Your kindnesses are from the world." In order to accomplish His purpose in creating the world, namely to do good to others, Hashem, the ultimate personification of kindness and mercy, "required" a medium in which His kindness could be expressed, just as a philanthropist requires poor people in order to fulfill the *mitzvah* of charity. Only by creating the universe was it possible for Hashem to bestow His mercy and kindness upon the needy.

In this light we can understand this plea as follows: Spare our universe from any misfortune or calamity, since it is only through that universe and its inhabitants — imperfect as they are — that Your kindness can reach fruition. (*Rosh Hashanah* 5645)

Shabbos Rosh Hashanah

The Gemara (*Rosh Hashanah* 29b) rules that when Rosh Hashanah occurs on Shabbos, the *shofar* is not sounded because of our concern that someone may carry the *shofar* four cubits in a public thoroughfare. In the following section, we will take the homiletic (דְּרוּשׁ) approach that when Rosh Hashanah coincides with Shabbos it is not necessary to sound the *shofar*.

◆§ A Time of Good Will

לכן בשבת א״יצ לתקוע כדאיתא בזוה״ק כי בשבת מתגלה עת רצון מעתיקא קדישא ומתהפך הדין לרחמים.

The Midrash (*Yalkut Emor* 645) relates that upon hearing the *shofar*, Hashem rises from the Throne of Justice and sits on the Throne of

Mercy. (For a more complete discussion of this theme refer to the section on *Shofar*). On Shabbos, depicted by the *Zohar* as an עֵת רָצוֹן, *a time of Divine goodwill*, Hashem's mercies are evoked even without the *shofar*.

(5652)

⋰§ Purity of Shabbos

לכן בש״ק א״י־ץ לתקוע בענין שאמרו חז״ל שא״יצ תפילין לאות
בשבת שהוא עצמו אות. כי נפשות בנ״י מתעלין בש״ק שהוא
יומא דנשמתין ולאו דגופא.

As discussed in the essay on *Shofar*, the wordless *shofar* represents the essential purity of the Jewish people. By contrast to the esophagus which contains food particles, the trachea which is the source of sound is free of any external matter. So too by sounding the *shofar*, we remind Hashem of the inner purity of the Jewish soul. On Shabbos, however, a day in which the soul predominates over the body, this reminder is unnecessary;[1] the mere verbalization of the *shofar's* theme through the verses of *Malchiyos*, *Zichronos* and *Shofaros* suffices. Just as *tefillin* are not donned on Shabbos since the Shabbos day itself is a sign (אות) of our relationship to Hashem as *tefillin* usually are, so too the inherent spirituality of Shabbos obviates any need for the *shofar*.

(5652)

⋰§ Revisiting Eden

ולכן בשבת שנק׳ מתנה טובה בבית גנזי ואין בשבת תערובת
פסולת אין צריכין לשופר.

In a similar vein, the pure sound of the *shofar* brings us back to the purity of Eden before Adam's sin (refer to our essay on *Shofar*). Prior to partaking from the Tree of Knowledge of Good and Evil (עֵץ הַדַּעַת טוֹב וָרָע), Adam lived in an ambience of only good, of knowledge of Hashem in its pristine form, undiluted by evil. On Shabbos, a day

---

1. The *mitzvah* of enjoying physical pleasures on Shabbos (e.g. partaking of meals) may be a form of tribute to the body which subordinates itself to the soul every Shabbos.

described by the Torah as לָדַעַת כִּי אֲנִי ה' מְקַדְּשְׁכֶם, *To know that I am Hashem Who makes you holy* (*Shemos* 31:12), as a time to acquire knowledge of Hashem even without benefit of the *shofar*, Israel returns to the world of Eden, to the world of good without evil. While all week long, good is often obscured by evil, on Shabbos good alone comes to the forefront. The renowned description of Shabbos as: מַתָּנָה טוֹבָה בְּבֵית גְּנָזַי (*Beitzah* 16a), *A goodly gift in My treasure-house,* may allude to the release of "good" from the clutches of "evil." Shabbos is a gift of *goodness* from Hashem's treasure-house (בֵּית גְּנָזַי). Hidden all week long, obscured amidst all other items in Hashem's treasure-house on Shabbos, Hashem extricates "good" and bequeaths it to Israel.　　　(5662)

◄§ Yisrael Not Yaakov

משפט לאלקי יעקב להמשיך חיות ואלקות גם בבחי' הגוף. ובזה
נלחם יעקב עם עשו ולבן. ובזה צריכין שופר . . . אבל בשבת
מתגלה בחי' ישראל. נחלה בלי מצרים.

David distinguishes between the impact of the *shofar* on Yaakov and Yisrael: כִּי חֹק לְיִשְׂרָאֵל הוּא מִשְׁפָּט לֵאלֹהֵי יַעֲקֹב *because it is a decree for Israel, a judgment [day] for the God of Yaakov* (*Tehillim* 81:5). Whereas, the physical aspect of every Jew, the body, is constantly waging battle against the Evil Inclination (יֵצֶר הָרָע), the soul containing the pure Divine spark is never tainted by evil. Thus, our primary concern when sounding the *shofar* is to assist the body in its eternal struggle against evil. The *body,* known as *Yaakov*, because of its constant struggles with evil — in the same manner that Yaakov battled those symbols of evil, Lavan and Esav — desperately needs the assistance of the *Shofar* in its noble battle (מִשְׁפָּט לֵאלֹהֵי יַעֲקֹב).[1]

However, the *soul,* depicted as יִשְׂרָאֵל, the name given to the Patriarch after he had triumphed over Esav, needs no such assistance. It remains pure as ever, unaffected by evil. The Divine spark remains permanently embedded in it. (According to this approach חֹק is related to חָקַק, *to engrave.*)

---

1. In fact, the *Zohar* interprets the requirement of sounding the trumpet when waging battle against the foe within you (עַל צַר הַצֹּרֵר אֶתְכֶם) to refer to the *shofar's* effectiveness against the יֵצֶר הָרָע.

On Shabbos, the day when the soul and the יִשְׂרָאֵל component of every Jew prevails, the *shofar* is not required. (5662)

✤§ Unity in Creation

נעשה שבת קודש שהוא התאחדות הבריאה ואין בה תערובת

רע . . . ולכן בשבת א׳׳צ לתקוע כי האחדות נתעורר מעצמו.

והתקיעה הוא לעורר בחי׳ האחדות

As mentioned in the essay on *Shofar*, one of the purposes of sounding the *shofar* is to return the universe to its original state. While Hashem throughout the Six Days of Creation gradually obscured His Presence in favor of His creations (allowing the universe He created to dominate), a process known as יֵשׁ מֵאַיִן, creating something, a material world, from sheer nothingness, on Shabbos the process is reversed. The יֵשׁ, the many-phased material world, is restored to its primeval simple beginnings, the אַיִן . At the conclusion of the sixth day — an eventful day in which Adam was created, sinned, and repented — Hashem viewed and approved of the universe in its entirety: וַיַּרְא אֱלֹהִים אֶת כָּל אֲשֶׁר עָשָׂה וְהִנֵּה טוֹב מְאֹד, *And God saw all that He had made and behold it was very good* (Bereishis 1:31). The fragmented segments, the many phases of the Six Days of Creation, were melded together. Now the stage was set for the perfection of Shabbos.

The *shofar*, too, generates אַחְדּוּת, *unity*. The *tekiah* sound, in particular, is associated with gathering the congregation (cf. *Bamidbar* 10:5,7).

Rosh Hashanah, in particular, evokes memories of the universe in its original state, at the commencement of Creation. While the Ten Days of Repentance correspond to the Ten Divine Statements (עֲשָׂרָה מַאֲמָרוֹת) through which the universe emerged, Rosh Hashanah parallels the first moments of Creation.

If Shabbos and the *shofar* both evoke memories of the beginning of Creation, we can now appreciate why on Shabbos Rosh Hashanah the *shofar* need not be sounded. (5642)

←§ The Gates of Shabbos Open

ואפשר דלכך בשבת אין תוקעין דביום השבת יפתח. וזה הפתח
אינו נכסה ולכך א״צ לתקוע בשבת.

Please refer to our essay entitled בַּכֶּסֶה in which we noted that the
Gates of Heaven, which usually open every *Rosh Chodesh* (cf.
Yechezkel 46:1: וּבְיוֹם הַחֹדֶשׁ יִפָּתֵחַ), remain closed on Rosh Hashanah. We
turn to the *shofar* instead, to evoke Hashem's Mercies so that He may
rise from the Throne of Justice and sit on the Throne of Mercy (עוֹמֵד
מִכִּסֵּא הַדִּין וְיוֹשֵׁב עַל כִּסֵּא רַחֲמִים).

On Shabbos, however, the other gate, described by Yechezkel as the
Gate of Shabbos, opens to Israel's pleas. On Shabbos Rosh Hashanah,
Israel does not require the *shofar* since the Gates of Shabbos remain
open.[1]   (5645, 5660)

←§ Unique to Israel

במלכות שמים באהבה ובשמחה כמ״ש ישמחו במלכותך שומרי
שבת. כי בזמן שליטת מלכות שמים המה ימים נוראים. ובנ״י
מקבלים הימים בשמחה ע״י שהם שומרי שבת. . . . רק בנ״י שהם
דבוקים בהשי״ת והמה למעלה מן הטבע. וזה אות השבת שבא
להם נשמה יתירה למעלה מהטבע ואז יכולין לקבל מלכות שמים
בשמחה.

As stated in the essay on *Tekias Shofar*, by blowing *shofar*, rather
than resorting to the Gates of Heaven which usually open on *Rosh
Chodesh*, Israel is following Hashem's Will that the Jewish people
evoke Hashem's Mercy upon all mankind. On Shabbos, however, a day
that is uniquely designated for Israel, following such a cosmic role
would be folly. Instead, on Shabbos Rosh Hashanah, Israel basks in
the joy of Shabbos. As we say in the Shabbos prayer: יִשְׂמְחוּ בְמַלְכוּתְךָ
שׁוֹמְרֵי שַׁבָּת, *They shall rejoice in Your Kingship — those who observe the*

---

1. In fact, the primary purpose of the *shofar* is to open the Gates of Heaven which usually
open on Shabbos. On Shabbos Rosh Hashanah, therefore, the *shofar* is clearly not necessary.

Sabbath. Generally, fear is the primary emotion at the time of the annual coronation of Hashem (בְּמַלְכוּתְךָ), but Israel, the nation that observes Shabbos, rejoices. Only those with the ability to surmount the numerous temptations of the physical world, only Israel blessed with an extra dimension of spirituality, נְשָׁמָה יְתֵרָה, every Shabbos, may rejoice. (5647)

Aseres Yemei Teshuvah

Haftarah of the
Fast of Gedaliah (דִּרְשׁוּ)

דִּרְשׁוּ ה׳ בְּהִמָּצְאוֹ קְרָאֻהוּ בִּהְיוֹתוֹ קָרוֹב
Seek HASHEM when He can be found; call Him when He is near (Yeshayahu 55:6).

In the following section, we shall examine a number of passages from the *Haftarah* we read at *Minchah* on the Fast of Gedaliah (and on all other fast days except for Yom Kippur). The Sages say that the opening phrase of this passage, *when He can be found*, is an allusion to the Ten Days of Repentance from Rosh Hashanah to Yom Kippur (*Rosh Hashanah* 18a). In particular, we shall consider why we are aware of Hashem's Presence more acutely during these days than at any other time of the year. We shall also explore the prophet's stirring call to repentance voiced in this *Haftarah*, focusing especially on the imagery of rain and snow falling on the soil.

◈§ When He Can Be Found

כי השי״ת בבריאות העולם כביכול עשה עצמו להיות נמצא
בעולם. כי צריך כל איש לידע ולהאמין כי הקב״ה הוא נעלם
ורחוק מכל רחוק וכמו כן הוא קרוב מכל קרוב . . . ובחי׳ זה
הקורבות נתחדש בבריאות עולם ובכל שנה מתחדש זה
המציאות. ובאמת זה הקורבות היא באמצעיות תורה ומצות

It is a fundamental tenet of Judaism that Hashem is both far beyond our comprehension and at the same time ever close to our pleas. As

Yirmiyahu admonishes the Jewish people (23:23): *Am I a G-d Who is close, and not a G-d that is distant?*.

The remote quality of Hashem's Presence has always existed in the infinite timelessness of eternity.[1] Only when the world came into being at His word did it become conceivable for Him to be close to His creations.

Just as we celebrate the renewal of the world itself each year during these ten days, so also we celebrate the renewal of Hashem's proximity to that world, and in particular the exceptional clarity with which we perceive that proximity. Indeed, perhaps it is precisely because His closeness to the world first came into being during this time that our perception of that closeness becomes especially palpable during the Ten Days of Repentance.

However, this sensation of closeness to Hashem does not come without effort, even at this special time of the year; Hashem allows us to come close to Him only in reward for our rededication to intensive Torah study and *mitzvos*. As we say in *Shemoneh Esrei*: הֲשִׁיבֵנוּ אָבִינוּ לְתוֹרָתֶךְ וְקָרְבֵנוּ מַלְכֵּנוּ לַעֲבוֹדָתֶךְ, *Bring us back, our Father, to Your Torah, and bring us near, our King, to Your service*.

(cf. *Shabbos Shuvah* 5655)

ובעשי״ת מתגלה בחי׳ אלקים חיים ושם הוי׳ לכן דרשו ה׳ בהמצאו.

It is noteworthy that the prophet's call uses the Name *Hashem*, which indicates Hashem's attribute of kindness and mercy (רַחֲמִים) rather than *Elokim*, which is associated with the quality of strict justice (דִין), suggesting that Divine kindness predominates during this critical period. On Rosh Hashanah not only do we celebrate the beginning of a new yearly cycle, we actually return to the very beginning of the universe — to the moment of *Bereishis*, before the emerging material world progressively obscured the majestic awesomeness of Hashem's Presence. The Sages relate that during that time Hashem was garbed in ten layers of "garments," corresponding to the Ten Utterances with which He created the world (cf. *Avos* 5:1).

---

1. *Editor's Note*: As we say in *Adon Olam*, אֲשֶׁר מָלַךְ בְּטֶרֶם כָּל יְצִיר נִבְרָא . . . וְאַחֲרֵי כִּכְלוֹת הַכֹּל לְבַדּוֹ יִמְלוֹךְ נוֹרָא, *Who reigned before any form was created . . . And after all has ceased to be He, the Awesome One, will reign alone*.

As Hashem's Presence becomes progressively veiled in His Creation, the name אֱלֹהִים, referring to the Divine Presence hidden in the (natural) world, becomes appropriate.

Thus this plea, *Seek Hashem when He can be found*, is really an eloquent call to the Jewish soul: Exploit this annual opportunity to penetrate beyond the material world, beneath the veil that hides Hashem's Presence. Armed with the mighty weapon of *teshuvah* and basking in the rarefied ambience of this time, we can achieve a closeness to Hashem's Presence as it was in the primeval beginning, before the material world came into being to obscure it. Armed with *teshuvah* we can come close to Hashem, to His Presence as it was manifested at the beginning of Creation.

The great opportunity of these days is captured sublimely in the Psalmist's song, that we read as a preliminary to blowing the *shofar*: שָׂשׂ אָנֹכִי עַל אִמְרָתֶךָ כְּמוֹצֵא שָׁלָל רָב, *I rejoice **over** Your utterances, like one who **finds** a great treasure* (119:163). Israel rejoices at passing *over* the barriers to perceiving Hashem's Presence interposed by the world, which was created with Ten Utterances. And when do we do this? **When** *I find a great Treasure*, clearly a reference to this period, *When He is to be found*, for surely Hashem is the greatest Treasure in existence.[1]   (cf. *Shabbos Shuvah* 5654)

⇜ Seek Out Your Roots

וקודם הקילקול הם דבקים בשורשם ונק' ממש בהמצאו שהם הם
ממוצא פי ה'

A lternatively, perhaps we can understand the word בְּהִמָּצְאוֹ, *when He can be found*, as an allusion to the classic verse in *Mishneh Torah*, כִּי עַל כָּל מוֹצָא פִי ה' יִחְיֶה הָאָדָם, *rather by everything that emanates from the mouth of HASHEM does man live* (Devarim 8:3). This verse in turn alludes to the moment in which man first received the Divine kiss of life from Hashem, וַיִּפַּח בְּאַפָּיו נִשְׁמַת חַיִּים, *And He blew into his nostrils the soul of life* (Bereishis 2:7). Taken together, these

---

1. *Editor's Note*: Alternatively, the phrase עַל אִמְרָתֶךָ may be interpreted in the singular, *Your utterance* — Israel rejoices at the single statement of בְּרֵאשִׁית — rather than the Ten Utterances.

three verses constitute a subtle reminder of the great potential Hashem
has imbued in us: *Seek out Hashem*, the prophet exhorts us, during the
annual observance of our creation, when we have the ability to find the
true roots of our life, the roots which emerge from the "mouth" of
Hashem. While we may have been sullied by sin throughout the year,
during these Ten Days the process of repentance cleanses us and enables
us to find our way back to the pristine purity of that moment when
Hashem first breathed life into the human soul.

בְּהִמָּצְאוֹ, *Seek out Hashem* during these hallowed days when the מוֹצָא
פִּי ה׳, the expression of Hashem's mouth that resulted in the first pure
soul, surfaces again, ready to reinvigorate Jewish souls. In fact, the
Heavenly origins of Israel's souls may be deduced from the term בְּהִמָּצְאוֹ
itself, if we interpret it as a compound word: הֵם, *they* (i.e. Israel), מוֹצָא,
are derived, from the expression of Hashem's will. During the course of
the year, the Jewish people are often confronted with temptation. We
successfully deflect the importuning of the יֵצֶר הָרָע by remembering the
purity of the first man's creation and of our annual recreation.

(*Likutim* 5629)

קְרָאֻהוּ בִּהְיוֹתוֹ קָרוֹב
Call Him When He Is Near

**דרשו ה׳ בהמצאו הוא התורה . . . קראהו בהיותו קרוב הוא
עבודה ותפלה**

The prophet continues, "Call Him when He is near." At the
beginning of this verse the prophet pleaded with us to renew our
commitment to Torah; here he urges us to call out to Hashem in prayer.
Indeed, these two expressions — *Call Him* and *Seek Him* — are
particularly apt as references to prayer and Torah study, respectively.
While much of the time Hashem may seem beyond our conception, at
least some of His greatness can be *found* in this period, through
intensive Torah study. Similarly His Presence also, although usually
remote, can be drawn close during these days, when He opens the gates
of Heaven to our earnest prayer. (5645)

◆§ Follow Hashem's Example

ואמרו חז״ל בהמצאו הוא בעשי״ת. כי פי׳ בהמצאו בזה
המציאות שהמציא לו כביכול הקב״ה בזה העולם בזה יש לבע״ת
כח לשוב כמ״ש לעיל.

Finally, and perhaps most profoundly, the prophet urges us to follow the powerful example set by Hashem. If Hashem maintains His Presence in this world (עוֹלָם הַזֶּה), despite all its foibles, this is indicative of His closeness (and accessibility) to mankind and to Israel, in particular. בְּהִמָּצְאוֹ: Reflect upon Hashem's Presence in this world, think of His intimate closeness to your own life, and bearing this in mind, return to Him. (5651)

יַעֲזֹב רָשָׁע דַּרְכּוֹ וְאִישׁ אָוֶן מַחְשְׁבֹתָיו

Let the wicked one forsake his way and the iniquitous man his thoughts (Yeshayahu 55:7).

וז״ש איש און מחשבותיו שעדיין לא חטא וע״י פחד החטא שב
מקודם. מצילין אותו מן החטא. שהרי החטא גרם לו התשובה
ותיקון מחשבותיו לכן נתרחק מן החטא.

After issuing a general plea for repentance, the prophet now outlines a step-by-step plan to achieve this goal, starting with a fundamental shift in direction on the part of the sinner: *Let the wicked one forsake his way* — let him abandon his evil deeds and return to the path of Hashem. True repentance cannot stop here; it must also include abandoning any sinful thoughts. Only after accomplishing both of these — rectifying thoughts as well as deeds — can a former sinner attain the coveted status of a true penitent and reap the benefits of the prophet's sweeping promise: וְיָשֹׁב אֶל ה׳ וִירַחֲמֵהוּ וְאֶל אֱלֹהֵינוּ כִּי יַרְבֶּה לִסְלוֹחַ, *and let him return to* HASHEM *and He will show him mercy; and to our God for He will be abundantly forgiving* (v. 7).

While repenting for evil thoughts may be difficult, it carries with it more than ample reward. The Sages tell us (*Yoma* 85b) that someone who justifies his sins with the intention, however sincere, to repent afterwards (a fallacy described in Hebrew as אֶחֱטָא וְאָשׁוּב, "I will sin and then repent") will never be allowed to repent, since he has abused this Divine gift. Now it is well known that Hashem's generosity in rewarding good deeds far exceeds His severity in punishing wrongdoing, as the Sages said, מִדָּה טוֹבָה מְרֻבָּה מִמְּדַת פֻּרְעָנוּת, *Hashem's goodwill exceeds His desire to punish* (cf. *Rashi Makkos* 23a). It follows that if someone has a genuine fear of sin and sincerely regrets any evil thoughts he may have had, he will certainly merit to be protected from further sins. (5651)

כִּי לֹא מַחְשְׁבוֹתַי מַחְשְׁבוֹתֵיכֶם . . . כִּי גָבְהוּ שָׁמַיִם מֵאָרֶץ כֵּן גָּבְהוּ
דְרָכַי מִדַּרְכֵיכֶם וּמַחְשְׁבֹתַי מִמַּחְשְׁבֹתֵיכֶם.

For My thoughts are not your thoughts . . . As the heavens are high above the earth, so My ways are high above your ways, and My thoughts above your thoughts (Yeshayahu 55:8,9).

העניין לידע ולהאמין כי הקב״ה שהוא נעלם מכל אעפ״כ הוא
מחי׳ ומנהיג הכל.
ויתכן לפרש כי לא מחשבותי בדרך אעפ״י.

Once a sinner succeeds in shifting his focus from material desires to his spiritual well-being, Hashem in turn returns to him. Perhaps, in this light, the prophet's statement that Hashem's ways are as distant from ours as heaven is from earth is really a call upon Israel to reorient our thoughts from earth to heaven. Perhaps the word כִּי, which usually means *because*, is to be rendered here as *despite*: "Despite the fact that My thoughts are so distant from yours, and the gap between Myself and Israel has been befouled by sins, it is still possible to bridge that distance with sincere repentance." (cf. 5651)

דבבריאות העולם כתיב אלקים שהי׳ ע״י צמצום בטבע.
פי׳ ע״ז צריכין לשוב כי רצונו ית׳ הי׳ שיהי׳ כל הדרכים
ומחשבות של בנ״י דבוקין בשורשם

Or, perhaps כִּי is to be understood in its more usual sense. *Because My thoughts are above your thoughts*, because Hashem's way of thinking is so different from ours, we have a sacred obligation to *seek Hashem when He can be found* and to direct all our mental energies towards Him. (5654)

וז״ש הכתוב כי לא מחשבותי מחשבותיכם. כי באותה הבחירה שבחר בנו הקב״ה ונתן לנו התורה דברי אשר שמתי בפיך הוא בחירה עולמית. והנה גם בנ״י בחרו בהקב״ה כמ״ש את ה' האמרת אבל בזה נעשה שינוים ע״י החטא. אבל אני ה' לא שניתי כתיב וזהו לא מחשבותי מחשבותיכם שאין בי שינוי רצון.

This phrase לֹא מַחְשְׁבוֹתַי מַחְשְׁבוֹתֵיכֶם, *My thoughts are not your thoughts,* may also hint at the unique connection which has always existed between Hashem and Israel. When this relationship was first formed with the Giving of the Torah at Mount Sinai, it was not one sided. Hashem chose us from the rest of mankind to serve Him, and we in turn designated Him as our only God. Never before had any nation made such a commitment to any god or idol, as Moshe proclaimed, אֶת ה' הֶאֱמַרְתָּ הַיּוֹם לִהְיוֹת לְךָ לֵאלֹהִים, *You have distinguished HASHEM today to be a God for you* (Devarim 26:17).

Sadly this relationship soon reverted into a one-sided situation. While Hashem's loyalty to us never wavered in the face of our many shortcomings, we forsook Him and strayed after other gods. It is this betrayal which spurs the prophet to exhort us to return, *for My thoughts are not like your thoughts* —unlike you who abandon Me, I will never forsake My people. As the prophet Malachi states (3:6), אֲנִי ה' לֹא שָׁנִיתִי, *I am Hashem, I have have not changed,* and have never wavered in my commitment to Israel. (5663)

כִּי כַּאֲשֶׁר יֵרֵד הַגֶּשֶׁם וְהַשֶּׁלֶג מִן הַשָּׁמַיִם וְשָׁמָּה לֹא יָשׁוּב כִּי אִם הִרְוָה אֶת הָאָרֶץ וְהוֹלִידָהּ וְהִצְמִיחָהּ וְנָתַן זֶרַע לַזֹּרֵעַ וְלֶחֶם לָאֹכֵל. כֵּן יִהְיֶה דְבָרִי אֲשֶׁר יֵצֵא מִפִּי לֹא יָשׁוּב אֵלַי רֵיקָם כִּי אִם עָשָׂה אֶת אֲשֶׁר חָפַצְתִּי וְהִצְלִיחַ אֲשֶׁר שְׁלַחְתִּיו.

For just as the rain and snow descend from heaven and will not return there — unless it waters the earth and causes it to produce and sprout, and gives seed to the sower and food to the eater — so shall be My word that emanates from My mouth; it shall not return to Me unfulfilled unless it will have accomplished what I desired and brought success where I sent it (Yeshayahu 55:10-12).

וכמו כן דברי תורה שהם שמותיו של הקב״ה ומתלבשין
באותיות התורה שלפנינו להחיות התחתונים והוא כמו הגשם
והשלג היורד משמים והוא מרוה הארץ ומוליד ומצמיח להוציא
הארץ מכח אל הפועל מעשיי׳.

This passage seems to serve as a rationale for the prophet's impassioned plea: *Seek Hashem when He can be found.* Although snow and rain originate in the remote heavens, their primary impact is on the soil, which they help bear fruit. So too while Hashem may appear at times distant from the vicissitudes of the world, in fact He gives close and loving attention to every minute detail of our lives, and earnestly waits for us to repent.

Understood properly, the comparison of Hashem's word to rain and snow is particularly apt. The Torah itself, which consists solely of arrangements of Hashem's various Names, is beyond human comprehension.[1] Just as precipitation descends from heaven to earth to make the physical world into a productive and fecund medium for growth, so too Hashem's word "descends" from the abstract, sublime form it takes in heaven to the Torah we know in this world which gives us the opportunity to reach our spiritual potential. (5651)

והקב״ה נתן בכל איש ישראל דברים שצריך להוציאם בעולם
מכח אל הפועל לעשות בהם פירות ואז ישוב בשליחותו לפניו
ית׳. והוא נשמת אלקי כמ״ש רז״ל הנשמה בגוף כאזכרות
בגווילין וכ״כ ואשים דברי בפיך.

Alternatively, perhaps the term דְּבָרִי, *My word*, alludes to the soul Hashem infused into our bodies, as the Torah relates, וַיִּפַּח בְּאַפָּיו נִשְׁמַת חַיִּים, *And He blew into his nostrils the soul of life* (Bereishis 2:7). Elsewhere we find another description of the connection between Hashem's word and the human soul: וָאָשִׂים דְּבָרַי בְּפִיךָ, *I have placed My words in your mouth* (Yeshayahu 51:16). Similarly there is a renowned statement (cf. *Zohar Noach* 66) הַנְּשָׁמָה בַּגּוּף כָּאַזְכָּרוֹת בַּגְּוִילִין, *the soul as it*

---

1. Cf. *Ramban's* introduction to his commentary on the Torah: "Though it is remote and inscrutable, the Torah can and must be studied by Israel in the physical form in which it was given to the Jewish people at Mount Sinai, consisting of sacred letters and words which subsume Hashem's Names."

is encased within the body is like Hashem's Name inscribed on the parchment of a Torah scroll.

Thus our verse can be interpreted as follows: Just as the rain and snow cannot return to the heavens until they have accomplished their mission of fructifying the earth, so too the soul (i.e. Hashem's word) will not return to its Creator until its innate potential bears the desired fruits. In this light, the prophet's plea to *seek Hashem* is really an impassioned cry to Israel: "Return to Hashem, and He will help you fulfill your potential for greatness." *Teshuvah* goes far beyond simply renouncing past sins; it both requires and promises something much greater, a return to our original mission, to the objectives Hashem designated for each of us when He sent our souls down to this world (*ibid.*).

פי' שכל רצונו ית' יתקיים בודאי וסוף הכל ישובו. לכן בכח הזה
יכול אדם לעורר בתשובה כי העומד להיות כאלו עשה.

Finally, the analogy between precipitation and Hashem's word also speaks to the inevitability of *teshuvah*. Just as rain and snow are assured that their mission will be completed, so too Hashem's word — the Torah — promises that the Jewish people will ultimately repent, as it says, וְשַׁבְתָּ עַד ה' אֱלֹהֶיךָ וְשָׁמַעְתָּ בְּקֹלוֹ, *You will return unto HASHEM, your God, and hearken to His voice* (*Devarim* 4:30). When an individual comes to the awareness that all mankind will return to Hashem at the time of *Mashiach's* arrival, it becomes much easier for him to return to the path of Torah and *mitzvos*, and *teshuvah* is transformed from an impossible task into a certain reality for everyone. (5658,5663)

Shabbos Teshuvah

Shabbos Teshuvah[1] occupies a central role in our experience of the Ten Days of Repentance. In the following section, we shall elaborate on the role of Shabbos, and in particular of this special Shabbos, in the *teshuvah* process.

⋖§ Return to Heavenly Roots

שבחול נעשה ע״י מלאכה בבחי׳ מלאכים ושלוחים וצמצום כחו
ע״י כמה אמצעיות.
ושבת עולה כל דבר לשורשו כמו״ש ויכלו כו׳ שכל הדברים
מיוחדין בש״ק להיות רק כלי א׳ להיות נעשה רצונו ית׳

In order to appreciate the pivotal role played by Shabbos in the process of *teshuvah*, let us consider the Torah's description of the first Shabbos: וַיְכַל אֱלֹהִים בַּיּוֹם הַשְּׁבִיעִי מְלַאכְתּוֹ אֲשֶׁר עָשָׂה וַיִּשְׁבֹּת בַּיּוֹם הַשְּׁבִיעִי מִכָּל מְלַאכְתּוֹ אֲשֶׁר עָשָׂה, *On the seventh day God completed His work which He had done, and He abstained on the seventh day from all His work which He had done* (Bereishis 2:2). The Torah here uses two different expressions to describe Hashem's cessation of work at the beginning of the first Shabbos — וַיְכַל, *He completed*, and וַיִּשְׁבֹּת, *He abstained*. Each of these conveys a different aspect of the essence of Hashem's "rest" at the completion of the Six Days of Creation.

---

1. While in contemporary times the Shabbos between Rosh Hashanah and Yom Kippur is commonly known as *Shabbos Shuvah*, the *Sefas Emes* consistently refers to it as *Shabbos Teshuvah*, and so we have chosen to follow his practice.

The word וַיְכַל can be understood in connection with the similar word כְּלִי, *vessel*. With the culmination of Creation, all Hashem's creatures, which had just come into existence, reached their pinnacle and stood poised to fulfill their potential. The diverse elements of the heavens and the earth united together around a common purpose — to act as a "vessel" for fulfilling Hashem's will and manifesting His Presence.

Similarly, the word וַיִּשְׁבֹּת, *and He rested*, describes Hashem's rest from His מְלָאכָה. While this word normally denotes physical labor, here we can understand it as referring to the *intermediaries* (from the word מַלְאָכִים, *angels* or *messengers*) through which His Presence manifested itself during the first six days. In the course of Creation, Hashem's Presence had grown increasingly obscured by His emerging creations (a theme discussed extensively in the essay on דְּרָשׁוּ). When the first Shabbos arrived, however, He ceased to express Himself through intermediaries and allowed the universe to return to its roots, and to perceive its Creator *directly* in His full glory.

Thus a return to one's heavenly roots is an essential aspect of Shabbos — and of *teshuvah* as well, as the very name *teshuvah* (literally "return") implies. We see from this that a *baal teshuvah* does far more than merely repent for his past transgressions — he also returns to his sacred roots.   (*Likutim Vayelech*, 5634)

ושיר לשון המשכה להיות נמשך כל הטבע . . . אותיות ישר
שהוא קו הישר כמו שור וחומה

In the Psalm (92) devoted to the Shabbos day, מִזְמוֹר שִׁיר לְיוֹם הַשַּׁבָּת, King David sings eloquently of the relationship between Shabbos and *teshuvah*. As the very name מִזְמוֹר שִׁיר attests, this is not merely a מִזְמוֹר, a *song* of praise, but also a שִׁיר. Shabbos is portrayed as a *straight chain*[1] linking the natural world to its heavenly roots.[2]

Surely returning to one's sacred roots is the essence of Shabbos, and equally so of *teshuvah*, as we said above. Thus tradition most fittingly relates that this Psalm was first composed by Adam after Hashem accepted his plea for forgiveness after partaking from the Tree of Knowledge.   (*Likutim Vayelech*)

---

1. From the words שִׁיר, *chain*, as in the Mishnah (*Shabbos* 5:1) וְכָל בַּעֲלֵי הַשִּׁיר יוֹצְאִים בְּשִׁיר, *And all that wear a neck chain may go out with a neck chain*; and יָשָׁר, *straight*.

2. Thus the Zohar states that this Psalm was sung by the material world to the upper worlds.

✑ Shuvah and Emunah

והוא אמונה מה שנמשך האדם אחר הש״י גם בעוה״ז שנסתר
האמת . . . אם אדם זוכר אשר הכל מהש״י ואלקי ממש בקרבי כי
לכל דבר יש חיות מהש״י ואז לא ישלוט בו כל און וזה תשובה
לבוא לזכור זאת

The Sabbath observer and the *baal teshuvah*, as well as all others who return to their spiritual roots, are privileged to enjoy another dividend — the capacity for belief in Hashem and His Torah. This ability rests on the same basis as Shabbos and *teshuvah*, a stronger feeling of attraction to Hashem than to the superficialities of the material world. As the Psalm cited above continues, וֶאֱמוּנָתְךָ בַּלֵּילוֹת, *and Your faith in the nights*, even in the night of exile, the Jew remains inspired by the message of Shabbos and of *teshuvah*, and continues to believe. While the wicked may seem to *flourish like grass*, this is only for a limited period of time, but ultimately they will be destroyed *for all eternity*, and then Hashem's sovereignty will be recognized and accepted by all mankind.

The Psalm continues further: וְאַתָּה מָרוֹם לְעֹלָם ה׳, *And You are exalted forever, HASHEM*. In this light, we can understand an otherwise puzzling dialogue between Hashem and Israel. In the final era before *Mashiach*, after Israel has weathered all the horrors predicted in the Torah, the Jewish people will awaken from their spiritual lethargy and proclaim, הֲלֹא עַל כִּי אֵין אֱלֹהַי בְּקִרְבִּי מְצָאוּנִי הָרָעוֹת הָאֵלֶּה, *"Is it not because my God is not in my midst that these evils have come upon me?"* (*Devarim* 31:17).

Nonetheless, Hashem spurns their *teshuvah*, a problem which has confounded many commentators. Really, however, His reaction is explained clearly in Israel's own words. By proclaiming that Hashem is *not* with them, they deny one of the foundations of *teshuvah*, the belief that Hashem never leaves the Jew and that whatever happens a Jew can never lose the latent spark of Divinity that awaits his efforts to fan it into a conflagration of desire to return to Hashem.

(Likutim Vayelech)

~§ The Extra Soul (נְשָׁמָה יְתֵרָה)

ולכן בשבת קודש בנקל לשוב יותר. . . . וזה ענין נשמה יתירה
שיש לבנ׳׳י בשבת שהוא כח השורש שאינו תלוי בעבודת האדם.
לכן נקראת יתירה שהיא יותר מכפי זכות ועבודת האדם וזה הכח
אינו נאבד ע׳׳י החטא לכן יכולין לשוב בשבת קודש.

In this light, the granting of a נְשָׁמָה יְתֵרָה, an *extra soul*, to the Jew on
Shabbos takes on new significance. The term יְתֵרָה, *extra*, implies that
the added spiritual dimension a Jew receives on Shabbos is more than he
strictly deserves. While spiritual rewards are normally granted in direct
proportion to one's performance of Torah and *mitzvos*, there also exists
an additional component of spirituality which is *not* contingent upon
individual merit. This is the extra soul of Shabbos, which is so deeply
entrenched that even the totally undeserving individual cannot
eliminate it, and which we tap every Shabbos. And it is this hidden
nugget which facilitates our return on the one Shabbos of the year
which is especially dedicated to *teshuvah*.   (5641)

~§ Shemoneh Esrei of Shabbos

אבל בשבת הוא עליות הכל אל השורש. ולבטל כל המעשים. לכן
אין מתפללין בשבת בקשת צרכי האדם והוא בחי׳ התשובה
בלבד לבקש התדבקות בשורש העליון.

This concept helps us explain another surprising feature of Shabbos.
While it might be expected that the *Shemoneh Esrei* of such an
elevated day would be longer than the weekday version, actually we
recite only seven blessings in place of the usual nineteen.

The explanation for this is clear, however. All week long we pray for
our material needs and plead with Hashem to overlook any barriers our
sins may have erected to the flow of His blessings. On Shabbos,
however, no barriers separate Israel from its Creator and our material
needs play no role in our prayers. Instead, we seek only to return to our
sacred roots and cling again to Hashem (הִתְדַּבְּקוּת בְּשׁוֹרֶשׁ עֶלְיוֹן), which is

indeed the theme of the truncated Shabbos prayer, as we say, וְטַהֵר לִבֵּנוּ
לְעָבְדְּךָ בֶּאֱמֶת, *Purify our heart to serve You sincerely.*   (5652)

וע״ז הדפיקה בחול הקב״ה פותח להם שער בשבת. וגם בימי
המעשה נוכל לעורר בחי׳ השבת

It should be noted that the special quality of Shabbos in no way
detracts from the importance of the remaining days of the week. On the
contrary, as a result of this reconnection with his roots on Shabbos, a
Jew can sanctify all aspects of his life, and elevate even the weekday to
the lofty status of Shabbos. Shabbos elevates the entire week from the
surface materialism of this world to the spirituality of the World to
Come.

Indeed, the initiative for true *teshuvah* must begin during the week.
As the liturgist writes (*Rosh Hashanah Mussaf*), פּוֹתֵחַ שַׁעַר לְדוֹפְקֵי
בִתְשׁוּבָה, Hashem opens the gates of *teshuvah* on Shabbos to those who
knock on them all week long imploring Hashem to accept them. Then,
once the gates of repentance are opened on Shabbos, they remain open
the rest of the week as well, as the prophet Yechezkel writes, וּבְיוֹם הַשַּׁבָּת
יִפָּתֵחַ, *On the Sabbath day it shall be opened* (46:1). It is significant that
the prophet does not write יְהִי פָּתוּחַ, which would imply that the gates
will be open only during that time, but rather יִפָּתֵחַ, the gates *will
remain open* all the time. By flinging open the gates of repentance on
Shabbos, we open other opportunities to do *teshuvah* and to return to
Hashem even during the week.   (5637)

⋞ The Teshuvah of the Soul

ושבת תשובה היא בבחי׳ הנשמה ובימי המעשה לתקן הגוף לב
טהור

The dual nature of *teshuvah* — perfecting of the body to make it into
a worthy receptacle for the soul — can help us appreciate the special
role of *Shabbos Teshuvah*. The first part of this process, the development of the body, occurs during the weekdays, while on Shabbos the
focus shifts to the restoration of the soul. As the Psalmist asks, לֵב טָהוֹר

בְּרָא לִי אֱלֹהִים וְרוּחַ נָכוֹן חַדֵּשׁ בְּקִרְבִּי, *Create for me a pure heart* [a purified body] *and then renew within me a steadfast spirit* (51:12).

We must understand a critical difference between these two phases of *teshuvah*: Whereas the *body* repents because it is afraid of the punishment that otherwise awaits it, the *soul* is prompted by a loftier motive — its love for Hashem. The soul realizes that it can achieve its deep-seated aspiration of clinging to Hashem only through *teshuvah*, and so it is only natural for it to return to Hashem.[1]

ותשובת הגוף היא תשובה מיראה. ותשובת הנשמה מרוב התשוקה להיות נכסף לחזור להתדבק בו ית'

As we have said, the *teshuvah* one does during the week is motivated primarily by the fear of Hashem's punishment and affects only the body. Thus it may appear that this is inferior to the more rarefied, spiritually motived, *teshuvah* achievable on Shabbos, but paradoxically this is not the case. Actually *teshuvah* done out of fear is a necessary precondition for the *teshuvah* from love. Only when Hashem sees that someone truly regrets repeating his sins and is genuinely afraid of repeating them will He bestow His most precious gift of all — the true love of Hashem — in the heart of the penitent and allow him to do *teshuvah* out of love on Shabbos.   (cf. 5655)

∞§ Spiritual Reinvigoration

פי' שבשבת נמשך כחות ונפש להחיות כל מעשה בראשית. ובנ''י זוכין לזה . . . כדי להתדבק בשורש מושכין משם חיות חדש. וזה עיקר התשובה.

Not only does a Jew return to his spiritual roots on Shabbos, he is also infused with a new, higher form of life. In this light we can better understand a particularly abstruse word used to describe Hashem's rest on the first Shabbos following the Creation: וַיִּנָּפַשׁ (*Shemos* 31:17). While

---

1. This theme is discussed further in our essay on *Teshuvah MeAhavah* beginning on page 243 below.   (5655)

this word is normally translated, *and He was refreshed*, it can also be related to one of the words for soul, נֶפֶשׁ, suggesting that Hashem imbues Israel with a new soul, and thus new life, every Shabbos. No other nation but Israel — the nation which once each week ceases all material labors in order to relocate and re-embrace its spiritual roots — can be privileged to such a weekly renewal of its existence. As the Torah states: בֵּינִי וּבֵין בְּנֵי יִשְׂרָאֵל אוֹת הִיא לְעֹלָם, *Between Me and the Children of Israel it is a sign forever* (ibid.). The Sabbath with its weekly rejuvenation and reinvigoration of Israel's soul are the supreme indication of the high esteem in which Hashem holds Israel, the eternal sign of the unique relationship between the Creator and His people.

This dual process — rediscovering one's spiritual roots and consequently experiencing a reinvigoration of one's spiritual life — is the essence of *teshuvah*.   (5651)

⏤§ Dismantling Barriers Between Hashem and Israel

ובשבת כתיב אות הוא ביני וביניכם והיא מבטל מסך המבדיל.
לכן יכולין לשוב לפניו בתשובה בנקל יותר.

One of the most potent effects of *Shabbos Teshuvah* is the removal of the barriers which have been erected between Hashem and Israel by our transgressions, thereby in turn facilitating our return to Hashem. In this light we can understand the Sages' comment (*Shabbos* 118b) that if a Jew observes Shabbos according to *halachah*, all his sins are forgiven. By meticulously observing all the laws of Shabbos, and especially on *this* Shabbos, we can remove all the barriers between ourselves and Hashem which have prevented us from repenting properly until now.

This connection between the effect of our sins and the uniqueness of Shabbos emerges clearly from an uncanny similarity in two verses that describe these seemingly different topics. In speaking of Shabbos the Torah says, אוֹת הִיא בֵּינִי וּבֵינֵיכֶם, *It is a sign between Me and you* (*Shemos* 31:13), while elsewhere the prophet Yeshayahu warns, עֲוֹנֹתֵיכֶם הָיוּ מַבְדִּלִים בֵּינֵכֶם לְבֵין אֱלֹהֵיכֶם, *Your sins were dividing between you and your God* (59:2). This suggests that the bond between Hashem and His people is far stronger than the barriers erected by our sins.[1]

(5654)

⧉ The Beginning of Creation

וכתיב בשבת זכרון למעשה בראשית ולכאורה אינו מובן כי אדרבא כל מעשה בראשית הכנה להשבת. רק שהשבת הוא הזכר והפנימיות של מעשה בראשית.

Shabbos is commonly called זְכָּרוֹן לְמַעֲשֵׂה בְרֵאשִׁית, *a remembrance of Creation*, but this is puzzling if we think about it, since it would seem that the Six Days of Creation were a prelude to Shabbos, rather than the reverse.

Perhaps, though, the expression "a remembrance of Creation" actually refers to the beginning of Creation. To understand this, let us remember that while each phase of Creation was accomplished by a separate Divine utterance beginning with the phrase, וַיֹּאמֶר אֱלֹהִים, *God said*, the very first stage is described by the one classic word בְּרֵאשִׁית, *In the beginning*. At that first moment of Creation, none of the latent multi-faceted universe had yet emerged, and nothing existed in heaven and earth but Hashem's Presence. The Sages have taught (*Avos* 5:1) that although Hashem chose to create the universe in a sequence of Ten Divine Utterances, really all of them, the whole Six Days of Creation, could have been telescoped into the very first Divine Word, בְּרֵאשִׁית, *in the beginning*.

This, then, is the מַעֲשֵׂה בְרֵאשִׁית of which Shabbos is a reminder — the first moment of Creation, the inner core at the very beginning of the universe when Hashem in total glory and unity alone dominated a world in which no trace of materialism had yet emerged. It is this aspect of Shabbos, the memory it evokes of the intensely spiritual

---

1. *Editor's Note*: It is noteworthy that the verse which speaks of the separations between Hashem and His people is phrased in the past tense, suggesting that any divisions that might have existed in the past have been nullified, presumably at the time when the sign of the Sabbath is renewed between Hashem and Israel each week. It is also noteworthy that two words in the verse are spelled "deficiently" (i.e. missing a *yud* which is normally included), namely מַבְדִּלִים, *dividing*, and בֵּינֵכֶם, *between you*, suggesting that any divisions that may exist between Hashem and His people are only weak and temporary.

core and origin of Creation, which has the power to arouse us to repent.[1]

(5648)

✺ The Hidden Light of the First Days of Creation

ואיתא במדרש אשר אור הגנוז שראה הקב״ה שאין כדאי
להשתמש בו בעוה״ז וגנזו, אעפ״כ נתעכב האור כל יום השבת.
שזה כח השבת שיוכל גם עוה״ז לקבל הארה שלמעלה . . . והוא
באמת ע״י נשמה יתירה . . . כי בה לא היה החטא.

This special Shabbos, which comes during the Ten Days of Repentance
when we observe the anniversary of the universe's Creation, enables
us through our *teshuvah* to recreate the special light Hashem created on
the first day of the universe's existence. Quickly, however, Hashem saw
that this luminosity was too brilliant and sacred to be revealed to anyone
but the righteous, and so He hid it for their use in the World to Come.
Nonetheless, according to the Midrash this light was still allowed to shine
on that first Shabbos, and indeed is revealed to Israel even today in the
form of the *extra soul* (נְשָׁמָה יְתֵרָה) which is granted to a Jew every
Shabbos. From the great purity of this light, we see that it can only
emerge from the same hidden source as the primeval light of Creation.

This radiant light of Creation which suffuses the universe every
Shabbos carries the Jew off to a different, more rarefied world, a microcosm of the World to Come which is so far removed from our universe
that our sins have no impact there. It is only natural that in such a world
we can reconnect with the true roots of our souls which have remained
ever pure even through our flirtation with sin. (5634, 5637)

ועתה יש עשרה ימים והיינו שמתגלה הארת הג׳ ראשונות שהם
נקראים ימי קדם. ואמת כי השבת יש בו מג׳ הראשונות ג״כ.

The Infinite created this world, establishing in it the natural הַנְהָגָה,
conduct. But even before that, He also created a parallel conduct which

---

1. *Editor's Note:* In this light, perhaps it is significant that the Sages did not say זֵכֶר לְמַעֲשֵׂי
בְּרֵאשִׁית in the plural, which would have connoted a remembrance to all the various *acts* of
Creation, but rather זֵכֶר לְמַעֲשֵׂה בְּרֵאשִׁית, suggesting a *single act*, namely the all-encompass-
ing *beginning* of the Creation, as described within.

is above the laws of Nature, comprising three levels of utmost purity. These three pure levels are symbolically called "יְמֵי קֶדֶם", *Primeval Days*, as their creation preceded that of our world. Their light is available to the *Baal Teshuvah*, who needs to detach himself from worldly matters in order to be able to overcome his natural inclinations. This light is revealed during the Ten Days of Repentance. An allusion to this can be derived from the simple calculation that the length of this period (ten days) consists of an ordinary seven-day week, which signifies the seven days of creation, to which three extra days are added, signifying those three "Primeval Days". Thus the repentant gets Heavenly help in these days to be able to connect to a higher conduct which will enable him to tear himself from his worldly attachments.

The Sabbath is permeated and illuminated by that light as well, and therefore it is always a help to *Teshuvah*.[1] The famed verse הֲשִׁיבֵנוּ ה' אֵלֶיךָ וְנָשׁוּבָה חַדֵּשׁ יָמֵינוּ כְּקֶדֶם, *Bring us back to You, Hashem, and we shall return, renew our days as of old [the beginning]* (Eichah 5:21) may hint at the relationship between *teshuvah* and the revelation of that pure light By returning to Hashem — הֲשִׁיבֵנוּ ה' אֵלֶיךָ — we merit to bask in the light of the three "Primeval Days" — חַדֵּשׁ יָמֵינוּ כְּקֶדֶם.

(5648, 5644, 5658)

◆§ Enhanced Awareness of Hashem

דעיקר התשובה הוא ע״י הדעת כמ״ש וידעת היום והשבות כו'.
. . . ולכן בש״ק שנק' סהדותא ומבורר אצל בנ״י כבוד מלכותו
ובא להם הדעת כמ״ש בש״ק לדעת כי אני ה'

Complete *teshuvah* is impossible without a recognition of Hashem's total omnipresence and omniscience. As the Torah says, וְיָדַעְתָּ הַיּוֹם וַהֲשֵׁבֹתָ אֶל לְבָבֶךָ כִּי ה' הוּא הָאֱלֹהִים בַּשָּׁמַיִם מִמַּעַל וְעַל הָאָרֶץ מִתָּחַת אֵין עוֹד, *You are to know this day and take to your heart that* HASHEM *is the [only] God — in heaven above and on the earth below — there is none other* (Devarim 4:39). Once we realize that no force exists other than Hashem — a realization which can only make us painfully aware of our own shortcomings — we become possessed by a sense of shame: "If Hashem

---

1. The three meals we are required to eat on Shabbos, which are derived from the three times that the verse says "הַיּוֹם" in connection with the Sabbath meal, are symbolic of these three primeval "days" of creation during which this Divine light enveloped the universe.

is so great and has done so much for me, how could I have ever have been so brazen as to transgress His will?" This new-found shame is really the first, and perhaps the most important, step in the process of *teshuvah.*

Surely no better time exists to enhance our awareness of Hashem's Presence — and to repent for our earlier lack of that awareness — than the weekly Sabbath. As the Torah makes clear: We are urged to observe the Sabbath each week לָדַעַת כִּי אֲנִי ה' מְקַדִּשְׁכֶם, *so that you will know that I am HASHEM, Who makes you holy (Shemos* 31:13). (5647)

◆§ A Sense of Shame

נראה כי זה הבושת א״י לפגום אפילו ע״י חטאים ועונות . . .
ובשבת שבו ניתנה תורה יכולין לשוב ע״י הבושת הנטוע בתוכינו.

Not only does Shabbos help us become more aware of our Creator, it also assists us in reawakening one of our greatest inner assets, the humility that comes from realizing how many are our short-comings and how brief our lives are in comparison to Hashem's eternity. The Sages said *(Nedarim* 20a) that anyone whose forefathers were present at the Giving of the Torah has an innate capacity for shame, and as long as this remains part of him, his sins will never leave a permanent stain on his soul. This understanding sheds a new light on Moshe's explanation of Hashem's appearance at Mount Sinai *(Shemos* 20:17): וּבַעֲבוּר תִּהְיֶה יִרְאָתוֹ עַל פְּנֵיכֶם לְבִלְתִּי תֶחֱטָאוּ, "So that awe of Him — the humility and shame that comes with the awareness of His presence — *shall be upon your faces so that you shall not sin,* and will not be permanently tainted by the sins you have already committed."

This innate sense of shame first came into being on Shabbos, the Shabbos on which the Torah was given, and every Shabbos this critical attribute is reinforced.[1] All week long, this sense of shame is somewhat obscured because of our preoccupation with our material pursuits. However, on Shabbos, freed from this preoccupation with material matters, this sense of shame comes to the forefront. Propelled by the newly found

---

1. An allusion to these two concepts of Shabbos and shame may be found in the word בְּרֵאשִׁית, whose letters can be arranged to spell both יְרָא בֹשֶׁת, *fear of shame*, as well as יְרָא שַׁבָּת, *fear of Shabbos*, suggesting that someone who fears violating the Sabbath will also have a strong innate sense of shame.

sense of its own limitations — imbued again by this oldest of virtues, shame — on *Shabbos Teshuvah* Israel returns to Hashem.   (5658)

Witnesses Doing Teshuvah

שבנ״י מעידין בו על הבורא ית׳״ש ועדים צריכין לשוב בתשובה
שיהיו כשרים לעדות כמו שמזהירין עדי הגט לתשובה. . . . כי זה
העדות אינו דוקא בפה אבל אתם עדי בעצמיכם. . . . וז״׳ש שובה
ישראל עד ה׳ אלקיך אל תקרי עד אלא עֵד לשוב אל זה העדות.

Moreover, it is impossible to observe this holy day fully without doing *teshuvah*. It is well known that an important purpose of observing Shabbos is to give testimony that Hashem created heaven and earth. In order for his testimony to be acceptable, then, the Jew must be of impeccable character and must, in fact, repent of any wrongdoing, like any witness in Torah law. Thus only by doing *teshuvah* can we properly fulfill the true purpose of Shabbos: testifying that Hashem created the world.

Indeed, the *teshuvah* we do on Shabbos and the resulting moral improvement are in themselves the greatest testimony we can give on Hashem's behalf. As the prophet Yeshayahu implores us (43:10): אַתֶּם עֵדָי, "You, Israel — not your verbal tribute — but *you* yourselves — through your personality and character, you testify about Me." The more exemplary our actions and the more effective our *teshuvah*, the more convincing our testimony will be.

This concept sheds a new light on the renowned Rabbinic dictum, cited above, that anyone who observes the Sabbath according to *halachah* is forgiven for all his sins. The mere fact that a Jew has the merit to observe the Sabbath and to attest that Hashem created the world is itself a clear indication that all his sins must have been forgiven. Elsewhere[1] we have suggested that the prophet Hosea's clarion call, שׁוּבָה יִשְׂרָאֵל עַד ה׳ אֱלֹהֶיךָ, *Return, O Israel, to HASHEM, your God*, can also be read שׁוּבָה יִשְׂרָאֵל עֵד ה׳ אֱלֹהֶיךָ, "*Return, O Israel, and you can be the witness of HASHEM, your God.*" By repenting on Shabbos, and especially on *this* Shabbos which is designated and designed for repentance, we can make ourselves into Hashem's witnesses.

---

1. See our commentary on the *Haftarah Shuvah Yisrael*.

Above we noted that an enhanced awareness of Hashem's rule of the world is a prerequisite to proper *teshuvah*. Moreover, there is a close connection between increasing our awareness of Hashem and bearing testimony to Him. Thus the Midrash (*Rashi, Devarim* 4:35) relates that at Mount Sinai Israel was privileged to witness Hashem's full glory when He opened the heavens and showed Israel that nothing existed in the universe except for Him. All of this was done for the sole purpose of showing Israel that Hashem alone exists, as the Torah says, אַתָּה הָרְאֵתָ לָדַעַת כִּי ה׳ הוּא הָאֱלֹהִים אֵין עוֹד מִלְבַדּוֹ, *You have been shown in order to know, that HASHEM, He is the God; there is none beside Him* (*Devarim* 4:35).

By demonstrating our awareness of Hashem's Presence in every aspect of our lives, we testify to His existence and His rulership of the world. The *teshuvah* we do all week long makes it abundantly clear that we do not forget Hashem, and even more so the *teshuvah* we do on Shabbos. In this light we can glean new meaning in the twin commandment to *remember* and to *safeguard* the Sabbath day. On this special day, when we have the opportunity to do a higher level of *teshuvah*, it is more than ever important to *remember* Hashem and to *safeguard* our awareness of His Presence. (5661)

◆§ Hashem Reveals Himself

בשבת מתגלה שם הוי׳. וכ״כ בזו״ח כי אחר פרשת ויכולו כתיב
ביום עשות ה׳ אלקים כו׳ ומקודם לא כתיב רק אלקים ע״ש.

The special revelation of Hashem's Presence which occurs during these ten days — as Yeshayahu says, דִּרְשׁוּ ה׳ בְּהִמָּצְאוֹ, *Seek Hashem when He can be found* — makes the path of *teshuvah* considerably easier at this time. Especially on this Shabbos Hashem's proximity can be felt. Thus the *Zohar* (*Zohar Chadash*) notes that throughout the Six Days of Creation the Torah uses only the name *Elokim*, indicating Hashem's quality of justice, but suddenly after the first Shabbos we also find the four-lettered Name of Hashem which indicates His attribute of mercy (*Bereishis* 2:4): בְּיוֹם עֲשׂוֹת ה׳ אֱלֹהִים אֶרֶץ וְשָׁמָיִם, *On the day that HASHEM God made earth and heaven.* (5654).

⋖§ Hashem Returns to Us

ומה שצריכין בנ״י בימי המעשה לתקן מעשיהם להכין הצורה
שיהי׳ הקב״ה יושב תהלות ישראל זה נעשה בשבת מעצמו.
נמצא הקב״ה מתחיל לשוב אלינו בשבת

In a well-known verse,[1] the prophet Yirmiyahu describes two phases of the process of *teshuvah*: Firstly, Hashem helps us return to Him — הֲשִׁיבֵנוּ ה׳ אֵלֶיךָ, *Bring us back to You, HASHEM*. This is followed by our promise, וְנָשׁוּבָה, *and we shall return*; on our own we shall repent and come back to Hashem.

The first and crucial phase, in which Hashem brings us back to Him, occurs every Shabbos, as is conveyed in an eloquent yet terse passage in the Shabbos liturgy, לָאֵל אֲשֶׁר שָׁבַת מִכָּל הַמַּעֲשִׂים, *To the God Who rested from all works*. The liturgist writes that בַּיּוֹם הַשְּׁבִיעִי נִתְעַלָּה וְיָשַׁב עַל כִּסֵּא כְבוֹדוֹ, *Who on the Seventh Day was elevated and sat on the Throne of His Glory*. During the week Israel's prayers are required to support Hashem on His throne, as the Psalmist sings (22:4), וְאַתָּה קָדוֹשׁ יוֹשֵׁב תְּהִלּוֹת יִשְׂרָאֵל, *You are the Holy One, enthroned upon the praises of Israel* — Hashem is supported on His Throne by Israel's praises. The Sages, describing Hashem's throne, suggest that the souls of Israel are engraved under the throne. In this light we may interpret that the prayers of the Jewish people *support* the Throne of Glory.

On Shabbos, however, Hashem "rises unto Himself" and mounts His Throne without respect to Israel's prayers. Shabbos, the day of the week when Hashem returns to us on His own initiative, is the most opportune time for Israel's *teshuvah*.   (5654)

ובאמת בכל עשרת ימי תשובה כך הוא שהקב״ה נקרא מלך
המשפט ויושב על הכסא לכן הוא זמן תשובה.

In this light, we can better appreciate the designation הַמֶּלֶךְ הַמִּשְׁפָּט, *the King of Judgment*, which we apply to Hashem in the *Shemoneh Esrei* of the Ten Days of Repentance. The rest of the year Hashem is

---

1. *Eichah* 5:21.

described as מֶלֶךְ אוֹהֵב צְדָקָה וּמִשְׁפָּט, *the King Who loves righteousness and judgment*, but now, when He sits on His Throne to judge His creations, He is described as the *King of Judgment* because His entire Being is focused on judgment. (5654)

⋙ The Gates of Torah Open

שבת מיוחד ביותר לתשובה כי בו נפתח שער התורה ונפתחים
לבות בנ״י לקבל התורה. לכן בשבת לחם משנה רמז לתורה
שבכתב ושבע״פ שנתגלה בו טעמי תורה. . . . לכן שבת ביני ובין
בנ״י אות כו' שהיא עדות על ישראל כמו שנפתחים למעלה שערי
תורה . . . ובו נפתחים לבות בנ״י אל התורה

In the essay on the *Haftarah* of this Shabbos[1] we discussed the important role Torah plays in the process of *teshuvah*, which in essence is a *return* to the Torah. Surely, then, there is no more opportune time to return to Torah than Shabbos. On Shabbos, the heart of a Jew — which often goes through the week preoccupied with the mundane concerns of the material world — is granted the tranquillity to delight in Torah thoughts.

Thus it has fittingly been said that *lechem mishneh*, the two loaves of bread we eat at each Sabbath meal, correspond to the Written and Oral components of Torah. Just as our taste and sensitivity to other physical pleasures is enhanced on Shabbos, so also is our ability to glory in the far more sublime spiritual treasures of the Torah which, although obscured during the week, are revealed and intensified to those who thirst to grasp their inner significance on Shabbos.

The renowned verse בֵּינִי וּבֵין בְּנֵי יִשְׂרָאֵל אוֹת הוּא לְעֹלָם, *Between Me and the Children of Israel it is a sign forever* (*Shemos* 31:17), suggesting that the Shabbos is a sign of the bond between Israel and Hashem may refer to this dimension. Both the Jewish people and their Creator come closer to Torah on Shabbos. An almost identical process occurs in heaven and earth — the gates of Torah are opened. Thus, Hashem granted the Torah to Israel on Shabbos and continues to do so every Shabbos. Similarly, the Jewish people's capacity to acquire and absorb

---

1. See our commentary on the phrase קְחוּ עִמָּכֶם דְּבָרִים, *Take words with you.*

Torah is heightened and increased every Shabbos. The fact that this process occurs simultaneously with Hashem is a sign of the intimacy between Israel and Hashem — אוֹת הוּא בֵּינִי וּבֵינֵיכֶם (v. 13).   (5660)

৵§ The First Shabbos

ויש להתחזק בשמירת שבת תשובה שהוא שבת ראשון בשנה מעין מ״ש חז״ל אילו שמרו ישראל שבת ראשונה לא שלטה בהם אומה ולשון.

The location of *Shabbos Teshuvah* in the annual calendar may explain some of its special significance. As the first Shabbos of the year just begun, it sets a precedent for the entire year. Thus the manner in which we observe this keynote Sabbath can ensure that we will be privileged to observe the remaining Sabbaths properly as well.

On a similar note, the Sages suggest (*Shabbos* 118b) that if Israel had properly kept the first Shabbos after they were first informed of the laws of this special day at Marah,[1] then no nation — not even the wicked Amalek — would have dared attack them. We may conclude also, then, that if all Israel were to observe this first Shabbos, all the wily attempts of the *yetzer hara* to corrupt us would come to naught.   (5653)

৵§ One of Two Extraordinary Sabbaths

ויש לרמוז מ״ש חז״ל אלו שמרו שתי שבתות מיד נגאלין שהוא שבת הגדול בחי׳ צדיקים. ושבת תשובה בחי׳ בעלי תשובות.

Elsewhere the Sages have said (*Shabbos* 118b) that if Israel would only observe two Sabbaths they would surely be redeemed. Perhaps the two Sabbaths they meant are *Shabbos HaGadol* (the Shabbos prior to Pesach) and *Shabbos Teshuvah*: While *Shabbos HaGadol* reminds us of the lofty purity attained by the Jewish people at the time of the Exodus, *Shabbos Teshuvah* celebrates the extraordinary accomplishment of ordinary people in repenting from their sins. In the merit of both groups — both the righteous who live their lives in total purity and *baalei teshuvah* — Israel will surely be redeemed.

An apparently redundant phrase we say in the Friday night *Kiddush* alludes to this interconnection between the totally righteous and *baalei teshuvah*: וְשַׁבַּת קָדְשְׁךָ בְּאַהֲבָה וּבְרָצוֹן הִנְחַלְתָּנוּ, *Who has bequeathed us the Sabbath with **love** and with **desire**.* "Love" refers to Hashem's love for the actions of *tzaddikim*, while "desire" refers to His wish to accept the repentance of the former sinner. As we say thrice daily in *Shemoneh Esrei*, Hashem is הָרוֹצֶה בִּתְשׁוּבָה, *The One Who **desires** repentance.*

(5654)

ואמרו חז"ל אלו שמרו ישראל שבת אחת נגאלין. הרמז שבת
אחת להיות כל הרצון תמיד לשבות ולהיבטל אל השורש. כמ"ש
אחת שאלתי כו' שבתי.

On this first, precedent-setting Shabbos it is our crucial task to rectify any past lapses in our Sabbath observance, not only as regards actual violations of the intricate laws of Shabbos but also in simply failing to remember and cherish this most sacred of days.

The *mitzvah* זָכוֹר אֶת יוֹם הַשַּׁבָּת לְקַדְּשׁוֹ (*Shemos* 20:8), *remember the Sabbath day to sanctify it*, is meant to be interpreted literally, that we are to keep the sacredness of this day in mind, remember it and not to forget it even for an instant. True, this may seem too much to ask of ordinary mortals, but really the most important thing is how we greet the day at its outset; if we welcome Shabbos joyfully, with determination to observe it as it should be, then we can be assured that the rest of the day will proceed as it should.

Particularly on this first Shabbos of the year it is important to remember the sanctity of the day and this specific Shabbos, to the fullest extent. Perhaps this is the true meaning of the Sages' statement cited above, "Were Israel to observe one Shabbos properly, they would surely be redeemed": If we were to muster the full concentration and singular focus required to observe Shabbos properly, then we would surely be redeemed. As the Psalmist sings (27:4), אַחַת שָׁאַלְתִּי מֵאֵת ה' אוֹתָהּ אֲבַקֵּשׁ שִׁבְתִּי בְּבֵית ה' כָּל יְמֵי חַיַּי, *I seek only one thing — my mind is totally focused on one objective — let me dwell in Hashem's House all the days of my life and to behold His sweetness.* (5651, 5660)

❧ A Reminder of the Exodus

השבת מסייע אל התשובה שהוא זכר ליצ״מ שביציאת מצרים
יצאו בנ״י משערי טומאה ונכנסו לשערי בינה.

One more aspect of Shabbos contributes to the process of return — its status as a "reminder of the Exodus."

True *teshuvah* is a gradual and sequential process, with the gates of comprehension and knowledge of Hashem opening slightly further at each stage, until finally all fifty gates of understanding are accessible to the *baal teshuvah*. Since this process was accomplished all at once on the night of the Exodus from Egypt, it can also be accomplished through the weekly reminder of that night, the Sabbath. On the weekly Sabbath the penitent is given the ability to achieve the level of Divine comprehension associated with complete *teshuvah*. (5653)

Haftarah of Shabbos Teshuvah
שׁוּבָה יִשְׂרָאֵל

In this essay we shall explore various aspects of *teshuvah* (repentance) as outlined by the prophet Hoshea in the renowned *Haftarah* from which *Shabbos Shuvah* takes its name.

שׁוּבָה יִשְׂרָאֵל עַד ה׳ אֱלֹהֶיךָ

Return, O Israel, to [until] HASHEM, your God (Hoshea 14:2).

פי׳ כי לעולם יש תשובה אף מי שהוא צדיק עד ה׳ אלקיך פי׳ עד
להיות מרכבה אליו ית׳ ממש. וכפי תיקון החטא בתשובה צריכין
אח״כ לשוב בתשובה מחדש.

By insisting that we return *until* Hashem, the prophet sets an exacting standard for Israel to meet. Repentance encompasses far more than forswearing past sins, and even a totally righteous person who rarely sins can participate in this endeavor. As the prophet pleads: *Return, O Israel, until HASHEM, your God* — until you have made yourself into an exalted bearer of the *Shechinah*, no less than the Patriarchs who brought Hashem's Presence into the world.[1] A Jew, whether he was wicked or righteous to start with, cannot fulfill his obligation to do *teshuvah* unless he attains this level of serving Hashem.

Moreover, *teshuvah* is an ongoing process, with continually new requirements and opportunities at every step of the way. Each stage of an individual's repentance brings a higher degree of spirituality, as well as a higher level of service he is expected to perform. The more the penitent purifies himself from his sins, the closer he is able to, and expected to, draw himself to Hashem through more intense devotion to Torah and *mitzvos*.

The prophet Yirmiyahu alludes to this process in his plea: הֲשִׁיבֵנוּ ה' אֵלֶיךָ וְנָשׁוּבָה חַדֵּשׁ יָמֵינוּ כְּקֶדֶם, *Bring us back to You, Hashem, and we shall return, renew our days as of old* (*Eichah* 5:21). Even after You have helped us return to You, we must still continue to return on our own. The primary purpose of the *mitzvah* we call *teshuvah* can be seen from the very words עַד ה' אֱלֹהֶיךָ — to return to Hashem and resume our role as bearers of the *Shechinah*, which is possible only *after* the initial process of repentance has been successfully accomplished.

(5638)

כי וודאי כפי מה שאדם שב בתשובה כראוי זוכה אח״כ לקבל
מלכות שמים כראוי. וזהו עד ה' אלקיך שצריך האדם לשוב עד
שיוכל לקבל אלקותו ית' כראוי ואז קבלת אלקותו ית' הוא עדות
על התשובה כנ״ל.

Thus the prophet's call is really a plea to renew our commitment to Hashem, for the *mitzvah* of *teshuvah* is not fulfilled until the penitent genuinely feels a renewal of his relationship with the Creator. Indeed,

---

1. Cf. *Bereishis, Rashi* 17:22 אָבוֹת הֵן מֶרְכַּבְתּוֹ שֶׁל מָקוֹם, the *Patriarchs were the bearers [chariot]* of the *Divine Presence*.

this spiritual reinvigoration one feels and the revival of one's awareness of Hashem's sovereignty may be the best indicators that one's *teshuvah* has been effective. (5638)

פי׳ ע״י שמתברר אצל האדם כי ה׳ הוא האלקים ואין חיות וכח נמצא בלתי מהשי״ת ממילא נופל בושה על האדם ושב

This is implied in the prophet's own words עַד ה׳ אֱלֹהֶיךָ, *to [until] Hashem, your God*. For our *teshuvah* to be complete, we must make Hashem into *our* God, and must realize that no other power exists in the universe besides Hashem. If we are truly aware of Hashem's total power over every aspect of life — and consequently aware also of the limitations of our own existence and power — surely we will be ashamed to sin again and stir ourselves to repent. (5647)

ואף שחטא והרשיע הרבה צריך להאמין כי עיקר נקודה ישראלית שבו היא במקומה.

The prophet's call is also a directive to each of us to look inside himself, to reflect on the Divine Presence which shines within every Jew, as we say daily in the morning blessings: אֱלֹהַי, נְשָׁמָה שֶׁנָּתַתָּ בִּי טְהוֹרָה הִיא, *My God, the soul that You placed within me is pure.* Although we may have been misled into sinning — כִּי כָשַׁלְתָּ בַּעֲוֹנֶךָ, *for you have stumbled through your iniquity* — the inner core of the Jew remains pristine pure. (5634)

כשאמר הקב״ה אנכי ה׳ אלקיך חל אלקותו ית׳ עלינו לדורות. רק עוונות מבדילין. לכן כתיב שובה כו׳ עד ה׳ אלקיך

This pure spark of Divinity within each Jew experienced its moment of exultation at the great convocation at Mount Sinai. While that Divine spark may have come to be tarnished by later sins, the process of *teshuvah* always has the power to revive this inner sanctity. Thus the summons, *Return to Hashem, your God*, may actually be exhorting us to return to the spark of Godliness Hashem implanted within each and every Jew when He first told us, אָנֹכִי ה׳ אֱלֹהֶיךָ, *I am Hashem, Your God.*

Indeed, those sacred words, (spurned by so many generations which have turned away from Torah), themselves anxiously await the day when we will return and again accept the Torah upon ourselves. (5652)

וזהו ג׳׳כ לשון הרמב׳׳ם שיעיד עליו יודע תעלומות. פי׳ יודע
תעלומות אף מה שנעלם מעיני האדם עצמו כמי׳ש

Pesikta interprets this phrase as if it said, עֵד ה׳, *Hashem is a Witness* — Hashem will testify to your repentance.

While mortals are usually aware of their *acts* of repentance, they may not be cognizant of their unfulfilled *thoughts*. Even those individuals who are able to repent fully enjoy stirrings of remorse (הִרְהוּרֵי תְּשׁוּבָה) of which they may not be fully aware. But Hashem — Who monitors man's innermost thoughts — knows. Consequently, the prophet implores us, *Repent!* Even if your intentions are thwarted and your *thoughts* of remorse are never translated into action, Hashem will still *testify* to the internal *teshuvah* that is taking place and reward you accordingly.

This interpretation gives us an insight into a famed statement of the *Rambam* (*Hilchos Teshuvah* 2:2): וְיָעִיד עָלָיו יוֹדֵעַ תַּעֲלֻמוֹת שֶׁלֹּא יָשׁוּב לְזֶה הַחֵטְא לְעוֹלָם, *The One Who knows hidden things will testify that the penitent will never again return to this sin.* Hashem knows man's deepest and most secret thoughts, even those which are hidden from the person himself, and He can testify that the faintest stirrings of return latent in the hidden recesses of every Jewish heart are sincere and that the penitent will never repeat his sin again. (5638)

כִּי כָשַׁלְתָּ בַּעֲוֹנֶךָ.
For you have stumbled through your iniquity (v. 2).

ובאמת שם ישראל לעולם אינו מתבטל לגמרי . . . והיא חלק
הנשמה שמסתלקת כשאדם חוטא אעפ׳׳כ יש בה כשלון ע׳׳י עונות
האדם

There seems to be an inherent contradiction in these words: The phrase *you have stumbled* suggests that any wrongdoing there may have been was unintentional, while *through your iniquity* clearly indicates a willful transgression of the Torah.

We can resolve this difficulty by referring to the dichotomy between the body and the soul in the Jewish makeup. When a Jew sins, it is only because his body has ignored the counsel of his soul and succumbed to the importuning of his *yetzer hara*, while the pure soul remains unsullied, and distances itself from the sinner rather than participate in the sin. Nonetheless, although the soul is not an accessory to the transgression, it also stumbles and suffers because of the sins of the body in which it is housed. In this phrase, then, the prophet is calling to the Jew: "Return to Hashem, for you — your pure soul — has *stumbled* (is affected) when the body in which it is encased sinned."

This immaculate and enduring purity of the Jewish soul is implied in a renowned saying of the Sages (*Sanhedrin* 44a): יִשְׂרָאֵל אַף עַל פִּי שֶׁחָטָא יִשְׂרָאֵל הוּא, *An Israelite, even though he has sinned, is still an Israelite.* It is significant that the Sages used the term יִשְׂרָאֵל, *Israelite*, rather than יְהוּדִי, *Jew*. While a sinner's body — depicted by the name Yaakov by which the Patriarch was known before he combatted Esav's angel — may indeed deviate from the path of purity, the soul — which is known by the name Israel, which was awarded to Yaakov after he consolidated his spiritual ascendancy over Esav — never leaves the fold. Thus it was specifically to the Children of *Israel* that Hashem proclaimed *I am* HASHEM, *your God*, and to whom the prophet calls, *Return, O* **Israel**, *to* HASHEM, *your God*.   (5665)

קְחוּ עִמָּכֶם דְּבָרִים וְשׁוּבוּ אֶל ה'

Take words with you and return to HASHEM (v. 3).

קחו עמכם דברים שע"י התורה בדחילו ורחימו נשאר ממנו
רשימה בלב האדם

Exactly which *words* did the prophet think would aid Israel in its return to Hashem? To the Jew, whose whole world revolves around the Torah, the term "words" always refers to the sacred letters and words of the Torah, unless there is reason to think otherwise. It is noteworthy that this plea is phrased in the most personal terms: *Take words* **with you** — take the words of the Torah, which can reach to the depths of your soul, as the vehicle for your *teshuvah*. Any *mitzvah* that involves the words of Torah, if they are studied with reverence and love for Hashem, cannot fail to leave a deep and lasting imprint on the Jewish soul. In the merit of taking within you the *words* of Torah, the Torah you have learned and made part of your soul, you will be given the ability to do complete *teshuvah* and to return to Hashem. (5636)

◆§ Every Jew's Capacity to Discuss Torah

כי בכל איש ישראל נמצא דברי תורה כמו״ש חז״ל. . . וע״י החטא
נסתר הארת הדיבורים הנ״ל. וע״י התשובה מתבררים.

Although many people think the ability to articulate original Torah thoughts is the exclusive province of an elite group of scholars, this is hardly true, for every Jew is blessed with an innate capacity to contemplate and discuss the Torah. The Midrash (*Yalkut Yirmiyahu* 315) interprets Hashem's fond memories of the Jewish people as expressed by the prophet Yirmiyahu, רַחֵם . . . עוֹד אֶזְכְּרֶנּוּ זָכֹר בּוֹ דַבְּרִי מִדֵּי אֲרַחֲמֶנּוּ, *Whenever I speak of him I remember him more and more . . . and I will surely take pity on him.* The expression דַבְּרִי בּוֹ refers to Hashem's word — the Torah — which He has implanted in His people and which by itself insures that we will return to Him. While it may seem at times that some Jews have forfeited their gift for expressing Torah thoughts, this is only a passing phase, the result of flirtation with sin. Once a Jew repents, however, the words embedded in every Jewish soul, the words Hoshea tells us to take with us, rise again to the surface, and again we regain our capacity to speak Torah thoughts. (5647)

◆§ Perfecting the Universe

ועיקר התשובה הוא בכח התורה כמו״ש תורת ה' תמימה משיבת
נפש. כמו שכל הבריאה הי' ע״י התורה. כן מתקנים כל הפגמים
ע״י התורה. וז״ש קחו עמכם דברים ושובו.

The Psalmist beautifully captures the relationship between *teshuvah* and returning to Torah in a few succint words: מְשִׁיבַת תְּמִימָה ה' תּוֹרַת נָפֶשׁ, *The Torah of HASHEM is perfect, it restores the soul* (19:8). It is only logical that Torah study should be an effective medium for doing *teshuvah*; for just as Hashem created the universe for the sake of Torah, so too He uses the Torah as His instrument for perfecting the universe and its inhabitants. Indeed, perhaps this is what the Sages meant in speaking of a person who studies Torah עַל מְנַת לַעֲשׂוֹת, *in order to practice it* (*Avos* 4:6 and 6:6); anyone whose intention in studying Torah is purely לַעֲשׂוֹת — to remake the universe to conform to Hashem's will, to conform to the spirit of the Torah — is assured of the ability not only to study and to teach the Torah, but also to observe it and to use it to perfect the world. (5653)

◆§ Torah Precipitates Teshuvah

ובכח התורה יכולין לשוב אליו ית״ש כדאיתא עבירה מכבה מצוה
ואינה מכבה תורה ולכן ע״י התורה יכולין לחזור ולהדליק נר
מצוה מאור התורה. והשי״ת הכין התורה לתקן על ידה כל
הקלקולים מאחר שהתורה האומן שבו נברא הכל מכש״כ שיכולין
לתקן הכל ע״י התורה.

The Sages have noted (*Sotah* 21a) that all of man's transgressions, however many they may be, can never extinguish the light of Torah. It is well known that the Torah is compared to a light and *mitzvos* to a lamp (cf. *Mishlei* 6:23, נֵר מִצְוָה וְתוֹרָה אוֹר). The light of the Torah is never extinguished and eventually stirs a Jew to repent, causing the lamp of *mitzvah* to be kindled. The Torah is called רֵאשִׁית, *the primary force*, because of its power to lift man out of the dregs of existence to the primary level of spirituality. Likewise, the Torah is compared to fire, as the prophet Yirmiyahu says, הֲלוֹא כֹה דְבָרִי כָּאֵשׁ נְאֻם ה׳ וּכְפַטִּישׁ יְפֹצֵץ סָלַע, *Is not My word like fire, says HASHEM, and like a hammer shattering stone* (23:29)? Like fire Torah has the power to incinerate man's impurities, and like a hammer it can shatter a person's facade and refashion it into a new, more spiritual personality.

Similarly, Hashem created the Torah before the material world so that if the survival of the universe was ever jeopardized by man's transgressions, it would be spared in the merit of Torah.

It is noteworthy that the prophet's call does not say explicitly to take the Torah, but rather to return with the *words* of Torah, as they leave an impact on the individual Jew. Often, however, the Sages understood the term דְּבָרִים to refer to words of reproof (cf. *Koheles* 1:1 and *Rashi*) —

take the impact of Torah on your soul, let the Torah chastise and humble you, for only then will you truly be able to return to Hashem.

This willingness to take the Torah's chastisements to heart is itself a great source of merit for Israel, a testimony to our unique nature. As the wise Shlomo *HaMelech* noted: בִּדְבָרִים לֹא יִוָּסֶר עָבֶד, *A servant cannot be disciplined with words* (*Mishlei* 29:19), for only physical punishment (or the threat of it) can move him. It is only the Jewish people — who are called Hashem's children — who are capable of returning to their Father through the vehicle of Torah. (5660)

∞§ Ten Commandments

קחו עמכם דברים הם עשרת הדברות שהם מתחדשים בכל יום

Perhaps also the term *words* mentioned by the prophet alludes to the Ten Commandments (in Hebrew the עֲשֶׂרֶת הַדִּבְּרוֹת can be rendered the *Ten Words*), which in turn correspond to the Ten Days of Repentance. On each of these ten days, Hashem pleads with us to return to the Ten Commandments and to perceive our sojourn at Sinai as an ongoing experience, a day-to-day, year-to-year renewal of the Torah, and especially to the Ten Commandments. Thus the Torah refers to הַדְּבָרִים הָאֵלֶּה אֲשֶׁר אָנֹכִי מְצַוְּךָ הַיּוֹם, *these **words** that I command you today* (*Devarim* 6:6), since the Divine command to return to Torah is renewed every day of our lives. (5665)

∞§ Return to Potential

קחו עמכם דברים כו' כי הנה עיקר התשובה הוא לתקן השליחות שנשתלח האדם לעוה״ז.

Finally, we can see the prophet's plea to *take words with you* as a heartfelt cry urging Israel to return to its inner potential. When Hashem implanted the Divine soul within us, He also charged each of us with a mission that every person is uniquely suited to accomplish. Until that mission has been accomplished, a soul cannot be restored to its Maker.

Thus the prophet is exhorting us to find our souls, to seek out the Divine Presence in our midst, so that we will be able to fulfill our Divinely endowed mission.

We find that the prophet describes the soul as Hashem's Word (cf. *Yeshayahu* 51:16 וָאָשִׂם דְּבָרַי בְּפִיךָ, *I put My Word in your mouth*). Likewise, the Sages depicted the relationship between the soul and the body as being comparable to God's Name (אַזְכָּרוֹת) inscribed on the parchment of a Torah scroll (גְּוִילִין).   (5651)

◄§ Good Beneath All Evil

תשא עון וקח טוב. כי בכל דבר יש תערובות טו״ר וצריכין לשוב
לבער הפסולת ולהוציא הנק״יד שנתערבו בהחטא. וזהו למדו
הטיב להטיב כדפרש״י שם.

אִמְרוּ אֵלָיו כָּל תִּשָּׂא עָוֹן וְקַח טוֹב

Say to Him, "May You lift up [forgive] every iniquity and take [accept] what is good" (v. 3).

The prophet continues his outline of the process of *teshuvah* by telling Israel to bear its sins and focus on the good in its soul. Rather than allow ourselves to be burdened by regret for our past misdeeds, we must strive to develop the inherent goodness which lies hidden in our souls beneath the layers of tarnish left by our sins. The Sages' dictum that a person does not sin unless he is obsessed by a deranged spirit (cf. *Yalkut Bamidbar* 605) actually implies man's innate and invincible goodness: Since only under the influence of external forces can a Jew be made to sin, by repenting, we *lift up* the outer veneer of sin to uncover and *take* the inner goodness that lies beneath.

Indeed, even sin itself, which we generally think of as totally bad, contains an aspect of inner goodness. By repenting and eradicating the outer facade of our transgressions, we actually uncover a hidden goodness latent in every sin.[1] In this light we can appreciate Hashem's warning to Kayin after he killed his brother Hevel (*Bereishis* 4:7),

---

1. *Author's Note*: Perhaps this refers to the fact that sin stimulates us to do *teshuvah*; only by having transgressed can we attain the level of *baalei teshuvah*, a status the Sages tell us is even greater than that of the totally righteous.

הֲלוֹא אִם תֵּיטִיב שְׂאֵת, *If you do good* [i.e. repent], *you will lift up* your sin and reveal the inner core of goodness underneath it.

This formidable undertaking, ferreting out the good component of sin, can be accomplished only through Torah, which gives Israel the power to extract the good from amongst the evil of the world. This esoteric and sublime concept — finding the good lurking beneath the sin — is also voiced by Yeshayahu (1:17), pleading with Israel to return, לִמְדוּ הֵיטֵב, *learn well.* As *Rashi* suggests, לִמְדוּ לְהֵיטִיב, *learn good* — learn to find the good in all evil. (5655)

⋙ Return to the Ten Commandments

וקח טוב כמ''ש רש''י למדנו דרך הטוב. ויחדש לנו עשרת
הדברות ואנכי ה' אלקיך.

E arlier we interpreted the phrase קְחוּ עִמָּכֶם דְּבָרִים, *Take words with you,* as an oblique call to return to the spiritual state we enjoyed when we first received the Ten Commandments. Perhaps we can understand the conclusion of this verse in a similar manner. In response to Hashem's plea (voiced through the prophet) to return to Him, Israel responds, כָּל תִּשָּׂא עָוֹן — "Forgive us our sins and do not allow them to prevent us from making a *complete* return" — וְקַח טוֹב — "Take us on the good path, back to Sinai, back to the Ten Commandments."

(5665)

⋙ Thanking Hashem for Bad as well as Good

דכ' טוב להודות. פי' לך נאה להודות כי כל הדברים שנראין
תמוהים בעוה''ז ולעתיד יתברר הכל כי הי' הכל הכנה ועצה
לטובה

R ashi offers a startling insight on this phrase וְקַח טוֹב :וְקַבֵּל הוֹדָיָה
מֵאִתָּנוּ שֶׁנֶּאֱמַר טוֹב לְהֹדוֹת לַה', *Accept gratitude from us, as the Psalmist says [in the Psalm, A Song for the Sabbath Day]," It is good to thank HASHEM"* (92:2). What good can we offer Hashem other than our gratitude, which the Psalmist also calls good?

This comment raises several immediate questions: Why would a repentant Jew go so far as to *thank* Hashem for having sinned? Also, what connection did *Rashi* see between *teshuvah* and Shabbos that led him to draw his source from the *Song to the Sabbath Day*?

According to *Rashi*, the prophet is trying to galvanize Israel to return to Hashem by evoking a picture of the glorious future. If we evaluate events and situations only from the narrow perspective of our world, it is difficult if not impossible to arouse ourselves to do *teshuvah*.[1] But some day, when mankind as a whole accepts Hashem's sovereignty, all our questions and doubts will be resolved. On that day, we will recognize that everything Hashem has done — both things which appeared bad at the time, as well as those which were obviously good — were all in Israel's best interests.

Indeed, all the baffling events of this world are really integral modules in the Divine master plan to prepare us for the great events of the future world. The prophet Yeshayahu alludes to the relationship between the muddle we see in the present and the brilliant clarity of the future world in these few words: מַגִּיד מֵרֵאשִׁית אַחֲרִית . . . עֲצָתִי תָקוּם, *He foretells at the outset what will occur in the end . . . My advice will be fulfilled* (46:10). While on the surface this verse speaks of Hashem's ability to foretell what will transpire in the world's final epoch, in light of our remarks we can also interpret it as follows: "The first events — those of the present era — are heralds and precursors of the events of the final period." Furthermore, the particular order in which events occur in the contemporary world is Divinely ordained, a form of heavenly *advice* which will eventually be accepted and *fulfilled* by all mankind.

Thus in citing the *Song for the Sabbath Day*, perhaps *Rashi* is alluding not to the weekly Sabbath (vital to our lives and dear to us as it may be), but rather to the future time, when the world will be in a permanent state of Sabbath and all evil will cease (cf. *Tamid* 7:4). At that time all humanity will pay homage to Hashem, as the prophet Tzephaniah promises: כִּי אָז אֶהְפֹּךְ אֶל עַמִּים שָׂפָה בְרוּרָה לִקְרֹא כֻלָּם בְּשֵׁם ה' לְעָבְדוֹ שְׁכֶם אֶחָד, *For then I will turn to the peoples with clear speech, to call upon all of them in the Name of Hashem to serve Him all together* (3:9).

Israel, however, need not wait so long; even now we believe with total faith in Hashem's guarantees of a better future and praise Him for

---

1. This is because Hashem has built so many apparent (but only apparent) injustices into the world, in order to mislead us and to increase the reward of those who maintain their faith in the Torah's view of existence, and who are not led astray by the world's illusions.

everything that occurs. We give thanks not just for events that are obviously good, but even for the ones that seem bad from our limited perspective. Hashem's assurance that better days lie ahead not only consoles us in the despair of exile, it also prods us to repent in the knowedge that eventually all mankind will return to Hashem.

All these many different meanings are subsumed in the prophet's terse call, וְקַח טוֹב, *take what is good* — "Seize the good!" Hoshea tells us. "Acknowledge that everything in our world, the world which seems so dark and murky to us, is truly good because it prepares humanity, and indeed the whole of creation, for its eventual climax. Take this good in your minds, and return to Hashem!"   (5658)

⋑ Forgive Us to Better Serve Hashem

שנעשה מכאן ולהבא. שצריך האדם לבקש שיתקבל לפני הבורא
ית' בתשובה.

We pray to Hashem, כָּל תִּשָּׂא עָוֹן וְקַח טוֹב, "Lift up and forgive our iniquities now so that in the future we may serve You in purity." The Psalmist alludes to a similar thought in different words, כִּי עִמְּךָ הַסְּלִיחָה לְמַעַן תִּוָּרֵא (130:4), "Forgive us now so that we may serve You and You may become feared in the world through our service." (5639)

⋑ Return to the Universe's Good Beginnings

הואיל והכל הי' צפוי לפניו ית' וראה שיש בזה ג"כ טוב הצפון.
ולכן לעולם יש תקנה. רק שצריכין רחמים שיתגלה הדרך איך
למצוא הטוב אחר החטא. וזה הבקשה שיורנו דרך הטוב.

The call, וְקַח טוֹב, also contains a plea to return to the path of that which was first called good in primeval times, when Hashem surveyed the universe whose creation He had just completed and declared (*Bereishis* 1:31), וְהִנֵּה טוֹב מְאֹד, *Behold, it is very good!* By itself, the word *good* would have neatly described a universe dominated by *tzaddikim; **very** good*, however, can only mean a much higher world, a world of the good that can be attained only after we have confronted evil and bested it, because only then is it possible to achieve the lofty status of *baal teshuvah*.[1]

Indeed, this satisfaction Hashem expressed with the totality of His handiwork, His final seal of approval for the universe, came only in the merit of those generations which would sin and do *teshuvah*. It was only when He looked at **everything** He created — at all the generations destined to emerge from the first man, including those who were to sink to the depths of sin and then pull themselves back up again — that He could say, "Behold, *it is* **very** good! Behold, eventually the Jewish people will return to Me and attain the preeminent status of **very good**".

Just as Hashem affirmed the supreme value of the universe He had just created, and its right to exist, on the basis of its glorious end, so too should the potential returnee, rather than succumb to depression and remain mired in sin, reflect on the lofty status he can attain after doing *teshuvah*. Certainly, it is no easy feat to think so far into the future from his perspective, to consider the world of *teshuvah* while the sinner is dealing with the consequences of his transgressions. With thoughts of our desire to do *teshuvah* in mind, we plead with Hashem, קַח טוֹב, "Teach us the good path, the path of *teshuvah* which at the very beginning of the world You called **very good**. (5644)

וּנְשַׁלְּמָה פָרִים שְׂפָתֵינוּ.

Let our lips substitute for bulls (v. 3).

ונשלמה פרים שפתינו ע׳׳י העסק בתורה מתקרבים אליו ית׳ כמו ע׳׳י הקרבן

While this phrase is usually understood as a plea to accept our prayers in compensation for the animal offerings we are unable to bring, through our many sins, the prophet may also be alluding here to the role of Torah study as a means of returning to Him. Just as the earlier call, קְחוּ עִמָּכֶם דְּבָרִים, *Take words with you*, also expressed a Divine request for Israel to return to the Torah, perhaps this phrase is also an assurance from the prophet that the Torah we study now can be just as effective a medium for returning to Hashem in complete *teshuvah* as were the bullocks we once offered on the Altar. (5653)

---

1. As we have discussed elsewhere in the essay on The Unique Standing of the Baal Teshuvah, the Sages said (*Berachos* 34b) that a penitent attains a much higher status than that of those who have always been totally righteous.

וְלֹא נֹאמַר עוֹד אֱלֹהֵינוּ לְמַעֲשֵׂה יָדֵינוּ

We will never again call our handiwork "our gods" (v. 4)

וז״ש ולא נאמר כו׳ אלקינו למעשה ידינו שזה עיקר התשובה
לשוב להתדבק בעיקר חיות אלקי שבו

From this pithy phrase emerges the essence of *teshuvah*: No longer is strength (one of the meanings of the word אֵל) to be defined as the force of one's hand; rather we must realize that true inner strength rests in the Divine soul Hashem has implanted in us. (5634)

אֹהֲבֵם נְדָבָה

I will love them charitably [willingly] (v. 5).

כמו כן מתנדב לאהוב השבים לפניו בתשובה. . . . אבל כמה
תשובות בדבר. א׳ כי המגעגע לבוא לאהבה זו מתהפך הלב
לאהבתו ית׳. וכמו כן הפרעון ע״ז התשוקה לבוא לאהבה זו.
השי״ת משלם מדה במדה להתנדב אהבה להם.

The prophet tells us that although Israel does not merit Hashem's love, He will nonetheless love us as an act of charity. This is a startling statement: How can someone be loved on the basis of charity? If Hashem feels no emotional bond linking Him to Israel, how can He love us "charitably"? Love has to be genuinely felt, not done out of charity or pity.

We must understand, however, that such a question may be asked only about ordinary mortals, but is inappropriate concerning Hashem. Just as He created the universe out of unfathomable love for His as yet non-existent creations, knowing that they might not prove worthy of that love, so too He can extend His loving "embrace" to those who repent, even if they do not deserve His love.

A similar question is asked about the requirement to love Hashem: How can love for anyone be compelled, even for Hashem? These two questions, although in a sense antitheses, can be answered in similar fashion. By yearning for Hashem, even though we do not know how to approach Him, we can develop genuine feelings of love and an emotional bond. Similarly, when Hashem generously offers us His love even though we do not yet deserve it, He knows that we will ultimately merit His love. (5634, 5639)

◆§ Mutual Love Between Hashem and Israel Never Ceases

רק ע״י הנקיון מגשמיות והתרחקות דברי עוה״ז מוציאין האהבה מכח אל הפועל. וכמו כן נמצא אהבת הבורא ית׳ לבנ״י עמו וחלקו. רק החטאים והעונות מבדילין.

In truth, both Israel's love for Hashem and His love for us have never completely lapsed. While the lures of the material world often obscure our inherent love for the Creator, they have never succeeded in totally eradicating it. The moment we make an effort to distance ourselves from the world, with its desires and obsessions, our deep-seated love for Hashem emerges again.

So too, Hashem's love for Israel has never faded. While our transgressions create a barrier between ourselves and Hashem, sincere *teshuvah* transcends that barrier and rekindles Hashem's innate love for us, as Hoshea says, אֶרְפָּא מְשׁוּבָתָם אֹהֲבֵם נְדָבָה כִּי שָׁב אַפִּי מִמֶּנּוּ, *I will heal their rebelliousness, I will love them willingly, for My wrath will be withdrawn from them* (v. 5). (5639)

◆§ Removing the Barriers to Divine Love

אבל גם זה נכון שכאשר נפתח שער הפנימיות האהבה המוסתרת אצל בנ״י כחודה של מחט פותח הקב״ה באהבה המוסתרת אצלו כפתחו של אולם וממילא עי״ז נפתח אח״כ בלב אדם עצמו ג״כ כפתחו של אולם.

Let us elaborate further on this metamorphosis, how a love which exists on both sides can be transformed from a deep, concealed feeling into a highly visible relationship. Imagine a remote and inaccessible gateway beyond which lie valuable treasures hidden within. Although enormous efforts are required to surmount the many barriers and obstacles which block the approach to it, the gateway nonetheless remains ready and open, its treasures available to those who earnestly seek them.

So too, the "gateway" of Hashem's love for Israel exists in a lofty spiritual site far beyond the reach of humanity. Only Israel — and only after we make gargantuan efforts to do *teshuvah* — can scale the heights and reach the summit. But still the gate remains open, and Hashem's love for Israel lives forever, despite the obstacles our sins have placed between ourselves and Him. Nor need these heights be scaled all at once; the gate of Hashem's love can be attained by degrees, through an incremental upward process of *teshuvah*. As we reveal our love for Hashem by stripping away layers of materialism, we collapse many of the barriers between our present station and our long-sought goal, and winning Hashem's eternal love.

This is not a vain, one-sided quest; as we dismantle the barriers we have created with our misdeeds, Hashem reciprocates by returning to His children and removing the impediments He has allowed to be erected to our return. Hashem's innate longing for us to simply begin the process of return is poignantly described by the prophet Yirmiyahu: זָכַרְתִּי לָךְ חֶסֶד נְעוּרַיִךְ אַהֲבַת כְּלוּלתָיִךְ, *I remember* — how can I ever forget! — *the kindness of your youth, the love of your bridal days* (2:2).

In this light, Hoshea's description of Hashem's love as אַהֲבַת נְדָבָה, "charitable love," assumes new significance. Hashem promises that He will act out of charity and dismantle the barriers which separate lowly creatures like ourselves from His Divine love — if we only take the initiative and return to Him.

Hashem has charted for us the path leading to the gateway of His love: (cf. *Shir HaShirim Rabbah* 5) "Open for Me an opening as wide as the eye of a needle, and I in return will open for you an opening as wide as the great chamber of the *Beis HaMikdash*. Open for Me the gates of your heart and allow My Presence to penetrate! Let the innate love every Jew has for the *Shechinah* emerge, and then I will open a much wider opening, like the opening of a great chamber, and I will enable you to reach the summit, to elicit My love for you and to bring it again to the forefront."

Indeed, the entire process of *teshuvah* may be envisioned as a rapprochement, through which we dismantle all those barriers which inhibit our innate love of Hashem. He in turn removes all factors that prevent His love of Israel from reaching fruition. This is what the Psalmist meant in calling Hashem שׁוֹמֵר יִשְׂרָאֵל, *the Guardian of Israel*

(121:4), that He eternally guards and protects His inner love for Israel, always awaiting the moment when we will return to Him.

(*Likutim Parshas Vayelech*)

אֶהְיֶה כַטַּל לְיִשְׂרָאֵל יִפְרַח כַּשּׁוֹשַׁנָּה וְיַךְ שָׁרָשָׁיו כַּלְּבָנוֹן: יֵלְכוּ יוֹנְקוֹתָיו וִיהִי כַזַּיִת הוֹדוֹ

I will be like the dew to Israel, it shall blossom like the rose and strike its roots like the [forest of] Lebanon. Its tender branches shall spread and its glory shall be like the olive tree (vs. 6-7).

וז״ש אהי׳ כטל כו׳ ויך שרשיו כלבנון ילכו יונקותיו כו׳ כל פרשת ההפטורה. הכוונה שיוכל להוציא מכח אל הפועל שיתקנו הדברים כל הגוף להפריח ולהצמיח לעשות פירות כנ״ל.

In these soothing words the prophet assures the repentant Jew that he will succeed in his assigned mission. As we have said, Hashem implants His Word, in the form of a Divine soul, into every Jew. Earlier the prophet pleaded with Israel to return to that Divine spark, as we explained on the verse, *Take with you words.*

Now, the prophet describes the great reward which awaits the returnee. By returning to the roots of his soul, the *baal teshuvah* can bring his vast innate potential to actualization. The various forms of symbolism employed here by the prophet — "I will be like the dew," it will "strike its roots like the [forest of] Lebanon" and so on — all these allude to the *baal teshuvah's* newly discovered ability to grow and achieve his full potential. Just as the prophet Yeshayahu asserts that the soul will not return to its Maker until it has accomplished its designated mission,[1] so too Hoshea exhorts Israel, "Repent and you will reap the full benefit of *teshuvah*, the flourishing of your inner potential."

(5651)

יָשֻׁבוּ יֹשְׁבֵי בְצִלּוֹ

Those who dwell in His shadow will return (v. 8).

---

1. This point is discussed in detail in the section on the *Haftarah* of the Fast of Gedaliah, on the verse, *My word that emanates from My mouth shall not return to Me unfulfilled unless it will have accpomplished what I desired and brought success where I sent it (Yeshayahu 55:11).*

תשובה ראשונה אל ה׳ שהוא עמנו בגלות בחי׳ אל אמונה ע״ז
נאמר ישובו יושבי בצלו. הגם דרש״י פי׳ שהיו יושבים בצלו מ״מ
גם בגלות מאמינים בנ״י ונמשכין אחריו אעפ״י שאין צלו ניכר.

This phrase is an allusion to the Jew mired in exile. Although he has
no visible manifestation of the Divine Presence to guide him, a Jew
nonetheless *believes* that Hashem is with him. This is what Moshe
meant when he described Hashem as אֵל אֱמוּנָה (*Devarim* 32:4), *the God
of faith*, the God in Whom we believe even when we do not feel His
Presence openly. In the merit of this belief, this willingness to follow
Hashem blindly in exile, eventually the *baal teshuvah* will merit to
actually feel Hashem's Presence when He reveals Himself to Israel and
the rest of the world at the ingathering of the exiles.

In this light, we can reinterpret a renowned verse at the end of
Eichah, הֲשִׁיבֵנוּ ה׳ אֵלֶיךָ וְנָשׁוּבָה, *Return us to You, Hashem and we will
return* (5:21). Allow us to return to You even when we lack a clear
perception of Your Presence, and in the merit of those initial steps
towards *teshuvah*, we — You and Israel together — will return from
our exile.
(5662)

Alternatively, the expression *those who dwell in His Shadow* may
refer to the special aura experienced by the Jew every Shabbos. As we
affirm in the Friday night prayers, הַפּוֹרֵשׂ סֻכַּת שָׁלוֹם עָלֵינוּ, [Hashem]
spreads His canopy of peace over us. Surely there is no more favorable
time to do *teshuvah* than the one day of the week we spend entirely in
Hashem's Shadow.[1]
(5641)

וַה׳ נָתַן קוֹלוֹ לִפְנֵי חֵילוֹ

*And HASHEM gave forth His voice [in prophetic warning]
before [sending forth] His army (Yoel 2:11).*

This selection from the prophet Yoel traditionally read as part of the
Haftarah of *Shabbos Teshuvah* is often taken as an allusion to the
sound of the *shofar*.

When a Jew hears the *shofar*, he is reminded of another momentous
sound, Hashem's thunderous proclamation which emerged from Mount
Sinai to fill the world: אָנֹכִי ה׳ אֱלֹהֶיךָ, *I am HASHEM, your God*. No matter
how far a Jew may have strayed from the voice of the Torah which is

---

1. For expansion on this theme, see our essay on *Shabbos Teshuvah*.

his inalienable heritage, these eternal words remain embedded in his soul. Always the sound of the *shofar* retains its power to arouse this latent spark, as Shlomo *HaMelech* sings, אֲנִי יְשֵׁנָה וְלִבִּי עֵר קוֹל דּוֹדִי דוֹפֵק, *I am asleep but my heart is awake. The voice of my Love knocks (Shir HaShirim* 5:2). However deep may be our slumber in exile, the voice of our Lover Hashem keeps trying to awaken us and to return us to His service. We may be asleep . . . but our hearts remain awake.

Hashem forever resonates together with the Jewish heart and seeks to arouse the spark of Torah which is never totally extinguished. Israel in turn responds, "I may appear to be asleep, my adherence to your Torah and *mitzvos* may have grown feeble, but the eternal sound of Torah pulsating in the Jewish heart has remained ever vibrant."

In a similar vein, the prophet Yeshayahu proclaims, וְאָנֹכִי לֹא אֶשְׁכָּחֵךְ, *I shall not forget you* (49:15). The Ten Commandments, which commence with אָנֹכִי ה' אֱלֹהֶיךָ, will never fade completely but will remain permanently embedded in the Jewish psyche, waiting to be aroused by the sound of the *shofar*. (5662)

תְּשׁוּבָה מֵאַהֲבָה
Teshuvah with Love

אָמַר רֵישׁ לָקִישׁ גְּדוֹלָה תְּשׁוּבָה שֶׁזְּדוֹנוֹת נַעֲשׂוֹת לוֹ כִּשְׁגָגוֹת . . . וְהָאָמַר רֵישׁ לָקִישׁ גְּדוֹלָה תְּשׁוּבָה שֶׁזְּדוֹנוֹת נַעֲשׂוּ לוֹ כִּזְכוּיּוֹת . . . לֹא קַשְׁיָא כַּאן מֵאַהֲבָה כַּאן מִיִּרְאָה

Reish Lakish said: Teshuvah is so great that deliberate [transgressions] are treated like inadvertent [transgressions] for [the repentant] . . . But Reish Lakish has [also] said: Teshuvah is so great that deliberate [transgressions] are treated like meritorious deeds for him . . . This is not a difficulty: Here [Reish Lakish refers to repentance] out of love; here [he refers to repentance] out of fear (Yoma 86b).

In the following essay, we will consider the nature of *teshuvah* conducted out of love of Hashem (תְּשׁוּבָה מֵאַהֲבָה). In particular, we will consider the circumstances that are conducive to תְּשׁוּבָה מֵאַהֲבָה and especially the baffling comment that through such repentance, sins are changed into sources of merit.

תְּשׁוּבָה מֵאַהֲבָה

Israel's innate love for Hashem "matches" Hashem's love for Israel.

אכן ע״ז נאמר מים רבים לא יוכלו לכבות כו׳ האהבה. דכמו דיש
אהבה לכנס״י ואין מים רבים של האומות יכולין לכבותה. כמו כן
יש מזה בכל נפש מישראל ג״כ.

While it may be difficult to comprehend how a sinner can already love Hashem, we should recall the splendid "love relationship" that has always existed between Hashem and the Jewish people. As *Shir HaShirim* (8:7) notes: מַיִם רַבִּים לֹא יוּכְלוּ לְכַבּוֹת אֶת הָאַהֲבָה, *Many waters [of heathen tribulation] cannot extinguish the fire of this love.* Paralleling Hashem's love for us is the innate love that every Jew — no matter how enmeshed in sin he may be — retains for Hashem. All the persecutions inflicted upon us by mankind will never extinguish that love.

This love stems from the Exodus when Hashem chose us as His nation. The comment of the *Zohar* that יְצִיאַת מִצְרַיִם is equivalent to the fifty gates of knowledge (חֲמִשִּׁים שַׁעֲרֵי בִינָה) may be understood in this light. The emotional bond between Hashem and us, created at the Exodus, is as effective as all the Torah knowledge that we could possibly acquire in ensuring that the special personality of the Jew — the heart and mind of Israel — will never be affected by the pressures of the world at large. (5639)

תְּשׁוּבָה מִיִּרְאָה / **Hashem Loves Him**
תְּשׁוּבָה מֵאַהֲבָה / **He Loves Hashem**

ונמצא השב מיראה השי״ת מקרבו ומתנדב לו אהבה בלבו. אבל
מי ששב מאהבתו הוא גדול יותר.

In truth, love of Hashem is a prerequisite for any form of repentance. The distinction between תְּשׁוּבָה מֵאַהֲבָה and תְּשׁוּבָה מִיִּרְאָה lies in the origin of this vital component of תְּשׁוּבָה – אַהֲבָה. Whereas the individual who returns to Hashem out of fear is granted אַהֲבַת ה׳ as a gift from Hashem Himself (in recognition of the penitent's first steps toward תְּשׁוּבָה albeit out of fear), one who repents out of love needs no Divine gift. His אַהֲבַת ה׳ is innate, and so powerful a presence that it inspires him to return to Hashem. As a result his reward is even greater — his sins become merits. (See our commentary on the *Haftarah* of *Shabbos Shuvah* and especially on אֹהֲבֵם נְדָבָה). (cf. 5634)

תְּשׁוּבָה מִיִּרְאָה / Initial Step
תְּשׁוּבָה מֵאַהֲבָה / Result of תְּשׁוּבָה מֵיִּרְאָה

התשובה מיראה השי״ת נותן לו בחי׳ אהבה במתנה כמ״ש אוהבם נדבה.

It is noteworthy that Hoshea's clarion call to *teshuvah* only insists that Israel return out of fear [cf. *Yoma* 86b cited partially in the introduction of this essay which interprets the verse כִּי כָשַׁלְתָּ בַּעֲוֹנֶךָ to refer to תְּשׁוּבָה מִיִּרְאָה (*Hoshea* 14:2)]. It is unrealistic to expect a sinner to *immediately* love Hashem. Rather, אַהֲבַת ה׳ is the end product of a process beginning with תְּשׁוּבָה מֵיִּרְאָה. As a result of the sinner's newly acquired fear of Hashem, Hashem grants him the gift of love, enabling the former sinner to now return on the basis of love. (5637)

תְּשׁוּבָה מִיִּרְאָה / All Week Long
תְּשׁוּבָה מֵאַהֲבָה / Shabbos

והאמת כי תשובה מיראה היא בימות החול ועי״ז זוכה לשוב מאהבה בש״ק.

The distinction between these two types of *teshuvah* may be in their timing. In the merit of repenting all week through fear of Hashem, we merit תְּשׁוּבָה מֵאַהֲבָה on Shabbos. It is well known that the primeval light existing at creation was eventually hidden by Hashem, Who perceived that this spiritual luminescence was too powerful for this world. Yet, Hashem did not remove this awesome force until after the first Shabbos. Shabbos, the day associated with the "extra soul" (נְשָׁמָה יְתֵירָה), is the singular occasion in which this world can absorb some of the radiance of the World to Come. It is on the Shabbos day, armed with the נְשָׁמָה יְתֵירָה basking in this glorious light, that Israel can come back lovingly to Hashem. (5637)

⊰ תְּשׁוּבָה מִיּרְאָה / Fear of Sin (יִרְאַת חֵטְא)
תְּשׁוּבָה מֵאַהֲבָה / Resulting from Shame (בּוּשָׁה)

> כי מקודם צריכין לשוב מיראת החטא לבקש רחמים להתקרב אל
> הבורא ית׳. ואח״כ כשזוכין להתקרב צריכין לשוב ע״י בושה
> מגודל חסד ה׳ שמקרב החוטא. וע״ז נאמר ונשובה כו׳.

The relationship between תְּשׁוּבָה motivated by fear and love is indicated by the verse הֲשִׁיבֵנוּ ה׳ אֵלֶיךָ וְנָשׁוּבָה, Bring us back to You, Hashem, and we shall return (Eichah 5:21). The first phase of תְּשׁוּבָה results from a fear of sin and its consequences (יִרְאַת חֵטְא). We plead: הֲשִׁיבֵנוּ ה׳ אֵלֶיךָ, Bring us back to You, despite the barrier created by our sins. But even after Hashem brings us back to Him, we have hardly completed our sacred task of doing teshuvah. Now we are propelled by a sense of shame (בּוּשָׁה). Hashem in His infinite kindness saw fit to welcome us back — despite our manifold transgressions and total unworthiness. Understandably, this creates a sense of inferiority and shame, but also a feeling of love appreciating how God displayed compassion despite the many times that we have wronged Him. The בַּעַל תְּשׁוּבָה can now complete the cycle. Loving Hashem again, he can return on his own initiative (וְנָשׁוּבָה), this time מֵאַהֲבָה. (5638)

⊰ תְּשׁוּבָה מִיּרְאָה / Noach
תְּשׁוּבָה מֵאַהֲבָה / Avraham

> נח הי׳ צריך סעד לתומכו ואברהם אבינו לא הי׳ צריך סעד כי זה
> מיראה וזה מאהבה.

The distinction between teshuvah based on love and that based on fear may be appreciated by considering Biblical personalities who epitomized each characteristic. Noach, who required Divine assistance to remain upright in an evil world (cf. *Bereishis; Rashi* 6:9), related to Hashem out of fear. Avraham, on the other hand, who stood alone against assorted evildoers, merited that distinction through his love of Hashem.

(5641)

§⊷ תְּשׁוּבָה מִיִּרְאָה / Negation of Evil (סוּר מֵרַע)
תְּשׁוּבָה מֵאַהֲבָה / Doing Good (עֲשֵׂה טוֹב)

כן תשובה מיראה בחי' סור מרע שמבקש להתנקות מלכלוך
העוונות. אבל מאהבה הוא בחי' עשה טוב

The admonition of David, סוּר מֵרַע וַעֲשֵׂה טוֹב, *Turn from evil and do good* (*Tehillim* 34:15), helps delineate the distinction between these types of *teshuvah*. While the returnee who comes back because of his fear of Hashem is seeking primarily to be cleansed of the impact of his sins — the negation of evil — one who returns out of love is motivated primarily to return to his previous capacity to perform good. The lingering impact of previous transgressions makes it difficult to cling to Hashem (דְּבֵקוּת). By doing תְּשׁוּבָה מֵאַהֲבָה, we hope to return to Hashem and the warm relationship that once existed before sinning. As Yirmiyahu pleads: חַדֵּשׁ יָמֵינוּ כְּקֶדֶם, *renew our days as of old* (*Eichah* 5:21).

(5641, 5662)

§⊷ תְּשׁוּבָה מִיִּרְאָה / Return of the Wicked
תְּשׁוּבָה מֵאַהֲבָה / Return of the Righteous

דתשובה מיראה היא תשובת הרשעים מאימת הגיהנם. ותשובת
הצדיקים הוא מתאוותם להתקרב אל ה' ולבקר בהיכלו בגן עדן.
ותשובה זו גם אל הצדיקים . . . וכל חטא קל פוגם שלא יוכל
לעלות במקום גבוה.

Typically, we associate *teshuvah* with evil, assuming that evildoers need to repent. In reality, the *teshuvah* of the wicked is but a preliminary form of repentance, *teshuvah* out of fear of punishment. On the other hand, the more rarefied forms of *teshuvah*, done out of love of Hashem, can only be attained by the righteous. As David voiced it so sublimely: לַחֲזוֹת בְּנֹעַם ה' וּלְבַ(קֵּר בְּהֵיכָלוֹ, *to behold the sweetness of* HASHEM *and to contemplate in His Sanctuary* (*Tehillim* 27:4). The righteous seek to come close to Hashem to visit his "palace," his inner chamber — the Garden of Eden enjoyed by them after the life of this world. While every *tzaddik* is assured a portion in the World to Come, many gradations and levels of reward are available, varying according to their achievement in this world. And significant differences exist between the various levels of spiritual bliss enjoyed by the righteous in Eden. The Talmud (*Bava Basra* 75a) notes that every *tzaddik* is "burned" (i.e. feels awed by the fiery presence) by the canopy (i.e. the spiritual reward) enjoyed by his even greater contemporaries. The תְּשׁוּבָה מֵאַהֲבָה is the avid and incessant longing of the righteous to attain the maximum possible spiritual reward and closeness to Hashem in the World to Come.

Each of us (even if we haven't attained the levels of sanctity of the righteous) are motivated to return to Hashem מֵאַהֲבָה as we experience the frustration of being unable to come close to Hashem — despite our persistent pleas and prayers. We reason, surely it must be the taint caused by our sins that prevent this intimacy from developing. Yet, rather than yield in our efforts to approach Hashem, we repent again — this time spurred by an even greater love of Hashem that is as yet unfulfilled.

In one of the Torah's first calls to *teshuvah*, Hashem urges Kayin (who had just murdered Hevel), אִם תֵּיטִיב שְׂאֵת, *Surely, if you improve yourself, you will be forgiven* (*Bereishis* 4:7). It can also be interpreted: If you will do good (i.e. repent), you will be uplifted (נשא). You will merit to lift up your soul, to let it soar from the confinement of the body. Every sacrifice offered when the Temple stood, every prayer, serves the same function — to satisfy the intense yearning of the Jew to come close to his Creator.   (cf. 5662)

§⇔ תְּשׁוּבָה מִיִּרְאָה / Body
תְּשׁוּבָה מֵאַהֲבָה / Soul

יש תשובה בבחי' הנשמה ובבחי' הגוף בחי' זכור ושמור. תשובה
מיראה על החטאים והם מצד הגוף בחי' סור מרע מל"ת. ותשובה
(מיראה) [מאהבה] על חסרון המעשים טובים

---

*I*n a similar vein, we may suggest that *teshuvah* based on fear is performed by the physical side of man, the body — fearing the impact of sins it had committed and the consequent punishment it may endure. On the other hand, תְּשׁוּבָה מֵאַהֲבָה, *return out of love,* is the plaintive cry of the soul (נְשָׁמָה) seeking to reassert its dominance over man's physical instinct.

(cf. 5662)

◆§ The Scales of Justice

◆§ תְּשׁוּבָה מִיִּרְאָה / Lifting up the Scales of Demerit
תְּשׁוּבָה מֵאַהֲבָה / Pressing down on the Scale of Merit

ולפעמים מתעורר האדם בתשובה ע״י אהבה שמתפעל איך בכח
אדם במעשים טובים לעשות נ״ר למעלה ועי״ז מתחרט על החטא
שעי״ז אין בכחו להתדבק . . . וזה כובש שכף הזכיות מתעלה
ומתגדל ומכריע. . . . נמצא ממש זדונות נעשין כמו זכיות שעי״ז
הוסיף כח ועוז בהזכיות כנ״ל.

---

*I*n order to understand the distinction between תְּשׁוּבָה מֵאַהֲבָה and תְּשׁוּבָה מִיִּרְאָה, let us recall an argument in the Gemara (*Rosh Hashanah* 17a) about the manner in which Hashem tilts the scales of justice (wherever possible) in favor of merit. While one opinion rules that Hashem lifts up the sinner's demerits (נוֹשֵׂא), the other argues that He "presses down" (כּוֹבֵשׁ; i.e. gives additional weight to) the scales of merit. These opinions are not necessarily opposites but rather are simply considering different contingencies. If the individual being judged had returned to Hashem out of fear, realizing the awesome consequences of his transgressions, he manages to weaken the effect of his sins. He lightens the scale of demerits about to be meted out. As *Michah* (7:18) describes Hashem's Attribute of Mercy, He is נֹשֵׂא עָוֹן , *lifting up the [scales of] sin.*

On the other hand, one who returns out of love of Hashem contemplates the "*nachas*" that Hashem derived from his *mitzvah*. He also realizes the negative impact of his sins, how they prevented him from clinging to Torah and *mitzvos*. It is this combination — the good accomplished by the *mitzvos* he had already performed as well as the harm caused by his sins — that generate his *teshuvah*. Inasmuch as the significance of his *mitzvos* that he had already performed propels him to do *teshuvah*, Hashem, too, gives additional weight (כּוֹבֵשׁ) to those *mitzvos*. He too deems the individual's past *mitzvos* to be of additional significance.

In this light, we can resolve the baffling mystery with which we opened this essay — how sins can be transmuted into *mitzvos*. The Talmud is alluding to the process of Divine Justice that we have just described. As a result of weighing the difference between past sins and the *mitzvos* already performed, the individual repents and gives additional weight to his *mitzvos*. Since the sins led to additional weight being given to his previous *mitzvos*, since his sins led to additional merit (*teshuvah*), we can truly say that transgressions — coupled with *teshuvah* based on love — have the effect of merit.

(5644)

⊷§ Additional Forms of Teshuvah
Teshuvah out of Truth / תְּשׁוּבַת אֱמֶת

וויש עוד תשובה למעלה מזה ונק׳ תשובת אמת לשמו ית׳ כי יש
לך אדם שירא מעונש ושב.

We have discussed in detail the two principle forms of *teshuvah*, out of fear and love. However, another even greater form of *teshuvah* exists: תְּשׁוּבָה מֵאֱמֶת — the individual who returns to Hashem not out of concern for his own fate but simply because he realizes the truth, how horrendous it was to defy Hashem's will. We can draw an analogy between the *Avos* and the various forms of *teshuvah*: Avraham epitomizing love of Hashem; Yitzchak, fear; and Yaakov, truth (תִּתֵּן אֱמֶת לְיַעֲקֹב). As Yaakov pleads: וְשַׁבְתִּי בְשָׁלוֹם אֶל בֵּית אָבִי, *let me return in peace to my Father's house* (Bereishis 28:21). Being aware of the "anguish" that Hashem receives from one's transgressions, the penitent forgets his own distress and focuses solely on his desire to give נַחַת to His Father in Heaven.

(5653)

⋅§ Returning to Torah and Divine Service

הֲשִׁיבֵנוּ אָבִינוּ לְתוֹרָתֶךָ וְקָרְבֵנוּ מַלְכֵּנוּ לַעֲבוֹדָתֶךָ

*Bring us back, our Father, to Your Torah, and bring us
near, our King, to Your service.*

דרשו חז״ל על תשובה מאהבה דיש בחי׳ בנים ובחי׳ עבדים. ועל
שניהם צריכין לשוב בתשובה. ועל זה מבקשין השיבנו אבינו
לתורתך שהוא הבחי׳ בנים. שנבחרו בנ״י בכח התורה. וקרבנו
מלכנו לעבודתך הוא בחי׳ עבדים.

This brief selection from the *Shemoneh Esrei* highlights two different
types of *teshuvah*, reflecting a varying relationship between Israel
and Hashem. As children (of אָבִינוּ, *our Father*) we return to the Torah.
As Yirmiyahu pleads: שׁוּבוּ בָּנִים שׁוֹבָבִים, *return wayward children [to the
Torah]* (3:14). We were designated as Hashem's children because of our
commitment to Torah. If we have strayed from Torah neglecting our
role as children of Hashem, we plead for His forgiveness so we may
return.

But we are also servants of Hashem. This role is ideally fulfilled in the
Beis HaMikdash. In this spirit, we plead: וְקָרְבֵנוּ מַלְכֵּנוּ לַעֲבוֹדָתֶךָ , as
servants of the King, return us to the intimacy with Hashem that Israel
enjoyed (more than any other nation) through our Divine Service in the
Temple. The renowned *tefillah:* שֶׁיִּבָּנֶה בֵּית הַמִּקְדָּשׁ . . . וְתֵן חֶלְקֵנוּ בְּתוֹרָתֶךָ,
that the Holy Temple be rebuilt . . . Grant us our share in Your Torah,
also reflects Israel's wish for the return of its two treasures. First is our
full commitment and immersion in Torah befitting our status as
Hashem's chosen children and second is the return of the sacrificial rite,
the designated mission of Hashem's servants in the *Beis HaMikdash*.
(Please also refer to our commentary on אִם כְּבָנִים אִם כַּעֲבָדִים in the essay
entitled "Tefillos".) (5645, 5655)

קְחוּ עִמָּכֶם דְּבָרִים suggests that the Torah is also a particularly effective
medium through which *teshuvah* is accomplished as well as the
objective of the *teshuvah* process.

Heavenly Throne

גְּדוֹלָה תְּשׁוּבָה שֶׁמַּגַּעַת עַד כִּסֵּא הַכָּבוֹד

Great is repentance because it reaches until the Throne of Glory (Yoma 86a).

⋅§ Returning to One's Roots

וז״ש שמגעת עד כסה״כ. וברמב״ם עד שיעיד עליו יודע
תעלומות שלא ישוב לדבר הזה. . . . אכן המכוון הוא כי התשובה
צריך להיות עד מדריגה זו. והיינו ביטול הבחירה לגמרי כי בוודאי
צדיקים זוכין בעבודתם עד שנקח מהם כמעט כל הבחירה.

Perhaps the simplest interpretation of this renowned tribute to the power of *teshuvah* is based on the theme which we have frequently emphasized, that every Jew's roots lie in heaven ensconced under the Throne of Glory. Even the most righteous person, the greatest *tzaddik*, and equally so the *baal teshuvah*, who feels that he has already completed the process of return, have not completely exhausted the potential to do *teshuvah*. Only the Jew who feels that he has discovered his heavenly roots, "engraved" under the Heavenly Throne, can say that he has achieved true *teshuvah*.

In a similar vein, the *Rambam* (*Hilchos Teshuvah* 2:2), states that the process of *teshuvah* is not completed until Hashem testifies that the sinner will not return to his sin. While lesser forms of *teshuvah*, even those that do not enjoy a Divine assurance, are certainly welcome, the *Rambam* is simply pointing out the consummation of the *teshuvah* process leading to negation of free will No greater reward exists for the truly righteous than the denial for them of the prerogative of free will. (5640; *Nitzavim* 5650)

৵§ The Impact of Teshuvah on the Heavenly Throne

דאיתא תשובה מגעת עד כסה״כ. והנה נשמתן של ישראל חקוקה תחת כסה״כ וכפי שלימות הכסא שבנ״י מבררין הצורה תחת כסה״כ אז כביכול הקב״ה יושב על הכסא כמ״ש יושב תהלות ישראל.

If we recall that the souls of Israel are engraved under the Heavenly Throne we can appreciate that by repenting and perfecting ourselves, we are also leaving an impact on Hashem's Throne. David describes Hashem as קְדוֹשׁ יוֹשֵׁב תְּהִלּוֹת יִשְׂרָאֵל, *the Holy One, enthroned upon the praises of Israel* (*Tehillim* 22:4). Through our prayers — and through our efforts at *teshuvah* — we who are the bearers of the Heavenly Throne, through our names that are inscribed on the Throne, enable the Divine Presence to sit on the Throne (see our remarks on *Shabbos Teshuvah* for further expansion of this theme and in particular, for the relationship between Shabbos and the Throne of Glory). (5654)

৵§ The Revelation of Hashem's Presence in This World

וזהו שכתבו חז״ל גדולה תשובה שמגעת עד כסה״כ. יתכן לפרש כי השי״ת מלא כל הארץ כבודו רק ע״י החטא כ׳ עונותיכם מבדילים. וע״י התשובה מתגלה כבוד מלכותו ית׳ בכל מקום.

By aiming to reach the Heavenly Throne, Israel is not only "connecting" with its own roots but it is also leaving an impact on this world, by enabling Hashem's Presence to be felt on earth as well as in Heaven. We are aware that Hashem's Presence suffuses the entire universe, as we pray: מְלֹא כָל הָאָרֶץ כְּבוֹדוֹ, *the whole world is filled with His glory*

(*Yeshayahu* 6:3). However, Yeshaya also prophesied: כִּי אִם עֲוֹנֹתֵיכֶם הָיוּ
מַבְדִּלִים בֵּינֵכֶם לְבֵין אֱלֹהֵיכֶם, *your sins have separated between you and
your God* (59:2). By repenting, Israel dismantles the barriers that have
prevented Hashem's Glory (emanating from His Throne) from being
perceived in this world. (5647)

⊷§ Rectifying Heaven as well as Earth

וכמה רחוק זה החוטא מכסה''כ . . . כי הקב''ה ברא מקומות
מעוקמים גם בעולמות עליונים שיצטרכו תקון ע''י עבודת האדם
. . . ע''י התשובה מתיישבין אותן המקומות ליישר העקמימות וזה
זכותו של בע''ת . . .

It would seem farfetched to say that the actions of the *baal teshuvah*
reach as far as Hashem's Throne. The sinner, even after repenting,
remains quite distant from Hashem's Throne.

However, upon creating the universe, Hashem deliberately left a void
in the heavenly stratosphere — a void that can only be filled through
teshuvah. By repenting, the *baal teshuvah* sets into motion a process
through which not only his own personal life but also the celestial
sphere, the spiritual world, attains a measure of perfection. It is a process
that begins on earth but ascends level upon level culminating in the
realization of the highest strata of spirituality, adjoining (according to
this approach the term מַגָעַת is derived from נוֹגֵעַ, *touching*) the
Heavenly Throne. (*Nitzavim 5635*)

⊷§ Teshuvah of the Soul

פ' דיש כמה מדריגות בתשובה. לכן נקראו עשרת ימי תשובה.
וצריכין לשוב לתקן פגם הנפש במעשה. והרוח בדיבור. והנשמה
במחשבה. וכשמגיעין לתשובת הנשמה שם אמרו שמגעת עד
כסה''כ.

As it is well known, the human soul consists of several components —
the נֶפֶשׁ, the active, physical side of man which attends to his material needs; the רוּחַ through which man attains the power of speech (cf.

Bereishis 2:7, Targum Onkelos on וַיְהִי הָאָדָם לְנֶפֶשׁ חַיָּה which is translated as לְרוּחַ מְמַלְּלָא); and the pure נְשָׁמָה, monitoring man's thoughts. Every sin taints each component of the Jewish personality. So too, for the process of return (teshuvah) to be effective it must involve all these components that had participated in sinning — the נֶפֶשׁ, רוּחַ, and נְשָׁמָה. By rectifying our misdeeds we repair the damage done to the נֶפֶשׁ; by verbalizing and confessing our sins (וִדּוּי) we rehabilitate the רוּחַ; and finally, by perfecting our *thoughts* (מַחֲשָׁבָה) we regain the purity of the נְשָׁמָה. At that point, when a Jew's innate purity has been restored, we can proudly state that our teshuvah has reached the Throne of Glory. (5653)

◆§ Reaching to the Avos

הנה עיקר התשובה הוא לחזור ולהתדבק בהקב"ה. כמו"ש חז"ל
עד כסה"כ עד ה' אלקיך. והאבות הן הן המרכבה אשר השכינה
שורה עליהם וכל איש ישראל צריך לומר מתי יגיעו מעשי למעשי
אבותי

The expression עַד כִּסֵּא הַכָּבוֹד may refer to the Patriarchs who are depicted as the מֶרְכָּבָה, *the Bearers of the Divine Presence* (cf. Bereishis, Rashi 17:22). While the primary function of teshuvah is to return to Hashem (שׁוּבָה יִשְׂרָאֵל עַד ה' אֱלֹהֶיךָ), this difficult mission is somewhat eased if we seek to attain the spiritual status of the Avos, who achieved דְּבֵקוּת to Hashem. As Tanna d'Vei Eliyahu implores us: מָתַי יַגִּיעוּ מַעֲשַׂי לְמַעֲשֵׂי אֲבוֹתַי, every Jew is required to ask, *when will my deeds reach the levels of my forefathers.*

This, too, then is the essence of teshuvah, returning to the levels attained by the Avos. While it is true that the merit of the Avos no longer exists (cf. Shabbos 55a), it is also true that through teshuvah — by reaching their levels — it is possible to revive this merit.

In this light, we can better comprehend the comment of the Midrash that the Jewish people will not succeed in doing teshuvah until the coming of Eliyahu HaNavi. The Midrash, however, is hardly denying the effectiveness of repenting *prior* to Eliyahu's arrival; instead it is reflecting on Eliyahu's role in restoring the Jewish people to the levels of their forefathers (cf. Malachi 3:24, וְהֵשִׁיב לֵב אָבוֹת עַל בָּנִים). What the Midrash maintains is that the ultimate teshuvah, attaining the Avos' stature, can only be accomplished with Eliyahu's arrival. (5652)

The Unique Standing
of the Baal Teshuvah

⊷§ Rectifying Past Misdeeds

מָקוֹם שֶׁבַּעֲלֵי תְּשׁוּבָה עוֹמְדִין צַדִּיקִים גְּמוּרִים אֵינָם עוֹמְדִין

*The place where baalei teshuvah stand, [even] the totally
righteous do not stand (Berachos 34b).*

וע״ז אמרו במקום שבע״ת עומדין אין צדיקים גמורים יכולין
לעמוד. כי הצדיק לא עבר במקומות האלה ובע״ת מתקן כל
הדרכים המקולקלים.

The expression מָקוֹם שֶׁבַּעֲלֵי תְּשׁוּבָה עוֹמְדִין may be taken literally: *The
place where the baalei teshuvah stand* — the returnee, reviewing
his life, rectifies all his past mistakes. The *tzaddik*, never having been
exposed to the experiences of the *baal teshuvah*, cannot possibly stand
in that place. The returnee, thus, enjoys a unique distinction, the
ability to improve and try to perfect himself, perhaps even to find
the good in all the evil that he was exposed to and maybe even
participated in. Having strayed off the straight path of the Torah, the
baal teshuvah not only repents but can even perfect and elevate to a
higher purpose all the wrong paths that he may have taken.

(cf. 5640)

✥ Create a New World

צדיקים מקיימים העולם כדכ׳ צדיק יסוד עולם. אבל בע״ת
מושכין דרך חדש למעלה מן העולם כדאיתא תשובה קדמה
לעולם.

Whereas the *tzaddik upholds* the universe (cf. *Mishlei* 10:25, וְצַדִּיק
יְסוֹד עוֹלָם), the *baal teshuvah*, merits through his *teshuvah* that
Hashem creates a new universe on his behalf. Whenever the natural
order governing this world would deny the *baal teshuvah* any hope of
returning to Hashem, Hashem supersedes all natural rules and creates a
new world for him. The Talmud (*Pesachim* 54a) alludes to the
superiority of *teshuvah* by noting that *teshuvah* preceded (and by
extension, supersedes) the limits of the universe.   (5658)

✥ Renewal

כי צדיקים מקיימים כו׳. ובעלי תשובות חוזרין ומחדשין העשרה
מאמרות. . . . א״כ כשהרשע שב בתשובה מחדש העשרה
מאמרות.

The renowned Mishnah in *Avos* (5:1) notes the power of the righteous
to uphold the universe which was created through Ten Divine
Statements (עֲשָׂרָה מַאֲמָרוֹת). The *baal teshuvah*, having conspired with
other evildoers, in effect, had destroyed the universe created through
Ten Divine Statements. By returning to Hashem, the *baal teshuvah* is
not merely upholding the Divine Statements, but is also causing
Hashem to create the universe, to *renew* the Ten Statements on his
behalf. No more opportune time exists to renew the universe than the
annual commemoration of Creation, Rosh Hashanah. By extending the
period of repentance to last ten days, ample time for the Ten Statements
to be renewed, Hashem allows the *baal teshuvah* to enjoy the full
benefit of a new created universe.   (5662)

✑ Enjoying the Light of the Three Primeval Days

במקום שבע"ת עומדין אין צדיקים גמורים יכולין לעמוד ולכן
לעולם יש רק ששת ימי המעשה ושבת. ועתה יש עשרה ימים
והיינו שמתגלה הארת הג' ראשונות שהם נקראים ימי קדם.

Teshuvah preceded the creation of our world. There were three higher levels of Heavenly conduct created even before our world, which are symbolically called יְמֵי קֶדֶם, *primeval days.* The sinner is strongly drawn by his natural inclinations, and in order to overcome them and repent he needs to reach up to those levels which are higher than, and above, Nature.

The Ten Days of Repentance consist of the natural seven-day week and an extra three-day period which signifies these three "primeval days." This alludes to the fact that in these ten days the special light of those three "days" is shining, enabling the repentant to rise above his nature and achieve the true state of *"baal teshuvah,"* which is even higher than the state of a צַדִּיק גָּמוּר, *the totally righteous.* (5648, 5644)

✑ Friday at Twilight

ובע"ש ביה"ש ע"י התשובה שעשה אדה"ר ניתקן הדרך של
בע"ת בתוספות מעלה בבחי' עשרה וכדאיתא בזוה"ק כי בע"ת
מתקנין ברגעא חדא . . . לכן בשעה אחת ניתקן אלה העשרה.
אשר הם יותר ממה שניתקן בכל ימי המעשה.

A renowned Mishnah (*Avos* 5:8) enumerates ten entities that were created Friday afternoon at twilight (בֵּין הַשְּׁמָשׁוֹת). The significance of these final "last-minute" creations becomes apparent if we recall that on the first Friday, Adam was not only created but also sinned by partaking of the Forbidden Fruit and had already repented from his sin by twilight. Thus, a new universe came into being that first Friday at twilight, the world of *teshuvah.* Just as ten days every year are reserved for *teshuvah,* so too, ten entities (עֲשָׂרָה דְבָרִים) were created in this new universe dedicated to *teshuvah.* Perhaps the most outstanding characteristics of all these creations is their usefulness to the *baal teshuvah* as can be seen from the ram utilized for the *Akeidah* (as Yitzchak's surrogate) which, even in contemporary times, serves as a source of merit and forgiveness for the Jewish people.

It is noteworthy that more entities were perfected in that short twilight than during all of the Six Days of Creation. This is in accordance with the *Zohar's* (*Parashas Vayeira*) assertion that a *baal teshuvah* can accomplish in a moment what others would require a week to do.

Every year we, too, have the capacity during the Ten Days of Repentance to accomplish more spiritually than has been achieved all year long. (*Rosh Hashanah* 5650)

✒ Constantly Beholding the Divine Presence

שודאי צדיק גמור חביב יותר לפני השי״ת . . . שעמידת צדיק
הישר בעוה״ז . . . אבל בעל תשובה צריך להיות תמיד יראת ה׳
על פניו

This *Chazal* should not be interpreted as in any way disparaging the *Tzaddik*. On the contrary, no one is as beloved as the *tzaddik*. To comprehend this *Chazal* properly, we need to focus on the term עוֹמְדִין, *[in the place] where they stand*. The *baal teshuvah* perceives himself to be constantly in Hashem's Presence. As Moshe reminds the generation of Jews poised to enter *Eretz Yisrael*: אַתֶּם נִצָּבִים הַיּוֹם כֻּלְּכֶם לִפְנֵי ה׳ אֱלֹהֵיכֶם (*Devarim* 29:9), *You are standing today, all of you, before Hashem, your God*. The *tzaddik*, however, while always mindful of Hashem's Presence, seeks to live in this world perfecting it. (*Nitzavim* 5633)

✒ Humility

כאשר זכה להתקרב לעלות במדרגות ע״י התשובה ואעפ״כ הוא
עומד בתשובה והכנעה.

While it is expected that a sinner, upon contemplating the dimensions of his sin, will be exceedingly humble, it is somewhat more surprising that the *baal teshuvah* having already repented still remains humble. Yet this is the case because he seeks to achieve even higher levels of return. As the Torah emphasizes after describing a process of repentance which had already led to an ingathering of exiles (cf. *Devarim* 30:8), וְאַתָּה תָשׁוּב, *Repent!* The *baal teshuvah* enjoys the distinction of humility, maintained despite great achievement.

(Nitzavim 5638)

◆§ Moshe and Aaron

מכאן אמרו חז״ל במקום שבע״ת עומדין אין צדיקים גמורים
יכולין לעמוד . . . א״י לכנוס לפני ולפנים רק ביו״כ שהוא בחי׳
בע״ת

Homiletically, the distinction between *baalei teshuvah* and the completely righteous may allude to the differing roles of Moshe and Aaron. While Moshe enjoyed unparalleled spiritual greatness, Aaron was unique in performing the Divine Service of Yom Kippur conducted in the inner sanctum, the קֹדֶשׁ הַקֳּדָשִׁים (Holy of Holies). As a *baal teshuvah*, having repented for his role in the Golden Calf and having influenced the Jewish people to repent, Aaron deserved this unique distinction.

In a similar vein, the Rabbinic statement that *teshuvah* reaches to Hashem's Throne may also allude to Aaron who through his *teshuvah* merited the Divine Clouds (עַנְנֵי כָבוֹד), a reflection on earth of the Glory of Hashem. *(Korach 5660; cf. Acharei 5664).*

Yom Kippur

Erev Yom Kippur
(Gateway to Yom Kippur)

◆§ Eating on Erev Yom Kippur

כָּל הָאוֹכֵל וְשׁוֹתֶה בַּתְּשִׁיעִי מַעֲלֶה עָלָיו הָכָּתוּב כְּאִילוּ הִתְעַנֶּה תְּשִׁיעִי וַעֲשִׂירִי

Whoever eats and drinks on the ninth [of Tishrei, Erev Yom Kippur], Scripture considers as if he fasted on both the ninth and the tenth [Yom Kippur] (*Yoma* 81b): In the following section, we will consider some of the reasons for the *mitzvah* of eating on *Erev* Yom Kippur.

◆§ Rectifying Eating of an Entire Year

כי באכילת יום זה מתקנים אכילת כל ימות השנה כשבשעת התשובה זוכרין בסיבה המביאה אל החטא עי״ז מתקן גוף החטא

It is an established tradition that by eating on *Erev* Yom Kippur we rectify any sins that may have arisen as a result of eating improperly all year long (e.g. eating without a *berachah*, eating non-kosher food, etc.). This statement is based on the realization that food and drink can often involve inordinate excess and many times are the root cause of sin (cf. *Devarim* 8:14, וְרָם לְבָבֶךָ וְשָׁכַחְתָּ אֶת ה' אֱלֹהֶיךָ, *and your heart will become haughty and you will forget Hashem your God*). By focusing on the cause — and seeking to elevate food and drink to a higher purpose[1] through involvement in a *mitzvah* immediately prior to the *teshuvah* of Yom Kippur — we are not merely repenting but also rectifying the very fact that led us to sin.[2]

(5640)

The Gateway to Yom Kippur

וצריכין להראות כי כוונת כל אכילה ושתייה רק להיות הכנה
ופרוזדור לע״הב

Just as the World to Come is so sacred that it cannot be approached without the preparatory phase of this world (cf. *Avos* 4:16 comparing this world to a corridor that opens into the palace), so too the most hallowed of days, Yom Kippur — which itself is compared to the World to Come — can only be approached through the intermediary of *Erev* Yom Kippur. By eating on *Erev* Yom Kippur with the intention of performing a *mitzvah* (not to satisfy physical cravings), we prepare ourselves on this earth for the microcosm of the World to Come — that totally spiritual occasion, Yom Kippur. By extension, we may argue that all the pleasures of this world are merely a prelude to — and a means of attaining — the true bliss of the World to Come.

The analogy to a cover or an outer layer of clothing would also be apt: This world and its comforts are little more than a surface cover, which when removed reveals an inner depth and beauty — the World to Come.

In this light, we can derive a new interpretation of the famed Rabbinical saying, מָקוֹם שֶׁבַּעֲלֵי תְשׁוּבָה עוֹמְדִין צַדִּיקִים גְמוּרִים אֵינָם עוֹמְדִין, *The place where baalei teshuvah stand, [even] the totally righteous do not stand* (*Berachos* 34b).

Whereas the righteous dwell in a totally spiritual world, the Jewish people prior to Yom Kippur successfully manage the transition from the material pleasure of *Erev* Yom Kippur to the rarefied spirituality of Yom Kippur itself.

(5640)

---

1. *Editor's Note:* The *berachos* we recite before partaking of food and drink elevate the "physical" act of eating to a more spiritual level (cf. *Berachos* 35a).

2. In a similar vein, the Mishnah relates that someone who sins with the express intention of repenting will not be able to repent. While *teshuvah* atones for most sins, it is ineffective if the concept of repentance is part of the sin itself, i.e. if the sinner is emboldened to transgress because of the option of *teshuvah* (cf. *Yoma* 81b).

✥ Clinging to the Joy of Yom Kippur

אך שאין יכולין להתדבק בשמחה זאת כראוי בעודנו בעוה"ז
צריכין להתדבק בהארת היו"כ לפניו ולאחריו.

It is noteworthy that the Talmud (*Yoma* 81b) derives two apparently distinct — even dichotomous — thoughts from the verse מֵעֶרֶב עַד עֶרֶב, *from evening to evening* (*Vayikra* 23:32), which implies that one commences the fast of Yom Kippur on the previous day. Firstly, the *mitzvah* of eating on *Erev* Yom Kippur we are told is tantamount to fasting. Additionally there is the requirement that one commence the fast early, not waiting until nightfall. In truth, these seemingly contradictory statements reflect the same theme, that the spiritual joy of Yom Kippur, so ethereal and otherworldly, can only be approached through the conduit of *Erev* Yom Kippur. It is through the rays of Yom Kippur's luminescence — the eating as well as the fasting of *Erev* Yom Kippur — that we are enabled to approach this holiest of days. (5641)

✥ Defeating Satan

ובודאי גם באחרונות עמד שטן בכל כחו . . . ואבותינו גברו עליו
. . . ולפי שעמדו על נפשם זכו לתשובה שלימה . . . שהשטן
מתגבר בעיו"כ

The joy of *Erev* Yom Kippur is associated not only with the atonement of Yom Kippur (cf. *Shaarei Teshuvah* 126a) but especially with the Giving of the Torah in the form of the Second Tablets (לוחות שניות) which were granted on Yom Kippur. [While we generally associate *Shavuos* with the Giving of the Torah, tragically the aura of that first Shavuos was dissipated when Moshe was compelled to shatter the First Tablets in response to Israel's veneration of the Golden Calf.]

One might assume that Satan strove mightily to thwart the Giving of the Second Tablets as he had successfully prevented the transmission of the First Tablets. It is also reasonable to assume that the maximum efforts of Satan to lure Israel into sinning occurred on *Erev* Yom Kippur, which was the final day of Moshe's forty-day stay on Mt. Sinai. Just as Satan lured Israel into worshiping the Golden Calf on the final day of Moshe's first absence, so too, he sought to repeat his success by causing Israel to sin on the final day of Moshe's second absence, on *Erev* Yom Kippur. But this time there was a radically different result. The Jewish people remained steadfastly loyal, refusing to succumb to Satan's importunings. This is true *teshuvah* — being exposed to the identical circumstances as those which had originally provoked one to sin, and withstanding it (cf. *Rambam Hilchos Teshuvah* 2:1).

To celebrate our triumph over such a mighty spiritual adversary, we rejoice on *Erev* Yom Kippur. The tradition that Satan is most powerful on *Erev* Yom Kippur (while powerless on Yom Kippur, cf. *Yoma* 20a) is probably based on the resilience of the powers of evil. Repulsed once, when foiled in its attempt to deny Israel the Tablets, it never gives up, and attempts every Yom Kippur to ensnare Israel. But, as occurred on the first *Erev* Yom Kippur, Satan is defeated. To celebrate our first and our perpetual triumph over evil on this day, we rejoice. (5662)

Immersion in Yom Kippur

◆§ Mikveh Yisrael

אָמַר רַבִּי עֲקִיבָא: אַשְׁרֵיכֶם יִשְׂרָאֵל, לִפְנֵי מִי אַתֶּם מִטַּהֲרִין? מִי מְטַהֵר אֶתְכֶם? אֲבִיכֶם שֶׁבַּשָּׁמַיִם, שֶׁנֶּאֱמַר: וְזָרַקְתִּי עֲלֵיכֶם מַיִם טְהוֹרִים וּטְהַרְתֶּם; וְאוֹמֵר: מִקְוֵה יִשְׂרָאֵל ה׳. מָה מִקְוֶה מְטַהֵר אֶת הַטְּמֵאִים, אַף הקב״ה מְטַהֵר אֶת יִשְׂרָאֵל.

R' Akiva said: "Praiseworthy are you, O Israel! Before Whom do you cleanse yourselves? Who cleanses you? Your Father in Heaven! As it is said: 'And I will cast pure waters upon you and you shall be cleansed' (Yechezkel 36:25), and He also says: 'The mikveh of Israel is HASHEM' (Yirmiyah 17:13). Just as a mikveh purifies the contaminated, so does the Holy One, Blessed is He, purify Israel (Yoma 8:9).

The analogy drawn between Hashem and the *mikveh* (used for ritual immersion) regarding the *purification of Israel*, placed at the conclusion of the Tractate *Yoma* (dealing with Yom Kippur), tells us a great deal about the nature of Yom Kippur. Consider one of the most important properties of a *mikveh*. To be effective, one must be *totally* immersed in the *mikveh* (even one infinitesimal hair emerging outside of the *mikveh* water invalidates the immersion). Similarly, Divine Service requires complete self-negation in favor of Hashem. This laudable objective is primarily achieved by the Jewish soul upon its departure from the body — in the hereafter. However, every Yom Kippur, which is a microcosm of the World to Come, the Jew attains a small measure of that *mikveh*-like characteristic — total self-negation and immersion in Godliness.

(5641)

✑ A Receptacle for Torah

The comparison between the *mikveh* and Hashem's purification of Israel may be based on a different property of a *mikveh*, its capacity to hold water. So too, to achieve purification on Yom Kippur, the Jewish people must return to its primary mission — serving as a receptacle (i.e. a platform) for the Torah. From its inception (the time of the Giving of the Tablets) Yom Kippur had already been designated as a day on which Israel becomes a receptacle for Torah. The verse from Yechezkel cited in the Mishnah — וְזָרַקְתִּי עֲלֵיכֶם מַיִם טְהוֹרִים וּטְהַרְתֶּם — may also allude to the Torah (cf. *Taanis* 7a stating that the term "water" refers to Torah).

(5662)

Perhaps we can synthesize both approaches, the concept of immersion as well as the intimate association between Torah and Yom Kippur. Only through immersion in Torah can Israel be purified. The analogy drawn between the *mikveh's* powers of purification and *Hashem's* purification of Israel every Yom Kippur may also be understood as pertaining to the Torah, inasmuch as the *Torah* itself (as described by *Ramban's* Introduction to the Torah) is comprised of various combinations of names of Hashem; much as הקב״ה is מְטַהֵר Israel, so too does Torah purify Israel. Similarly the *Zohar* states הקב״ה וְאוֹרַיְיתָא כּוּלָא חַד, *Hashem and the Torah are* [considered as if they are] *one* (cf. *Acharei Mos* 73a).

(5656)

◄§ Heavenly Waters

דיש מים עליונים ותחתונים . . . ולכן בעלי תשובות הקב״ה זורק
עליהם ממים עליונים והיא הארת העוה״ב שמתגלה ביו״כ

Let us consider further the process of purification that the Jewish people experience every Yom Kippur. Close examination of the Mishnah cited above reveals two distinct methods of purification — the *mikveh*, consisting of waters gathered together through human intervention (cf. *Bereishis* 1:9, וְיִקָּווּ הַמַּיִם מִתַּחַת הַשָּׁמַיִם אֶל מָקוֹם אֶחָד), and heavenly waters cast upon Israel by Hashem, מַיִם הָעֶלְיוֹנִים. The verse quoted by the Mishnah (*Yechezkel* 36:25), וְזָרַקְתִּי עֲלֵיכֶם מַיִם טְהוֹרִים, "I will *cast upon you* pure waters" (i.e. cast from above, from Heaven, to Earth), clarifies this concept — a Divine infusion of purity, being showered from heaven to earth.

Unlike the *mikveh* and the מַיִם תַּחְתּוֹנִים, *the waters below* (i.e. the efforts of mankind to achieve purity), which are far from perfect, these heavenly waters represent the pristine purity that only Hashem can provide. This then is Hashem's gift to a repentant Israel on Yom Kippur — purity. Such unadulterated purity can only be achieved in the World to Come, but nonetheless is bestowed upon His repentant people on Yom Kippur.

(5647)

Rosh Hashanah and Yom Kippur — Comparison and Contrast

⋅§ Rosh Hashanah: Tefillah
Yom Kippur: Teshuvah

ור״ה הוא בחי׳ תפילה ויוה״כ תשובה

Rosh Hashanah (noted for its elaborate *Malchiyos, Zichronos,* and *Shofaros* prayers) is a day dominated by *tefillos.* Yom Kippur (though certainly an opportune time for Israel's prayers) possesses an additional component — the sweeping power of *teshuvah.* Whereas Israel's prayers are not always effective, its sincere efforts to achieve repentance are *never* spurned. Please refer to our commentary on תְּשׁוּבָה תְּפִלָּה וּצְדָקָה (in the section on *tefillos* of Rosh Hashanah) for the full text of a Midrash which compares *tefillos* to a *mikveh* which is not always accessible and *teshuvah* to the ever-present sea (יָם). Yom Kippur is an open-ended opportunity for *teshuvah* as open as the ocean's waters.

(cf. 5647)

⋅§ Rosh Hashanah: Enlightening the Earth (אוֹרִי)
Yom Kippur: Israel's Heavenly Roots (יִשְׁעִי)

בר״ה הקב״ה מאיר לבנ״י מקום שהם לכן היא בכסה וישעי הוא
ישועה מלמעלה

David alludes to the distinction between these two great occasions by proclaiming, ה׳ אוֹרִי וְיִשְׁעִי, *Hashem is my light and my salvation*

(*Tehillim* 27:1). אוֹרִי, *my light*, refers to Rosh Hashanah, a day in which Israel, subject to judgment along with all of mankind, basks in Hashem's light. Though the Jewish people may be obscured (as the *Yom Tov's* description of בַּכֶּסֶה implies) amongst mankind, Hashem illuminates the darkness and remembers His people on the day of judgment.

Something far more profound occurs on Yom Kippur. Not only is Hashem אוֹרִי, *my light*, He is also יִשְׁעִי, *my salvation*. While on Rosh Hashanah Hashem may light up the darkness in which Israel is engulfed on earth, on Yom Kippur He *saves* the heavenly roots, the Jewish soul which has always been firmly implanted in heaven.[1]

(5647)

⋅§ Rosh Hashanah — The Righteous (צַדִּיקִים)
⋅§ Yom Kippur — The Intermediate (בֵּינוֹנִים)

צדקתך הוא צדיקים גמורים משפטך תהום רבה הרשעים אדם
ובהמה הם הבינונים

As it is well known (cf. Rosh Hashanah 16b) the righteous (צַדִּיקִים גְּמוּרִים) are written in the Book of Life on Rosh Hashanah. These worthy individuals can be vindicated on the basis of their own merit, they do not need to be saved. It is the intermediate category, the בֵּינוֹנִים, individuals who are neither totally virtuous nor totally evil, who are saved (i.e. spared through Hashem's Mercies) on Yom Kippur.

There is a verse (recited during Shabbos *Minchah*) that groups the various categories of individuals awaiting Hashem's judgment:

צִדְקָתְךָ כְּהַרְרֵי אֵ-ל — *Your righteousness is like the mighty mountains* alludes to the *tzaddikim*.

מִשְׁפָּטֶיךָ תְּהוֹם רַבָּה — *Your judgment is like the vast deep waters* refers to the wicked who will be condemned to the vast abyss of *Gehinnom* and, in accordance with our assertion that it is the בֵּינוֹנִים who require Divine Salvation, אָדָם וּבְהֵמָה תּוֹשִׁיעַ ה', *man and beast You Save*,

---

1. Another version of the Midrash suggests that אוֹרִי, *my light*, refers to the Exodus and יִשְׁעִי, *my salvation*, to the Splitting of the Red Sea. Whereas the Egyptians themselves were vanquished and Israel liberated during the Exodus, the complete salvation and destruction of Egypt's angel and the spiritual renaissance of the Jewish people only occurred at the Sea. (5647)

HASHEM, those individuals who face the constant conflict between their human (and finer) instincts (אָדָם) and their material (baser) instincts (בְּהֵמָה) receive Divine Salvation on Yom Kippur. (5649)

◈§ Rosh Hashanah — Strict Justice
Yom Kippur — Mercy in Implementing Justice

בר״ה הוא המשפט וכמ״ש צדיק ה' בכל דרכיו ביו״כ הוא
הסליחה בחסד וזה וחסיד בכל מעשיו

The renowned verse, צַדִּיק ה' בְּכָל דְּרָכָיו וְחָסִיד בְּכָל מַעֲשָׂיו, *Righteous is Hashem in all His ways and magnanimous in all His deeds* (*Tehillim* 145:17), points out an important distinction between Rosh Hashanah, the occasion on which our fate is determined, and Yom Kippur when the sentence is actually implemented. While Hashem's pronouncement of the verdict is just as are all His ways (צַדִּיק ה' בְּכָל דְּרָכָיו), He tempers the actual implementation of His verdict with mercy displayed on Yom Kippur. As the verse concludes וְחָסִיד בְּכָל מַעֲשָׂיו, He is exceedingly generous (חָסִיד). As far as the actual implementation of the element of Divine Mercy, Hashem is far more lenient. His sentence is carried out with mercy (חֶסֶד).

Unlike mortals who are much easier to influence *before* a verdict is decided, but once the verdict is pronounced and is at the implementation stage it is extremely difficult (if not impossible) to change, Hashem's Ways (His *verdict*, גְּזַר דִּין) are based on strict justice but enforced (implemented) with mercy.

The well-known verse, וּלְךָ ה' חָסֶד כִּי אַתָּה תְשַׁלֵּם לְאִישׁ כְּמַעֲשֵׂהוּ, *and Yours, HASHEM, is kindness, for You reward each man in accordance with his deeds* (*Tehillim* 62:13), may be interpreted in the same light. While Hashem's Judgment is based on His evaluation of our merit — rewarding everyone according to their deeds (לְאִישׁ כְּמַעֲשֵׂהוּ) — He demonstrates kindness when implementing His verdict (וּלְךָ ה' חָסֶד). [Please refer to our commentary on this verse in the essay entitled "Justice" in the Rosh Hashanah segment.]

Mortals would do well to emulate Hashem's ways in this regard. They should strive for the proper *intention* in carrying out the ideal even if the actual *implementation* falls short of that ideal. (5649)

◄§ Rosh Hashanah — For All Mankind
Yom Kippur — Unique to the Jewish People

כי בר״ה באי עולם עוברים לפניו ויוהכ״פ מיוחד רק לבנ״י

Whereas Rosh Hashanah is a day of judgment for all mankind, Yom Kippur's atonement is reserved for the Jewish people.   (5656)

◄§ Rosh Hashanah — Covenant of the Tongue (בְּרִית הַלָּשׁוֹן)
Yom Kippur — Covenant of Morality (בְּרִית הַמָּעוֹר)

ור״ה ויוהכ״פ הם בחי' ברית הלשון המעור

The distinction between Rosh Hashanah and Yom Kippur may be in the covenant (בְּרִית) that is emphasized on each occasion. Rosh Hashanah's *shofar*, symbolic of the "voice of Yaakov" (please refer to our commentary on Shofar), symbolizes the covenant of the tongue, in which Israel improves its manner of speech. On Yom Kippur, we stress the covenant of morality (בְּרִית הַמָּעוֹר). This can be demonstrated by the emphasis placed on the *bris milah* of Avraham which occurred on Yom Kippur. Observance of the ritual of circumcision, the best safeguard of morality, is one of the best indicators of Israel's uniqueness. Just as the *bris milah* is uniquely practiced by the Jewish people, so too Yom Kippur is enjoyed solely by Israel. On the other hand, the covenant of the tongue (בְּרִית הַלָּשׁוֹן) implies not only using proper speech but also the proper use of the Sacred Tongue (לְשׁוֹן הַקּוֹדֶשׁ) and could theoretically be shared by all mankind (cf. *Rashi, Bereishis* 11:1, stating that all mankind at the Tower of Babel spoke לְשׁוֹן הַקּוֹדֶשׁ).   (5656)

The Most Unique Day

יָמִים יֻצָּרוּ וְלֹא אֶחָד בָּהֶם.

When [Hashem] created days, the most unique (Yom Kippur) was not one of them (Tehillim 139:16).

זה יוה״כ שבו מתגלה ציור הפנימי אל איש ישראל . . . וביו״כ הסיר זה הגשמיות

This verse is interpreted by the Midrash (*Yalkut Tehillim* 888) to refer to Yom Kippur.

We can appreciate the uniqueness of Yom Kippur (and this verse's allusion to Yom Kippur) by recalling (cf. *Rashi, Bereishis* 2:7) that Hashem created man with a double soul — his *material* instincts propelling him to satiate himself with the pleasures of this world while his *spirituality*, the Divine Soul, is focused on the World to Come. But this conflict within man occurred later. At the very beginning of creation — before the Divine Plan for the universe unfolded — one of those conflicting instincts — man's material nature did not yet exist. When the days of creation were still before Hashem (יָמִים יֻצָּרוּ) — prior to the beginning of creation — only man's soul and not the other (וְלֹא אֶחָד בָּהֶם) instinct, his material side, were present. At the conclusion of the Six Days of Creation when man was created, he was permanently burdened with a material instinct prompting him to sin. Once a year, every Yom Kippur, we reverse the process and return man to his pristine state that existed before creation.

In the light, we can readily understand the prohibition against eating or drinking on Yom Kippur. Once our material instincts have been curbed, we no longer require food and drink to sustain us. Instead we are nurtured as angels who are totally spiritual beings.

Indeed the true inner personality of every Jew, his innate goodness comes to the forefront every Yom Kippur as the outer veneer of materialism is purged.

The famous verse, שְׁחוֹרָה אֲנִי וְנָאוָה, *I am black with sin, but beautiful nonetheless* (*Shir HaShirim* 1:5), may also refer to Yom Kippur. Though I am besmirched by my transgressions (שְׁחוֹרָה אֲנִי) this is only an outer surface. Every Yom Kippur this facade gives way to our true nature, the inner goodness (נָאוָה) of every Jew. (5649)

✌§ A Supernatural Occasion

דרשו לעשות לכפר מעשה פרה ומעשה יוהכ״פ. והכל ענין אחד
בחי׳ . . . התשובה שהיא למעלה מהנהגת ימי בראשית כמ״ש

The essence of Yom Kippur is captured best by the requirement that the *Kohen Gadol* (High Priest) be secluded for seven days prior to performing the Divine Service, for one (unique) day (פְּרִישַׁת שִׁבְעָה לְיוֹם אֶחָד, cf. *Yoma* 2b). This process of intensive preparation is derived from a similar seven-day separation period observed by Aaron and his children that culminated in the Tabernacle's dedication on the eighth day. Every Yom Kippur, the supernatural atmosphere of the day of the *Mishkan's* dedication is revisited. Not only were the outward trappings of the *Mishkan's* dedication and Yom Kippur similar (e.g. the fire emanating from heaven and the High Priest attaining the status of an angel; cf. *Yalkut Vayikra* 578), but — and of greater importance — the root cause, *teshuvah*, is what enabled Israel to soar to such heights and is present on both occasions. It is through *teshuvah* — whether it be Israel's collective repentance, after having venerated the Golden Calf, or our annual return to Hashem prior to Yom Kippur — that is the catalyst for the supernatural aura of the day. *Teshuvah*, created prior to the universe itself (cf. *Pesachim* 54a), establishes an environment in which all natural law can easily be superseded. (5644)

✣A Taste of the World to Come

צריכין לבטל כל הימים אל זה היום ולערב אותם כדי שיהי׳
לכולם יניקה מזה היום וזהו הרמז מערב עד ערב

The verse cited previously (*Tehillim* 139:16) may also allude to the other-worldly character of Yom Kippur. Hashem created "days" (יָמִים יֻצָּרוּ) and assigned them to serve in this world as finite units of time, except for one of them (וְלֹא אֶחָד בָּהֶם). The "one" of them is Yom Kippur and it was not relegated to serve in this finite, imperfect world, but instead retained the trappings of the World to Come. Every Yom Kippur a very small quantity of the radiance of the World to Come penetrates this world.

In the milieu of Yom Kippur, deeply rooted in the hereafter, it becomes apparent that the Satan loses his power to tempt Israel to sin (cf. *Yoma* 20a). For the forces of evil, by their very nature, are confined to this world and have no influence in the future world.

The Jew's challenge, however, is to somehow preserve a bit of Yom Kippur's other-worldly favor and infuse it into the other 364 days of the year. While this is a formidable and daunting task, Yom Kippur can be integrated into daily life. One only has to realize that Yom Kippur's supernatural, other-worldly ambiance is the *ideal* and consequently, should seek to integrate and blend the rest of the year with Yom Kippur's sacred ambience. Under ideal circumstances all the days of the year are sustained and nurtured by the greatest of days, Yom Kippur.

The concept of מוסיף מחול על הקודש requires that the fast of Yom Kippur be commenced during the final daylight hour of the previous day (9th of Tishrei). By extension when Yom Kippur ends, we should channel its sanctity into the post- (as well as the "pre-") Yom Kippur world. In fact, the term מֵעֶרֶב עַד עֶרֶב (literally, *from evening to evening*) may be related to תַּעֲרֹבֶת, *a mixture*, alluding to the importance of blending Yom Kippur's sacred ambience into the entire year.   (5652)

ופי׳ ולו אחד בהם קרי וכתיב לו בוא״ו ובאל״ף

Returning to the verse in *Tehillim* (139:16) which suggested the theme that Yom Kippur is a day truly distinct from the rest of the year, we notice that while it is written (כְּתִיב) as וְלֹא אֶחָד בָּהֶם, "It [Yom Kippur] is *not* one of them" (the days)," implying the distinctiveness of the day, the word לא is read (קרי) as לוֹ — וְלוֹ אֶחָד בָּהֶם, "*it is* one of them" (the days). By integrating some of Yom Kippur's otherworldliness into the year, we can truly say that Yom Kippur *is* one of the days of the year.

(ibid.)

Atonement

כִּי בַיּוֹם הַזֶּה יְכַפֵּר עֲלֵיכֶם לְטַהֵר אֶתְכֶם מִכֹּל חַטֹּאתֵיכֶם לִפְנֵי ה׳ תִּטְהָרוּ.

For on this day he shall provide atonement for you to cleanse you; from all your sins before HASHEM shall you be cleansed (Vayikra 16:30).

לכן אמרו חז״ל דיוהכ״פ בעי תשובה וע״י התשובה גם מיראה הזדונות נעשין שגגות ואז היוהכ״פ מכפר על השגגות

This verse, which is the primary source for Yom Kippur's extraordinary capacity for atonement, may also be the source for the ruling (cf. *Yoma* 85b) that Yom Kippur alone cannot atone for Israel's sins. Rather, the day of Yom Kippur together with the Jewish people's *teshuvah* causes Hashem to forgive our sins. This symbiotic relationship between *teshuvah* and Yom Kippur may be derived from the phrase מִכֹּל חַטֹּאתֵיכֶם, *from all your sins*. It is well known that חֵטְא always connotes unintentional transgression. As a result of our *teshuvah*, all our premeditated sins (זְדוֹנוֹת) are mitigated and become unintentional transgressions (חֲטָאִים) (cf. *Yoma* 86b stating that through *teshuvah*, זְדוֹנוֹת נַעֲשׂוּ כִּשְׁגָגוֹת). Once that has been accomplished, Yom Kippur itself atones, erasing any remnant of sin.

(5645)

באמת הנפשות . . . קרובין רק ע״י החטאים בא הריחוק . . .
ויתכן לפרש מבדילין . . . וגם בין אלקיכם כנ״ל רק עבירות
שגרמו פירוד . . . כמו לא תשנא כו' . . . שירצה את חבירו . . .
שיחזור להיות רוצה ואוהב את חבירו

This verse also limits Yom Kippur's capacity for forgiveness to those sins committed between man and God (בֵּין אָדָם לַמָּקוֹם). As the verse concludes, לְפְנֵי ה' תִּטְהָרוּ, *before HASHEM shall you be cleansed*. Those sins committed between peers (בֵּין אָדָם לַחֲבֵרוֹ) cannot be absolved until the offender appeases the aggrieved party (cf. *Yoma* 85b). The reason for this requirement is not only based on the importance of redressing any wrongs committed, but also because of the paramount importance of unity (אַחְדוּת) amongst Jews. The verse cited previously, וְלֹא אֶחָד בָּהֶם, which alludes to Yom Kippur, places emphasis on achieving unity (אֶחָד) as a prerequisite for Yom Kippur's forgiveness.

In truth, all Jews are inherently united through our common belief in Torah. Disunity — friction between Jews — is only possible when we sin and veer away from the Torah which unites us. Yeshayahu notes כִּי אִם עֲוֹנֹתֵיכֶם הָיוּ מַבְדִּלִים בֵּינֵכֶם לְבֵין אֱלֹהֵיכֶם, *Your sins have separated between you and your God* (59:2).

In light of our assertion that sins — even between man and Hashem — cause dissension and disunity among Jews, we can interpret this verse as referring to two effects of sin. Your sins caused disunity among yourselves (בֵּינֵכֶם) — as well as between you and Hashem (לְבֵין אֱלֹהֵיכֶם). By conciliating our peers, not only for outright offenses such as theft, but for any of our actions that may have promoted disunity, we eradicate both the *effect* of sinning (disunity, hatred) and the sins themselves.

In this light, we may redefine the Mishnah's conclusion עַד שֶׁיְרַצֶּה אֶת חֲבֵרוֹ. While this phrase is usually interpreted to refer to the need to reconcile with one's peers (which would atone for the sin itself), it may imply that *teshuvah* is not accomplished until the offender *wants* (שֶׁיְרַצֶּה, i.e. loves) to re-establish a relationship with his peer. *Achdus* cannot be accomplished merely by placating the offended party. It is critical that the offender yearn to love his peer again, that the spirit of וְאָהַבְתָּ לְרֵעֲךָ כָּמוֹךָ prevail again.   (5651)

Second Tablets:
Atoning for the Golden Calf

✑ Achdus (Unity)

ביוהכ״פ שמתכפרין העבירות נעשין בנ״י אחד ולכן זכו ללוחות
אחרונות
ביוה״כ שמקודם ע״י החטא כ׳ כי פרוע הוא ונתפרד

It is well known that the Second Tablets were given to Israel on Yom Kippur. Our previous assertion — that the Jewish people, no matter how fragmented they may be all year long, unite every Yom Kippur — can help us appreciate why the Second Tablets were granted then. Unity is a prerequisite for Torah. When Israel flirted with idolatry, worshiping the Golden Calf, disunity and fragmentation quickly ensued (cf. *Shemos* 32:25, כִּי פָרֻעַ הוּא, the people had become exposed and disorganized as a result of worshiping the Calf). It was not until the Jewish people's natural tendencies toward *Achdus* had returned that the Torah could be given again. The renowned Rabbinic saying, וְאָהַבְתָּ לְרֵעֲךָ כָּמוֹךָ זֶה כְּלָל גָדוֹל בַּתּוֹרָה (*Yalkut Vayira* 613), conveys the same theme. *Love your neighbor as yourself, this is a great principle* (and an essential prerequisite) for the study *of Torah.* Appropriately enough, Moshe's first initiative after descending from Sinai bearing the Second Tablets was to *gather* the Jewish people (cf. *Shemos* 35:1, וַיַּקְהֵל מֹשֶׁה). (5651)

~§ Taking the Initiative

מה שבראשונה הקדימו נעשה לנשמע וע״י החטא איבדו בחי׳
נעשה ועתה ע״י התשובה הקדימו נעשה לנשמע שקבעו לעצמם
יום תענית . . . מה שעתיד הקב״ה אח״כ לצוות להם

According to *Tanna d'Vei Eliyahu*, the Jewish people, anxious to
avoid repeating the Sin of the Golden Calf, fasted for forty
consecutive days while Moshe ascended to Mt. Sinai to receive the
Second Tablets. On the final day of this forty-day period, the Jewish
people proclaimed a 24-hour fast. In recognition of Israel's initiative,
Hashem not only accepted their *teshuvah*, but instituted the annual
anniversary of their fast as Yom Kippur.

By taking the initiative and fasting even though they weren't obliged
to do so, Israel recaptured the spirit of נַעֲשֶׂה וְנִשְׁמַע. Henceforth their
conduct would be one of *doing* before *hearing* the Divine command
(נִשְׁמַע), which had been dissipated when the Jewish people worshiped
the Golden Calf.

(5655)

~§ Engraving the Torah on the Jewish Heart

וכתיבות הלוחות הוא החקיקה בלבות בנ״י כמ״ש כתבם על לוח
לבך וע״י החטא לא יכלו לקבל הלוחות. ואחר שנמחל להם . . .
נחזור להם זו החקיקה בלב

Whereas the Jewish people *heard* the Ten Commandments, the
Tablets were not merely given but actually permanently *inscribed*
(i.e. they left a permanent imprint) on the Jewish heart. While it appeared
that the Ten Commandments were merely inscribed on the Tablets, they
were actually a means of inscribing and permanently embedding the
Divine word upon the heart of every Jew. *Mishlei* (3:3) implores us "to
write the Torah upon the tablets of your heart" (כָּתְבֵם עַל לוּחַ לִבֶּךָ).

This highly laudable goal of permanently embedding the Torah upon
the Jewish conscience was only possible after Israel repented from the Sin
of the Golden Calf. The words of Torah can only be imprinted upon a
heart cleansed of sin.

While it may appear that the events of Israel's first Yom Kippur — the absolution of the Sin of the Golden Calf as well as the Giving of the Second Tablets — are merely of historical interest, in reality they occur annually. The Sin of the Golden Calf was never totally forgiven (cf. *Rashi, Shemos* 32:34). Instead, an incremental process occurs, in which a small portion of this grave transgression is forgiven every Yom Kippur. As this gravest of sins is gradually forgiven, the impact of the Tablets first given on Yom Kippur increases every year. (5655)

שאין פקודה שאין בו מחטא העגל . . . לפי שעי״ז נסבבו אח״כ כל
החטאים . . . שאין סליחה שאין בו סליחת העגל

Upon further contemplation, we can appreciate the reason for the gradual expiation of the Sin of the Golden Calf. Inasmuch as that transgression was the root cause of all other sins (had Israel not sinned then, they would have enjoyed so great a spiritual existence that they would *never* have been tempted to sin), it follows that whenever the Jewish people commit any other sin, they are held accountable for the Golden Calf as well.

Since Hashem's attribute of rewarding good is far greater than His desire to punish evil (cf. *Makkos* 5b, *Rashi* s.v. על; מרובה מדה טובה), it follows that every time that Israel's sins are forgiven, a portion of the Sin of the Golden Calf is also absolved. Just as we attribute the Sin of the Golden Calf to the first generations of Jews in the wilderness (דור הַמִּדְבָּר), so too every time our prayers for forgiveness are accepted, it is in the merit of that first generation who established the precedent of doing *teshuvah*. If our repentance is accepted in *their* merit, it follows that a portion of their sin (worshiping the Golden Calf) should also be forgiven whenever we repent. (5663)

⋖§ The Uniqueness of the Second Tablets

והראשונות היו בבחי' קדושה כמ״ש וקדשתם . . . והשניות היו
בבחי' טהרה

The Second Tablets, while identical in substance to the First Tablets, represented a very different ideal. Whereas the Torah was originally given to a generation of sacred individuals (cf. *Shemos* 19:10, וְקִדַּשְׁתָּם הַיּוֹם וּמָחָר, *and sanctify them today and tomorrow*) who had never sinned, at the time of the giving of the Second Tablets the Jewish people, having repented from the Sin of the Golden Calf, attained a different state, טָהֳרָה, *purity*.

Only those who have been exposed to an impure environment and became טָמֵא could, upon their return, attain the status of טָהֳרָה. The verse (*Yechezkel* 36:25) cited in the final Mishnah of *Yoma*, וְזָרַקְתִּי עֲלֵיכֶם מַיִם טְהוֹרִים, pertains particularly well to the Second Tablets.

For a further discussion of the uniqueness of the Second Tablets, please refer to our remarks on Elul.

(5645)

The Yom Kippur Dance

והרמז שיש צדיקים . . . והם היפיפיות ויש פשוטים שחל עליהם כח
השורש מאבותינו . . . ויש עוד בח׳ מה שעושין לשם שמים

The well-known Mishnah (*Taanis* 4:8) describing a dance held on Yom Kippur is actually an allusion to the critical importance of Jewish unity.

Many of the details cited in the *Baraisa* of this Mishnah corroborate this approach. For example, the requirement that all participants in the dance wear borrowed clothing suggests that only by surrendering one's individualism on behalf of the community can Yom Kippur's full atonement be achieved.

The chants of the dance's participants are also indicative of the need for collaboration among Jews of various ranks. The most beautiful participants would sing, תֵּן עֵינֶיךָ בַּיוֹפִי, *look closely at our beauty*. Isn't that an allusion to the righteous whose deeds are deemed to be beautiful in Hashem's eyes? Other participants would point out their distinguished roots, *yichus* (תֵּן עֵינֶיךָ בַּמִּשְׁפָּחָה), alluding to Jews who at least enjoy the merit of their fathers (זְכוּת אָבוֹת). Finally, those who were ugly

— whose *mitzvah* observance was insufficient — would proclaim, קְחוּ מְקַחֲכֶם לְשֵׁם שָׁמַיִם, at least our intentions were sound. (5664)

Attaining the Status of Angels

ומסתמא כן הוא באדם . . . שאין יצה"ר שהוא השטן שולט בו
וכמלאכים שאין להם רק . . . לב א'. לכן א"צ אכילה ושתי'.

The Midrash (*Yalkut Vayikra* 578) relates that on Yom Kippur the Jewish people are comparable to angels (shunning food and drink, dressing in white). Let us consider some of the implications of this comparison between mortals and angels.

This Midrash may be alluding to the virtual annihilation of the Satan on Yom Kippur. As we mentioned previously, the forces of evil are impotent on Yom Kippur, equally unable to prosecute the Jewish people as they stand in judgment or to tempt the individual Jew to sin. In this respect, enjoying freedom from evil and even the temptation to do evil, man emulates angels every Yom Kippur. (5649)

והוא אות שעתידין ישראל להיות קדושים ובני ישראל מתענים
בשמחה לומר שמצפים לחזור למדרגה זו הראשונה

In our previous discussion, we emphasized that every Yom Kippur, Hashem forgives yet another portion of the Sin of the Golden Calf. When this process will be complete and the entire measure of Israel's gravest sin will be atoned for, we will be ready to resume the status that we enjoyed before sinning — that of angels. As David sings, אֲנִי אָמַרְתִּי אֱלֹהִים אַתֶּם, *I said* [before the Sin of the Golden Calf] *you are angelic* (*Tehillim* 82:6). Every Yom Kippur, the Jewish people are granted a foretaste of their future status, enjoying the status of angels once a year and feeling confident that this heavenly state will become their permanent lifestyle once the Sin of the Golden Calf has been fully atoned. (5663)

וזוכה מרע״ה את כל בנ״י והוא נקרא איש האלקים . . . ומשה
רע״ה נשאר בזה המדרגה ולא כולם . . . רק ביום הכפורים נדמו
כל בנ״י למלאכי השרת בכח הארת מרע״ה שהכניס עצמו בכלל
ישראל . . .

Finally, we suggest that every Yom Kippur the Jewish people attain the
status of Moshe, who is depicted as אִישׁ הָאֱלֹהִים (*Devarim* 33:1), a man
with God-like characteristics. Not only did Moshe bring down the Tablets on Yom Kippur, but also by fasting for forty days when he stood on
Mt. Sinai, he set a precedent for the Jewish people to at least fast for the
final day of that forty-day period. In fact, the first Yom Kippur was a
"gift" from Moshe to the Jewish people, allowing them to share in his fast.

Just as the first Yom Kippur fast was made possible by Moshe's
willingness to allow Israel to participate, so too every year a few rays of
Moshe's luminescence are enjoyed by the Jewish people. While Moshe
remained a אִישׁ הָאֱלֹהִים all his life, we at least can attain angel-like
characteristics through his largesse on Yom Kippur.   (5664)

Shabbos and Yom Kippur

The following remarks are particularly appropriate when
Shabbos coincides with Yom Kippur.

✺§ Shabbos — Divine Spirit Joins Us
Yom Kippur — We Ascend Heavenward

בכל שבת כתיב ביני ובין בנ״י . . . ובזוה״ק ויקהל איתא כי רוח
עליון היורד מיוחד לבנ״י . . . כן עתה מעלה הכח את נפשות בנ״י
להיות להם אחיזה בחלק העליון

The Torah implies that every Shabbos an unusually intimate relationship is formed between Israel and Hashem: בֵּינִי וּבֵין בְּנֵי יִשְׂרָאֵל אוֹת

הִיא לְעֹלָם (*Shemos* 31:17), *between Me and the Children of Israel it is a sign forever*. While this relationship continues on Shabbos Yom Kippur, its formation assumes radically different properties. Whereas on an ordinary Shabbos, Hashem delights in Israel's enjoyment of the Shabbos (cf. *Zohar Vayakhel* stating that the Divine Spirit delights from עֹנֶג שַׁבָּת), when Shabbos and Yom Kippur coincide it is very different. Israel subsists then on spirituality rather than food and drink, and reverses direction and soars heavenward, temporarily leaving This World and joining a world of supreme spirituality.

Rather than simply being passive participants in the process of spiritual ascent, the Jewish people are required to at least give their assent. The *mitzvah* of fasting on Yom Kippur, described as וְעִנִּיתֶם אֶת נַפְשֹׁתֵיכֶם, *and you shall afflict yourselves [your souls]* (*Vayikra* 16:31), may also be related to *answering* (עוֹנֶה, e.g. עֲנִיַּת אָמֵן). The Jewish people should *respond* positively to the challenge of this unique day. Attracted by the spiritual aura of Yom Kippur (and Shabbos), they should allow the full impact of the day to affect them.   (cf. 5653)

⋅§ Shabbos — Gates of Understanding
Yom Kippur — The Fiftieth Gate

כי יש נ' שערי בינה וביוהכ"פ נפתח שער הנ'

The Talmud (*Rosh Hashanah* 21b) notes the existence of fifty gates of intuition, נ' שַׁעֲרֵי בִינָה. The most opportune time to gain insight into Hashem's ways is on Shabbos. It is reasonable to assume that every Shabbos, one of these gates open. On Yom Kippur, however, the fiftieth and most profound of all gates opens. In fact, the primary purpose of fasting, of abstaining from material pleasures, is to attain a sufficiently high level to be deserving of Hashem's Insights.

(5653)

⋄§ The Root of all Sabbaths

וגם בכל שבת אמרו חז"ל שהוא מעין עוה"ב ויוהכ"פ הוא שורש
כל השבתות לכן הוא יום אחד בשנה. ובנפש כל רק עבודות
יוהכ"פ אין כשרים רק בכ"ג שהוא אחד . . . ובמקום המיוחד
בקדשי קדשים

Yom Kippur is known as שַׁבַּת שַׁבָּתוֹן (ibid. *Vayikra*), the root of and
greatest of all the Sabbaths. Recalling the trilogy of עוֹלָם, שָׁנָה, נֶפֶשׁ
(*time, space,* and the *soul*), we can appreciate Yom Kippur's uniqueness
in each regard.[1] In the realm of *time*, it is the greatest of all Sabbaths,
its Divine service is performed by that great *soul* the *Kohen Gadol* in
the most sacred *space* on earth, the Holy of Holies (קֹדֶשׁ הַקֳּדָשִׁים).

(5653)

⋄§ The Impact of Fasting on Shabbos

גז"ד של ע' שנה לכן בנ"י . . . שמתענין בשבת שבתון נמחל להם
כל העונות

The *Zohar* states that by fasting on Shabbos we effectively nullify
any harsh verdict that may have been destined for us. If this is so for
an *individual* who fasts on an ordinary Shabbos, imagine the impact of
all Jewry fasting on the "Shabbos of Shabbos" (שַׁבָּת שַׁבָּתוֹן) — Yom
Kippur.

(5653)

---

1. *Editor's Note:* The terms עוֹלָם and שָׁנָה are interchangeable with מָקוֹם and זְמַן used
elsewhere.

Tefillos of Yom Kippur

הֵן יַעֲבִיר זָדוֹן לְמְשׁוּגָה כִּי לְכָל הָעָם בִּשְׁגָגָה

*Behold, He transforms willful sin into error, because the
entire people acted through carelessness (Selichos, Maariv
Yom Kippur).*

כולם עושין תשובה עכ״פ מיראה

This stanza implies that the entire Jewish people had sinned
unintentionally. While our implication may seem strange that no
one had committed a *deliberate sin*, we should recall that *teshuvah* of
any sort — even if motivated by fear of retribution (תְּשׁוּבָה מִיִּרְאָה), —
has the effect of mitigating sins from the status of deliberate
transgression (זְדוֹנוֹת) to unintentional sins (שְׁגָגוֹת). Trusting that by the
advent of Yom Kippur the Jewish people have repented, we can
justifiably state, כִּי לְכָל הָעָם בִּשְׁגָגָה. What had been a malicious
transgression is now no more than an unintended misdeed.   (5645)

זדון למשוגה שמתפללין שיחשב מזיד כשוגג ואין מובן הסיום כי
לכל העם בשגגה שהרי מבקשין מחילה גם הזדונות . . . בבנ״י
כתיב ועמך כולם צדיקים כי החטא בעצם בישראל במקרה לא
בעצם

In a somewhat similar vein, we may suggest that the Jewish people
are innately righteous (cf. *Yeshayahu* 60:21, וְעַמֵּךְ כֻּלָּם צַדִּיקִים). If they
sin occasionally, it is an unfortunate deviation, not the norm, and is
immediately followed by regrets for having sinned. Surely any
transgression performed by a Jew is accidental, a rare occurrence, not
innate. It is noteworthy that the final letters (in scrambled order) of the

phrase מִילָה are כִּי לְכָל הָעָם בִּשְׁגָגָה. Any nation observing the rite of *milah* could not possibly engage in a pattern of willful sinning. (5656)

מְחֵה וְהַעֲבֵר פְּשָׁעֵינוּ וְחַטֹּאתֵינוּ מִנֶּגֶד עֵינֶיךָ

Wipe away and remove our willful sins and errors from before Your eyes.

הלשון מנגד עיניך הלא הבקשה הוא לכלות . . . ולמחות כל
החטא רק הפי' שבאמת עי"ז שמתקרבין לפני השי"ת וזוכין
להתוודות לפניו . . . עי"ז נמחה החטא

This prayer, recited in the *Shemoneh Esrei* of Yom Kippur, seemingly requests that our sins be merely erased from *Hashem's Presence* (מִנֶּגֶד עֵינֶיךָ). In reality, we seek the complete obliteration of all of our sins. However, this prayer should be understood in reverse order. Since we merit to stand in Your Presence — particularly so in the *Beis HaMikdash* during the Divine service of Yom Kippur — this exposure to the *Shechinah* in itself expunges the sin. The verse quoted to support our plea, אָנֹכִי אָנֹכִי הוּא מֹחֶה פְשָׁעֶיךָ לְמַעֲנִי, *I, only I, am the One Who wipes away your willful sins for My sake* (Yeshayahu 43:25), may also be understood in this fashion. לְמַעֲנִי — through the Revelation of My Sanctity — this alone helps to eliminate sin. (5647)

אָנֹכִי אָנֹכִי הוּא מֹחֶה פְשָׁעֶיךָ

I, only I, am the One Who wipes away your willful sins.

וב"פ אנכי הם אנכי שבעשרת הדברות בדיבור ואנכי שבלוחות
בכתב

The double expression אָנֹכִי אָנֹכִי, *I, only I*, may allude to the First Commandment, אָנֹכִי ה' אֱלֹהֶיךָ, conveyed twice — orally through the עֲשֶׂרֶת הַדִּבְּרוֹת and in writing on the Tablets. (5656)

כפי מה שמכניסין עצמם לתוך התורה שנקראת מים כך נמחין
הפשעים

Finally, the expression מְחֵה meaning *erase* is closely related to the theme of Hashem purifying Israel through a *mikveh* (please refer to our

previous remarks). By immersing our sins in the purifying waters of the
mikveh, Israel literally *erases* its transgressions. (5656)

◆§ Why Is the Sin of Not Studying Torah (בְּטוּל תּוֹרָה) Omitted in the Confession

לא נזכר חטא ביטול תורה . . . וי׳׳ל כי על חטא שחטאנו בבלי
דעת . . . גם י׳׳ל פריקת עול הוא עול תורה

Few sins can compare to the lethal offense of בִּיטוּל תּוֹרָה, neglect of
Torah study. Although it is not mentioned explicitly in the
confession of sins (וִדּוּי), it is implied in our confession of sins that were
committed בִּבְלִי דָעַת (literally translated as *without knowledge,
unintentionally*) which may refer to sins caused by a lack of Torah
knowledge (since the Torah is the means to obtain knowledge of
Hashem). Alternatively, the plea for forgiveness of פְּרִיקַת עול, *casting
off the yoke*, may refer to our casting off and weakening our
commitment to Torah. (*Likutim*)

The Torah Reading: Shacharis

◆§ Yom Kippur Morning

אַחֲרֵי מוֹת שְׁנֵי בְּנֵי אַהֲרֹן . . . דַּבֵּר אֶל אַהֲרֹן אָחִיךָ . . . וְלֹא יָמוּת
*After the death of Aaron's two sons . . . Speak to Aaron,
your brother . . . so that he should not die (Vayikra 16:1,2).*

ונראה כי זכו בנ׳׳י לעבודת יו׳׳כ על ידיהם . . . כי הי׳ אפשר
שימסור אהרן נפשו לכנוס אף שימות

It is noteworthy that the Torah feels compelled to plead with Aaron
not to enter the Holy of Holies. Apparently, a powerful, almost

irresistible urge existed to enter the *Mishkan's* inner sanctum. In fact, it was this urge that consumed Nadav and Avihu, Aaron's children, driving them to enter the *Mishkan* inappropriately (cf. *Eruvin* 63a citing different opinions as to the exact nature of the sin). Moreover, this overwhelming urge to come exceedingly close to Hashem was not necessarily evil. On the contrary, Nadav and Avihu were extolled by Moshe as being greater than Aaron and himself (cf. *Rashi, Vayikra* 10:3 s.v. הוא). While their personal flaws prevented them from satiating their yearning for closeness to Hashem (please refer to the above citation from *Eruvin* for a litany of their sins), they succeeded to accomplish in death what they couldn't while alive. While they themselves were never able to enter the Holy of Holies, their death — which was a great sanctification of Hashem's Name — enabled the Jewish people, through their representative the *Kohen Gadol*, to enter it every Yom Kippur. In fact, the entire Divine service of Yom Kippur was granted to Israel in their merit. [Thus, the opening phrase אַחֲרֵי מוֹת שְׁנֵי בְּנֵי אַהֲרֹן may refer to the justification for Aaron's entry into the קֹדֶשׁ הַקֳּדָשִׁים. In tribute to their death, you Aaron may enter the Holy of Holies under specific conditions.] Perhaps this opening segment of the Torah reading dealing with Nadav and Avihu is read on Yom Kippur (rather than beginning with the verses dealing *specifically* with the sacrifices of Yom Kippur) to remind us that it was in the merit of those two great sons of Aaron, who loved Hashem so much that they risked their lives to gain intimacy with Him, that we can benefit from Yom Kippur's service.

It is conceivable that Aaron, driven by the same overwhelming urge to approach Hashem, was willing to risk the same fate as his children. To forestall such an option the Torah admonishes Aaron, וְלֹא יָמוּת — Hashem desires that you *live* and not *die* as a result of His service.

(*Acharei* 5636)

בְּזֹאת יָבֹא אַהֲרֹן אֶל הַקֹּדֶשׁ

Only with this may Aaron come into the Sanctuary (v. 3).

בכח אהרן . . . החזיר אותם בתשובה ולכן נמסר כפרת היום ביד
אהרן כה״ג

Aaron earned the distinction of performing the Yom Kippur service on the basis of his splendid *teshuvah*. Having participated (to some extent) in the Sin of the Golden Calf, Aaron was not content with his personal repentance but rather wanted to ensure that the Jewish people would repent as well. As a reward for leaving so sweeping an impact on the Jewish people, Aaron was granted the distinction of performing the Yom Kippur service. *(Yom Kippur 5655)*

בזה עצמו שאל יבא בכל עת בזה הכח יבא אל הקודש

The question arises, what is the antecedent for the term בְּזֹאת, *only with this?* To what does בְּזֹאת refer? While the verse does indicate that Aaron offers sacrifices (a bull and a ram), these are only mentioned at the verse's conclusion. The term בְּזֹאת seems to refer to something previously cited.

It may refer to the immediately preceding admonition, וְאַל יָבֹא בְּכָל עֵת אֶל הַקֹּדֶשׁ , *he may not come at all times into the Sanctuary.*

In the merit of not entering on any other occasion, Aaron will be able to successfully enter the Holy of Holies on Yom Kippur. This combination of *mitzvos* — not entering on any other occasion and being obliged to enter on Yom Kippur — is typical of a Jew's relationship to Hashem: serving Him from a remote vantage point all year long (רָחוֹק) and approaching Him closely (קָרוֹב) on Yom Kippur. *(Acharei 5648)*

וזה הרמז אל יבא בכל עת כי לכל זמן ועת וכו', אבל בנ"י ואני תפלתי וכו', עת רצון

Homiletically, we may interpret the prohibition against coming at any time to the Holy of Holies, the abode of the *Shechinah,* as a warning against focusing only on our material needs when we stand in Hashem's presence (which we related to the concept of time; cf. *Koheles* לַכֹּל זְמָן). Elevate your mundane requests (for sustenance, health) by praying that *all* needs be granted through Hashem Himself (rather than through apparently natural means). Pray that you can come to the realization that all of the material blessings of this world are a Divine gift. As David reminds us, וַאֲנִי תְפִלָּתִי לְךָ ה' עֵת רָצוֹן, *But as for me, my prayer is to You, Hashem, [may it be] at a time of favor (Tehillim 69:14).*

My prayers are not for material abundance itself, not for an עֵת, but for the עֵת רָצוֹן, the realization that all that is perceived of as being עֵת —

merely material — actually stems from Hashem's will (רָצוֹן). As David prays elsewhere (27:4): אַחַת שָׁאַלְתִּי מֵאֵת ה' . . . שִׁבְתִּי בְּבֵית ה' כָּל יְמֵי חַיַּי, *I have only one request of HASHEM . . . to dwell in the House of HASHEM all the days of my life.* Our fondest wish is to come to the realization that everything emanates from Hashem. (5654)

מכאן אמרו חז״ל במקום שבעלי תשובה עומדין צדיקים גמורים יכולין לעמוד

The famous principle, מָקוֹם שֶׁבַּעֲלֵי תְּשׁוּבָה עוֹמְדִין צַדִּיקִים גְּמוּרִים אֵינָם עוֹמְדִין, *In the place where baal teshuvah stand [even] the totally righteous do not stand* (*Berachos* 34b) may be derived from here. All year long, even on Shabbos and *Yom Tov*, the *Kohen Gadol* may not enter the Holy of Holies. Only on Yom Kippur, representing penitents — returnees to Hashem — when he merits unusual closeness to Hashem, may Aaron (the *Kohen Gadol*) enter. (5664)

אבל הענין שיש מצות כלליות ונק׳ חבילות

Commenting on בְּזֹאת יָבֹא אַהֲרֹן, the Midrash (*Yalkut Vayikra* 16) enumerates numerous *mitzvos* that are depicted with the word זֹאת, categorizing them as חֲבִילוֹת שֶׁל מִצְוֹת, *bundles of mitzvos.* The Midrash is hardly implying that some *mitzvos* are more significant than others, but rather is suggesting that certain commandments — identified by the term זֹאת — are so broad based that they contain other *mitzvos.* (5638)

בִּגְדֵי קֹדֶשׁ הֵם

They are sacred vestments (v. 4).

רק שבגדים הם המלבושים,,ונהפך מלבוש הגוף שהוא לבוש להנשמה ונתלבש במלבושי קודש

The Midrash (cited by *Rashi* on v. 34, וַיַּעַשׂ כַּאֲשֶׁר צִוָּה ה') notes that Aaron did not wear the priestly vestments (בִּגְדֵי כְּהוּנָה) for his own glory, but solely to fulfill Hashem's commandment. It would seem rather unlikely that the sainted *Kohen Gadol* would don the בִּגְדֵי כְּהוּנָה for his own eminence. Therefore why does the Midrash tell us this?

It appears that the Midrash is hinting at the effect upon Aaron of wearing these sacred garments. As soon as he donned the בִּגְדֵי כְּהוּנָה, Aaron's *body*, which ordinarily served as a לְבוּשׁ, a covering for his soul, was subsumed by these garments. Thus, the בִּגְדֵי כְּהוּנָה took over the traditional function of the body, the role of sheltering the soul. Appreciating now the full impact of these garments, transforming Aaron from an ordinary, though great, human being into a totally spiritual being whose soul was encased in equally sacred garments, we can appreciate how even the slightest personal enjoyment derived by Aaron would have made it impossible to don these garments.[1] It is evident from here and other sources that the *Kohen Gadol* attained supernatural characteristics when adorned in these sacred vestments.

(Yom Kippur 5644)

לְשַׁלַּח אֹתוֹ לַעֲזָאזֵל הַמִּדְבָּרָה.

By sending it for Azazel to the desert (v. 10).

החטאים נשלכים במצולות ים דשם שורש כל החטאים .. וזהו ענין השעיר המשתלח שמקבל כל עונות בנ"י.

By casting the goat off a cliff, we are demonstrating that sins — even if committed by the Jewish people — are extraneous, and hardly an innate trait. The *Zohar* suggests that our sins are cast in the depths of the sea (cf. *Michah* 7:19, וְתַשְׁלִיךְ בִּמְצֻלוֹת יָם כָּל חַטֹּאתָם).

When sinning, the individual gives the Evil Inclination a foothold. Every transgression allows the forces of evil to penetrate a bit farther into the sacred soul of the Jew. By designating the Azazel goat (שָׂעִיר לַעֲזָאזֵל) as the bearer of all sins, we are returning all perpetrators of Israel's sins to their origin, on some distant cliff in the wilderness, far removed from the core of the Jewish soul. (*Yom Kippur* 5645)

כִּי בַיּוֹם הַזֶּה יְכַפֵּר עֲלֵיכֶם

For on this day he shall provide atonement for you (v. 30).

---

1. The liturgical piece מַרְאֵה כֹהֵן, describing the splendid appearance of the *Kohen Gadol* upon departing the Holy of Holies, alludes to the role of these garments in supplanting the body. For example, כְּהוֹד אֲשֶׁר הִלְבִּישׁ צוּר לִיצוּרִים, the *Kohen Gadol's* appearance was *like the majesty in which the Creator clothed the creatures.* כְּעֹז אֲשֶׁר הִלְבִּישׁ טָהוֹר לַמְטַהֵר, It was also comparable to *the strength that the Pure One* (Hashem) *garbed the one who became pure* (Israel).

All other occasions when Hashem forgives our misdeeds (e.g. for transgressions where simply repenting suffices) are only effective because of the existence of the Day of Atonement: כִּי בַיּוֹם הַזֶּה יְכַפֵּר should be interpreted as *through* this day rather than restricting the definition to *on* this day. All other occasions (days) for atonement are effective because of (through) Yom Kippur.   (*Acharei 5664*)

Torah Reading: Minchah
Don't Emulate Pagans

כְּמַעֲשֵׂה אֶרֶץ מִצְרַיִם אֲשֶׁר יְשַׁבְתֶּם בָּהּ לֹא תַעֲשׂוּ וּכְמַעֲשֵׂה אֶרֶץ
כְּנַעַן אֲשֶׁר אֲנִי מֵבִיא אֶתְכֶם שָׁמָּה לֹא תַעֲשׂוּ

Do not perform the practice of the land of Egypt in which you dwelled; and do not perform the practice of the land of Canaan to which I bring you (Vayikra 18:3).

It seems somewhat surprising that the Jewish people need to be admonished not to act as the Egyptians or the Canaanites. Moreover, if the verse is referring to the laws of prohibited marriages (עֲרָיוֹת), detailed subsequently, these relationships are inherently אָסוּר — not merely because they are pagan practices. Let us consider several interpretations of this verse and their ramifications for a Torah life.

✑ Don't Live a Superficial Lifestyle

בנ״י יכולין לעשות כל המעשים בקדושה ע״י המצות

Unlike the Egyptians and Canaanites who lived a superficial lifestyle, you, the Jewish people, are able to understand the inner purpose

(פְּנִימִיוּת) of everything. By virtue of observing *mitzvos* (mentioned in the following verse, אֶת מִשְׁפָּטַי תַּעֲשׂוּ, *carry out My laws*) we are able to grasp the inner significance of every aspect of life. As *Avos* (2:12) urges us, וְכָל מַעֲשֶׂיךָ יִהְיוּ לְשֵׁם שָׁמָיִם, *all your deeds should be for the sake of Heaven*. The pagan, clinging to a non-Torah lifestyle, could only understand the surface aspects of life. For him, everything was a חֹק (as the Torah exhorts, וּבְחֻקֹּתֵיהֶם לֹא תֵלֵכוּ), a statute devoid of meaning.

(*Acharei 5635*)

אף דברי רשות לא יהיו נעשים כמעשה ארץ כנען

If the Torah were merely encouraging us to observe Hashem's commandments and not commit the transgressions of the Egyptians and Canaanites, it would have simply said מַעֲשֶׂה, *the actions* (*practice*). By stating כְּמַעֲשֶׂה, the כ implies anything *similar* to their actions. We can deduce therefore that the Torah is referring to mundane secular deeds, and that those too should be conducted in a different manner than that of the pagans. Even our wishes, our desires and aspirations should be uniquely Jewish! Perhaps the best way to fulfill such a laudable goal is to somehow relate every act — no matter how secular and remote from Torah it may appear to be — to a *mitzvah*. This brings to mind the famous verse: בְּכָל דְּרָכֶיךָ דָעֵהוּ, *Know Him through all your actions* (*Mishlei* 3:6).

(5638)

לאכול ולשתות להוסיף כח בעבודת הבורא

Even eating and drinking, seemingly only physical acts, can — and must — be undertaken for a higher purpose, to give us the fortitude to serve Hashem.

(5639)

◆§ Character Perfection

והוא תיקון המדות .. פרישה מקנאה תאוה וכבוד

Alternatively, the verse may refer to the ignoble character traits of the pagan world. The concept of תִּקּוּן הַמִּדּוֹת, *character development*, is a prerequisite to Torah study (cf. *Yalkut Bereishis* 3, דֶּרֶךְ אֶרֶץ קָדְמָה לַתּוֹרָה). In particular, the verse may be referring to the character traits denounced in *Avos* 4:21 — קִנְאָה תַּאֲוָה וְכָבוֹד. *Jealousy, Lust, and Glory* [*remove a man from the world*]. The Torah is exhorting us to reject those basest of character traits and replace them with the מִדּוֹת טוֹבוֹת of the Jew. (5642)

✍§ The Challenge and the Reward

שע״י שיצ״מ הי׳ בכח מרע״ה והי׳ בתיקון השלימות לכן התורה
נשאר לנו לעולם וכן זכינו אח״כ לבטל יצרא דע״ז מכל וכל

By singling out the Egyptians and the Canaanites, the Torah is challenging the Jewish people to defeat and eliminate the vices that distinguished each of these nations. Instead of bypassing Egypt and Canaan — instead of trying to avoid dealing with their pagan travesties — we accepted the challenge, met and conquered the Egyptian and Canaanite foe and eliminated (or at least curtailed the effect of) their vices. By defeating the Egyptians who were known for their infatuation with idolatry, the Jewish people helped mitigate mankind's lust to worship idols. In fact, ultimately — perhaps as a result of their forefathers having overcome the Egyptian threat — the Men of the Great Assembly (אַנְשֵׁי כְּנֶסֶת הַגְּדוֹלָה) were able to eliminate any temptation to worship idols (cf. *Sanhedrin* 64a).

Likewise, by vanquishing the Canaanites who were known for their licentious ways, the Jewish people were able to eventually eliminate certain aspects of גִּלּוּי עֲרָיוֹת, especially incest.

However, a crucial distinction existed between the *complete* elimination of the Egyptian threat (to the extent that the Jewish people not only left Egypt but may never return) of idolatry and the excessive tolerance of the Canaanites who were only *partially* eliminated. Perhaps for that reason, the Men of the Great Assembly only succeeded in eliminating the lust for idolatry but not that of prohibited relations. The distinction between the total elimination of the Egyptian threat and only partial curtailment of the Canaanites and their vices may lie in the unique power of Moshe to eliminate evil, whereas the following generation lacked the capacity to expunge the Canaanites.

Consider the rewards accruing to the Jewish people as a result of rising to the challenge and eliminating the Egyptian and Canaanite threat. Almost immediately after the Exodus, we received the Torah. In the merit of conquering Canaan, we took title to *Eretz Yisrael* and eventually, the *Beis HaMikdash.* Again, the reward is commensurate to the manner in which the challenge was dealt with. The Torah, which was granted after Egypt's total elimination as a spiritual threat, is perpetual. On the other hand, possession of *Eretz Yisrael* and the *Beis HaMikdash,* granted as rewards for *partially* eliminating the Canaanite threat, were eventually lost.

In this verse, the Torah refers to two of the greatest threats, Egypt's paganism and the promiscuity of the Canaanites. However, other equally lethal dangers exist, threatening the viability of the Jewish people. Among them, murder (שְׁפִיכַת דָּמִים), symbolized by Sichon and Og, the two mighty warriors crushed by the Jewish people (cf. *Makkos* 9b suggesting that in Gilead, the territory conquered from Sichon and Og, murder was commonplace), evil talk (לָשׁוֹן הָרָע) and baseless hatred (שִׂנְאַת חִנָּם) — which are equivalent to the combined effect of paganism, prohibited marriages, and murder — represented by Esav (who hated Yaakov). Only the Final Redemption will eliminate the perpetual threat of baseless hatred. (5641)

ᴈ Intrinsic Beauty of Eretz Yisrael vs. the Total Evil of Egypt

---

הגאולה ממצרים . . . והוא ערלת החיתוך שמשליכין לעפר
וארץ כנען . . . והוא עור הפריעה שצריכין להסירו כדי לגלות
העטרה.

While the Torah *seems* to equate the two nations as threats, a major distinction exists between Egypt and Canaan, a difference that can be appreciated in the context of *bris milah.* The Egyptian threat required total elimination (cf. *Devarim* 17:16 prohibiting our return to Egypt) which is analogous to the *orlah* (foreskin) which is totally excised. On the other hand, *Eretz Yisrael* is intrinsically good: Once the outer veil, the dissolute Canaanites are purged, the great spiritual light of the Land comes to the forefront. This is comparable to the פְּרִיעָה, the retraction of the foreskin (cf. *Yevamos* 71b stating that the *mitzvah* of פְּרִיעָה was observed upon the Jewish people's entrance into *Eretz Yisrael*. In light of our suggestion that the פְּרִיעָה symbolizes the inherent goodness of *Eretz Yisrael*, we can appreciate why this *mitzvah* was only granted upon entering the Land).

Yet another component exists — extricating some of the blood of the *bris milah* (הַטָּפַת דַּם בְּרִית).

This goal, avenging the blood spilled by Esav and his cohorts, will not be realized until the Final Redemption. Then, Esav's territory (known as הַקֵּינִי הַקְּנִיזִּי וְהַקַּדְמֹנִי; cf. *Bereishis* 15:19), historically off-limits to the Jewish people, will be ours. (5651)

⋖§ First Thorns, then the Straight Path

כי במעשה הרשעים הוא הדרך שתחילתו מישור וסופו קוצים . . .
ודרך התורה הוא להיפוך

While the pagan, licentious path of the Egyptians and Canaanites appear to be *good*, they are eventually proven to be only a mirage, an outer facade of glitter obscuring a great deal of evil and falsehood. The Midrash describes their lifestyle as a straight path that eventually degenerates into a bed of thorns. On the other hand, the Torah's path may appear to be fraught with difficulties *at first*, but eventually our way is proven to be the right way. As the following verse (4) indicates, אֲשֶׁר יַעֲשֶׂה אֹתָם הָאָדָם וָחַי בָּהֶם, *which man shall carry out and by which he shall live*, the Torah is the true path of life. (5647)

⋖§ Subject to No Angel

כי כל אומה יש לה שר בשמים אבל הנהגת בני למעלה מכל
השרים

Whereas every other nation — even the Canaanites while they were dwelling in *Eretz Yisrael* — were subject to the angels that Hashem appointed to regulate their natural existence (cf. *Ramban*, *Vayikra*, elaborating on this theme), the Jewish people, directly under

Hashem's sovereignty, are immune to such constraints. Consequently, our conduct befits that of a nation chosen by Hashem to be His.

(5659)

אֲשֶׁר יְשַׁבְתֶּם בָּהּ

In which you dwelled (v. 3).

וז"'ש אשר ישבתם בה כעין שדרשו אשר שברת יישר כוחך

The term אֲשֶׁר may be interpreted as יִישַׁר, a form of Divine appreciation (cf. *Rashi, Devarim* interpreting אֲשֶׁר שִׁבַּרְתָּ as יִישַׁר כֹּחֲךָ שֶׁשִּׁבַּרְתָּ). Hashem is *thanking* Israel for having dwelled in Egypt and in Canaan. During their sojourn in these lands, the Jewish people were able to extricate sacred sparks (i.e. souls of converts who joined the faith). [Refer to our remarks in *The Pesach Haggadah with Ideas and Insights of the Sfas Emes* pp. 90-91, for an elaboration of this theme.] Hashem is thanking Israel for having endured the Egyptian *galus* for so long in order to attract these souls.

(5649)

אֲשֶׁר אֲנִי מֵבִיא אֶתְכֶם שָׁמָּה

To which I bring you (v. 3).

Toras Kohanim (an ancient Midrash dating back to the Mishnaic era) comments that the very fact that the land belonged to the Jewish people was a major factor in causing the Canaanites to sin. The Talmud (*Sotah* 47a) states a similar theme: חֵן מָקוֹם עַל יוֹשְׁבָיו, the place can only find favor [in Hashem's eyes] if its inhabitants are suitable for it. A land as sacred as *Eretz Yisrael* — linked to its heavenly roots — cannot possibly tolerate individuals who are steeped in materialism. Of course, the Jewish people were not immune to the same criticism levied against their Canaanite predecessors: If they emulated the Canaanite ways and lost contact with their own heavenly roots, they too would be ejected from the land. In fact, Israel's temptation to sin may have been greater in *Eretz Yisrael* than anywhere else. Just as *Chazal* (*Succah* 52a) say, כָּל הַגָּדוֹל מֵחֲבֵירוֹ יִצְרוֹ גָּדוֹל מִמֶּנּוּ, *the greater the person, the greater the temptation to sin*, so too, the greater and more sacred the land, the greater the temptation to sin.

(5648)

ঙৃ Avoiding Temptations of the Natural World

וּבְחֻקֹּתֵיהֶם לֹא תֵלֵכוּ

And do not follow their traditions (v. 3).

פ׳ חקה שנטבע באדם . . . שלא להיות נמשך אחר הטבע

The term בְּחֻקֹּתֵיהֶם does not necessarily refer to idolatrous practices, but to the danger of slavishly following the natural order without recalling Hashem's capacity to supersede the natural order. Instead, you should *guard My mitzvos* (אֶת חֻקֹּתַי תִּשְׁמֹרוּ), ensure that nothing should distract you from your objective of following Torah and *mitzvos*. In the merit of not being lured by the natural world, you will ascend to the level of לָלֶכֶת בָּהֶם, in which you will *walk* (i.e. become accustomed) with *mitzvos* and no longer be tempted to follow the natural order.

(*Likutim*)

לָלֶכֶת בָּהֶם
To follow them (v. 4).

**וצריך האדם להתעלות תמיד ממדרגה למדרגה ויש לו תמיד
תורה חדשה וחיות חדש וזה ללכת בהם**

This phrase emphasizes the importance of constantly ascending rather than being content with one's present level of spiritual achievement. At each phase of one's personal growth, one is rewarded with new insights into Torah. (5644)

**צריך להיות המכוון לבוא עי״ז ליותר קדושה שיוכל להוסיף בכל
עת ממדריגה למדרגה**

Rashi comments, אַל תִּפָּטֵר מִתּוֹכָם, *do not take leave of them* — you can never be exempt from *them* (from *mitzvos*). Please refer to our commentary on כְּמַעֲשֵׂה אֶרֶץ מִצְרַיִם, in which we emphasized the importance of conducting every sphere of life — even such seemingly mundane acts as eating and drinking — from the perspective of Torah. In this spirit, we may also interpret לָלֶכֶת בָּהֶם. Eating and drinking are perfectly permissible if it is motivated by the desire to gain strength to walk in Hashem's ways (לָלֶכֶת בָּהֶם). For those on a higher level of observance, לָלֶכֶת בָּהֶם implies observing *mitzvos* so that we may merit to do even more *mitzvos* (cf. *Avos* 4:2, שְׂכַר מִצְוָה מִצְוָה). Thus, it is *Rashi's* intention to tell us that we should observe *mitzvos* not only for the purpose of discharging one's obligation (לִיפָּטֵר מֵהֶם), but on the contrary perform *mitzvos* so that in their merit you will continue to perform even more *mitzvos*.

(5639)

שישאר בו חיות מן המצוה כל היום

Alternatively, לָלֶכֶת בָּהֶם implies that through performance of a *mitzvah*, we obtain enough spiritual strength to last us the entire day. For example, the hand upon which *tefillin* was placed, during the morning prayers, attains a degree of sanctity that remains with it all day. (5660)

אֲנִי ה' אֱלֹהֵיכֶם

I am HASHEM, your God (18:2).

אֲנִי ה' אֱלֹהֵיכֶם

I am HASHEM, your God (18:4).

רמז לדבר בההוא עובדא במס' מנחות שבאו הציצית לאותו תלמיד והצילו מחטא ערוה ואמר שכי' בפ' ציצית ב"פ אני ה' אלהיכם

Why the apparent repetition of the words אֲנִי ה' אֱלֹהֵיכֶם, *I am HASHEM, your God?*

We recall a renowned Gemara (*Menachos* 44a) about the individual who almost succumbed to a prostitute's lures. However, as he was preparing to meet her, he was hit on his head by four *tzitzis* strings. As he explained later to the prostitute, he was reminded then of the repetition of אֲנִי ה' אֱלֹהֵיכֶם contained in the portion of *tzitzis* (cf. *Bamidbar* 15:41: *I, HASHEM, your God will punish those who violate My commandments, and I will reward those who obey them*). Considering the ramifications of sinning and the rewards obtained by not sinning, the individual desisted from sinning (cf. the complete story in the Gemara stating how the prostitute was so impressed with his rationale that she converted and then was permitted to marry the individual she had tempted).

Similarly, the best safeguard against prohibited marriages (which is the subject of the portion read on Yom Kippur afternoon) is the message conveyed by the repetition of אֲנִי ה' אֱלֹהֵיכֶם — we are obliged to keep His decrees even under difficult circumstances and should remember the reward and punishment that will result.　　　(*Yom Kippur 5656*)

ב"פ אני ה' . . . אני ראשון ואני אחרון

Alternatively, the repetition of אֲנִי ה' אֱלֹהֵיכֶם alludes to His Eternity. As Yeshayahu states (44:6) more explicitly, אֲנִי רִאשׁוֹן וַאֲנִי אַחֲרוֹן, *I am first* (i.e. prior to Creation) *and I am last* — I am your God in this world and I am your God in the World to Come.　　　(*Acharei 5657*)

אני ה' אלקיכם . . . שבנ"י צריכין עזר מקודש הן בסור מרע . . . (תרס) שממשיכין כח אלקות ע"י שמירת ל"ת . . . וע"י מ"ע (תרסא)

Perhaps the double phrase אֲנִי ה' אֱלֹהֵיכֶם refers to the two challenges granted to Israel in this reading: כְּמַעֲשֵׂה אֶרֶץ מִצְרַיִם . . . לֹא תַעֲשׂוּ, which admonishes us not to follow the mores of the pagans, and also אֶת מִשְׁפָּטַי תַּעֲשׂוּ וְאֶת חֻקֹּתַי תִּשְׁמְרוּ, *Carry out My judgments and observe My decrees* (v. 4), we are obligated to perform Hashem's statutes. As Hashem our God, He grants us sufficient fortitude to rise to meet both challenges, to resist evil (סוּר מֵרַע) and also to do good (עֲשֵׂה טוֹב).　　　(5660, 5661)

If we extend this theme even further, we may suggest that אֲנִי ה' אֱלֹהֵיכֶם is not only the means of preventing transgressions and performing *mitzvos* but also the *result* of our superior performance. By withstanding evil and through performing *mitzvos*, we earn the distinction of אֲנִי ה' אֱלֹהֵיכֶם, that Hashem can say *I am your God*. Both the negative commandments (מִצְוֹת לֹא תַעֲשֶׂה) as well as the positive commandments (מִצְוֹת עֲשֵׂה) bring the Jew closer to Hashem; they facilitate דְּבֵקוּת, the clinging of the soul to its God. In contrast to the prohibited marriages mentioned in this portion, which lead to a severing of the link between man and God [as indicated by the penalty of כָּרֵת, *excision*, the cutting off of an individual from his spiritual core (cf. *Ramban, Vayikra* 18:29 s.v. ונכרת)], *mitzvos* lead to an even more intimate relationship. The double usage of אֲנִי ה׳ אֱלֹהֵיכֶם, recalls the verse (*Yirmiyahu* 23:23). הָאֱלֹהֵי מֵרָחֹק ... מִקָּרֹב אָנִי ... וְלֹא אֱלֹהֵי מֵרָחֹק. Hashem states emphatically that *I am God* through those *mitzvos* that bring the Jew *closer* to Hashem (מִצְוֹת עֲשֵׂה) as well as *distancing* Myself from עֲבֵרוֹת.

(5661)

שלא יקבלו שום שנוי מאלה המקומות

Perhaps the greatest assurance that we will not emulate the pagan practices of the Egyptians and Canaanites is this simple (yet profound) statement, *I am HASHEM, your God.* Just as Hashem is immutable (cf. *Malachi* 3:6, אֲנִי ה׳ לֹא שָׁנִיתִי), so too the Jewish people will never succumb.

(ibid.)

וָחַי בָּהֶם
Living Through Mitzvos

אֲשֶׁר יַעֲשֶׂה אֹתָם הָאָדָם וָחַי בָּהֶם

Which man shall carry out and live by them (v. 5).

This renowned verse lends itself to numerous interpretations which have ramifications for many aspects of Jewish life. In the following segment we will explore some of these explanations and insights.

✺§ The Life of the Soul

שהמצות ממשיכין החיות להאברים ... רמ״ח מ״ע נגד רמ״ח אברים .. ויגרש את האדם ... הכל הוא באדם עצמו שנעשה מסך מבדיל בין הנפש והנשמה שרומז לג״ע ולעץ החיים ובין הגוף

In order to appreciate the Torah's perspective on life, let us first turn to the creation of man who is described in these terms, וַיִּפַּח בְּאַפָּיו נִשְׁמַת חַיִּים וַיְהִי הָאָדָם לְנֶפֶשׁ חַיָּה, *and He blew into his nostrils the soul of life; and man became a living being* (Bereishis 2:7).

While Hashem "blew" a soul of life into man, He then assigned man an additional task, to be a נֶפֶשׁ חַיָּה, a vehicle (כְּלִי) through which the life of the soul (נִשְׁמַת חַיִּים) could penetrate the entire body. Prior to the first sin, Adam, ensconced in Eden, was the epitome of the נֶפֶשׁ חַיָּה concept, he truly lived! Every limb of his body was infused with the spiritual life of the soul. The Torah's description of man's expulsion from Eden and the fiery revolving blade that prevented his return (ibid. 3:24) refer not only to his *physical* departure but also to the barrier between the body and the soul that occurred as a result of sinning.

The Garden of Eden and the Tree of Life were not only physical entities, but also symbolized man's ability to be immersed in a totally spiritual milieu — the body being dominated by the soul. Adam's expulsion from Eden and especially the emplacement of a fiery blade preventing access to Eden are the Torah's way of depicting the barriers that now existed between the soul, still in Eden, and the body on the outside. However, by heeding our verse's call to observe Torah and *mitzvos* (וּשְׁמַרְתֶּם אֶת חֻקֹּתַי וְאֶת מִשְׁפָּטַי, *you shall observe My decrees and My judgments*), man can be restored to his original function, to infuse the life of the soul into the body. As the verse continues and urges us, אֲשֶׁר יַעֲשֶׂה אֹתָם הָאָדָם וָחַי בָּהֶם, *by performing them* (the statutes and *mitzvos*), *we can live*. Appropriately, each of the 248 limbs (רמ"ח אֵבָרִים) corresponds to one of the 248 positive commandments, suggesting that each limb is sustained through the *mitzvos* it performs. Through Torah and *mitzvos*, the Jew can regain what Adam lost — a body wholly nurtured and kept alive through the life of the soul.   (5661)

◆§ Clinging to the Tree of Life

וּבֶאֱמֶת הַתּוֹרָה נק' עֵץ חַיִּים וּכְפִי הָעֵסֶק בַּהַתּוֹרָה זוֹכִין לְהִתְדַּבֵּק בַּחַיִּים.

As we have frequently discussed, one of the effects of Adam's sin was the blurring of good and evil. By partaking of the Tree of

Knowledge of Good and Evil, it became virtually impossible to discern between good and evil. Yet, another tree remains, the Tree of Life (עֵץ הַחַיִּים), symbolic of the purity that existed before the first sin and that is still attainable by clinging to the Torah which is called a "Tree of Life" (cf. *Mishlei* 3:18). By resisting the Evil Inclination and by observing Torah and *mitzvos*, the Jew is able to overcome Adam's sin and the consequent blurring of good and evil. Such a person can cling to the "Tree of Life," וָחַי בָּהֶם. (5654)

⋅§ Reversing Adam's Sin

אך אחר החטא נתלבש בגוף שיש בו מיתה. וע״י המצות זוכין
למלבוש הראשון.

The concept of mortality stems from Adam's sin (cf. *Bereishis* 2:17, כִּי בְּיוֹם אֲכָלְךָ מִמֶּנּוּ מוֹת תָּמוּת, *for on the day you eat of it, you shall surely die*. Prior to partaking from the Tree of Knowledge, Adam's body was merely an adjunct to his soul, and was blessed with immortality. Even today, by fulfilling the 248 positive and 365 negative commandments which correspond to the limbs and sinews of the human body, we can sanctify our body to the extent that it reacquires the spirituality and immortality that it once enjoyed. This may be the intent of *Rashi's* comment that the verse pertains to the World to Come. Through Torah and *mitzvos* the Jew regains the immortality Adam once enjoyed. While it may appear that man expires, in reality he lives eternally in the World to Come. (5653)

⋅§ A Sight Never Seen

ועתידין בנ״י להתלבש בציור רוחני שאין מושג לשום ברי׳ . . .
והכל באמצעיות המצות בעוה״ז

Perhaps one may draw a parallel between the term יַעֲשֶׂה utilized in this verse and Yeshayahu's description (64:3) of the World to Come: עַיִן לֹא רָאָתָה . . . יַעֲשֶׂה לִמְחַכֵּה לוֹ, *No one has ever seen . . . what Hashem will do for those who wait for Him*. The Talmud (*Berachos* 34b) notes that no one — not even the greatest prophet — could visualize the reward granted to the righteous in the World to Come. Here too, the Torah is alluding to the indescribable reward and the spiritual profile to be attained by the Jew in the World to Come as a reward for observing *mitzvos* in this world. Every Shabbos, described as a microcosm of the World to Come, he enjoys a taste of this great reward. (5653)

⋞ Live Now on the Basis of Future Mitzvos

לכן כתיב אשר יעשה לשון עתיד וחי בהם קודם העשי'

It is noteworthy that the Torah utilizes the future tense, אֲשֶׁר יַעֲשֶׂה אוֹתָם, *which man shall carry out* — the *mitzvos* that a person *will* perform *already* sustain him (וָחַי בָּהֶם).

The mere intention and desire to perform a *mitzvah* sustains an individual. (5660)

⋞ Appreciating a Mitzvah Retroactively

פ' אחר המעשה ימצא שחי בהם

Whereas we discussed above the affect of a future *mitzvah*, let us reinterpret the verse as pertaining to the *retroactive* effect of a *mitzvah*, אֲשֶׁר יַעֲשֶׂה אֹתָם וָחַי בָּהֶם. It is only after one performed a *mitzvah* that one realizes that he had indeed *lived* through the *mitzvah* (וָחַי בָּהֶם). (5647)

⋞ Choose the Path of Life

כי זה עצמו המצוה על בנ״י לראות להתדבק בדרך החיים כמ״ש
ובחרת בחיים . . . .

The Torah's plea of וָחַי בָּהֶם is strikingly similar to another such Divine request, וּבָחַרְתָּ בַּחַיִּים, *you shall choose life* (*Devarim* 30:19). Even the Torah itself, if utilized improperly, can induce death and not life. As the Talmud (cf. *Shabbos* 63a) states, לַמַּשְׂמְאִלִים בָּהּ סַמָּא דְמוֹתָא, for those who abuse the Torah and (literally) *approach it from the left,* it can prove to be lethal. Observe Torah and *mitzvos* so that you *will live.*

(5659)

◆§ The Permanent Impact of Mitzvos

חי הוא כמו מים חיים שדבוק במקורו ולא יתבטל לעולם ולא
שימות בהם כי העושה בקרירות . . . נקרא מיתה

Alternatively, the term חַי may be related to מַיִם חַיִּים, *naturally flowing water.* Just as water emanating from a natural source rarely, if ever, ceases, so too our involvement with Torah and *mitzvos* should never be transitory. Instead, we should be so immersed that every *mitzvah* performed leaves a permanent impact. The Talmud's ruling (cf. *Yoma* 85b), וָחַי בָּהֶם וְלֹא שֶׁיָּמוּת בָּהֶם, *one must live through Torah and not die through Torah* (which is interpreted halachically that *mitzvos* are superseded in case of mortal danger), may be interpreted homiletically in the same vein. Perform *mitzvos* with such devotion that you will cling permanently to the *mitzvah.* Anything less than stellar performance — performing *mitzvos* haphazardly — is the spiritual equivalent of death.

(5659)

◆§ Attain Perfection Through Mitzvos

כי השלמת האדם ע״י המצות וחי בהם משלים עי״ז צורת האדם

The term חַי also connotes *perfection* (cf. *Berachos* 51a requiring the cup used for *Bircas HaMazon* to be חַי and *Tosafos'* [50b s.v. מוֹדִים] interpretation that the cup not be chipped or dented in any fashion). Only through Torah and *mitzvos* may one attain perfection.

Utilizing this connotation of חַי meaning *completion,* one may suggest that man attains the supreme honor, the distinguished accolade of being called an אָדָם through Torah and *mitzvos.* The verse should be interpreted in the following manner: אֲשֶׁר יַעֲשֶׂה אֹתָם הָאָדָם, by performing them (the חֻקִּים and מִשְׁפָּטִים previously mentioned), וָחַי בָּהֶם

one *completes* and perfects the אָדָם. The title אָדָם, *man*, is ultimately earned through *mitzvos.* (5658)

⋖§ Completing the Mitzvah

שהאדם משלים המצוה בעשייי'

In a similar vein, utilizing וָחַי בָּהֶם in the context of completion, we suggest that *mitzvos* themselves are "completed" — through the Jewish people's actions (אֲשֶׁר יַעֲשֶׂה אֹתָם). While *mitzvos* exist in all realms — *thought* (מַחֲשָׁבָה), *speech* (דְבּוּר), as well as *action* — a *mitzvah* cannot be completed until it is actually performed (מַעֲשֶׂה). [Refer to our commentary on *shofar* for a further discussion of the various realms of *mitzvos.*] (5658)

⋖§ In This World or the World to Come?

והנפש פושטת צורה ולובשת צורה וע״י המצות מכין אדם לנפשו מלבוש וחלוקא דרבנן בעוה״ב ז״ש וחי בהם שיתלבש החיות אח״כ מהם ממש.

The Midrash interprets the verse וָחַי בָּהֶם to be referring to the World to Come (עוֹלָם הַבָּא). Yet, the simple meaning (פְּשַׁט) of the verse clearly refers to this world. In reality these explanations are not dichotomous. Undoubtedly, the primary effect of observing *mitzvos* is to prepare the Jew for the hereafter. Death is merely a transition from the body (which enveloped the soul in this world) to another, more spiritual form of protection for the soul, known as the חֲלוּקָא דְרַבָּנָן (cf. the prayer recited before donning the *tallis*), *the garment of the Rabbis.* This garb is literally comprised of the Torah studied and the *mitzvos* performed while one was alive in this world. In this sense, וָחַי בָּהֶם may be interpreted quite literally — וָחַי, *you will live,* בָּהֶם, *through them,* through the Torah and *mitzvos* you perform.

However, a glimpse, a foretaste of the "spiritual garb" (the חֲלוּקָא) that will enclothe us in the World to Come is enjoyed by the worthy in this world. As stated frequently in this commentary, every individual not only enjoys physical presence in this world but also has heavenly roots. Every time we perform *mitzvos* in this world we sustain our heavenly roots (וְחַי בָּהֶם). If a *mitzvah* has been performed properly, one can sense even in this world a bit of the bliss attained by our spiritual roots. The renowned Mishnah stating כָּל יִשְׂרָאֵל יֵשׁ לָהֶם חֵלֶק לָעוֹלָם הַבָּא, *All Israel has* (present tense, rather than יִהְיֶה, *will have*) *a portion in the World to Come*, implies the same theme. While the primary effect of *mitzvos* is to nurture and protect us in the World to Come, one can enjoy a foretaste in this world as well. (5657)

◆§ Living or Dying for Torah

כפי מה שממית עצמו עליי כך התורה מחיי אותו . . . וכל הכוחות
שאדם ממעט . . . בשביל התורה משיבה התורה אליו

As previously cited, the Talmud (*Yoma* 85b) deduces וְחַי בָּהֶם וְלֹא שֶׁיָּמוּת בָּהֶם, *one must live through Torah and not die through Torah.* This seemingly contradicts the renowned Talmudic saying (*Shabbos* 83b) that Torah only clings to those who are willing to die for its sake (אֵין הַתּוֹרָה מִתְקַיֶּמֶת אֶלָּא בְּמִי שֶׁמֵּמִית עַצְמוֹ עָלֶיהָ).

Upon further contemplation, no contradiction exists. The Torah sustains those who are willing to die for it. This is corroborated by the famous verse in *Tehillim* 19:18: תּוֹרַת ה׳ תְּמִימָה מְשִׁיבַת נָפֶשׁ, *the Torah of HASHEM is perfect, it restores the soul.* All the efforts that one expends for Torah is restored by the Torah itself. In fact, "dying" for Torah is not merely a fair exchange. On the contrary, by sacrificing some of the transient material pleasures of this world in order to study Torah, one gains eternal life. Isn't that what our forefathers experienced at Sinai? As the Talmud (*Shabbos* 89a) relates, their souls expired as they heard the Commandments (יָצְאָה נִשְׁמָתָן), only to have them replaced. (See our commentary on Shavuos, *The Three Festivals*, p. 194, for expanded discussion of this theme.) In other words, their physical, material soul expired, to be replaced by a new spiritual identity. (5654)

◆§ Restoring the Trilogy of Hashem, Torah and Israel

ובאמת בנ"י הם כלים וכלי אומנות שלהם הוא תורה ומצות
ובאמצעיותם חל נועם ה' ובכלל שלש הכוחות נגלה חיות הפנימי

In light of the *Zohar's* famous insight that הקב״ה וְאוֹרַיְיתָא וְיִשְׂרָאֵל כּוּלְהוּ
חַד, *Hashem, Torah and Israel are all one (Acharei Mos* 73a), we can
appreciate that this verse alludes to the power of *mitzvos* to restore this
trilogy. וּשְׁמַרְתֶּם אֶת חֻקֹּתַי וְאֶת מִשְׁפָּטַי should be interpreted in the
following manner: By longing to observe My *mitzvos* (שמר in this
context is related to וְאָבִיו שָׁמַר אֶת הַדָּבָר, *Bereishis* 37:11, Yaakov waited
for Yosef's dream to come true),you merit to restore that intimate
relationship between Israel, Hashem and Torah. As the verse continues,
אֲשֶׁר יַעֲשֶׂה אֹתָם, by fulfilling *mitzvos* (and studying Torah), הָאָדָם, the
person, the Jewish soul, וָחַי בָּהֶם אֲנִי ה', I Hashem will grace your efforts;
I (Hashem) will help you (Israel) fulfill the *mitzvos*.

This perfect trilogy between Hashem, Torah and Israel may not be
necessarily realized in contemporary times. But as this verse emphasizes,
יַעֲשֶׂה אֹתָם הָאָדָם, *man will do*; eventually, as Israel perfects its performance of *mitzvos*, Hashem, Torah and Israel will be one again.

David sings (*Tehillim* 90:17): וִיהִי נֹעַם ה' . . . עָלֵינוּ וּמַעֲשֵׂה יָדֵינוּ כּוֹנְנָה
עָלֵינוּ וּמַעֲשֵׂה יָדֵינוּ כּוֹנְנֵהוּ, *May the pleasantness of HASHEM . . . be upon us
— our handiwork, establish for us; our handiwork, establish it.*

Each phrase may refer to one partner in this trilogy.

וִיהִי נֹעַם ה' refers to Hashem Himself; וּמַעֲשֵׂה יָדֵינוּ refers to the *mitzvos*
performed by our hands through Torah. Finally, וּמַעֲשֵׂה יָדֵינוּ כּוֹנְנֵהוּ is
referring to Israel and the Jew's effort in preparing to perform the
mitzvos.   (5651)

◆§ Sustaining the Human Body

שכל אבר מקבל חיות ע"י המצוה המיוחדת לו

Every limb is nurtured by its *mitzvah*. Quite simply, the verse implies
that by performing *mitzvos* (אֲשֶׁר יַעֲשֶׂה אֹתָם הָאָדָם), the limbs of the

human body are sustained (וְחַי בָּהֶם). As mentioned previously, the 248 positive *mitzvos* correspond to the 248 limbs. This is not intended merely as a symbolic relationship but on the contrary, to emphasize that the body — and every one of its limbs — is nurtured by its corresponding *mitzvah*. (5649).

⋖§ Finding Hashem's Voice in Every Mitzvah

וכן הוא בכל מצוה בפרט שבכח העשי׳ זוכין לשמוע קול דברו
הגנוז בה

David sings: עֹשֵׂי דְבָרוֹ לִשְׁמֹעַ בְּקוֹל דְּבָרוֹ, *who do His bidding, to obey the Voice of His word* (*Tehillim* 103:20).

By performing *mitzvos* (עֹשֵׂי דְבָרוֹ), we merit to hear Hashem's Voice (קוֹל דְּבָרוֹ) that is embedded in the *mitzvah*. According to this approach, וְחַי בָּהֶם may be understood that by performing the *mitzvah*, one elicits the Voice of Hashem (the feeling of intense spirituality) that the *mitzvah* contains. This inner force, the Godliness subsumed in every *mitzvah*, can be appreciated — but only after performing the *mitzvah* itself. And it is this inner voice that sustains the *mitzvah* (i.e. *mitzvos* would be meaningless without the Divine Command embedded in them). וְחַי בָּהֶם — it is this voice that is the life of the *mitzvah*.

By proclaiming נַעֲשֶׂה וְנִשְׁמַע, *we will do and we will hear*, the Jewish people agreed to perform *mitzvos* even before they could hear the inner Divine Voice latent in every *mitzvah*. (For further discussion of this theme refer to *The Three Festivals*, p. 238.) (5647)

⋖§ First Thorns, then the Straight Path

דרך התורה היא להיפוך אשר יעשה וכו׳, ואח״כ וחי בהם כמ״ש

Refer to our commentary on כְּמַעֲשֵׂה אֶרֶץ מִצְרַיִם in which we emphasized that the path of *mitzvos* is marked by momentary difficulties followed by eventual rewards, comparable to a path which is dotted with thorns at its beginning but eventually becomes clear and straight. This thought can also be deduced from the verse, אֲשֶׁר יַעֲשֶׂה אֹתָם; first

one performs the *mitzvah* faithfully, despite any surface difficulties, וָחַי
בָּהֶם, and then realizes how it enlivens and inspires us.   (5647)

⇜ Shabbos and the Weekdays

אשר יעשה הוא בימי המעשה וחי בהם בשבת מעין עוה״ב ונשמה
יתירה . . . היא בחי׳ החיים

H omiletically, one may suggest that by performing *mitzvos* all week
long (אֲשֶׁר יַעֲשֶׂה אוֹתָם), he can appreciate a sample of the eternal life
every Shabbos (וָחַי בָּהֶם) which is a microcosm of the World to Come.
Certainly, the additional soul (נְשָׁמָה יְתֵירָה) enjoyed by Israel every
Shabbos is an indication of the perpetual life that Torah provides.
                                                                    (5647)

⇜ Your Life Is Torah

שיניח האדם עיקר החיות בתורה ובמצות . . . אבל הצדיקים . . .
התורה ומצות הם החיים שלהם

T he *Chiddushei HaRim* interpreted this verse quite simply. Doing
mitzvos (אֲשֶׁר יַעֲשֶׂה אֹתָם) constitutes the totality of a Jew's life (וָחַי
בָּהֶם). Whereas the evildoer's *raison d'etre* is to benefit from the physical
pleasures of this world, the righteous live for the sole purpose of doing
mitzvos.   (5647)

Expanding on this concept, we can say that by observing *mitzvos*, the
Jew attains life. As the Mishnah (*Avos* 6:7) says: גְּדוֹלָה תוֹרָה שֶׁהִיא נוֹתֶנֶת
חַיִּים לְעוֹשֶׂיהָ בָּעוֹלָם הַזֶּה וּבָעוֹלָם הַבָּא, *Great is Torah, for it confers life
upon its practitioners, both in this world and in the World to Come.*

Whereas the wicked subsist solely on food and drink, the righteous,
whose sole motive (as the *Chiddushei HaRim* pointed out) is to serve
Hashem, are sustained through Torah and *mitzvos*. This thought is
voiced during the *Maariv* service, כִּי הֵם חַיֵּינוּ, *for they* (the words of
Torah) *are our life.* While the Torah is rooted in heaven (and existed
before the Creation), nonetheless, through the Jewish people's *mitzvos*
and Torah study, it sustains us on earth as well. In fact, the primary

reason for giving us the Torah is that we be sustained through it in this world.   (5647)

↩§ Growing Through Torah

רק אדרבא לזכות עי"ז למצות אחרות . . . וליקח מהם חיות
כמ"ש וחי בהם

It is well known that the evildoers are deemed dead, even while physically alive. It follows then that life is defined in terms of involvement in Torah and *mitzvos*; not merely involvement, but also constant growth. As one becomes increasingly immersed in Torah, his life is renewed (וָחַי בָּהֶם).   (5639, 5644)

↩§ Sanctifying the Material World

באמצעיות המשפטים והחוקים יתקן כל בחי' העשי' ואז מעורר
החיות שיש בכל המעשים

Please refer to our commentary on כְּמַעֲשֵׂה אֶרֶץ מִצְרַיִם and especially the interpretation that even secular deeds must be conducted in a uniquely Jewish fashion. Ideally, every facet of Jewish life should be sanctified by being used in the context of a *mitzvah*.

שע"י התשוקה וההכנה אל המצוה זוכין מיד להמשיך חיות

In this vein, we may interpret וּשְׁמַרְתֶּם אֶת חֻקֹּתַי וְאֶת מִשְׁפָּטַי אֲשֶׁר יַעֲשֶׂה אֹתָם as follows: With the assistance of the statutes (חֻקִּים) and laws to which the word אֹתָם refers (אֹתָם being equivalent to אִתָּם, *with them*), true meaning is given to the universe through man's performance [עֲשֶׂה] of *mitzvos*.   (5638)

The future tense יַעֲשֶׂה, *will make* or *do*, delineates the great challenge to not only perfect the material world through our involvement with *mitzvos* but also to be constantly *thinking* about possible future opportunities to elevate the entire universe through *mitzvos*. The renowned term שְׁמִירַת הַמִּצְוֹת signifies far more than mere observance of mitzvos. Rather, it implies eagerly waiting for the opportunity to fulfill Hashem's will. This may even be the intent of the verse וּשְׁמַרְתֶּם ... וָחַי בָּהֶם. By waiting for opportunities to fulfill mitzvos, this alone — this sacred form of anticipation — brings life. (5648)

◄§ Creating Angels

כמ״ש ז״ל וחי אלו המלאכים . . . וכן בעשית המצות שנברא
מלאך מכל מצוה

Homiletically, the term וָחַי may refer to the angels that are created through the performance of every mitzvah (cf. Avos 4:11). (Likutim)

וְלֹא תָקִיא הָאָרֶץ אֶתְכֶם . . . כַּאֲשֶׁר קָאָה אֶת הַגּוֹי אֲשֶׁר לִפְנֵיכֶם

Let not the land disgorge you . . . as it disgorged the nation that was before you (v. 28).

אך הכל לפי המדרגה . . . כן בנ״י . . . צריכין לשמור את חוקם
שתסבול הארץ אותם

While it seems inconceivable that the Jewish people would perform the same abominations that caused the expulsion of the Canaanites, the Torah expects more of Israel dwelling in Eretz Yisrael than from the Canaanites. Yet, the analogy to the Canaanites is still appropriate. Just as the Canaanites, possessing only the seven Noahide commandments, were held responsible for their misdeeds, so too Israel, equipped with the entire Torah, would be held responsible for its higher standard while living in Eretz Yisrael. (5644)

מוֹצָאֵי יוֹם כִּפּוּר
The Night After Yom Kippur

וקשה ג״כ וכי בערב מתענין הלא ביום מתענין. רק האוכל ושמח
במוצאי יוהכ״פ כאלו התענה.

Just as the Talmud (*Yoma* 81b) interprets the phrase מֵעֶרֶב עַד עֶרֶב as alluding to the *mitzvah* of eating on עֶרֶב יוֹם כִּפּוּר, so too we may derive from here the *mitzvah* of eating and rejoicing on the night *after* Yom Kippur (מוֹצָאֵי יוֹם כִּפּוּר). Clearly, one is not required to fast עַד עֶרֶב until the evening *after* Yom Kippur. Instead we fulfill this requirement by eating a festive meal on מוֹצָאֵי יוֹם כִּפּוּר. The purpose of the post-Yom Kippur meal is to channel the joy of Yom Kippur (associated with forgiveness) into the rest of the year; the transition being the meal after Yom Kippur. (5652)

מאי לשון כבר . . . והקב״ה שרואה עתידות מצרף עבודת האדם
אחר כפרה לכפר לו בזכות זה

The Midrash relates that a heavenly voice (בַּת קוֹל) rings out after Yom Kippur proclaiming, לֵךְ אֱכֹל בְּשִׂמְחָה לַחְמֶךָ וּשְׁתֵה בְלֶב טוֹב יֵינֶךָ כִּי כְבָר רָצָה הָאֱלֹהִים אֶת מַעֲשֶׂיךָ, *Go, eat your bread with joy and drink your wine with a glad heart, for God has already approved your deeds* (*Koheles* 9:7).

The expression כְּבָר, *already*, suggests that already prior to Yom Kippur, Hashem, looking into the future and foreseeing the joy through which the Jewish people *will* perform *mitzvos* in the year ahead, takes these future deeds into account and forgives their sins *now*. (5651)

Index

❧ Index

תורה

נביאים

כתובים

תלמוד

מדרשים

תפילה

This volume is part of
THE ARTSCROLL SERIES®
an ongoing project of
translations, commentaries and expositions
on Scripture, Mishnah, Talmud, Halachah,
liturgy, history and the classic Rabbinic writings;
and biographies, and thought.

For a brochure of current publications
visit your local Hebrew bookseller
or contact the publisher:

Mesorah Publications, ltd

4401 Second Avenue
Brooklyn, New York 11232
(718) 921-9000